ISBN 978-1-332-13511-0
PIBN 10289416

1 MONTH OF
FREE
READING

at
www.ForgottenBooks.com

By purchasing this book you are eligible for one month membership to ForgottenBooks.com, giving you unlimited access to our entire collection of over 700,000 titles via our web site and mobile apps.

To claim your free month visit:
www.forgottenbooks.com/free289416

A HANDBOOK

OF

LOCAL GOVERNMENT
IN IRELAND:

CONTAINING

AN EXPLANATORY INTRODUCTION TO THE LOCAL
GOVERNMENT (IRELAND) ACT, 1898;

TOGETHER WITH

The Text of the Act, the Orders in Council, and the
Rules made thereunder relating to County Council,
Rural District Council, and Guardians' Elections.

WITH AN *INDEX*.

BY

JOHN J CLANCY, M.P.,
M.A., Barrister-at-Law.

DUBLIN:
SEALY, BRYERS AND WALKER,
MIDDLE ABBEY STREET.

M. H. GILL & SON,
UPPER O'CONNELL STREET.

1899.

DUBLIN :
PRINTED BY SEALY, BRYERS AND WALKER,
MIDDLE ABBEY STREET.

PREFACE.

THE following pages contain the text of the Local Government (Ireland) Act of last year, and of the Orders made under it by the Lord Lieutenant in Council, and by the Local Government Board (the GRAND JURY ORDER excepted), together with an Introduction in which I have endeavoured to present, within a moderate compass, a connected view of the new system of local self-government established by those enactments.

The principle I have followed in the Introduction, is that of bringing together, under appropriate heads, all the chief provisions relating to each subject dealt with, whether they are to be found in the Act itself, in the Orders, or in the Rules. In this way, it is hoped, and by the aid of the Index, the reader will be enabled to find, without much trouble or delay, any of those provisions of which he may be in search. In every case in which it seemed necessary I have given the authority for the statements made.

I have to express my grateful acknowledgments to Mr. G. A. Mahon, of the Local Government Board, for the courtesy with which he has several times allowed me to avail myself of his wide and accurate knowledge of the new, as well as of the old, system of Local Government in Ireland, and for many valuable suggestions.

J. J. C.

DUBLIN, *March 9th*, 1899.

ERRATA.

P. 74, line 16, for " Order in Council, dated October, 1898, Article 20," read " Local Government (Application of Enactments) Order 1898, Article 21."

P. 87, under head of " First Rural District Councils, for " Article 6," read " Article 10."

P. 88, line 4 from top, for " after election," read " after the triennial election."

P. 88, line 9 from top, for " *Ibid.*," read " Local Government (Transitory Provisions), No. 2 Order, 1898, Article 15 (1)."

P. 95, line 30, add : " (*d*) To existing collectors who hold a pensionable office, and have expressed their willingness to serve, but are not continued in office " (sec. 115, sub-sec. 12 (*a*)).

P. 96, line 18, for " changed," read " charged."

CONTENTS.

I.—EXPLANATORY INTRODUCTION.

PART I.—COUNTY COUNCILS.

PART II.—COUNTY BOROUGHS.

PART VI.—FINANCE.

PART VII.—OFFICERS.

PART VIII.—TEMPORARY PROVISIONS.

A HANDBOOK

OF

LOCAL GOVERNMENT IN IRELAND

Explanatory Introduction.

PART I.

COUNTY COUNCILS.

I.—Establishment of County Councils.

"A Council shall be established in every administrative county, and be entrusted with the management of the administrative and financial business of that county, and shall consist of a chairman and Councillors" (sec. 1).

(1) An "administrative" county is that throughout which the County Council has authority for the purposes of the Act (sec. 68, sub-sec. 2). It is not necessarily conterminous in every case with the Parliamentary County. But, with a few exceptions, the administrative and Parliamentary counties are actually conterminous.

The first Councils are to be elected for the counties as existing at the passing of the Act (called in the Act "existing judicial counties,") except in the case of a county which, for Grand Jury purposes, has been divided into ridings, each of which is to have a Council for itself (sec. 68, sub-sec. 1); but the Local Government Board is given power, within six months after the passing of the Act, to alter the boundaries of any existing county (sec. 68, sub-sec. 1); and that body has, accordingly, made alterations in the boundaries of several counties (see Appendix III. *post*).

As Tipperary is the only county divided into ridings for Grand Jury purposes, it is the only county, therefore, which will have two County Councils. But as will be seen, except for County Council purposes, Tipperary will continue one county.

(2) As to what is "the administrative and financial business" of a county, see "Powers and Duties of County Councils," *post*.

(3) As to "the Chairman and Councillors" of a County Council, see "Constitution of County Councils," *post*.

(4) A County Council is a corporate body by the name of the county, and has a perpetual succession and a common seal (Order

B

in Council, (Application of Enactments), dated 22nd day of December, 1898, Article 13, sub-sec. 1). It may, therefore, sue and be sued in its corporate name; and where any land used to be conveyed or granted to, or any contract or agreement made in the name of the Secretary of the Grand Jury, Clerk of the Peace, or other person or body, on behalf of the county or any part of it, it must now be conveyed to or made with the Council of the county concerned (same Order, Article 12, sub-sec. 2).

It may be added that the Grand Juries were *not* incorporated bodies.

II.—Constitution of County Councils.

A County Council consists of a chairman and councillors (sec. 1).

1.—THE CHAIRMAN AND VICE-CHAIRMAN.

(*a*) A chairman is elected annually from among the Councillors, and the Council may also elect a vice-chairman annually, if it thinks fit. The chairman, by virtue of his office, becomes a justice of the peace for the administrative county, but, before acting as such, must take the oaths required by law to be taken by a justice (sec. 3, sub-sec. 4). The oaths required to be taken by a justice are the oath of allegiance and the judicial oath (31 & 32 Vic., c. 72, s. 6; 34 & 35 Vic., c. 48). If a person is re-elected chairman "on the expiration or other determination of a previous term of office," he need not take the oaths afresh (sec. 95).

(*b*) The term of office of both the chairman and the vice-chairman is one year, but he will hold office till his successor is appointed, and has made and subscribed the required declaration (Order in Council (Application of Enactments), dated 22nd day of December, 1898, Article 37, sub-sec. 1). The election of chairman and vice-chairman must be the first business transacted at each annual meeting of the Council, except the first annual meeting after a triennial election at which it will be the second business, the first being the question of co-opting additional members, same Order, Article 35, sub-sec. 5 (*a*) (*b*)). In the case of an equality of votes at the election, the chairman of the meeting, although not entitled to vote in the first instance, shall have the casting vote in case of a tie (same Order and Article, sub-sec. 5 (*c*)).

2.—THE COUNCILLORS.

The Councillors for each county will be ordinarily of three classes :—

    (*a*) Elected Councillors,
    (*b*) Ex-officio,
    (*c*) Co-opted.

For the First Councillors there will also be Nominated Councillors.

·(*a*) .The elected Councillors are elected for the county electoral divisions, in the proportion of one for each, except where an urban district forming one such division returns more than one Councillor; and the number of divisions and Councillors are to be fixed by an order of the Local Government Board, but so that the divisions shall be as nearly as conveniently may be equal as regards population, and that, in forming them, regard shall be had to a proper representation of the rural and urban population (sec. 2, sub-sec. 3 (*a*) and (*b*)). They may thus be unequal as regards area. A list of the County Electoral Divisions for each of the 33 administrative counties, and of the number of County Councillors fixed for each urban district forming one county electoral division will be found in Appendix III. *post*.

(*b*) The *ex-officio* Councillors will be the chairmen of the Rural (*not* Urban) District Councils (as to which see *post*), and, if the chairman of a Rural District Council is already a member of the County Council, or is disqualified (as to which see "Qualifications and Disqualifications of Councillors" *post*), then some other member of the District Council may be chosen in his stead by the District Council (sec. 3, sub-sec. 1).

(*c*) The co-opted Councillors may number one or two who may be chosen by the County Council itself from persons qualified to be Councillors. As to who are qualified to be Councillors, see *post*. Those additional members are to hold office only during the term of office of the Council by whom the choice is made (sec. 3, sub-sec. 2), and the question of electing such additional members is the first business to be considered after the election of a Council (sec. 3, sub-sec. 3), and Order in council (Application of Enactments), 22nd December, 1898, Art. 35, sub-sec. 5 (*a*)).

(*d*) The nominated Councillors to serve only on the County Councils *first* elected are to number three in each case, and they are to be selected by the Grand Juries, or by a committee appointed by the Grand Jury for the purpose at the next Spring Assizes, and in the case of the County of Dublin, at the next Easter presenting term. The persons selected must be then serving, or have, during the previous three years, served as Grand Jurors (sec. 113, sub-sec. 1).

III.—Period of Existence of County Councils.

The term of office of all classes of County Councillors is three years, at the end of which period all must retire together, and new Councils must be elected (sec. 2, sub-sec. 2).

IV.—Electors of County Councillors.

The elected members of every County Council are elected by "the Local Government electors" for the county (sec. 2, sub-sec. 1). Those electors are defined to be, "as respects any county, or borough, district, electoral division, ward, or other area, the persons for the time being registered in the local government register of electors in respect of qualifications within such county, district, borough, ward or other area" (sec. 109); and the expression "local government register of electors" is itself defined to be, "as respects any county, borough, district, electoral division, ward, or other area in Ireland, the register of Parliamentary electors, or the portion of that register which relates to such county, or borough, district, electoral division, ward, or other area, together with the local government supplement" (sec. 98, sub-sec. 10). "The local government supplement" which is thus made part of "the local government register of electors," should contain the name of every person who would, but for being a peer or a woman, or being registered as a Parliamentary elector elsewhere, be entitled to be entered in the list of Parliamentary electors (61 Vic. c. 2, Registration (Ireland) Act, 1898, sec. 1, sub-sec. 2).

In other words, the local government electorate will consist of all Parliamentary electors and of all peers and women who, but for their being peers or women, would be entitled to be Parliamentary electors.

The following is a list of the qualifications for the Parliamentary franchise :—

1. Actual possession or receipt of the rents and profits for at least six months before the 20th July in the current year, of a freehold estate in lands or tenements, of the net annual value of £50;

2. Ditto, of a freehold estate of the net annual value of £20;

3. Actual possession, or receipt of the rents and profits, for at least twelve months before the 20th July in the current year, of a leasehold estate worth £20 a year, less rates and taxes, provided the lease was originally for a term of not less than fourteen years;

4. Ditto, of a leasehold estate worth £10 a year, less rates and taxes, provided the lease was originally created for not less than 60 years;

5. Actual possession, or receipt of the rents and profits, for six months before the 20th July in the current year, of a freehold estate rated at £5 or upwards, and worth £5 a year at least, net, less taxes;

6. Occupying and being rated for, during twelve months before the 20th July in the current year, as tenant or owner, premises rated at £10 a year—occupation in this case not meaning, but not being inconsistent with residence;

7. Inhabiting, as owner, tenant, or servant, a dwelling-house of any valuation, for twelve months before the 20th July in the current year, provided the house is rated in some person's name, and that the rates are paid by someone;

8. Inhabiting by virtue of office, service, or employment, for a similar period, a dwelling-house exempt from rating;

9. Occupying separately as lodger and as sole tenant, for twelve months before the 20th July in the current year, apartments worth at least £10 a year unfurnished;

10. Ditto, as joint lodgers, provided that the apartments unfurnished are worth £10 a year for each lodger (*two* joint lodgers only can be registered out of the same premises);

11. Being on the "Freeman's Roll" of a city, town, or borough, where the freemen franchise exists.

(See Hunt's "Franchise and Registration Law," pp. 76-81, new and revised edition, and the enactments there mentioned).

Any peer or woman, as well as any other person, who possesses any of the foregoing qualifications is entitled, as has been said, to be registered as "a local government elector," and to vote for County Councillors. The local government register of electors is to be completed and on sale to the public, and is to come into operation on the same day as the Parliamentary register of electors, that is on the 1st January in every year, and is to continue in force for the same period—that is, for a year (sec. 98, sub-sec. 1).

V.—Elections of County Councillors.

1.—THE MODE OF ELECTION.

The mode of election of County Councillors is to be such as may be prescribed by rules to be made by the Local Goverment Board (Order in Council (Applied Enactments), Article 5 sub-sec. 1). But it will be the same except in a few respects as that for Municipal and Parliamentary elections—that is to say, all polls will be taken by ballot, and the Ballot Act, 1872, and the Municipal Elections (Corrupt and Illegal Practices) Act, 1884, and other enactments regulating municipal elections will apply (Order in Council (Applied Enactments), Article 5, sub-sec. 3)

The law, however, regulating county council elections (same Order, Article 5, sub-sec. 1) will differ in some respects from that regarding Parliamentary elections. No more than two persons —one as proposer, the other as seconder—may sign a nomination paper (same Order, Article 5, sub-sec. 2 (*a*)); no elector may subscribe a nomination paper or vote in more than one electoral division, nor nominate nor vote for more than one candidate, unless in an urban district where as many votes may be given as there are seats to be filled (sec. 2, sub-sec. 4, and same Order, Article 5, sub-sec. 2 (*b*)); the Local Government Board, by rules, may fix, or enable the County Council to fix, the days and hours of polling, so, however, that the poll shall always be open between 6 p.m. and 8 p.m. (same Order, Article 5, sub-sec. 2 (*c*)); may, if convenient, provide for the polls being taken simultaneously in the same place for all local government elections held at the same date and in the same area (same Order, Article 5, sub-sec. 2 (*d*)); and may provide for the appointment of returning officers (same Order, Article 5, sub-sec. 2 (*e*)). If the same person is elected for more than one electoral division he must, within three days after notice of his election, declare, in writing, to be delivered to the secretary of the council, for which division he will sit, or if he does not so declare, the chairman shall within three days after the time of choice has expired, declare for him (same Order, Article 5, sub-sec. 5).

The returning officer may use for nominations, polls, and counting of votes, all schools receiving grants from Parliament, or any room the expense of maintaining which is payable out of a local rate, except one adjoining a church or a conventual or other religious establishment (same Order), Article 5, sub-sec. 3 (*a*)).

2.—Official Expenses.

The official expenses of a County Council election will be borne out of the county fund as county-at-large charges—that is, may be levied off the whole county (same Order, Article 6, sub-sec. 2 (*a*)); and it must not exceed a scale to be fixed by the County Council with the approval of the Local Government Board (sec. 94, sub-sec. 16 and same Order in Council, Article 6, sub-sec. 1). The Council must advance to the returning officer for such expenses such sum, not exceeding £10 for every 1,000 electors, as he may require (same Order, Article 6, sub-sec. 3). The returning officer must make a detailed return of his expenses to the Council within twenty-one days after the return of the persons elected is made and must annex to his account a notice of the place where the vouchers may be seen by the Council or by any agent of the Council, and he will not be allowed for any charges not included in his account (same Order, Article 6, sub-secs. 4 and 5). The Council may, within one month after the receipt of the account, apply for a taxation of it to the County Court, and that Court may, accordingly, tax it or depute the duty to the registrar or other principal officer of the court (same Order, Article 6, sub-secs. 6 and 7); and, if the returning officer has not, when he could have, made use of ballot boxes and the other apparatus for a poll belonging to any other public authority, the fact will be taken into account against him (sec. 99, sub-sec. 2). An appeal from the County Court to a taxing officer of the High Court is allowed to either party, and any taxation or review of taxation is subject to an appeal to the High Court as in the case of any ordinary taxation of costs (same Order, Article 6, sub-secs. 12, 13, 14). Ballot boxes and other apparatus for elections must be provided by the County Council for its elections at the expense of the rates, and may be used at Parliamentary elections, and any damage caused to them other than reasonable wear and tear must be paid as part of the expenses of the election in which they are used (sec. 99, sub-sec. 1).

3.—EXPENSES OF CANDIDATES.

As to the Expenses of Candidates at elections, it is provided that the provisions of the Municipal Elections (Corrupt and Illegal Practices) Act, 1884, shall not apply to local government elections regulated by rules of the Local Government Board, as far as regards

(a) The payment of any money, or the incurring of any expense, by or on behalf of any candidate on account of the conduct or management of an election;

(b) The time for sending in and paying claims;
(c) The maximum amount of expenses allowed; and
(d) The return and declaration of expenses.

(same Order, Article 5, sub-sec. 3 (b); but any person having a claim against a returning officer must transmit it to such officer within fourteen days after the election, and that claim may be investigated and adjudicated upon by the County Court where application is made for taxation (same Order in Council, Article 6, sub-secs. 8 and 10). The notice of any election held under the Ballot Act must contain a notification that such claim may be made within the time mentioned (same Order in Council, Article 6, sub-sec. 9).

It would thus seem that there is no limit to the amount that may be spent by a candidate at a County Council election for the purposes of the election; that he need make no return and no declaration of his expenses; that there is no time limited for sending in claims against candidates, nor any for paying them; and that a candidate may, subject to his not committing bribery, or treating, or any other corrupt practice, pay anything he likes to any one for services in connection with the election. But the amounts paid must be *reasonable*, and not made for the purpose of influencing voters, which, if the sum were too large, might be implied.

4.—ELECTION PETITIONS.

County Council elections may be questioned, like Parliamentary elections, on petition, and the procedure in regard to election petitions is that prescribed by Part IV. of the Municipal Corporations Act, 1882, as amended by the Municipal Election (Corrupt and Illegal Practices) Act, 1884 (same Order in Council Article 5, sub-sec. 3). In accordance with that procedure, a petition may be presented on any one or more of four specified grounds by any four or more voters or electors, or by a candidate ; the Election Court will be a barrister of at least fifteen years' standing, selected from five such barristers to be annually appointed for the trial of election petitions by the judges of the High Court, who, however, will have no appellate jurisdiction over the Election Court, except upon a question of law reserved by that court itself; and the remuneration of the election judge and his staff will, in the first instance, be borne by the Treasury, which is to be recouped out of the county fund, unless the Election Court orders it to be paid, as it may in certain cases, by either the petitioner or the respondent (same Order and Articles).

5.—MISCELLANEOUS PROVISIONS.

Some Miscellaneous Provisions regarding County Council Elections remain to be mentioned.

(*a*) The ordinary day of election, in the case of a County Council is to be the 1st June, or such other day, a week earlier or a week later, as may be fixed by the County Council (sec. 94, sub-sec. 7); each district electoral division which will be the poor law electoral division (sec. 22, sub-sec. 4), shall be a polling district, unless the Local Government Board, on the representation of the County Council

otherwise direct (sec. 94, sub-sec. 6); the old Councillors will
retire the day after the election of their successors, and on
the same day the new Councillors will come into office (sec.
94, sub-sec. 8); and the day of the annual meeting and of
the election of chairman and vice-chairman shall be the
twelfth day after the election (sec. 94, sub-sec. 7).

(b) When difficulties arise as respects the election of any
individual Councillor, and there is no provision for holding
another election, or when difficulties arise as to any election
of councillors, or as to the first meeting after any triennial
election, or as to any Council not being properly constituted
or being unable to act, the Local Government Board may
solve them, and for the purpose of doing so, may go to the
extent of modifying not only their own rules, but the Act
itself and any applied enactments ; and when similar difficulties occur in the case of any other Council or body, the
County Council, acting either by itself or by a Committee,
shall have similar powers. (Local Government (Application
of Enactments) Order, 1898, Article 7.)

(c) Casual vacancies in any County Council are to be filled
by the Council (sec. 94, sub-sec. 4); a person appointed to
casual vacancy shall hold office until the time when the
person in whose place he is appointed would regularly have
gone out of office (same Order, Article 11, sub-sec. 2).
Casual vacancies may be created by non-acceptance of office,
as well as in other ways (same Order in Council, Article 11,
sub-sec. 3).

(d) As to the special provisions regarding first elections
see *post*.

VI.—Qualifications & Disqualifications of County Councillors.

1.—QUALIFICATIONS.

" A person shall not be qualified to be elected or to be a
Councillor for a County, unless he is a local government
elector for such county " (sec. 2, sub-sec. 5).
This provision makes every local government elector eligible
for the position of County Councillor; and, consequently, a
person registered in one county electoral division may be elected
for that or any other division.

2.—DISQUALIFICATIONS.

The following classes of persons, however, are disqualified for being elected or being County Councillors, although they may be local government electors :—

(*a*) A County Coroner in the county for which he is coroner (sec. 14, sub-sec. 5);

(*b*) Clergymen and regular ministers of any religious denomination (sec. 94, sub-sec. 1);

(*c*) Women (Local Government (Application of Enactments) Order, 1898, Article 12, sub-sec. 1);

(*d*) An infant or an alien;

(*e*) Anyone who has received union relief since his election or within twelve months before;

(*f*) Anyone who, within five years before his election, or since his election, has been convicted of any crime and has been sentenced to imprisonment with hard labour without the option of a fine, or to any greater punishment, and has not been pardoned;

(*g*) Anyone who, within or during the same time, has been adjudged bankrupt, or has made a composition or arrangement with his creditors, unless his bankruptcy is annulled, or he obtains a certificate that it was due to misfortune, or unless, in the case of a composition or arrangement, he pays his debts in full;

(*h*) Anyone who holds any paid office or place of profit under the Council;

(*i*) Anyone who, by himself or his partner in business, enters into or participates in the profit of a contract with the Council, except in the following cases—that is, unless he is a person interested in a newspaper publishing advertisements of the Council, or in the sale or lease of any land to the Council, or in supplying, for public works, stone, gravel, or other such materials from his own land, or in the transport of such materials for the repair of public works in his own immediate neighbourhood, or in a contract between the Council and a joint stock company in which he is a shareholder. (Same Order in Council, Article 12, sub-secs. 4, 5, 6, 7.)

In addition to the classes of persons disqualified by the Act or Order in Council, all paid officers in the service of the Boards of Guardians have been disqualified by an Order of the Local Government Board (Appendix III., *post*), made by virtue of the general powers vested in that body to regulate the conditions under which such officers may hold office; and, of course, any other public department having a similar power may exercise it in a similar way in regard to its own employés.

As to the general principle to be taken account of in determining whether a person has a disqualifying interest in a contract or other dealings with a public body such as a County Council, the case of Nutton *v.* Wilson (20 Q. B.D.) may be referred to.

3.—ABSENCE.

Absence on the part of any Councillor from the meetings of the Council for twelve months makes his seat vacant, unless it be due to illness or some reason approved by the Council; and any vacancy created by disqualification or absence must be notified by three members of the Council and the Secretary in such manner as the Council may direct. (Same Order in Council, Article 12, sub-secs. 9, 10.)

4.—OUTGOING CHAIRMAN AND COUNCILLORS.

An outgoing Councillor will not be disqualified from remaining in office till the ordinary day of retirement, even though he may have ceased to be a local government elector on the previous 1st January (when the new register of electors came into force), and under similar circumstances an outgoing chairman may continue in office till his successor has made a declaration accepting office (sec. 94, sub-sec. 14).

5.—PENALTY FOR ACTING WHEN DISQUALIFIED.

Any Councillor who acts as such when disqualified is liable on summary conviction, to a fine of £20 for each offence (Order in Council (Applied Enactments), Article 12, sub-sec. 10); and, when convicted, will be ineligible for being elected or being a member of the same or any other council, board, or body of commissioners for seven years (sec. 94, sub-sec. 3). But a person who is disqualified by reason only of the fact that he was not entitled to be registered as a local government elector, shall not be liable to a fine for acting when disqualified, if he was in fact registered (same order, Article 12, sub-sec. 5).

VII.—Acceptance and Resignation of Office by County Councillors.

1.—MODE OF ACCEPTANCE.

Acceptance of office by a County Councillor must be signified by making and subscribing, within three months after notice of the election, before any Justice of the Peace or Commissioner for taking Oaths, or before any two members of the Council, or the Secretary, the prescribed declaration, and, except to take such a declaration, no Councillor can act as such till he has made and subscribed the declaration in the manner mentioned. (Same Order, Article 9, sub-secs. 1, 5).

Every person elected Councillor, or chairman, or vice-chairman, must either accept office by making the prescribed declaration within three months, or pay a fine to the Council; and the fine, in the case of a chairman or vice-chairman, is such a sum not exceeding £100 as the County Council by bye-law may determine, and in the case of a Councillor a sum not exceeding £50, to be paid in each case to the Council (same Order, Article 9, sub-sec. 2); but, if there is no bye-law regulating the matter, the penalties will be £50 and £25 respectively (same Order, Article 9, sub-sec. 2).

Persons disabled by lunacy or imbecility of mind, or deafness, or blindness, or other permanent infirmity of body are exempt from this penalty; and so is any person who is either over sixty-five years of age, or has, within five years, either already served in office, or paid a fine for non-acceptance, *and* claims exemption (same Order, Article 9, sub-sec. 3). The fine is recoverable on summary conviction (same Order, Article 9, sub-sec. 4). When a Councillor or chairman becomes disqualified by absence he is liable to the same fine as for non-acceptance of office (same Order, Article 10, sub-sec. 3).

2.—RESIGNATION.

A person elected Councillor or chosen (that is, presumably co-opted), may resign by writing to be delivered to the secretary, on payment of the fine prescribed for non-acceptance of office (same Order, Article 10. sub-sec. 1). On his so resigning, the fact must be notified in the same manner as the creation of a vacancy by absence (same Order, Article 10, sub-secs. 2, 3).

VIII.—Powers and Duties of the County Councils.

The powers and duties of the County Councils may be treated of under five heads—viz.:

1. Those transferred from the Grand Jury,
          „   „   „ the Boards of Guardians,
          „   „ justices,
          „   „ wholly or partly from other bodies, and
2.   „ specially assigned by the Act.

1.—POWERS AND DUTIES OF THE GRAND JURY TRANSFERRED.

All the business of the Grand Jury, not excepted (as to which see *infra*), and all the business of the County at large present-ment sessions are transferred to the County Councils, with all the powers and the duties of the jury and the sessions and without the necessity of obtaining for the acts of the Council any fiat or other sanction of a judge (sec. 4, sub-sec. 1), but subject to any provisions or limitations affecting those powers and duties, whether contained in the Act or in any Order in Council made under Part VI. of the Act (sec. 72, sub-sec. 1); and with the powers and duties of the bodies from which the business is trans-ferred there are also transferred to the Councils the powers and duties of all the officers of the superseded bodies except the treasurers (sec. 72, sub-sec. 2). All the property of the Grand Juries, in whatever name or names held, which is for the public uses and purposes of a county or any division of a county, is vested in the County Councils, but subject to all debts and liabilities affecting it (Local Government (Applied Enact-ments) Order, 1898, art. 15, sub-sec. 1); but the existing records of, or in the custody of, the Court of Quarter Sessions shall continue to remain in the same custody as at the pass-ing of the Act, and so will the records of the Court of Assize, so far as they do not relate to the business trans-ferred to the county, or unless the court otherwise orders (same Order, sec. 15, sub-sec. 1 (*a*)), and the Grand Jury may retain any property or chattels presented to it or bought with the private funds of its members, and not held for public pur-poses, and any differences on this subject between the Councils and the Grand Juries are to be referred to and settled by the Local Government Board (same Order, art. 15, sub-sec. 1 (*b*)). There are also transferred to the Councils the debts and liabilities of the Grand Juries (same Order, art. 15, sub-sec. 2).

The principal business of the Grand Jury transferred may be summarised under the following heads:

(*a*) The construction and repair, maintenance, enlarge-ment, and improvement of roads, bridges, pipes, arches, gullets, railings, fences, walls, and any other public work, such as the erection and repair of court and sessions houses for which presentments might have been made by any county at large presentment sessions, or any Grand Jury under the Grand Juries' Acts, 1816 to 1895 (sec. 109), except the business of the Grand Jury in relation to public works in urban districts which are not maintained wholly or partly at the expense of the county at large, this latter business being transferred to the Urban District Councils (sec. 27, sub-sec. 1 (*b*)).

(*b*) Making contributions to the maintenance of Lunatic Asylums, County Infirmaries, and Fever Hospitals, under 6 & 7 William IV. c. 116, as to which, however, changes are made by the Act (see *infra*).

(*c*) Making contributions (under 7 & 8 Vic., c. 106, 31 & 32 Vic. c. 59, 31 Vic. c. 25, 44 & 45 Vic. c. 29, and 48 & 49 Vic. c. 19), to the establishment and maintenance of Reformatory and Industrial Schools.

(*d*) Paying the salaries and fees of county officers under the Grand Juries' Acts, 1816 to 1895 ;

(*e*) Exercising under the Public Works Act, 1853 (14 & 15 Vic. c. 90), the power of borrowing money from private sources for public works, and taking over public works constructed wholly or partly with public money (but see as to borrowing powers of County Councils, *post*).

(*f*) Giving guarantees under the Tramways Acts and Light Railways Acts, the Irish Loans Act, 1880, and guaranteeing harbour loans under 50 & 51 Vic. c. 37.

(*g*) Repaying under 37 & 38 Vic. c. 70 the sum therein fixed as the proportion of the counties for revising the valuation ;

(*h*) Providing local standards of weights and measures under 41 & 42 Vic. c. 49, and 52 & 53 Vic. c. 21 ;

(*i*) Administering the Food and Drugs' Act of 1875 (38 & 39 Vic. c. 63), the Sale of Food and Drugs' Act Amendment Act, 1879 (42 & 43 Vic. c. 30), the Margarine Act, 1881, and the Fertilizing and Feeding Stuffs Act, 1893 ;

(*j*) Making imperative presentments for extra police, repayment of loans, and payment of debts to the Crown and Government departments, as to which see the new provisions made by sec. 80, *infra*.

(*k*) Appointing, under 19 & 20 Vic. c. 62, trustees for the management of the navigation of the districts of Ballinamore and Ballyconnel, the Corrib, and the upper and lower Bann (the only persons, however, who are qualified to be trustees being such as have a leasehold or a freehold property of £100 a year, or are agents to an estate of £2,000 a year).

2.—THE BUSINESS OF THE PRESENTMENT SESSIONS.

The business of the county at large presentment sessions was to *initiate* the presentments for public works, the expense of which was to be levied off the county at large. This business will now be discharged in the manner described *infra*.

3.—THE BUSINESS OF THE GRAND JURY NOT TRANSFERRED.

The business of the Grand Jury *not* transferred, is of three classes, viz.—

(*a*) Criminal business;

(*b*) Business relating to compensation for malicious injuries (which is transferred to the County Court, see *post*);

(*c*) The business of appointing Visiting Committees for prisons (sec. 4, sub-sec. 2).

4.—POWERS AND DUTIES TRANSFERRED FROM THE BOARDS OF GUARDIANS.

The business transferred to the County Councils from the Boards of Guardians is the following :—

(*a*) The business of making, levying, collecting, and recovering the poor rate in the rural districts of the county (sec. 6 (*a*)); as to the procedure to be followed in regard to which see *infra*;

(*b*) The business of administering the Destructive Insects Act of 1877 (40 & 41 Vic. c. 68)—that is, assessing and paying compensation for the destruction of crops ordered by the Privy Council to be destroyed for the purpose of preventing the spread of the Colorado beetle (sec. 6 (*b*));

(*c*) The business of the Guardians under the Diseases of Animals Act, 1894 (57 & 58 Vic. c. 58) (sec. 6 (*b*));

(*d*) Appointing under the Military Manœuvres Act, 1897 (60 & 61 Vic. c. 43), members of Military Manœuvres Commissions, to determine what lands, roads, and sources of water supply are to be used for military manœuvres, and to determine the mode in which compensation for any injury done in execution of the Act is to be claimed and paid (sec. 73).

5.—THE BUSINESS TRANSFERRED FROM JUSTICES.

The business transferred from the justices in petty sessions is that transacted under the Explosives Act, 1875 (38 & 39 Vic. c. 17), except the power of appointing officers which shall cease (sec. 6 (*c*)). Under this Act, in places where no Corporation existed, or where there was no urban authority exercising Grand Jury powers, the justices in petty sessions were entitled to license the erection of firework factories and gunpowder stores, to charge fees for such licenses, and to obtain a licence for the erection by themselves of magazines for any explosives at the cost of the poor rates, to acquire land for that purpose, and to let such magazines at a rent to others.

6 –The Business Transferred Wholly or Partly from other Bodies.

The business transferred wholly or partly to the County Council from other bodies relates to the Lunatic Asylums and the County Infirmaries and Fever Hospitals.

(a) Lunatic Asylums:—

1. As regards Lunatic Asylums, the powers of the Lord Lieutenant and the Inspectors of Lunatics as to the officers of asylums, the expenditure, land and buildings, and appointment of governors, cease, and the Board of Control is abolished (sec. 9, sub-sec. 5). Instead of these authorities, the County Councils are henceforth to provide for and manage the asylums, and to appoint and remove the officers and regulate the expenditure (sec. 9, sub-sec. 1 and 5), subject to the approval of the Lord Lieutenant as to plans and contracts for buildings and land (sec. 9, sub-sec. 4).

2. The County Council, however, must act in this matter through a Committee, the number of which may be fixed by the Lord Lieutenant, if he pleases, and the Committee may consist either wholly or in part of members of the Council, but no more than one-fourth of the entire number may be persons who are *not* members of the Council (sec. 9, sub-sec. 2).

3. Where a Lunatic Asylum District comprises two or more counties, the Committee is to be a Joint Committee, representing the different counties in the proportion of the expenses to be defrayed by each, and the expenses are to be in proportion to the number of lunatics for each county in the asylum according to the average of the three local financial years before each triennial election (sec. 9, sub-sec. 7); and such Joint Committees may sue or be sued in the names of the Councils represented (sec. 9, sub-sec. 9). The Committee of a single county is capable of suing or being sued in the name of the Council representing that council.

4. The County Council, and, in the case of two or more counties being represented in an asylum district, the Councils of these counties, may also provide an auxiliary lunatic asylum for chronic and harmless lunatics, and may take over, and use for that purpose, a workhouse (if an amalgamation of unions takes place) or any other building of the Guardians, on paying for it (sec. 76, sub-sec. 1, 2, 4); and, if this power is exercised in any county, lunatics in that county can no longer be sent to a workhouse (sec. 76, sub-sec. 3).

5. In aid of the expenses of ordinary lunatic asylums, the grant from the Local Taxation (Ireland) Account will henceforth be one-half of the net charge for each lunatic, or 4s. a week, whichever is least, provided, however, that the net charge is itself equal to or over 4s. a week (sec. 58, sub-sec. 2 (c)). The grant in aid from the same source in the case of an auxiliary asylum for chronic and harmless lunatics is to be half the net charge for each lunatic when that charge equals or exceeds 3s. 6d. a week, but is not to exceed 2s. a week for each lunatic (sec. 76, sub-sec. 1).

6. The County Council, acting through the Committee, *must* appoint for each lunatic asylum a resident medical superintendent and at least one assistant medical officer, and *may* appoint any other officers whom it considers necessary (sec. 84, sub-sec. 1); but, in the case of the medical superintendents and medical officers, the appointment is subject to the approval of the Lord Lieutenant (sec. 84, sub-sec. 4). The salaries of the medical superintendents and medical officers may be fixed only with the approval of the Lord Lieutenant (sec. 84, sub-sec. 4 (b)); in every other case they may be fixed by the County Council alone, acting through its Committee (sec. 84, sub-sec. 1 (b)). The medical superintendents and medical officers may be removed only with the consent of the Lord Lieutenant (sec. 84, sub-sec. 4); every other officer may be removed by the Council, acting through its Committee (sec. 83, sub-sec. 6); and the Council, without waiting for the approval of the Lord Lieutenant or of the Inspectors of Lunatics, may grant superannuation to any asylum officer or servant who has become incapable from confirmed sickness, age, or infirmity, or has served fifteen years, and is sixty years of age (sec. 84, sub-sec. 3, and 53 and 54 Vic., c. 31).

(b) County Infirmaries and Fever Hospitals :—

As to these it is provided as follows :—

1. The County Councils *must* henceforward contribute annually to such of these institutions and their officers as the Grand Juries were empowered to contribute to, the Waterford City and County Infirmary excepted (sec. 15, sub-sec. 12), a sum not less than was contributed by the Grand Juries in the standard financial year—that is, 1896-7— or any less minimum fixed by the Local Government Board (sec. 15, sub-sec. 1); but it may contribute up to £1,400 per annum in any case (sec. 15, sub-sec. 9, and 6 and 7 Wm. IV., c. 116, sec. 88), and the power to contribute to fever hospitals

established by private subscriptions and donations, and the power of the Grand Juries to appoint Boards of Superintendence for charitable institutions supported by presentments (2 and 3 Wm. IV., c. 85), are both abolished (sec. 15, sub-sec. 13).

2. The control and management of both infirmaries and fever hospitals so supported are to be in the hands of a Joint Committee, composed of a certain number of Governors elected by the governing bodies existing at the passing of the Act, and of a certain number of persons appointed by the County Council, the number in each case to be determined by the Local Government Board from time to time, regard being had, *inter alia*, to the sum contributed out of the county-cess and the poor-rate to the building and maintentenance of the institutions (sec. 15, sub-secs. 2 and 4); when more than one county supports one such institution, each shall be represented on the Committee (sec. 15, sub-sec. 3); and where any ecclesiastical person has been an *ex-officio* governor of any infirmary or fever hospital, he shall cease to be so (sec. 15, sub-sec. 11).

3. A County Council *may* contribute to the rebuilding, enlargement, or erection on a new site of any county infirmary, or to the re-opening of a closed infirmary, a sum not exceeding one-third of the sums received from private sources for such purposes (sec. 15, sub-sec. 6).

7.—APPLICATION OF ACTS RELATING TO BUSINESS TRANSFERRED.

As to all business transferred from any authority to the County Council it is provided that all Acts relating to such business shall be applicable to the County Council as the authority for the execution of those Acts and to the committees, members, and officers of the County Councils. (Order in Council (Application of Enactments), Article 33).

8.—NEW POWERS AND DUTIES.

The new powers and duties assigned to the County Councils are as follows :—

(*a*) TECHNICAL INSTRUCTION :—

Administering either by itself, or in conjunction with any other local authority already having jurisdiction in the matter, the Technical Instruction Acts 1889 and 1891 (52 & 53 Vic. c. 76, and 54 Vic. c. 4), under which a local authority may supply or aid the supply of instruction in the principles of science and art applicable to industries, the expenditure not to exceed what would be produced, by a rate of 1d. in the £ (sec. 7). The rate, except in the case of a county borough, must be the poor rate, and the amount expended is to be treated as county at large or district-expenses—that is, must be levied over the county at large, or on a particular district, according as the County Council directs (sec. 74, sub-sec. 2); the rate levied by any other authority than a County Council must not, together with the rate levied by the County Council, exceed the limit mentioned; but existing schemes are not affected (sec. 7 (*a*) and (*b*)).

(*b*) SUDDEN DAMAGE:—

Arranging for the repair of sudden damage to any "public work" (see definition, section 109), maintained at the cost of the county or any rural district; but, if the cost is to be borne by a district and not by the county, it must not exceed £50, unless the district does not object within the prescribed time (sec. 11, sub-sec. 1), and the county surveyor must certify that the execution of the work cannot be delayed without prejudice to the public (sec. 11, sub-sec. 2).

(*c*) EXCEPTIONAL DISTRESS:—

Relieving exceptional distress out of the workhouse, if the Council chooses to exercise the power, and if the Local Government Board consents to the borrowing of the necessary money, half the expense (which is not to exceed 3d. in the £) to be levied off the county at large, the other half off the district electoral division in which the poor persons relieved reside (sec. 13, sub-secs. 1 and 3). Persons holding more than a quarter of an acre of land are not to be excluded from relief under the section (sub-sec. 2), and the County Council is enabled to appoint a member of its body to act as an additional guardian of the Union concerned for the period for which the relief is to be given (sub-sec. 3).

(*d*) COUNTY CORONERS:—

The election of county coroners (sec. 14, sub-sec. 1), the alteration of coroners' districts (sec. 14, sub-sec. 2), and fixing the salaries of coroners (sec. 14, sub-sec. 6), but *not* the removal of a coroner (sec. 14, sub-secs. 3 and 4).

(*e*) BYE-LAWS:—

Making bye-laws for the good order and government of the county, or any part or parts thereof. except a borough, and for the prevention of nuisances, in the same way and tc the same extent as is enacted for corporations by sections 125 to 127 of the Municipal Corporations (Ireland) Act, 1840 (3 & 4 Vic., c. 108), to which bye-laws section 224 of the Public Health (Ireland) Act, 1878 (41 & 42 Vic., c. 52), shall apply (sec. 16). The effect of this last-mentioned provision is to make confirmation of all such bye-laws by the Local Government Board necessary. In determining the validity of such bye-laws the courts will be slow to hold that a bye-law is void for unreasonableness, or that it ought not to be supported, unless it is manifestly partial, or unequal in its operation between different classes, or unjust, or made in bad faith, or clearly involving an unjustifiable interference with the liberty of those subject to it (Kruse *v.* Johnson, 1898, 2 Q. B. 91). A County Council cannot make bye-laws for a *borough* which is part of the administrative county (sec. 16, sub-sec. 2). But, apparently, it may do so for any other urban district.

(*f*) LEGAL PROCEEDINGS :—

The same power of opposing (but not *promoting*) Bills in Parliament, and of prosecuting and defending legal proceedings as is conferred on municipal bodies by the Borough Funds (Ireland) Act, 1888, for the exercise of which power no approval of voters shall be required (sec. 17).

(*g*) MARINE WORKS :—

Power, with the consent of the Congested Districts Board and the Board of Works respectively, to take over any " marine work "—that is, any harbour, dock, pier, quay, wharf, beacon, light, and any similar work, including the approaches thereto — constructed or acquired by those Boards, and to maintain or reconstruct such works, subject to making compensation for same to any person other than the Congested Districts Board, all the powers of the Board of Works or Congested Districts Board as to tolls, rates, and regulations in relation to such works, being also given to the Councils (sec. 18).

(*h*) EXPENSES :—

Supplying Rural District Councils and Boards of Guardians (as to which see *post*), with their respective expenses (sec. 51, sub-sec. 1); apportioning the amounts to be raised for county-at-large charges and union charges between any urban districts in the county or union and the rest of the county or union, and also apportioning every amount to be raised for county-at-large charges, partly between any urban district and partly between any rural district in the county (sec. 51, sub-sec. 2).

(*i*) COURTHOUSES :—

Power to manage, alter, and enlarge, and, with the consent of the Local Government Board, to sell any of its land or buildings, including courthouses [Local Government (Application of Enactments) Order, 1898, Art. 15, (1) (3)], and, subject to the use of any courthouse or sessions house for the administration of justice, to use the same for its purposes as a Council (sec. 72, sub-sec. 3).

(*j*) OFFICERS :—

The power of appointing, paying, and removing the officers of the Council.

A County Council *must* appoint a secretary, a treasurer, and a county surveyor; and *may* appoint such assistant surveyors and such further officers as it thinks necessary for the performance of the duties of the Council (sec. 83, sub-sec. 1), but the appointment of a secretary and a county surveyor, and the appointment of an assistant surveyor, if made, must be approved by the Local Government Board (sec. 83, sub-sec. 4).

It may provide for a deputy for any of its officers in case of illness, absence, or incapacity (sec. 83, sub-sec. 2).

It *may* take from a treasurer when a banking company, and *must* take from any other officer who receives or pays money on behalf of the Council, such security as may be approved by the Local Government Board (sec. 83, sub-sec. 3).

In the case of the secretary, county surveyor, and assistant surveyor (if appointed), the salaries can only be fixed or altered with the concurrence of the Local Government Board (sec. 83, sub-sec. 4), while in all other cases the County Council may fix any salaries it pleases, subject to any existing statutory limitations (sec. 83, sub-sec. 1).

The Council may not remove the secretary, the county surveyor, or the assistant surveyor (if appointed) without the concurrence of the Local Government Board (sec. 83, sub-sec. 4), but it may remove any other of its officers without that concurrence (sec. 83, sub-sec. 6), except the Coroner as mentioned *supra*, p. 19.

Finally, the County Council possesses the same powers of superannuating any of its officers but the county surveyor.

as is conferred on Boards of Guardians by the 28 & 29 Vic. c. 26 (sec. 83, sub-sec. 11), the existing law regarding the superannuation of county surveyors remaining untouched; and section 83 and the law relating to treasurers of counties are applied to the County of Dublin (sec. 83, sub-sec. 12), which hitherto had been exempt from the operation of that law.

(k) STAGE PLAYS :—

The County Council of Dublin may apply to the Lord Lieutenant for, and the Lord Lieutenant may grant, an occasional license for the performance of any stage play in any theatre, room, or building, if the profits arising from the performance are to be applied to charitable objects, or in aid of the funds of any scientific or literary society (sec. 89), this power being necessary in the City and County of Dublin, because of the provisions of the 26 Geo. III., c. 57, which prohibit any dramatic performance there in any but a licensed theatre, and being unnecessary in any other county where there is no restriction in such matters.

(l) VOTERS' AND JURORS' LISTS :—

The County Council, through its Secretary, shall have the preparation of the lists of voters and jurors as far as respects rural districts (sec. 83, sub-sec. 7), except during the lives of existing clerks of unions, or unless such clerks agree not to perform the duties in relation thereto (sec. 121); and the Council shall arrange by contract, as in the case of works leviable off the county at large, for the printing of such lists, whether such printing is required by the Secretary, the Clerk of the Peace, the Clerk of the Union, or Town Clerk (sec. 96, sub-sec. 2 and 3).

(m) DIFFICULTIES IN THE CASE OF OTHER BODIES :—

Powers to remove difficulties arising as respects the elections to other local bodies, or as to the first meetings of such other bodies after a triennial election, or as to any Council not being properly constituted, or being unable to act (see *infra*, p. 220).

(n) COMMITTEES :—

Power to delegate to Committees, either general or special, any business which, in the opinion of the Council, would be better regulated and managed by a Committee, the acts of such Committees, however, to be confirmed by the Council (Local Government (Application of Enactments) Order, 1898, Article 36, sub-sec. 4).

(*o*) OATHS :—

Power to administer oaths in the administration of such business as the examination of tenders and the making of contracts, that power having been possessed by the Grand Jury, and not having been reserved from the Councils when the transfer of the business was made from the one set of bodies to the other.

(*p*) TRAMWAYS AND RAILWAYS:—

Power, with the approval of the Privy Council, to enter into an arrangement with any railway or tramway company, with any of whose railways or tramways an undertaking which becomes or has become the property of the Council under the Tramway Acts is connected, for the working of such undertaking on such terms as may be agreed upon (sec. 92).

(*q*) MAIN ROADS :—

Power to regulate the expenditure on main roads, as to which, whether situate in a rural or urban county district or not (sec. 8, sub-sec. 11), the following are the provisions :—

(1.) Main roads are roads which, at the passing of the Act, were maintainable partly or wholly at the expense of the county at large (sec 8, sub-sec. 2).

(2.) One-half the cost of maintaining such roads is to be borne by the administrative county at large, and one-half by the districts through which it runs (sec. 8, sub-sec. 1).

(3.) Where a road has been wholly maintained at the cost of the county at large, or where more than half the cost of a road has been borne by the county at large that arrangement may continue, whether the road is a main road or not, and this provision applies to a bridge (sub-sec. 12).

(4.) The County Council may, on the report of the County Surveyor, declare what roads are main roads, and may make new declarations, at intervals of not less than five years (sub-sec. 3), and make and declare a new road a main road, and after that declaration at like intervals (sub-sec. 4); but such declarations shall be provisional till the District Councils concerned have considered them, and made representations to the County Councils concerning them, after which they may. modified or unmodified, be finally adopted (sub-secs. 5, 6). A District Council may appeal to the. Local Government Board against such a declaration, and that body, in that case, will finally decide (sub-sec. 8), and till the appeal is decided the declaration is suspended (sub-sec. 7); but if the declaration is eventually confirmed it will operate from the date on which it was originally made, or from such later date as the Local Government Board fix (sub-sec. 10).

(5.) The County Council, for the purpose of maintaining roads, may purchase or take on lease land where road materials exist, and may purchase or take on hire any machines (such as steam rollers) for the repair of roads, and may place both materials and machines at the disposal of road contractors (sec. 12, sub-sec. 1), and the power to obtain materials (6 and 7 Wm. IV., c. 116, s. 162) is extended to taking such materials out of a river or brook at a distance of at least 150 feet above or below any bridge, dam, or weir, provided no injury is done thereby (sec. 12, sub-sec. 2).

(6.) The County Council may, by resolution, stop up or abandon an old road or work, subject to objection by any ratepayer, in which latter case the resolution of the Council must be confirmed by the Local Government Board (sec. 82, sub. sec. 2), and Local Government (Procedure of Councils) Order, 1899, Art. 30 (1).

(7.) Fresh expenditure on roads proposed by Rural District Councils cannot exceed one-fourth the average amount of the expenditure for the last three years, without the consent of the Local Government Board, which may fix a new limit for any particular road or any particular year (sec.7, sub-sec. 2).

(*r*) TAKING OF LANDS :—

Power, for the purpose of any of the powers or duties of a County Council, to acquire, purchase, take on lease, or exchange any land, or any rights or easements in or over land, including rights to water, within or without the county, and to acquire, hire, erect, and furnish such halls, buildings, and offices as are required within or without the county (sec. 10, sub-sec. 1, 2); and where a County Council wishes to take land, or any easement or right over land compulsorily for widening an old road or making a new one, it may do so, provided it be not demesne land, or a pleasure ground, or land situate in a borough or town, and provided the judge of assize, and, on appeal, the Privy Council, thinks the proposed work of public utility, an elaborate procedure in this matter being prescribed by the Act (sec. 10, sub-sec. 3).

(s) OBLIGATION TO MAINTAIN WORKS —:

The obligation to keep all public works maintainable at the cost of the county in good condition and repair (sec. 82, sub-sec. 1).

(t) COMPULSORY EDUCATION :—

The same power as is possessed by urban authorities under the Irish Education Act, 1892, to compel the attendance of children at school, and to appoint members of School Attendance Committees ; such power to be exercised, however, only on the application of a Rural District Council, and the expenses to be borne by the rate out of which the expenses incurred in the execution of the Act by the County Council are to be borne (sec. 74, s.s. 1, and see Irish Education Act, 1892, sec. 15, sub-sec. 2).

IX.—Procedure of the County Councils.

• The proceedings of County Councils and committees thereof are regulated by Articles 35 to 38, of the Local Government (Application of Enactments) Order 1898, and by the Local Government (Procedure of Councils) Order, 1899. The principal points to be noted as to procedure as so regulated are the following:—

1. The County Council must hold an annual meeting on the twelfth day after the day of election (s. 94 (7) of Act and Act 35 (4) of Application of Enactments Order), four quarterly meetings on such days between the annual meeting and the 1st June next following as it may fix by standing order, and such other meetings as it may consider necessary for the transaction of its business.

2. At the annual meeting (after a triennial election) the order of business will be:—

(a) Election of additional Councillors;
(b) Election of Chairman and Vice-Chairman;
(c) Election of members of a joint committee or board;
(d) Other business.

3. The quorum shall be one-fourth of the whole number of the Council.

4. The Council may appoint committees for any purpose

except to make a rate or borrow money, and fix the quorum, proceedings, and place or places of meetings of such committees.

5. Minutes of the proceedings of every meeting of a Council or a committee must be kept and signed in the usual way.

6. The chairman may call a meeting of his own motion or in obedience to a requisition of five members of the Council, and if he refuses to obey such requisition, or does not act on it within seven days without actually refusing, any five members may call a meeting.

7. Three days' notice of the meeting and of the business to be done must be given to every member, and no other business can be transacted, except that of which notice has been given.

8. The name of every member present at a meeting, and his vote on any question, must be recorded.

9. The chairman is to have a casting vote.

10. For the county at large presentment sessions there is substituted a Proposal Committee of the County Council, and instead of the Baronial Sessions the Rural District Councils are to be substituted; and all applications for county at large works must be made to the Proposal Committee, and all applications for district works in rural districts to the Rural District Councils.

11. The Proposal Committees and the Rural District Councils may either reject the applications made to them respectively, in which case there will be an end of them; or they may adopt them in whole or in part, in which case they will send on proposals in regard to them to the County Councils.

12. The County Councils will then either reject the proposals or adopt them, or send them back to be modified, and, on their being modified to their satisfaction, may then adopt them;

13. Every work must be done by contract, and tenders are invited and adopted by the Proposal Committees and the Rural District Councils before the proposals are submitted to the County Councils; and, if no tenders have been received after having been invited, the County Council may give the work into the charge of the County Surveyor;

14. Payments are to be made to contractors only on the certificate of the County Surveyor;

15. The regulations relating to Proposal Committees, Rural District Council proposals, contracts, and tenders, apply only to the business transferred from the Grand Juries and

Presentment Sessions, unless the standing orders of the Council apply them to any other business; so that, except in that event, the County Council may act, as regards all other than Grand Jury business, without the intervention of the Proposal Committee and the Rural District Council;

16. All printing must be done by contract;

17. Every meeting of the County Council, Proposal Committee and Rural District Council must be open to the public during the consideration of proposals and applications.

It will thus be observed that the old distinction between the Presentment Sessions and the Grand Jury—namely, that the former *initiated* expenditure, and the latter merely *sanctioned* or *rejected* it—is preserved as between the Proposal Committees and the Rural District Councils on the one hand and the County Councils on the other.

PART II.
COUNTY BOROUGHS.
I.—List of County Boroughs :—

"Each of the boroughs mentioned in the Second Schedule to this Act shall be an administrative county of itself, and be called a county borough" (sec. 21, sub-sec. 1).

The boroughs which are mentioned in the Second Schedule, and, therefore, become county boroughs, are :—

1. Dublin
2. Belfast.
3. Cork.
4. Limerick.
5. Londonderry.
6. Waterford.

These boroughs being made counties, their Corporations will have the powers and duties of a County Council (sec. 21, sub-sec. 2), but will retain their present name or title (sec. 22, sub-sec. 1).

II.—County Council Provisions which do not apply to County Boroughs.

The provisions regarding County Councils apply to the Councils of County Boroughs, with the following exceptions, viz., the provisions relating to

1. Main roads;
2. Coroners (except in one particular noticed *post*);
3. Bye-laws;
4. The Borough Funds (Ireland) Act, 1888; sec. 21, sub-sec. 2 (*b*).
5. The constitution, number, and duration of office of the corporations, and the office of Lord Mayor, or Mayor, section 21, sub-sec. 2 (*a*);
6. Casual vacancies (sec. 94, sub-sec. 4), casual vacancies

in the corporations of the six county boroughs being thus
filled up as in the past—namely by an ordinary election;

7.   The time of election of members of the Corporations,
which is to be the 15th day of January (sec. 94, sub-sec. 10).

8.   The procedure of County Councils as regulated by
Local Government (Application of Enactments) Order, 1898,
except as regards business transferred from the Grand Jury
or Presentment Sessions.

9.   The keeping of accounts so as to charge expenditure
to proper area (Local Government (Application of Enactments) Order, Article 17, sub-sec. 3).

10.   Payments out of funds of Councils, when acting as
County Councils (same Order, Article 18, sub-sec. 4);

11.   Borrowing, except when Corporations act otherwise
than as County Councils (same Order, Article 22, sub-sec. 12);

12.   Meetings and proceedings of Councils and appointment of Committees and keeping of Minutes (same Order,
Article 36, sub-sec. 1.)

13.   The annual budget, except as regards the receipts
and expenses of a Corporation as a County Council.   (Same
Order, and Article 21, s.s. 4.)

III.—County Council provisions which do apply to County Boroughs.

As the enactments regarding County Councils apply to the
Councils of County boroughs with the foregoing exceptions, it
follows that the following amongst others do apply, viz., the
provisions relating to

1.   Election petitions;

2.   The electorate, of which qualified women and peers
shall henceforth be a portion (sec. 21, sub-sec. 2 (a);

3.   The qualification of Aldermen and Councillors (sec. 21
sub-sec. 2 (a), sec. 94, sub-sec. 2);

4.   The mode of election of Aldermen and Councillors
(sec. 21, sub-sec. 2 (a));

5.   The expenses of elections as regulated by Local
Government (Application of Enactments) Order, 1898, Art. 6;

6.   Making up and audit of accounts (as to which see *post*);

7.   Future alterations of certain boundaries (Local
Government (Application of Enactments) Order 1898,
Article 25);

8.   Appointment of joint committees (Local Government
(Application of Enactments) Order 1898, Article 38).

County Boroughs retain the power to appoint *by resolution
of Council* a Banking Company to receive moneys on receivable
orders issued by the Borough Treasurers and in such cases the

receipts given on behalf of the Treasurer shall be a good discharge to the person paying the amount, and similarly to appoint the Chief Officer of the Dublin Rates Department to receive rates and give a good discharge for same. Section 47 does not diminish or limit the previous powers of the Council to make, such regulations, but provides that all receipts shall be accounted for to the Treasurer.

IV.—New Provisions as to County Boroughs.

The following are the new provisions enacted as regards County Boroughs in addition to any that may be involved in the conversion of Corporations into County Councils with the powers and duties thereof :—

1. The Dublin Corporation obtains the collection of the non-municipal rates, the collection of which has hitherto been in the hands of the Collector-General and his staff (sec. 66, and as to which see further *post*);

2. A general revaluation of property in the county boroughs may be made on the application of the Corporations, which is to bear such portion of the cost, not exceeding one-half, as the Treasury direct, and on such revaluation the land in county boroughs is to be valued as houses and buildings are valued under sec. 11 of the Valuation (Ireland) Act, 1852 (sec. 65, and as to which see further *post*);

3. The Corporations lose the power of assessing compensation for malicious injuries (sec. 21, s.s. 2 (*e*), and sec. 5);

4. The Dublin Corporation obtains the duties paid by pawnbrokers under sec. 66 of the Dublin Police Magistrates Act of 1808, in the city (sec. 67);

5. The qualification for jurors in all county boroughs is henceforth to be the same as in Dublin and Cork—that is, £20 valuation for common, and £50 for special jurors, and separate jurors' books must be made out for such boroughs (sec. 69, s.s. 7);

6. No person can be appointed to any paid ofhee, except that of mayor or sheriff, under a Council who is a member of the Council, or has been such within six months prior to his appointment, and this disqualification extends to the partner in business of any such person (Local Government (Application of Enactments) Order 1898, Art. 12 (3) (4));

7. A Corporation may make regulations respecting the use and speed of bicycles and similar machines (sec. 88);

8. The Corporation of Dublin will have the same power as the County Dublin Council and the Urban District Councils of that county to apply for licences for the performance of stage plays (sec. 89).

V.–Special Provisions as regards Belfast and Londonderry.

Some special provisions are enacted regarding Belfast and Londonderry :—

(1) A sheriff and lieutenant are to be appointed for those two county boroughs as for the other counties of cities mentioned in section 4 of the Municipal Privileges (Ireland) Act, 1676, the sheriff to be elected, as in those counties of cities, by the Corporations (sec. 69, s.s. 1);

(2). The offices of Clerk of the Crown and Clerk of the Peace for the County of Antrim and for the City of Belfast are to be held by the same person, and a similar provision is made regarding the County and City of Londonderry (sec. 69, s.s. 5).

VI.–Special Provisions as regards Mayors and Sheriffs.

The Mayors in the County Boroughs are to be elected and to come into office on the 23rd January, and the outgoing Mayor is to continue in office till his successor has made a declaration accepting office; but the Council may, by resolution, fix the 23rd February as the ordinary day of retirement of the Mayor, in which case that day will be the ordinary day for the retirement of the Mayor (sec. 94., s.s. 11).

As respects the sheriffs of counties of cities or towns, the selection of three persons to fill the office of sheriff is to take place at the quarterly meeting in January (sec. 94, s.s. 12). The outgoing sheriff remains in office till his successor is appointed (39 and 40 Vic. c. 76).

VII.–Opposing Bills in Parliament.

A council of a county borough may henceforth oppose a Bill in Parliament without any approval of voters (sec. 21, s.s. 2 (c)).

PART III.
DISTRICT COUNCILS, BOARDS OF GUARDIANS AND TOWN BOARDS.

I.—Establishment of District Councils

Two kinds of District Councils are established—namely, URBAN DISTRICT COUNCILS and RURAL DISTRICT COUNCILS.

(a.)—URBAN DISTRICT COUNCILS:—

All Corporations and all Town Boards which, at the passing of the Act, were urban sanitary authorities, became URBAN DISTRICT COUNCILS, and the area in which they will have authority become URBAN DISTRICTS ; but a corporation will not lose that title by becoming an URBAN DISTRICT COUNCIL (sec. 22, sub-sec. 1).

Excluding County Boroughs, those places in which urban sanitary authorities have hitherto existed, and in which, consequently, Urban District Councils will now exist by virtue of the Act, are the following :—

(1) Towns Corporate—that is, those having Corporations (Public Health (Ireland) Act, 1878, sec. 4).

(2) Towns with Town Boards under 9 Geo. IV., c. 82, the Towns Improvement Act, 1854, and the 3 & 4 Vic., c. 108, and with a population exceeding 6,000 (P. H. (I.) Act, 1878, sec. 4;

(3) Towns with Town Boards created under Local Acts (see same sec. of Public Health Act, 1878);

(4) Towns which, having town or township Commissioners and a population of less than 6,000, have been constituted urban sanitary districts by a provisional order of the Local Government Board (Public Health (Ireland) Act, 1878, sec. 7).

(For a list of *all* urban districts in Ireland, County Boroughs included, with the Acts under which they are so constituted, see Appendix V., *post*).

In addition to those places which were urban sanitary districts at the passing of the Act, and which will now in consequence possess Urban District Councils, any town having a population of over 1,500, and not being an urban sanitary district, may become an urban district and have an Urban District Council by order of the Local Government Board, if a petition is not presented against such order within three months by (1), if the petition is presented *before* the first election of Rural District Councils, at least one-fourth of the *Parliamentary* electors of the town or the guardians of the union in which the town is situate, and, (2) if the petition is *after* the first election of Rural District Councils, by at least one-fourth of the local government electors within the town or the Board of Guardians or the Rural District Council of the district (sec. 42, sub-sec. 1). This process is called "urbanising." The Local Government Board has had power under the Public Health Act, 1878, sec. 7, to add to an urban sanitary district, or to create a new one, but only by provisional order, which required confirmation by Parliament, and the cost of which to the local authority might be considerable. The change now made is to dispense with Parliaméntay sanction if there is no petition, and if the population is over 1,500. As to the financial effect of "Urbanising," see *post*.

(b.)—RURAL DISTRICT COUNCILS.

Rural District Councils are established for all rural sanitary districts (sec. 22, sub-sec. 2), which includes all areas not comprised in urban sanitary districts (sec. 6 P. H. (I.) Act, 1878). It may be added that a rural district comprises the Union if such Union be situated wholly in one county, but if the Union extends into two or more counties the portion in each county becomes a rural district. In both cases urban sanitary districts are excluded.

But, just as a town may become "urbanised," so it may become "disurbanised"—that is, may cease to be an urban district, and may become part of a rural district. This process is called "Disurbanising," as to the financial effect of which see *post*. The town, however, must be one having less than 5,000 inhabitants, and the Order of the Local Government Board constituting it part of a rural sanitary district must have been made within six months after the passing of the Act, and before the powers of the Grand Jury in respect of roads have been transferred to the town (by the provisions of the Act in relation thereto being declared to be in force). If there is no petition from either one-fourth of the Parliamentary electors or from the Board of Guardians against such an Order within three months after it is published, the Order will take effect without the authority of Parliament Once a town has become disurbanised it cannot be urbanised again for ten years (sec. 42, sub-sec. 2). As a matter of fact no such Order was made by the Local Government Board within the six months, nor was there any application for such an Order.

(c.)—INCORPORATION OF DISTRICT COUNCILS.

All District Councils, *except the Council of a borough*, become like County Councils, bodies corporate by the name of the Councils, with the addition of the names of the districts; they have each a common seal and perpetual succession; and they may hold land for the purposes of their powers and duties (Local Government (Application of Enactments) Order, 1898, Article 13, sub-section 1); but any District Council, with the sanction of the County Council, may change its name and the name of its district (same order, Article 14, sub-sec. 1). The Councils of boroughs were bodies corporate before the Act.

II.—Constitution of District Councils.

(a) As to URBAN DISTRICT COUNCILS. :—

As to Urban District Councils, the Act makes no change in the

(1) Constitution of the existing urban authorities,
(2) Number of their members,
(3) Duration of office of the members,
(4) Mayor or chairman

(sec. 23, sub-sec. 1); but, if an Urban District Council in any place where previous to the passing of the Act one-third of the Corporation or Town Board was elected annually, pass a resolution, by a majority of two-thirds of the members voting, for the extension to that District Council of the provision by which all the members of County Councils are elected triennially, an order carrying out that resolution may be made by the Local Govern-ment Board (sec. 23, sub-sec. 1).

In every case the quorum of an Urban District Council must be one-fourth of the total number of the Council (sec. 23, sub-sec. 2).

In an urban district which contains more than 5,000 popula-tion the Chairman of the Urban District Council, and in a borough *which has not a separate Commission of the Peace*, the Mayor will be *ex-officio* a justice of the peace for the county during his term of office on taking the oaths, unless, in the former case, the chairman is a woman or personally disqualified by any Act, or unless, in the latter case, the Mayor is personally disqualified (sec. 26). In boroughs having a separate Commission of the Peace there will be no change. The Mayor will be a justice of the peace *ex-officio*.

(b) As to RURAL DISTRICT COUNCILS.

(1) Each Council is to consist of a chairman and Councillors (sec. 23, sub-sec. 3 (a)); the district electoral divisions, which are to be the same as the existing Poor Law Electoral Divisions (sec. 22, sub-sec. 4), are each to elect two Councillors, unless where the Local Government Board assign more than two Councillors to a town or part of a town which forms one electoral division (sec. 23, sub-sec. 3 (b)) (see Local Government Board Order, Appendix III., fixing the number for such places); and every elector may vote for as many Councillors as there are seats to be filled, and no more (sec. 23, sub-sec. 3 (c)); and all rural district Councillors will continue in office, like County Councillors, for three years, and will then retire together, when there will be a new election (sec. 23, sub-sec. 3 (d), and sec. 94, sub-sec. 8).

D

(2) In addition to the *elected* District Councillors there may be three co-opted Councillors, who may be chosen from persons qualified to be Councillors—that is, persons who are Local Government electors or resident in the district (see *post* p. 35)— who will hold office during the term of office of the Council by whom they are co-opted, and the consideration of whose election shall be the first business after every triennial election (sec. 25, sub-secs. 1 (*a*) and 2).

(3) The chairman is to be chosen annually, and, if the Council think fit, a vice-chairman (sec. 25, sub-sec. 1 (*b*)); and such chairman, if the rural district over which he presides has a population exceeding 5,000, shall be a justice of the peace during his term of office, unless the chairman be a woman or a person personally disqualified by any Act (sec. 26, sub-sec. 1) on taking the oaths (sec. 26, sub-sec. 3, and see *supra* p. 2).

III.—Electors of District Councillors.

The electorate for all District Council elections, urban and rural, is the same as for County Council elections (sec. 23, sub-secs. 1 and 3 (*b*)).

IV.—Elections for District Councils.

(*a*) The provisions regarding the mode of elections (sec. 23, sub-sec. 1), the expenses at elections, and election petitions, which are enacted for County Councils, apply to all district Council elections (sec. 23, sub-sec. 1).

(*b*) Casual vacancies in urban district Councils are to be filled as hitherto in boroughs and towns, the Act making no change in that respect; but casual vacancies in rural district Councils are to be filled by those Councils themselves (sec. 94, sub-sec. 4).

(*c*) The ordinary day of election and the day of the annual meeting for urban district Councils are to be the 15th January and the 23rd January respectively (sec. 94, sub-sec. 9); in rural districts the Councils will be elected on the same day (*supra* p. 8), as the County Council elections, and the two sets of elections shall be held together (sec. 94, sub-sec. 6), and the day of the annual meeting, and the ordinary day of election of chairman and vice-chairman shall be the fifth day after the day of election (sec. 94, sub-sec. 7).

V.—Qualifications and Disqualifications of District Councillors.

(*a*) In an urban district, the qualifications for a Councillor shall be either the same as that for a County Councillor, that is, he need only be registered as a local government elector; or he must have resided in the district for twelve months before the election, and continue to reside there (sec. 23, sub-sec. 4, and sec. 94, sub-sec. 2), and this provision applies to an alderman as well as to a Councillor (sec. 23, sub-sec. 1); and a woman, married or single, may be a Councillor for any urban district except a borough (Local Government (Application of Enactments) Order, 1898, Article, 12, sub-sec. 2). A "borough" by section 109 is defined to mean a municipal borough having a Town Council. As neither the Act nor any Order in Council made under it removes the ineligibility of women for the urban district council of a borough, they remain excluded from Town Councils or Corporations.

(b) In a rural district the qualification for a Councillor is the same as that in an urban district which is not a borough (sec. 23, sub-sec. 4).

(c) The disqualifications for County Councillors exist also for urban and rural district Councillors (supra p. 10 and the Orders in Council there quoted); and a person disqualified for being a poor law guardian shall also be disqualified for being a rural district Councillor (Local Government (Application of Enactments) Order, 1898, Article 12, sub-sec. 8; and see also section 23 (4) of Act.).

(d) If a person is a local government elector for a rural district, or has resided therein for the twelve months preceding the election, he is qualified for being elected a rural district Councillor for any poor law electoral division comprised in such rural district. The same principle applies to wards in urban districts.

VI.—Acceptance and Resignation of Office by District Councillors.

The provisions relating to both these matters are generally the same for urban and rural district Councillors as for County Councillors (see supra, p. 11, and the enactments and orders in Council there quoted), except that the fine for non-acceptance of office, in the event of there being no bye-law regulating the matter, shall be £25 in the case of a Councillor and £50 in the case of a chairman or vice-chairman (Local Government (Application of Enactments) Order, 1898, Article 9, sub-sec. 2), and a rural district Councillor shall not be obliged to pay any fine on resignation of office (same Order, Article 10, sub-sec. 1). The proceedings consequent on vacancies occurring from any cause are also practically the same in the case of district Councils as in that of County Councils. These provisions do not apply to boroughs to which 3 and 4 Vic., c. 108, still applies (same Order, Article 8).

VII.—Business of District Councils.

(*a*) As to URBAN DISTRICT COUNCILS.

(*a*) The business of the Urban District Councils is the following :—

(1) The business of the baronial presentment sessions so far as respects the various districts, that is, the business of *initiating* in each urban district, such public works and expenditure as were dealt with at baronial sessions; the assignment of this business operating only so far as the new bodies, as the representatives of the old urban sanitary authorities, are not concerned with that business already (sec. 27, sub-sec. 1 (*a*));

(2) The business of the Grand Jury in relation to public works which are maintained exclusively at the cost of the district—that is, the business of finally deciding on presentments or proposals in reference to such works, so far as it is not already their business (sec. 27, sub-sec. 1 (*b*));

The reference in the expression "so far as the business is not already the business of the District Council" is to the fact that several urban authorities managed their own roads before the passing of the Act, and, in fact, were totally disconnected with the Grand Jury. Now such urban authorities as have not hitherto managed their own roads are given the power to do so; but, as regards roads in urban districts, the cost of the maintenance of which is partly leviable off the county at large and partly off the urban district, the Urban District Council will have only the same power as the Rural District Councils—that is, the power of making proposals to the County Council (Local Government (Procedure of Councils) Order, 1899, Article 29, made under sec. 106 (1).

(3) An Urban District Council may, if it pleases, undertake the *whole* cost of any road hitherto maintainable partly at the expense of the county at large, on such terms as may be agreed upon or, in default of agreement, on such terms as may be fixed by the Local Government Board (sec. 27, sub-sec. 6), but an order of the Local Government Board dealing with that matter will be provisional only if a petition against it is presented by either the County Council or the District Council concerned, or by at least a fourth of the Local Government electors of the county or district concerned (sec. 27, sub-sec. 7); but if any arrangement has been made by any local Act or provisional order confirmed by an Act respecting the maintenance of any road in an urban district or the liability of such a district to contribute to the maintenance

·of any road outside the district, it will not be disturbed (sec. 27, sub-sec. 8), unless after the expiration of 15 years the Local Government Board alter them (sec. 71);

(4) The business of making, levying, collecting, and recovering the poor rate in Urban Districts (sec. 28);

(5) The business of the Poor Law Guardians as Burial Boards in those towns which because they .have Town Boards under Local Acts, and not under any general Act, are excluded from sec. 160 of the Public Health Act, 1878, which constitutes the sanitary authority in each sanitary District, the District Burial Board (sec. 29);

(6) The business of the Board of Guardians in the case ·of the execution of regulations for preventing the spread of ·epidemic and infectious diseases (sec. 32);

(7) Their own proper business as sanitary authorities ·(sec. 22), which mainly consists of the following matters:—

(a) Drainage;
(b) Sewerage;
(c) New buildings;
(d) Scavenging and cleansing;
(e) Water and gas supply;
(f) Cellar dwellings;
(g) Common lodging houses;
(h) Houses let in lodgings;
(i) Markets and slaughter houses;
(j) Nuisances, offensive trades, and unsound meat;
(k) Infectious diseases;
(l) Burials;
(m) Locomotives on roads;
(n) Baths and wash-houses;
(o) Artizans' dwellings;
(p) Explosives;
(q) Alkali, etc., works;
(r) Factories, workshops, and bakehouses, dairies, and ·cowsheds;
(s) Infectious diseases notification;
(t) Open spaces;
(u) Certain matters in relation to railway and canal traffic;
(v) Sale of horseflesh;
(w) Technical instruction;
(x) Cleansing of persons;
(y) Electric lighting; and
(z) Rivers pollution.

(See the Public Health Act 1878, and amending and extending

Acts, and Acts relating to the several matters aforesaid not dealt
with by the Public Health Acts).

(8)   The powers of a County Council in reference to the
acquisition of lands or rights in or over land for any purposes.
transferred to Urban District Councils from the Grand Jury
(sec. 27, sub-sec. 4);

(9)   Power to establish recreation grounds or public
walks, or contribute towards the cost of, and make regulations for, the same (sec. 36);

(10)   Power, in addition to the power to purchase markets.
from a market company (Public Health Act, 1878, sec. 104),
to purchase from anyone any market rights (sec. 31);

(11)   Power to contribute towards the funds of the conservators of Fisheries in their several districts at the request
of the conservators, a sum not more in any year than the
produce of a ½d. in the £ on the valuation of the district,
with the right to appoint such a number of Conservators for
the several districts as the Lord Lieutenant may determine,.
the number, however, being less than the number appointed
under the Fisheries (Ireland) Act, 1848, (sec. 37);

(12)   The powers and duties of any body from which
business is transferred to the Urban District Councils and
of the officers of such bodies other than the treasurer (sec.
72, sub-secs. (1) (2);

(13)   Power to guarantee any loss sustained by the
establishment or maintenance of any post or telegraph
office or provision of additional facilities (postal or other) by
the Postmaster-General in an urban district which the
Council think would be beneficial (sec. 75);

(15) The duty of maintaining all public works within the
district in good condition and repair (sec. 82, sub-sec. 1), and
the power to propose to the County Council to stop up or
abandon an old road in the district which is useless (sec.
82, sub-sec. 2); and the power to appeal to the Local
Government Board against the refusal of a County Council
so to act (sec. 82, sub-sec. 3);

(16) Power to the Urban District Councils of the County
of Dublin to apply to the Lord Lieutenant and to license a.
place for the performance of stage plays (sec. 89, and see
supra, p. 22);

(17) Duty to send, through the clerk of the Council, to
every Board of Guardians, without payment and within such
time after the making of the poor rate as may be prescribed
by the Local Government Board a copy of so much of the
rate-book as relates to the Union (sec. 96, sub-sec. 1); and.

to provide and keep ballot boxes and other apparatus for holding elections in each urban district (sec. 99, sub-sec. 1.)

(18) Power to Urban District Councils *which are the Corporations of Boroughs*, to elect a coroner as heretofore (sub-sec. 40, sub-sec. 3) from which it follows that a borough like Galway, where the coroner is elected not by any council but by the electors of the borough, does not come within the provision (see also sec. 117 (2)).

(19) Power to the Urban District Council of Carrickfergus as successors of the Municipal Commissioners of that town, to take over the business and property of the Carrickfergus Municipal Commissioners (sec. 41, sub-sec. 3).

(b) As to RURAL DISTRICT COUNCILS.

The business of Rural District Councils is the following :—

(1) The business of the baronial presentment sessions for each district (sec. 27, sub-sec. 1 (*a*)).

(2) The business of the rural sanitary authority in each district (sec. 33, sub-sec. 1), and see the Public Health Act, 1878, and amending and extending Acts, the Labourers' Acts, 1893 to 1896, and the list of powers and duties of urban district Councils *all of which are assigned to rural as well as urban district Councils except those relating to the following matters:*—

(*a*) Baths and wash-houses ;
(*b*) Labourers' lodging-houses ;
(*c*) Artizans' dwellings ;
(*d*) Explosives.

(3) Such business of the *urban* sanitary authorities under the Public Health Acts, or any other Act, as the Local Government Board may direct by general order, *provided the County Council makes the application* (sec. 33, sub-sec. 2, 3).

(4) Power to purchase by agreement lessors' interest in lands already held by the sanitary authority for the purposes of the Labourers' (Ireland) Acts, 1883 to 1896 (sec. 34);

(5) Power, if authorised by the Local Government Board, to provide public walks and recreation grounds and making bye-laws for the regulation thereof, and to defray the expenses thereof as if they were expenses under the Public Health Act, 1878 (sec. 36);

(6) The same power as an urban district Council has to contribute to the funds of a Board of Conservators of Fisheries, with the same right to representation on such Board (sec. 37);

(7) Power to appoint, for any purpose of the Public Health Acts, for a dispensary district or other part of their district, a committee composed either of members of the Rural District Council, representing the particular place, or partly of such persons and partly of persons resident or interested therein, with power to the Committee to do anything which the Council itself might have done for the said purpose, except to raise or spend any money beyond the limit fixed by the Council, or to appoint, remove, or alter the remuneration of any officer ; and the appointing body may revoke, in whole or in part, its appointment or authority ; and, on the application of the Committee (if appointed), a District Council may authorise any expenditure by the Committee which would be general expenses under the Public Health Acts on the condition that it be levied as special expenses off the particular area in which the money is spent (sec. 39) ;

(8) The business of the Board of Guardians under sec. 150 of the Public Health Act, 1878, in reference to epidemic diseases, in respect of which sec. 3 of the Epidemic Diseases Prevention Act, 1883, is repealed (sec. 32) ;

(9) The same power as is given to an Urban District Council to recommend the stopping up or abandonment of an old road which has become useless (sec. 82, sub-sec. 2) ;

(10) Appointment and payment of its officers, subject to certain restrictions ;

(11) Power to fill up casual vacancies (sec. 94, sub-sec. 4) ;

(12) The same power as is possessed by towns, under the Towns Improvement (Ireland) Act, 1854, as amended by the Local Government (Ireland) Act, 1872, to make bye-laws in relation to boats plying for hire (sec. 35) ;

(13) The same duty as is imposed on Urban District Councils to provide ballot boxes and other apparatus for Rural District Council elections (sec. 99, sub-sec. 1).

(14) The power to apply to the County Council, to put in force in the district the compulsory provisions of the Irish Education Act, 1892, with which application the County Council must comply (sec. 74 sub-sec. 1 and 55 and 56 Vic., c. 42, sec. 15 (2)).

VIII.—Procedure of District Councils.

The following are the principal provisions relating to the procedure of District Councils :—

(a) As to URBAN DISTRICT COUNCILS.

(1) All such Councils, whether the Councils of Boroughs or not, must transact the business transferred to them

from the baronial presentment sessions, and the Grand Jury in the manner prescribed by general rules of the Local Government Board (sec. 27, sub-sec. 3, and Local Government (Procedure of Councils) Order, 1899, Article 19) ; as to which see *supra* under head of " Procedure of County Councils."

(2) Urban District Councils which are *not* the Councils or Corporations of Boroughs, must hold an annual meeting, and one each month at least, and as many more as may be necessary for the transaction of their business (Local Government (Application of Enactments) Order 1898, Art. 35 (1);

(3) The annual meeting of Urban District Councils shall be held on the 23rd January (sec. 94, sub-sec. 9) ;

(4) The procedure of the Councils of *Boroughs*, so far as they are unaffected by the aforesaid regulations, will, of course, continue in force.

(*b*) As to RURAL DISTRICT COUNCILS.

(1) The rules regulating for County Councils the meetings, annual and other, of the Council, the election of chairman and vice-chairman, the co-option of additional Councillors, the quorum, the appointment of special and general Committees, minutes of proceedings, the calling of meetings, and the procedure at meetings, apply to Rural District Councils, except that the ordinary day of the annual meeting and election of chairman and vice-chairman of a Rural District Council is to be the fifth, and not the twelfth day after the election (sec. 94, sub-sec. 7) ;

(2) As to the procedure to be followed in the case of business transferred to the Rural District Councils from the baronial presentment sessions (see *supra* and the provisions of the Order in Council there referred to).

The several kinds of representation which may be made by a County Council to the Local Government Board to enable that body to exercise its power regarding boundaries are set out in the Local Government (Application of Enactments) Order 1898, Article 25, which provision, however, seems to give the Board an absolute discretion as to whether it will entertain a representation or not (see also Articles 26-31 of the same Order).

IX.—Place of Meetings of Rural District Councils.

(a) Where a rural district is co-extensive with a union, the meeting and business of the Rural District Council and of the Board of Guardians may be held and transacted at the same place (sec. 79, sub-sec. 1 (c)) ;

(b) Where a rural district is comprised in, but not co-extensive with, a union, the District Council will be entitled, under conditions to be prescribed by the Local Government Board, to use the board-room and the offices of the Guardians, and, if such board-room and offices are outside its district, to hire a board-room and offices within it (sec. 79, sub-sec. 2). The meeting of a Rural District Council may be held at such place either within or without their district as the council from time to time direct (Local Government (Application of Enactments) Order, 1898, Article 36 (3)).

X.—Boards of Guardians.

Poor Law Unions continue to exist and to embrace the same areas as heretofore (except where their boundaries are altered as mentioned *post*); and for those Unions Boards of Guardians will continue to be appointed, but in a different manner, and with diminished powers.

(a) CONSTITUTION OF BOARDS OF GUARDIANS.

The provisions relating to the constitution of Boards of Guardians are the following :—

(1) In a rural district the Rural District Councillors shall, without further election, be the guardians for the electoral divisions which they represent (sec. 24 (a));

(2) In an urban district each district electoral division will *elect*, separately, a guardian or guardians to represent it on the Board of the Union (sec. 24 (b); and see Local Government Board's Order, fixing the number of guardians for urban districts, Appendix III., *post*).

(3) There shall be no *ex-officio* guardians after the commencement of the Act (sec. 24), but each rural district Council may, if it pleases, co-opt three persons who shall be additional guardians as well as councillors (sec. 25, sub-sec. 1 (a) and 3).

(4) The Local Government Board are authorised to constitute an urban district, or a part of such a district, or a part of a county borough, a district electoral division, and to assign to such new district two or more members (sec. 24 (c)); and that body has, accordingly, constituted every

municipal ward a district electoral division, except in the case of Dungannon (see Orders of Local Government Board, Appendix III., *post*).

(5) The elections of guardians for urban districts will take place at the same time as those for rural district Councillors—that is, the 1st June (sec. 24 (*b*) and sec. 94, sub-sec. 7)—unless the County Council fix a day seven days earlier or seven days later (sec. 94, sub-sec. 7);

(*b*) PERIOD OF EXISTENCE, ELECTORATE, AND ELECTIONS OF GUARDIANS.

The provisions for County and Rural District Councils repecting all those matters apply to Boards of Guardians. (sec. 24 (*b*), sec. 23, sub-sec. 3 (*b*), (*c*), (*d*)). A person elected both a guardian and a district Councillor in the same union must elect which he will be (Local Government (Application of Enactments) Order, Article 5 (5)).

(*c*) CASUAL VACANCIES IN BOARDS OF GUARDIANS.

Casual vacancies amongst the guardians elected separately as such—that is, amongst the urban guardians—may be filled by the Board (sec. 94, sub-sec. 5); those amongst the guardians who are guardians because they are also rural district. Councillors will be filled by the rural district Council or Councils (see *supra*, as to casual vacancies in Rural District Councils).

(*d*) QUALIFICATIONS OF GUARDIANS.

The provisions enacted in respect of those matters for Rural District Councillors, apply to poor law guardians who have to be separately elected—that is, to the guardians for urban districts (sec. 24 (*b*)).

(*e*) ACCEPTANCE AND RESIGNATION OF OFFICE BY GUARDIANS.

The provisions in respect of those matters enacted for county and district Council elections (regarding which see *supra*) apply to poor law guardians except that the fine for non-acceptance of office (if there is no bye-law on the subject) is to be £25 for a guardian and £50 for a chairman or vice-chairman of a board of guardians, and that there is to be no fine for resigning office in the case of a guardian or of a chairman or a vice-chairman of a Board of guardians or district councillors (Local Government (Application of Enactments) Order, 1898, Articles, 9 (2) and 10 (1)).

(*f*) BUSINESS OF BOARDS OF GUARDIANS.

The following will henceforth be the business of the Boards of Guardians:—

(1) Their primary business of administering the laws for the relief of the poor which, as it is not transferred to any other bodies by the Act, remains with them;

(2) Any other business of the Boards which is not expressly taken away from them;

(3) The business of the dispensary committees which will cease to be appointed (sec. 30); and a. lease to a Board of guardians made under the Dispensary Houses (Ireland) Act, 1879, may be for any term not less than sixty years which the lessor has power to grant (sec. 91).

(4) Power to appoint a committee of members or non-members resident or interested in the district for the admission of paupers to the union workhouse (sec. 39); to fix a limit of expenditure, and to revoke the appointment.

(5) Power to convert the workhouse hospitals into district hospitals, to transfer their powers over them to a committee of hospital governors to be appointed by them, and to arrange the payment and accommodation under which private patients may be admitted into such hospitals (sec. 90).

(g) PROCEDURE OF BOARDS OF GUARDIANS.

Neither the Act nor the Orders in Council made under it provide for any change in the mode of carrying on the business of the Boards; and it is expressly provided that the power of a Board of Guardians to choose its chairman and vice-chairman shall remain unaltered (sec. 25, sub-sec. 4).

(h) POWERS OF LOCAL GOVERNMENT OVER GUARDIANS.

Nothing in the Act is to affect the powers of the Local Government with respect to guardians and their officers (sec. 101. sub-sec. 1).

XI.—Town Boards (not Urban District Councils).

The following are the changes made in reference to Town Boards which do not become Urban District Councils :—

(a) The electorate is enlarged and made the same as that for County and District Council elections (sec. 97. sub-sec. 1);

(b) The same electorate is to be electorate for

(1) Petitioning for a provisional order in relation to the government of the town or for a charter, or

(2) Petitioning, presenting a memorial, or voting for the adoption of any enactment capable of being applied

to the town unless the persons entitled to petition or vote are a Council elected under the Act (sec. 97. sub-sec. 1);

(c) The qualification for a member of such Town Board is: *either* to be a local government elector, *or* to be a resident in the township area for 12 months before the election, and to continue such (sec. 97, sub-sec. 3, and sec. 94, sub-sec. 2) women, consequently, being qualified (see also Local Government (Application of Enactments) Order 1898, Article 12 (2) and Article 4).

(d) When a poll of the electorate is taken with reference to the adoption of any Act, it must be by ballot (sec. 97, sub-sec. 2);

(e) The power of the Lord Chancellor under sec. 29 of the Towns' Improvement (Ireland) Act, 1854, to appoint a Town Commissioner to act as justice of the peace is abolished (sec. 26, sub-sec. 4), but the chairman of the Town Board, unless the chairman be a woman or be personally disqualified by any Act, shall be a justice of the peace, just as if he had been appointed under the enactment just quoted by the Lord Chancellor (sec. 26. sub-sec. 2), and a person so becoming a justice must take the oaths required by law (sec. 26, sub-sec. 3), and as to what the oaths required by law are (see *supra*, p. 2).

(f) The Towns' Improvement (Ireland) Act, 1854, is applied to the town of Carrickfergus and to the towns (eight in number) having Commissioners under the 9 Geo. IV., c. 82 (sec. 41, sub-sec. 1). The number of Commissioners shall be the same as at present, but the Local Government Board may, if it think fit, divide any of those towns into wards, apportion the commissioners, and vary their number, so as to be in accordance with sec. 15 of the Towns Improvement Act, 1854 (sec. 41, sub-sec. 2).

PART IV.

THE COUNTY COURT.

I.—Compensation for Criminal Injuries.

The only business of the Presentment Sessions and the Grand Jury (except its criminal business), which is not transferred to the County Councils, is that of dealing with, and assessing compensation for, criminal injuries. This business is transferred by the Act to the County Court, and its jurisdiction in the matter is extended somewhat in respect of the injuries for which compensation may be given (sec. 5, sub-sec. 1).

I.—Procedure in Applications for Compensation for Criminal Injuries.

The provisions regarding the procedure in applications for compensation for malicious injuries are the following:—

1. The person or persons applying for compensation for malicious injuries are to apply to the County Court (sec. 5, sub-sec. 3);

2. When the application is made, the Council of the County, or the Council of the district, in or within one mile of which the injury is committed, and also any ratepayer may appear and be heard by the County Court in relation to the application (sec. 5, sub-sec. 3);

3. The County Court may either refuse the application or make such decree as the Presentment Sessions might have proposed, and the Grand Jury sanctioned (sec. 5, sub-sec. 1, 2), and where the Judge of Assize has had power to apportion the compensation between two or more counties under sec. 140 of the 6 and 7 Vic., c. 116—that is, when the injury is committed on the verge, or within one mile of the boundary, of any two or more counties, the County Court will have a similar power of apportionment (sec. 5, sub-sec. 2); *quere* whether it will have that power where the injury is committed on the verge of a county and a county borough;

4. When the decree is made or the application is refused, the applicant or the County Council, or any one who appeared or might have appeared before the County Court Judge, or, where the area to be assessed is less than the whole county, the Council of the district which comprises that area may appeal to the Judge of Assize, and any such appeal will be tried like any other appeal from the County Courts (sec. 5, sub-sec 4) ; the judge in the case of Dublin City and County being any Judge of the High Court (sec. 109);

5. The Judge of Assize on the appeal will have power to vary the decree (sec. 5, sub-sec. 4), and he may, if he thinks fit, empanel a jury to try any question of fact, and, if any party to the proceedings so requires, the jury, if the judge allows a jury, must be a special jury (sec. 5, sub-sec. 5);

6. Rules of court will prescribe the procedure in all such cases, but the County Court and the judge will, nevertheless, have a large discretionary power in matters of procedure (sec. 5, sub-sec. 7), and to give costs to or against any party (sec. 5, sub-sec. 6);

7. Except the fees allowed to be taken by an existing Clerk of the Peace, no court fees will be payable in such proceedings (sec. 5, sub-sec. 8).

8. The enactments relating to compensation for criminal injuries will apply to Belfast and to the County of Dublin, as well
as to the rest of Ireland (sec. 5, sub-sec. 9, and sec. 21, sub-sec. 2
(e)).

II.—ALTERATIONS OF THE LAW RELATING TO COMPENSATION FOR
CRIMINAL INJURIES.

The law regarding compensation for criminal injuries is
altered in two respects :—

(a) Hitherto where a presentment for a criminal injury
was *disallowed* and the judge gave leave to traverse, there
should be a jury (see Brett's Grand Jury Law, 2nd Edn., p.
56); now there need not be a jury in any case unless the
judge thinks fit to have one (sec. 5, sub-sec. 5);

(b) Hitherto compensation could only be obtained for
maliciously setting fire to, destroying, or injuring the particular kinds of property mentioned in sec. 135 of the 6 and
7, Wm. IV., c. 116 ; henceforth compensation may be obtained for maliciously setting fire, destroying or injuring
property of any description, real or personal, provided that
the malicious act done was a crime punishable *on indictment*
under the Malicious Damage Act, 1861 (sec. 5, sub-sec. 1,
and 24 & 25 Vic., c. 97).

III.—TAXATION OF COSTS.

The County Court are also entrusted with the duty of taxing
costs incurred at Local Government elections (see *supra*, pp. 6, 7).

PART V.

BOUNDARIES.

I.—Alteration of Boundaries.

I.—POWERS OF THE LOCAL GOVERNMENT BOARD.

(a) The first County Councils elected under the Act will be
elected for the existing judicial counties—that is, the counties as
bounded at the passing of the Act for Grand Jury purposes, as
already mentioned *(supra*, p. 1*)*. The Local Government Board,
however, has power not only to alter the boundaries of such counties
for the purposes of the first elections (sec. 68, sub-sec. 1), but to
alter permanently for the purposes of the Act not only the boundaries of counties, but also those of all other areas dealt with by the
Act, on the representation of the Council of any county or
borough (Local Government (Application of Enactments) Order
1898, Article 25. See also Articles 26-31 on same subjects);

but any orders it may make in respect of such matters must be confirmed by Parliament (same Order and Article, sub-sec. 2).

(b) The discretion of the Board, however, in altering boundaries is not unlimited. They are bound to have regard to the following considerations :—

(1) The existing boundaries of counties at large are to be preserved unless their preservati n would cause substantial inconvenience (sec. 68, sub-sec. 3 *(a)*) ;

(2) The same rule applies to the boundaries of unions, with the addition that unions shall not, if it is conveniently possible to avoid it, be divided between more than two counties, and shall not in any case be divided amongst more than three counties (sec. 68, sub-sec. 3 *(b)*), and that where a union is divided between two counties or more, the area of each part outside an urban district shall be of sufficient size and rateable value to constitute a suitable rural sanitary district (sec. 68, sub-sec. 3 *(c)*) ; and such an area when separated from the union to which it belonged, shall be a separate rural sanitary district (sec. 68, sub-sec. 4) ;

(3) A district electoral division must be situated wholly in one district (sec. 68, sub-sec. 3 *(d)*) ;

(4) A county district must be wholly situate in one county (sec. 68, sub-sec. 3 *(c)*).

(c) The Local Government Board have long had the power to amalgamate unions. In future, when they exercise that power, they may, after communication with the County Council and the rural District Councils concerned, either amalgamate the rural districts in the same county which may be comprised in the amalgamated unions, or direct that those districts shall continue as separate rural districts, with protection for the interests of existing officers (sec. 68, sub-sec. 5).

(d) The power of the Local Government Board to divide a poor law electoral division into wards or to combine such divisions, for the purpose of elections only, will cease, but the Board will retain the power in reference to the alteration of sanitary districts under section 7 of the Public Health (Ireland), 1878, and its general power to combine, divide, or otherwise alter district electoral divisions, and, in exercising that power, will have the further power of dividing any townland, which it has not had up to the present (sec. 68, sub-sec. 6).

(e) When an order of the Local Government Board alters the boundary of a *borough*, it may also increase or decrease the number of the wards of the borough, and alter their boundaries, and alter the proportion of Councillors for each ward, and their total number (Local Government (Application of Enactments) Order 1898, Article 25, sub-sec. 3).

II.—POWERS OF THE COUNTY COUNCILS.

Besides the Local Government Board the County Councils also have certain powers in the matter of the future alteration of bounderies of urban districts (other than boroughs), rural districts, the establishment of urban districts, and the creation or alteration of wards in urban districts.

Whenever a County Council, as respects any county district *not a borough*, is satisfied that a proposal is made out for

(1) The alteration or definition of the boundary thereof;

(2) The division of an urban county district into wards; and

(3) The alteration of the number of wards, or of their boundaries, or of the members of any Urban District Council, or of the apportionments of such members among the boards,

the County Council may, after inquiry, and if satisfied that such proposal is desirable, make an order accordingly (Local Government (Application of Enactment) Order, 1898, Article 26, sub-sec. 1); and any such Order must be confirmed by the Local Government Board if no petition is presented against it, or, being presented, is withdrawn (same Order and Article sub-sec. 4); if a petition is presented against it, and is not withdrawn, the Local Government Board is to determine, after inquiry, whether the Order is to be confirmed or not (same Order and Article, sub-sec. 3); and whatever order is finally made must be forthwith laid before both Houses of Parliament (same Order and Article, sub-sec. 6).

III.—POWERS OF PRIVY COUNCIL.

See for powers of Lord Lieutenant in Council in relation to Division of Borough into wards, &c., (Local Government (Application of Enactments) Order, Article 31.)

III.—Purposes of County Boundaries.

The purposes for which county boundaries exist are not those only relating to County Councils, the elections therefor, and the business thereof. They relate also to the administration of justice—that is, the holding of assizes and of quarter and petty sessions, the preparation of jury lists, police, militia, registration of electors, coroners, clerks of the peace, and other county officers, and any other matter (with one exception only) in reference to which the "County" is made the area of administration.

Consequently, if any place or district is taken by an alteration of the boundaries of administrative counties, from the county as it has hitherto existed, and added to another, it is to be for the future a part of the latter county for all the purposes mentioned, with one exception, as mentioned (sec. 69, sub-sec. 1), and as Belfast and Londonderry are added to the number of counties of cities and are made county boroughs, and as those two places have not hitherto had separate lieutenants and separate sheriffs, such officers are henceforth to be appointed for each of them by their respective Corporations at the same time and in the same manner as in the counties of cities (sec. 69, sub-sec. 1.)

It would follow, therefore, if there were no express provision to the contrary, that as the County of Tipperary is to have a County Council for each of its two ridings (*supra*, p. 1), it would consist for all the purposes mentioned of two separate counties. It is, however, expressly enacted that, subject to the variation of boundaries, it shall continue to be one county for all purposes (but one) so far as it was one county at the passing of the Act (sec. 69, sub-sec. 2 (*a*)).   Tipperary, at the passing of the Act, was one county in everything except that it had two grand juries and two courts of assize.   It will, consequently, have two County Councils, and will continue to have two courts of assize, but it will have only one sheriff and one lieutenant, and one County Court.   The one purpose in respect of which the boundaries of counties (and boroughs also) are not to be changed is that of electing members of Parliament.   As regards both the areas for which, and the persons by whom, members of Parliament are to be elected, the law remains unaltered (sec. 69, sub-sec. 2 *(b)*).

Neither the County of Cork nor the County of Galway will be divided into two counties for any purpose, for, though each has an East and West Riding, it is only for the appointment of county surveyors and the disposition and management of its police force, and in the case of Cork, for the purposes of the County Court.

The courthouse of a county, if situate in the county of a city or town, is deemed for the trials of prisoners and causes to be part of the county, and it is deemed to be part of such city or town when it is used as a city or town courthouse (sec. 69, sub-sec. 3).

IV.—Position of Cities and Towns (not County Boroughs.)

It will be convenient here to state the effect of the creation of " administrative counties " on all towns and boroughs which are not made " county boroughs."

Any such town or borough will be merged, for county purposes, in the county in which it is situate or which it adjoins, or
if it adjoins more than one such county, then it will merge in
such one of those counties as the Local Government Board order
(sec. 40, sub-sec. 1.) In all county matters it will be governed
by the county to which, as a county district, it will send representatives; but if it is an urban district it will govern itself by
means of its urban district council in all district affairs (sec. 40
sub-sec. 2), and, if it has a Corporation, that body will, as has
been already mentioned, retain its present name (sec. 22, sub-sec.
1.)

It follows that any town or city, which does not now become
a county borough, and which has hitherto been a county of a
city or a county of a town, and, as such, has had a separate lieutenant, a separate sheriff, a separate commission of the peace, a
separate court of assize or quarter sessions, a separate coroner,
and soforth, will now lose those marks of local distinctness and
be treated, in respect of them, like any other district of a
county.   Thus, the Corporations of Drogheda and Kilkenny
will no longer elect sheriffs (sec. 69, sub-sec. 1).   Those
towns will be subject to the jurisdiction of their respective
county sheriffs.   Galway loses its sheriff, its Clerk of the Crown
and Peace, its local justices, and its coroner, the right, however,
of the existing Clerk of the Crown and Peace and Coroner being
preserved (sec. 117, sub-sec. 1, 2), and the local justices being
made county justices for the town district (sec. 117, sub-sec. 3);
and Carrickfergus, Drogheda, Kilkenny, and Galway, shall no
longer have separate assizes.

The following provisions, however, which are in the nature
of exceptions to the general rule as to the consequences of merging
a county of a city or town in an administrative county are to be
noted :—

(1) Wherever a municipal borough having a town council
has hitherto, through that council, elected its own coroner,
it will continue to do so (sec. 40, sub-sec. 3 and sec. 109),
a provision which does not apply to Galway, as Galway is
not a borough ;

(2) Drogheda and Kilkenny will continue to have their
separate Civil Bill Courts (sec. 69, sub-sec. 6.)

V.—Proceedings Consequent on Altera-
tions of Boundaries.

Inasmuch as the Act provides that the administrative county
shall be the county for all purposes except that of the election of

members of Parliament, when the boundaries of any area are altered provisions are made for all necessary administrative and judicial changes of a consequential character (Local Government (Application of Enactments) Order, 1898, Article 27), and for adjustment of property and liabilities (same Order, Article 30); but unless an order under the Act altering boundaries, or the Act itself, or the Registration (Ireland) Act, 1898 otherwise provides, the same local authorities—that is to say, the sheriff, the Clerk of the Peace, and the County Council—as would have had authority in any place if there were no alteration of boundaries affecting that place, shall continue to have authority in that place for the purpose of Parliamentary elections and the registration of Parliamentary voters, in the event of such alteration being made (same Order, Article 27, sub-sec. 3.)

Where any county of a city or town becomes a part of a county at large, any urban or rural district council may apply, within a time to be fixed by the Local Government Board, for a financial adjustment by the Board between the area which it represents, or any part of it, and the county, in respect of county at-large charges and main roads (sec. 70, sub-sec. 1); but any such adjustment shall be subject to an appeal to the Appeal (Boundary) Commission (sec. 70, sub-sec. 2.)

VI.—General Provision as to Alteration of Boundaries.

In every alteration of boundaries care must be taken that, so far as practicable, the boundaries of any area shall not intersect any other areas (Local Government (Application of Enactments) Order, 1898, Article 28).

VII.—Appeal in Boundary Matters.

If within six months after an Order effecting an alteration of county boundaries is made a petition against the order, so far as it affects any county, is presented to the Local Government by the Council or the Grand Jury Board, or by any District Council, sanitary authority, or guardians, or by not less than 100 Parliamentary electors for the county, such petition is to be referred to the Appeal Commission for determination (sec. 103.) As to the Constitution of the Appeal Commission, see the same section. But an order of the Appeal Commission shall not have effect till after the first election unless it otherwise provides (sec. 103, sub-sec. 2). The Commission has thus no jurisdiction to deal with any alterations but those of *County* boundaries.

VIII.—Effect of Alteration of Boundaries on Elections and Registration of Electors.

Whenever any electoral districts are combined, divided, or altered, the alteration, if made after 1st May in any year, is not to take effect as regards registration of electors or elections till the following year (sec. 68, sub-sec. 6).

PART VI.
FINANCE.
I.—Area of Rating.

(a) THE UNION:—

1. Before the passing of the Act the area of rating in Poor-Law Unions was the whole union or each electoral division comprised within the union, according as an equal rate was made or was not made upon the whole union; and as the expenses in a great many cases were chargeable against the electoral divisions and not against the unions, and as the electoral division charges varied greatly from year to year, so, therefore, did the rates levied in those districts, the towns nearly always being taxed more heavily than the country districts.

Now there is to be union rating for all the expenses of the Poor-Law Guardians—that is, the expenses of administering the Acts for the Relief of the Poor; and all those expenses are to be called UNION CHARGES, and this enactment is to apply whether the union be divided between more than one county or not, the divided parts (in case of division) being treated as separate unions, and the total amount to be levied being apportioned amongst the several parts in proportion to the rateable value (sec. 43).

2. When any amount to be raised for union charges has to be apportioned between an urban district and the rest of the the county, the apportionment is to be made by the County Council in proportion to rateable value (sec. 51, sub-sec. 2), which, moreover, is to divide the amount apportioned to a rural district between the agricultural land and the other hereditaments (that is, the buildings) in that district (sec. 51, sub-sec. 3).

(b) THE COUNTY:—

1. Hitherto in counties the area of rating and taxation has been, according to chargeability, the county at large, the barony

or half barony, and the townland. Now all the expenses of a County Council are to be raised equally over the whole county, and are to be called COUNTY AT LARGE CHARGES, unless they are—

    (1) Union charges, or

    (2) District charges (as to what are such, see *post*),

    (3) Excluded charges (as to which see *post*), or

    (4) Unless it is provided in any case that a particular charge shall be made on a district and not on the county at large (sec. 45, sub-sec. 1, and sec. 5, sub-sec. 2).

2. Wherever any particular charge may be levied off a particular portion of a county, it rests with the County Council to say on what area it will be levied, but, whatever the area may be, it must be raised equally over the whole of that area (sec. 45, sub-sec. 3).

3. If any expenses incurred by a County Council may be levied off an URBAN district, they are to be called URBAN CHARGES (sec. 45, sub-sec. 2).

4. Whenever any amount to be raised for county at large charges, or for union charges, has to be apportioned between any urban district and the rest of the county or union respectively, the apportionment is to be made by the County Council in proportion to rateable value, and it is to perform the same duty in the case of any amount to be raised partly off any urban and partly off any rural district (sec. 51, sub-sec. 2); and whenever any division has to be made of any amount to be raised for county at large charges or for union charges, between agricultural land and other hereditaments in the county, and when no portion of the amount is apportioned to any urban district that division is to be made by the County Council also, in proportion to rateable value (sec. 51, sub-sec. 3).

(*c*) THE RURAL DISTRICT :—

1. Rural District Councils being entrusted with all the business of the Boards of Guardians (except the relief of the poor and the portion of that business which is transferred to the County Councils, and also with the business of the Baronial Presentment Sessions, the areas of rating for all those purposes would be so different if the law regarding that subject remained as it was before the passing of the Act that the work of assessment would be very difficult.

Accordingly, all the expenses of the Rural District Councils (with one exception). are now to be levied equally over the whole district, and are to be called DISTRICT CHARGES (sec. 44); and amongst the charges which are to be so levied are the expenses (incurred after the passing of the Act) of building labourers' cottages, whether the transactions in respect of those buildings were *commenced* before or after the passing of the Act (sec. 57, sub-sec. 4). The exception is the group of " excluded charges" (mentioned *post*), which may be raised as heretofore off any area less than a district or union (sec. 56, sub-sec. 2, and sec. 57, sub-sec. 2).

2. As to the charges to which rural districts are subject in common with other areas and the apportionment thereof, see *supra,* under heading " The County."

(*d*) THE COUNTY BOROUGH AND OTHER URBAN DISTRICTS:—

The area of rating and levy in urban districts before the passing of the Act was the whole county of a city or town, or other district, and the law in that respect remains unchanged. the Act not touching the point.

(*e*) GENERAL RESULT:—

It thus appears that there is to be, speaking broadly, union rating for union charges; county rating for county at large charges; district rating for rural district charges; town or city rating for all urban (including county borough) charges.

II.—Raising of Expenses.

The area of rating being determined, the next question is how and by what rate are the expenses of the bodies created or dealt with by the Act to be raised.

1. As regards RURAL DISTRICTS:—

The County Council is to raise by means of the poor rate such an amount of money as after allowing for the agricultural grant (see *post*), will be sufficient to meet (*a*) its own county at large charges for the rural districts in the county ; (*b*) the union charges or expenses of the Boards of Guardians for the rural districts; (*c*) and the district charges or the expenses of the Rural District Councils (sec. 51, sub-sec. 5); and such poor rate is to be made twice a year—namely, at the beginning of or prior to the first and the second six months of the year respectively (sec. 51, sub-sec. 6).

2. As regards URBAN DISTRICTS:—

(*a*) In the case of Urban District Councils, the expenses incurred in meeting the demands of the respective County Councils—that is, the sums to be contributed by the districts of these Councils for union charges, county at large charges, and their proportion of charges leviable partly off urban districts and partly off rural districts (sec. 51, sub-sec. 2) *and* expenses in connection with the poor rate, are to be met out of the poor rate (sec. 46, sub-sec. 1), and that poor rate is to be raised by the Urban District Councils twice a year, as in the case of the County Councils (sec. 51, sub-sec. 9 (*a*)); while the expenses of the Urban District Councils, incurred in carrying out the business transferred to them by the Act—that is, the business of the baronial presentment sessions and of the Grand Jury as regards their respective districts only (sec. 27, sub-sec. 1)—are to be defrayed out of the same rate or fund out of which the cost of paving and cleansing the streets are or can be defrayed (sec. 46, sub-sec. 2); and those charges are not to be taken into account in considering whether or not the limit imposed by law upon such rate has been exceeded or not (sec. 46, sub-sec. 2). Such a limit is imposed by the Municipal Corporations Act, 1840, the Towns Improvement (Ireland) Act, 1854, and Local Improvement Acts.

(*b*) In the case of the Council of a county borough, the expenses incurred for union charges or in connection with poor-rate, are to be defrayed out of the poor-rate, and so also are the expenses incurred in relation to any business transferred to such Councils by or in pursuance of the Act or done by them as County Councils, unless such expenses have been hitherto defrayed out of any rate other than the Grand Jury cess, in which case they shall continue to be so defrayed (sec. 46, sub-sec. 3); and the poor-rate is to be made for those purposes by the Council of the County borough as if it were the County Council of an ordinary county, but, while it may may make the poor-rate twice a year like the ordinary County Councils, it may also make it once a year and collect it in two moieties (sec. 51 sub-sec. 9).

(*c*) Two important consequences follow from those provisions:—

First, the Poor-Rate, which is a personal tax payable (with certain exceptions) by the person in actual occupation of the rateable property at the time of the making of the rate, and, on his default, by the person subsequently in occupation (Guardians of Midleton Union *v.* M'Donnell (1896), 2 I. R. 228), and which is regarded as a specialty debt, and may, therefore, be recovered within twenty years (Magherafelt Guardians *v.* Gribben, 24 L. R. I., 520), is substituted for the Grand Jury cess, which was a charge on land or premises.

Secondly it would seem that, in boroughs and all urban localities where municipal rates are levied, all persons may qualify for the franchise for local government elections therein by paying only the rate known as poor-rate, which in those places will be more than the poor-rate, as it has existed in the past, but which will not include the principal municipal impost—namely, the borough or town rate ; for, to be enabled to vote at local government elections, it is only necessary to be registered as a Parliamentary elector, and, to qualify for the Parliamentary franchise, it is only necessary to pay the poor-rate. It may be otherwise, if the rates are consolidated.

III.—Payment of Expenses.

1. The money to meet the expenses of Rural District Councils is to be supplied by the County Councils (sec. 51, sub-sec. 1), these latter being the sole rate-collecting authority in rural districts.

2. The money to meet expenses of the Boards of Guardians are also to be supplied by the County Councils (sec. 51, sub-sec. 1), they first receiving from the Urban District Councils what is leviable upon their districts for those expenses, and the Councils of county boroughs, by virtue of their being County Councils, have the same duty towards the Guardians in respect of the portions of Poor-Law Unions within their jurisdiction.

3. The money to meet county at large expenses is also, of course, to be supplied by the County Councils, those Councils first receiving from the Urban District Councils the amount due for such expenses for their respective districts (sec. 51, sub-sec. 2).

4. The money to meet charges leviable in urban districts only are to be supplied by the Councils of Urban Districts and county boroughs respectively, they being the rate-collecting authorities within their respective districts.

IV.—The Agricultural Grant.

It has been stated that the amount of money which the County Councils are to raise to meet the various charges imposed on the rural districts is to be the amount required less by the amount of the Agricultural Grant given in each case. It is now necessary to explain the provisions regarding that subvention, and the manner in which it is to be distributed.

1. The Local Government Board is to certify how much poor-rate and how much county cess may be taken as having been raised in each administrative county off agricultural land (which does not include land in urban districts), (sec. 48, sub-sec. 4), and off other hereditaments respectively, in the financial year, 1896-7, in respect of county at large, union, urban, and rural district charges respectively, on the assumption that equal rating prevailed over the county, the union, and the district in that year,

and that an average sum was raised in that year in each **case** (sec. 49, sub-secs. 1, 2); each part of a union which is divided between more than one county being for this purpose treated as a separate union (sec. 49, sub-sec. 2), and the expenses incurred in the standard year, 1896-7, in building labourers' cottages being deemed for the same purposes not to have been special expenses within the meaning of the "Excluded Charges," (sec. 57), but district charges (sec. 57, sub-sec. 4).

2. The sums raised off agricultural land—that is, agricultural land in rural sanitary districts—for county at large, union, and rural district charges respectively having been thus determined, there is to be paid every year to the County Council of each county, out of the Consolidated Fund, half the amounts so determined in respect of such county (sec. 48, sub-secs. 1, 2, and sec. 49, sub-sec. 3), the first payments to be made in the half-year ending 31st March, 1899, for the service of the ensuing six months (sec. 48, sub-sec. 3).

In other words, and broadly speaking, half the average county cess and half the average poor-rate *levied off land as distinguished from buildings, in rural and not in urban districts* in 1896-7, will be paid each year out of Imperial Funds in relief of local taxation, the total annual amount to be paid being estimated at about £730,000.

3. Each County Council having received its share of the Agricultural Grant, is to apply it to the relief of agricultural land in rural, not urban, districts, as follows:—It is to deduct from the amount of the rates on such agricultural land for county at large, union, and rural district charges, the amount of the Agricultural Grant made in respect of those charges respectively; and the balance will be the amount to be levied off such agricultural lands (sec. 51, sub-sec. 4).

4. As has been already mentioned, a place which, before the passing of the Act, was situated in a rural sanitary district, may become urbanised—that is, may be added to or erected into an urban district. Such a place will not thereby lose the benefit of the Agricultural Grant. The portion of that grant which would, if the place had remained part of a rural district, have been applied in relief of the poor-rate and the county cess, will, in the event of the place becoming urbanised, still be devoted to the reduction, *pro tanto*, of the local rates levied in such place or otherwise spent for the benefit of such place (sec. 50, sub-sec. 1), and this provision will apply in the event of the boundaries of a county borough being extended into a rural district, the portion of the Agricultural Grant available in that case for the council of the county borough being paid direct to that Council, and not to the Council of the county at large (sec. 50, sub-sec. 2).

5. Any adjustments that may be made (in consequence of alterations of boundaries) for the purpose of determining each county's share of the Agricultural Grant are to be made by the Local Government Board on the report of the Commissioners of Valuation (sec. 49, sub-sec. 4); that body may also amend or vary its certificates as to the share of each county (sec. 49, sub-sec. 6); and it may, if necessary, issue provisional certificates for enabling the first payments to be made out of that grant (sec. 49, sub-sec. 7).

V.—Change in Incidence of Rating.

One of the principal objects of the Act was to sweep away the landlord's liability to local rates.

(a) Accordingly, it is now provided that the poor-rate shall for the future be made on the occupier and not on the landlord of a hereditament (sec. 52, sub-sec. 1), except in two cases, viz.:—

(a) Where the landlord is the immediate landlord of a house let in separate tenements or lodgings;

(b) When under sec. 63 of the Poor Relief (Ireland) Act, 1838, and sec. 10 of the Poor Relief (Ireland) Act, 1849, a person is in receipt of rent from property which is exempt from taxation because of its being of a public or charitable nature, but where, nevertheless, such person is liable for half the rates made in respect of such rent.

In those two cases the poor-rate is to continue to be levied as heretofore (sec. 52, sub-sec. 1).

(b) A consequent provision is that the occupier or tenant shall not, for the future, be entitled to deduct from his rent any part of the poor-rate, notwithstanding any contract to the contrary (sec. 52, sub-sec. 2); but special provision is made as to existing tenancies. (See post.)

(c) It is important to note that those provisions regarding the poor-rate, together with the substitution of the poor-rate for the Grand Jury cess, involve the repeal of the provisions of the Land Act of 1870, which in the case of tenancies created after the passing of that Act made the landlord liable for half the county cess and, where the holding was valued under £4, to the whole of the county cess; and accordingly, those provisions are expressly repealed (sec. 110, sub-sec. 2, 6th schedule, part VI.).

(d) It is important also to note that the provisions exempting landlords from liability to the poor-rate apply to buildings in rural districts and to houses in towns (sec. 52, sub-sec. 1), although in neither case is any part of the poor-rate paid out of the Agricultural Grant (sec. 48, sub-secs. 1, 4).

(*e*) In cases in which the net annual value of any holding in a town was not more than £4, the assessment, under sec. 64 of the Towns Improvement (Ireland) Act, 1854, was to be made on the immediate landlord, and not on the tenant. In these cases, and in any other cases in any city, urban district, or town, in which the local authority can, independently of this Act, make a rate on the landlord or the immediate lessor, and not on the occupier, the latter alone is to be liable henceforth for all such rates, except in the case of apartments or lodgings or a half rate mentioned above (*supra*, p. 59), but this enactment is not to apply to a rate under any local Act in any county borough—such a rate, for instance, exists in Belfast—unless the Council of the borough, by a majority of not less than two-thirds present at a meeting specially summoned for the purpose, so resolve (sec. 53, sub-sec. 1).

(*f*) An urban District Council which, before the Act, could make a rate on the same basis as the poor-rate, may now, if it pleases, raise that rate as poor-rate, but as a separate item, and any right to deduct any part of such separate item from rent shall continue (sec. 53, sub-sec. 2 (*a*)).

(*g*) An urban District Council may also consolidate and collect together as one rate any rates which it could, before the Act, raise on the same basis, provided that basis was different from the basis of the poor-rate (sec. 53, sub-sec. 2 (*b*)).

(*h*) "The same basis" means "the same property, the same rateable value, and subject to the same exemptions" (sec. 53, sub-sec. 3).

VI.—Adjustment of Rents.

The removal from the landlord of all liability to rates, and making the tenant alone liable to them (except in the cases mentioned above), necessitated, of course, an adjustment of rent as regards *existing* tenancies. Accordingly, the following provisions are to have effect as from the gale day next after the 1st April, 1899, unless, after the election of the first County Councils, the County Council of any county apply that a date, twelve months earlier or twelve months later, be fixed, and unless the Local Government Board accede to such application (sec. 54, sub-sec. 1, and sec. 124, sub-sec. 1):—

I.—WHERE AND WHAT ALTERATIONS OF RENT MADE.

1. If an occupier has been entitled by law or contract (sec. 54, sub-sec. 3) to deduct from his rent either

    (*a*) The whole *cess*, or
    (*b*) The half of it, or
    (*c*) Less than half (as where his rent is less than the valuation),

his rent will be reduced by a corresponding amount of cess for 1896-7 of the standard amount (as to which see *post*); and a person who has not been liable to any cess will be in the same position as if he were entitled to deduct the whole—that is, his rent will be reduced by the whole of the standard amount (sec. 54, sub-sec. 3).

2. If any occupier has been entitled to deduct from his rent either

(*a*) The whole of the *poor-rate*, or
(*b*) The half of it, or
(*c*) Less than half,

his rent will be reduced, in the first case, by the whole of the standard amount of the poor-rate on the *buildings*, and by half the standard amount of the poor-rate on the land; in the second case, his rent will be reduced by half the standard amount of the rates on the buildings, but will not be reduced at all in respect of the rates on the land; and, in the third case, his rent will be reduced by an amount proportionate to half the standard amount of the rates on the building, but will not be reduced in respect of the rates on the land (sec. 54, sub-sec. 2).

In order to understand the provisions of sec. 54, the following considerations must be borne in mind :—

(*a*) Wherever a liability is now cast by law or contract (sec. 54, sub-sec. 3) on the landlord, it is transferred by the Act to the tenant (sec. 52), the poor-rate in that section meaning the county cess as well as what has hitherto been known as the poor-rate;

(*b*) The payment out of the Agricultural Grant in respect of cess is made for the benefit of the tenant;

(*c*) The payment out of the Agricultural Grant in respect of the poor-rate is intended for the benefit of the landlord;

(*d*) The payment out of the Agricultural Grant extends only to agricultural land—that is, land in rural, not urban, districts, and does not extend to buildings, either in urban or in rural districts.

All this being presupposed, the adjustment of Rent Section, so far as it concerns all agricultural holdings, consisting of both land and buildings, outside urban districts, may be explained in a more detailed manner as follows :—

(*a*) As regards cess (where the tenant benefits) :—

1. If the tenant is entitled, by law or contract, to deduct the whole of the cess from his rent—that is, if he in reality pays none of it—his rent, now that he is to be liable for the whole of it, will be reduced by the amount of the whole—that is of the appropriate standard amount on the entire holding—which change will place the landlord and the tenant in practically the same position as each was in before the Act, the benefit to the tenant coming to him when half the cess will be paid out of the Agricultural Grant, and thus will not be levied;

2. If the tenant is entitled, whether by law or contract, to deduct half the cess—that is, if he pays only half of it—his rent, now that he is to pay the whole, will be reduced by the amount of half the cess of the standard year, which will place both parties in the same position as before, the benefit to the tenant coming to him when half of the whole cess is paid out of the Agricultural Grant and thus will not be levied;

3. If the tenant is entitled to deduct less than half—that is, if he pays in reality more than half—his rent will be reduced by the proportionate standard amount, whatever it is, of the additional burden thrown upon him, the benefit arising to him when half of the whole cess is paid out of the Agricultural Grant, and is thus not levied;

4.—If the tenant is not entitled to deduct any part of the cess —that is, if he in reality pays the whole of it (which is the common case)—there will be no change in the rent, because there will be no change in the incidence of the rate, the benefit to the tenant arising when he gets half of the whole cess which he alone has hitherto paid out of the Agricultural Grant, and half of which will thus not be levied.

(b) As regards poor-rate (where the landlord benefits):—

1. If the tenant is at present entitled to deduct from his rent the whole of the poor-rate—that is, if he pays none of it—his rent will be reduced by the amount of the whole of the poor-rate on the buildings (the landlord and the tenant being thus placed in the same position as before, so far as regards the buildings), and by half of the amount of the poor-rate on the land the land-lord thus benefiting to that extent, while the tenant does not suffer, because half is paid out of the Agricultural Grant, and will not be levied;

2. If the occupier is entitled to deduct half of the poor-rate— that is, pays only half of it (which is the common case)—his rent will be reduced by half of the poor-rate on the buildings, the tenant and the landlord being placed in the same position as before as regards the buildings, but will not be reduced as respects the additional poor rate on the land, the landlord thus benefiting to the extent of half the poor-rate on the land, while the tenant will not suffer, because that half will be paid out of the Agricultural Grant and will not be levied;

3. If the occupier is entitled to deduct less than half the poor-rate—that is, if he pays more than half (as where his valua-tion is less than his rent)—his rent will be reduced by a propor-tionate amount of the additional poor-rate on the buildings, which he will now have to pay, the tenant and the landlord being thus placed in the same position as before as regards

the buildings, but there will be no change in the rent as respects the additional poor-rate in the land; the result being that the landlord will gain to the extent of the appropriate standard amount hitherto deducted for poor-rate on the land, while the tenant will be in the same position as before, as half the whole poor-rate on the land will be paid out of the Agricultural Grant, and will not be levied;

4. If the occupier is not entitled to deduct any part of the poor-rate—that is if he pays the whole of it—his rent will remain as it is so far as regards the buildings, because there is no additional burden thrown upon him, and it is not intended that, as regards buildings, the landlord shall benefit by the Agricultural Grant; but, as regards the land, his rent will be increased by the amount of half the poor-rate on the land, the landlord thus benefiting to that extent, while the tenant will be no worse off than before, because half the poor-rate will be paid out of the Agricultural Grant and will not be levied.

The poor-rate and cess referred to in all cases is that of the " standard " year, and, of course, the observation that the tenant will not, in certain cases, be "·worse off than before " applies only where the rates are not increased beyond those of the standard year.

2. Two Excepted Cases.

There are two exceptions to the foregoing rules :—

(1) Whatever deduction any tenant has hitherto been entitled to make from his rent in respect of any railway, harbour, navigation, or public health charge, he will be entitled to make till his tenancy is determined or till a new statutory term (in the case of an agricultural holding) begins (sec. 54, sub-sec. 9), because, as will be seen *post*, there is to be no relief given to either party out of the Agricultural Grant in respect of those charges ;

(2) If a holding in an urban district, consisting of land or buildings, is held under a lease for lives or for a term of years of which five years at least will be unexpired when the provisions respecting this matter come into force (as to which see *infra*, p. 97), there shall not be any alteration of rent, and the tenant shall be entitled to make from his rent the same deductions in respect of cess and poor-rate as he was entitled to make before the Act, till a new tenancy arises (sec. 54, sub-sec. 11).

3. The Case of Middlemen.

Where, in the case of a non-agricultural holding, the rent received by a middleman from his tenant is reduced in consequence of a readjustment of rent following on a change in the incidence of rating, there is to be a reduction in the rent he pays to the head landlord bearing the same proportion to the amount of that reduction as the rent he pays bears to the rent he receives, unless by the terms of his contract he is precluded from making any deductions in respect of rates (sec. 54, sub-sec. 4).

4. TOWN HOLDINGS.

Where a tenant of a holding in an urban district, consisting of land or buildings, becomes liable to pay any rate other than the poor-rate, and where that rate was previously made on the landlord, a proportionate reduction from the rent will be allowed until the existing tenancy determines, unless the terms of the contract forbid it (sec. 54, sub-sec. 12).

5. HOW FIXING OF RENTS IS AFFECTED.

In fixing fair rents the Land Commission has hitherto been bound to take into consideration the rights and liabilities of the parties in relation to cess and rates (Bruce v. Steen; 14 L.R.I., 408). In fixing rents after this Act comes into operation that body is to assume that the poor-rate is equal to the combined poor-rate and cess of the standard year 1896-7. It is, furthermore, not to increase the tenant's rent because half the old cess is paid for him out of the Agricultural Grant, nor to cut it down because the landlord is benefiting in every case out of the same funds to the amount of half the old poor-rate; but this provision does not apply to fixing rents on holdings in urban districts, for in the case of those holdings no relief is given to either party out of the Agricultural Grant (sec. 55).

6. HOW OCCUPYING OWNERS ARE AFFECTED.

Owners of agricultural land—that is, of land to which the Agricultural Grant extends—and who occupy that land themselves, will derive the double benefit from the Agricultural Grant. As owners, they will have half the poor-rate paid for them, and as occupiers they will be relieved of half the cess. Amongst such owners, of course, are tenants who have purchased under the Land Purchase Acts.

7. MISCELLANEOUS PROVISIONS.

Some miscellaneous provisions relating to readjustment of rents remain to be noticed.

(1) The "standard amount" of cess or poor-rate by comparison with which the amount of the Agricultural Grant is to be ascertained means the amount which would be produced in 1896-7 by a rate equal to "the standard rate" (sec. 54, sub-sec. 6); and that "standard rate" is to be ascertained by the Local Government Board at the same time as they ascertain the amount of poor-rate and county cess raised in the standard year 1896-7 or taken to have been then raised, and it is defined to be "the rate in the pound at which poor-rate and county cess is respectively to be taken for the purposes of the Act as having been levied off agricul-

tural and off other hereditaments respectively, in each union or district, in respect of county at large and union and urban or district charges added together" (sec. 49, sub-sec. 1 (c));

(2) When any change of rent under the readjustment of rent section of the Act would amount to less than sixpence, no change is to be made, and where it would amount to more than sixpence and a fraction of sixpence, if the fraction is under threepence, the fraction will not count, and, if it be threepence or over, the fraction will count as a full sixpence (sec. 54, sub-sec. 7); and any difference which may arise as to any amount to be deducted or paid will be finally decided by the Commissioner of Valuation (sec. 54, sub-sec. 8);

(3) The secretary of the County Council for the county at large and the town clerk for a county borough are to give, when asked either by landlord or tenant, certificates of the rateable value of any holding, and of the standard rate for the proper union or district (sec. 54, sub-sec. 10).

VII.—Excluded Charges.

In estimating the sums raised or taken to have been raised for county cess and poor rate in the standard year, and, therefore, in determining the amount of the Agricultural Grant, certain special charges are to be excluded from the calculation (sees. 56 & 57), and the charges so excluded are called EXCLUDED CHARGES (sec. 57, sub-sec. 1).

Those charges are defined by secs. 56 and 57 to be the following :—

1. Charges for extra police ;
2. Compensation for malicious injuries ;
3. Railway and harbour charges ;
4. Charges for drainage and navigation works ;
5. Special Public Health Charges, which are to be distinguished from General Public Health Expenses, and the most important of which are those incurred for sewers, water supply, lighting, labourers' cottages in towns (not in rural districts),

all which charges are henceforth to be raised as a part, but as a separate part, of the poor-rate, and may be charged to any particular area as hitherto, but levied equally off that area ; and no relief will be given in respect of them to either landlord or tenant. As to items 3, 4, and 5, an increase or decrease in them

F

is to be taken into account as usual in fixing rents under the Land Acts (sec. 57, s.-s. 3), while items 1 and 2 are not to be so treated, there being no provision that they shall be.

VIII.—License Duties and Local Grants.

According to the precedent set in England, certain grants in aid for local purposes which have hitherto been made annually are to cease, and instead there are to be given for similar purposes the produce of certain "Local License Duties" and a sum of £79,000 a year (sec. 58, sub-sec. 1).

The Grants withdrawn are the following, the items ·being taken from the Estimates for the current financial year, 1898-9:—

Page of Estimate where item will be found.	Service for which provision made.	Amount.
187 -	Medical Officers of Workhouses and Dispensaries - - -	£54,900
186 -	Schoolmasters and Schoolmistresses in Workhouses - - -	9,360
187 -	Medicines, and Medical and Surgical appliances - - - -	19,500
187 -	Sanitary Officers - -	16,700
476 -	Pauper Lunatics - - -	143,653
	Total -	£244,113

The Local License Duties, the produce of which is to be henceforth given in aid of local taxation, are set forth in the Third Schedule to the Act.

The Pawnbrokers' License Duties, payable in the Dublin Metropolitan Police District, is the subject of a special enactment. Those duties, levied under the Dublin Police Magistrates Act, 1808, sec. 66. and the local Act therein mentioned (44 Geo. III., c. xxii.), amounting to £100 (Irish) on each pawnbroker, are henceforth to be payable to, and collected by, the Council of the county borough or by the Council of the urban or rural district in which the place of business of the pawnbroker is situate (sec. 67).

Instead thereof there are to be paid out of the Local License Duties and out of the sum of £79,000 a year (which is added, the following sums:—

1. To each County Council (on behalf of the Poor Law Guardians):—

   (a) One-half the salaries of medical officers of workhouses and dispensaries;

   (b) One-half the salary of a trained nurse for each workhouse;

   (c) The whole of the salaries of the teachers in workhouses;

   (d) One-half the cost of medicines and medical and surgical appliances;

2. To the County Councils (on behalf of the Rural District Councils) :—

   One-half the salaries of sanitary officers in rural districts;

3. To Urban District Councils :—

   One-half the salaries of sanitary authorities in urban districts;

4. To the County Councils (for the Lunatic Asylums):—

   One-half the net charge (or four shillings a week, whichever is least) for each lunatic in lunatic asylums, provided the net charge amounts to or exceeds four shillings a week;

5. To the County Councils (for the counties concerned):—

   A sum equal to one-half of the excess over 6d. in the pound of any railway, tramway, or harbour charge connected with any guarantee given before the passing of the Act, wherever such charge at pressnt exceeds 6d. in the pound.

   (Sec. 58, sub-sec. 2, 3, 4.)

If the money available is not sufficient to meet those charges, the payments in respect to them are to be abated; if it should be more than sufficient, the unused balance will be hung to meet future deficiencies as Parliament may direct (sec. 58, sub-sec. 5); but it is all hypothecated in the first instance to meet possible deficiencies in the repayment of advances by purchasers under the Land Purchase Act (sec. 58, sub-sec. 6).

IX.—Other Grants in Aid.

1. As some misapprehension seems to have existed on the point, it may here be mentioned that the other parts in aid of local rates which are not given in the list of grants withdrawn

will continue to be made, with one exception. Amongst them may be mentioned particularly "the Exchequer Contribution" under the Land Purchase Act of 1891, the Estate (or Probate) Duty Grant of 1888, and the Local Taxation. Duties Grant of 1890.

1.—THE EXCHEQUER CONTRIBUTION.

The Exchequer Conntribution amounts to £40,000 a year. It is intended in the first place for the purpose of meeting losses. by defaulting purchasers under the Land Purchase Acts, and it was provided by the Land Purchase Act of 1891, that it should be carried every year to a reserve fund till it reached the sum of £200,000, after which, if it was not required for the purpose mentioned, it was to be divided between the municipal boroughs of Dublin, Belfast, Cork, Limerick, Londonderry, and Waterford, and the counties of Ireland in the proportions in which they were to share in the first Probate Duty Grant, the share of the counties to be spent on labourers' cottages. (see Purchase of Land (Ireland) Act,1891,sec.5,Land Law (Ireland) Act, 1896, sec. 39). Accordingly, for five years after the passing of the Act of 1891 no benefit was derived by any local authority in Ireland from the Exchequer Contribution. Last year it was made available for the first time, and paid in the prescribed proportions to the authorities entitled. Henceforward the share of the counties will be paid to the County Councils on behalf of the Rural District Councils which, for the future, are to have the administration of the Labourers' Acts.

2.—THE PROBATE DUTY GRANT OF 1888.

The Probate Duty Grant of 1888 is not to be confounded with the Estate Duty of 1896 (as to which see *post*). This grant was at first 9 per cent, of one-third—afterwards 9 per cent. of one-half—the total amount of the produce of the Probate Duties. of the United Kingdom. By the Finance Act of 1894, the Estate Duty was substituted for Probate Duty, and a different method of calculating the amount to be paid out of the duty in aid of local rates was adopted, but the amount remained practically the same. The sum payable was originally divided as follows:—

    (a) £5,000 a year to the Royal Dublin Society for improvements in the breed of horses and cattle;

    (b) One-half of the balance amongst Boards of Guardians in proportion to the sums expended by them during the financial year ending 29th September, 1887, in the salaries, remuneration, and superannuation allowances of union officers in connection with the relief of the poor or under the Poor Relief (Ireland) Act, 1851, the money to be applied in aid of the poor-rate;

(c) The remaining half of the balance amongst the Road Authorities in Ireland in proportion to the sums expended by them out of any cess or rate on roads and bridges during the year ending the 31st December, 1887, the money to be applied in aid of the cost of roads and bridges.

Those payments are to be made in future as follows :—

(a) £5,000 a year to the Royal Dublin Society, as hitherto ;

(b) Half the balance to the County Councils for the Boards of Guardians ;

(c) The other half of the balance to the new road authorities, viz..:—the County Councils in all rural districts, and the Urban District Councils in all urban districts, to be used as hitherto.

3.—THE LOCAL TAXATION DUTIES OF 1890.

The Local Taxation (Customs and Excise) Duties Grant of 1890 was a grant to England, Scotland, and Ireland, of certain additional duties on beer and spirits. Ireland's proportion then was fixed at 9 per cent. of the whole, and it was set apart for educational purposes, £78,000 going to the support of the National Schools, and the rest to the Intermediate Education Board for fees to schools and prizes to pupils. Part of the £78,000 has been paid to the Boards of Guardians of Unions which have contributed to the payment of salaries of National School Teachers in workhouses, and has been applied in the reduction of the poor-rate. Henceforth these sums will be paid to the County Councils, and will be used in the same way.

4.—THE ESTATE DUTY GRANT OF 1896.

The one grant, in addition to these specified as to be withdrawn, which will cease to be made, is the Agricultural Grant originally made under the Local Taxation (Ireland) Estate Duty Act, 1896, which amounted to about £180,000 a year (sec. 48, sub-sec. 1). No part of this sum has yet been paid out of the Treasury, but the present Act creates two charges on the fund. Half the gratuities paid to existing officers who may cease to be employed are to be paid out of it (sec. 115, sub-sec. 13), and so are the remuneration and expenses of all officers appointed to make adjustments under the Act, or to do any other work to carry the Act into effect, provided the adjustment is made or the work done within twelve months after the passing of the Act (sec. 122, sub-sec. 1). The balance remaining stands to the credit of the Local Taxation (Ireland) Account, and is to be disposed of in manner to be hereafter provided by Parliament (59 & 60 Vic., c. 41, s. 2).

X.—Borrowing Powers.

1. As to COUNTY COUNCILS :—

(a) County Councils may borrow, on the security of their county fund or revenues, such sums as may be required for—

(1) Consolidating the debts of the county ;

(2) Purchasing any land or erecting buildings ;

(3) Any permanent work or any other thing which they are authorised to do, and the cost of which ought, in the opinion of the Local Government Board, to be spread over a number of years ; and

(4) Any purpose for which the County Councils are authorised by any Act to borrow, or the cost of which the Grand Jury were authorised by any Act to spread over a number of years ;

in all which cases the consent of the Local Government Board must be obtained ; and, before giving that consent, the Board are to take into consideration any representation made on the subject by any ratepayer (Local Government (Application of Enactments) Order, 1898, Article 22, sub-sec. 1) ;

(5) Paying off prior loans ; and

(6) Re-borrowing a part of a loan paid off otherwise than out of capital money ;

in both which cases the consent of the Local Government Board shall not be necessary ; and, for the purpose of this provision, capital money includes any instalments, annual appropriations, sinking fund, and the proceeds of the sale of any property, but not money borrowed for the purpose of repaying a loan (same Order and Article, sub-sec. 3).

(b) The limit of borrowing is one-tenth of the rateable property in the county, excluding sinking fund, and any debt or capital liability incurred on account of lunatic asylums ; but that limit may be extended by a Provisional Order made by the Local Government Board, and confirmed by Parliament, where the proposed loan is for the purpose of a lunatic asylum (same Order and Article, sub-sec. 2).

(c) The means of borrowing by County Councils shall be either by the issue of stock (*post*), or by mortgage which must be by deed, truly stating the date, consideration, and the time and place of payment, and signed with the seal of the Council, and of which a register must be kept, open to public inspection, without fee or reward, in the office of the Council (same Order and Article, sub-sec. 9); but where a County Council has borrowed by means of stock, they are not to borrow by means of mortgage for more than five years (same Order and Article, sub-sec. 10).

(d) Loans to County Councils may be repaid within a period of 60 years, the exact time in each case to be determined by the Councils, with the approval of the Local Government Board, regard being had to the duration of the work or object for which the loan is required (sec. 60). Loans, however, incurred to pay off prior loans must be paid within the time originally fixed in each case (Local Government (Application of Enactments) Order, 1898, Article 22, sub-sec. 4).

The foregoing provisions do not apply to county boroughs, except where they are acting as a County Council, and does not authorise the Council of a County Borough to raise any loan by stock issued under the Local Government Act (same Order and Article, sub-sec. 12).

2. As to BOARDS OF GUARDIANS :—

(a) Money may be borrowed, as usual, by Boards of Guardians, under the Poor Relief Acts and the Medical Charities Acts, the Act containing no provision affecting that matter.

(b) But some alterations are made as to the time for repayment :—

In the case of Boards of Guardians, loans may be repaid either by equal yearly, or equal half-yearly payments of principal, or of principal and interest, or by means of a sinking fund (sec. 61, sub-sec. 1); and where the sinking fund method is adopted, the provisions of the Public Health Act, 1878, sec. 238, as regards the sinking fund, will apply (sec. 61, sub-sec. 2)—that is, the Guardians must every year invest in government securities at compound interest such sum as will, with such interest, suffice, after payment of all expenses, to pay the sum borrowed within the time fixed.

It may be here mentioned that the difference between those two methods of repayment is that, in the case of the former, known as the annuity system, the principal and interest are combined and paid off by equal half-yearly instalments, *constant in amount for the whole period for which the loan is made,* while in the latter case the payments are *larger at first,* being composed of equal instalments of the principal, together with interest on the portion of the principal outstanding at the time of each payment. Labourers' Acts loans have hitherto been on the former plan, sanitary loans on the latter, and the repayments of both have been half-yearly.

(b) Outstanding loans obtained by Boards of Guardians under the Poor Relief Acts and the Medical Charities Acts,

may be repaid by fresh loans (sec. 61, sub-sec. 3); outstanding loans, meaning loans which cannot be repaid on either of the two systems mentioned, or by means of a sinking fund, or out of capital money other than money borrowed for the purpose (sec. 61, sub-sec. 5); but the repayment of the first loan—that is, of re-borrowed money—must be made within the time originally fixed, unless the Local Government agree to extend the time to any period not exceeding sixty years (sec. 61, sub-sec. 4). The advantage of this provision lies in the smaller interest which will be chargeable under recent legislation.

(c) The limit to which Boards of Guardians may borrow under the Poor Relief Acts and the Medical Charlties' Acts must not, together with the other debts under the same Acts, exceed one-fourth of the total rateable value of the Union, except with the consent of the Local Government Board, which may extend it to one-half by means of a Provisional Order (sec. 61, sub-sec. 6). Hitherto they could not borrow more than £400 to be expended on workhouses, except on the consent in writing of the majority of the Guardians.

XI.—Issue of Stock by County Councils.

County stock may be created, issued, transferred, dealt with, and redeemed in such manner as the Local Government Board may prescribe; but the regulations of the Local Government Board in reference to this matter must be laid before Parliament, and, if disapproved of by either House, will be of no avail (Local Government (Application of Enactments) Order, 1898, Article 23).

XII.—Accounts and Audits.

1.—ACCOUNTS OF COUNTY AND DISTRICT COUNCILS.

(a) The accounts of all county and district councils, and of their committee and officers are to be audited by the auditors appointed to audit the accounts of the Poor Law Unions. Such audit is to take place once every year, except in the case of the County Councils and their committees and officers, whose accounts must be audited half-yearly, as must also accounts of receipts from and expenditure out of the poor-rate—that is, in the case of Urban District Councils, as well as County Councils (Local Government (Application of Enactments) Order, Article 19, sub-sec. 2).

Hitherto the boroughs of Cork, Kilkenny, and Waterford have been exempt from the general law regarding the auditing of accounts of public bodies in Ireland (Local Government (Ireland) Act, 1871 (34 & 35 Vic., c. 109, sub-sec. 11). The provision of the Order in Council just quoted, together with the repeal of the exemption in s. 11 of the 34 & 35 Vic., c. 109 (Sixth Schedule, Part II. of Act), now put those three municipalities on the same level in respect of this matter as all other municipalities.

(b) The provisions of the Local Government (Ireland) Act, 1871, as to the procedure to be followed in the auditing of the accounts of public bodies—that is, the sections from 12 to 18 (both inclusive) of that Act—are to apply to the auditing of the accounts of County and District Councils (Local Government (Application of Enactments) Order, 1898, Article 19, sub-sec. 2). The provisions referred to relate to the recovery of sums disallowed by the auditors, the power of auditors to call for books and accounts, and to summon and examine witnesses, the imposition of penalties for giving false evidence and other offences, the notice to be given by the local body of the holding of an audit, the publication of the accounts as audited, the remuneration of the auditors, and the procedure in cases in which persons dispute a decision of an auditor; but the Local Government Board have power to make rules modifying the provisions relating to notices, abstracts of accounts, and reports of auditors (Local Government (Application of Enactments) Order, 1898, Article 19, sub-sec. 3). The procedure in disputing an auditor's rulings is for the person or persons aggrieved to obtain a writ of *certiorari*, removing the question involved in any particular allowance, disallowance, or surcharge into the Queen's Bench Division of the High Court of Justice in Ireland, which has full power to vary or reverse the decision of the auditor and to award costs. An alternative course is to appeal to the Local Government Board (34 & 35 Vic., c. 109, sub-sec. 12). (See further powers to Local Government Board in sec. 63 (2)).

2.—ACCOUNTS OF BOARDS OF GUARDIANS.

As to the audit of the accounts of Boards of Guardians, there are some alterations of the law.

(1) Hitherto an expenditure authorised by a Board of Guardians must have been first declared illegal by the Court of Queen's Bench before it could be disallowed by the auditor (1 & 2 Vic. c. 56, sub-sec. 114). Now it may be questioned by the auditor, like the expenditure of any other public body, and the like appeal lies, as the case of the accounts of a town, to the Queen's Bench Division (sec. 63, sub-sec. 1).

(2) An appeal will lie to the Local Government Board;

which is empowered to decide according to the common sense of the case and on equitable principles, and the decision of which shall be final (sec. 63, sub-sec. 2 *(a) (b)*).

(c) The cost of auditing the accounts of a County Council in any year is limited to a sum not exceeding £100 (sec. 64), which is to be paid by the Council as the successor of the Grand Jury.

3.—ANNUAL BUDGET.

At the beginning of every local financial year—that is, in April (Local Government (Application of Enactments) Order, 1898, Article 19, sub-sec. 1), there must be presented to every County Council an estimate of all its probable receipts and expenditure, whereupon it will determine what amount of money is to be raised by rates; but if that estimate should prove too large or insufficient at the end of the first half of the year, it may be revised (Order in Council, Oct.—1898, Article 20); but this provision does not apply to the Council of a county borough, except as regards its receipts and expenses as a County Council (same Order, Article 21).

4.—MAKING UP OF ACCOUNTS.

(a) All accounts of County and District Councils must be made up to the 31st March in each year, except where by law they are to be audited half-yearly, in which case they are to be made up to the 30th September and 31st March every year, and the accounts must be in the form prescribed by the Local Government Board (Local Government (Application of Enactments) Order, 1898, Article 19, sub-sec. 1);

(b) The accounts of Boards of Guardians are to be made up as hitherto, not being dealt with by the Act or the Order in Council;

(c) Any local government elector may inspect and take copies of any accounts, or of the books and documents relating thereto (same Order and Article, sub-sec. 4).

XIII.—Remission of Rates in Certain Cases.

Under the Poor Law Acts (Ireland) Amendment Act, 1890, the Boards of Guardians have had power to forgive a person, rated for any premises, who ceases to be the owner or occupier of the premises before the termination of the period for which the rate is made, a portion of the rates due by him proportionate to the period during which he does *not* occupy or own them, and to require any successor in ownership or occupation to pay only the poor-rate for the period during which that successor *has been* in occupation; and the same Act further provides that, in recovering the rates due by the person who has quitted or ceased to own the premises as mentioned, the Guardians are not to distrain or sell any goods or chattels except the goods or chattels of such person.

The present Act provides that the power to charge only the abated sum from the person who succeeds another as mentioned shall not exist, unless the County Council or Urban District Council, as the case may be, determine to charge his predecessor with the abated sum mentioned. In other words, they must forgive the one portion of the rate before they can take less than the whole from the other (sec. 62). This provision applies to the city portions of the North or South Dublin Union, sec. 3 of the Act of 1890 being repealed by the Act of 1898. The reason of the change made by the latter Act is probably to be found in the case of Riddall v. Quigley [1894], 2 Ir. Rep. 144.

XIV.—Re-valuation of County Boroughs.

(a) It has hitherto been held by the Valuation Department that it had no power to undertake a general re-valuation in cities and towns; in consequence of which many inequalities of rating now exist in places like Dublin, many houses which are let out in offices or shops or stores being rated at sums far below the rents received in respect of such lettings.

(b) It is now provided that in any of the six cities of Dublin, Belfast, Cork, Limerick, Waterford, and Derry, a general re-valuation may be made of rateable hereditaments, if the Council or Corporation of the city applies for it. Such re-valuation is to be made on the principle of estimating the annual value, whether of land or buildings, at the rent which the particular hereditament might reasonably be expected to bring, one year with another, in its actual state, on the supposition that the tenant paid all taxes, rates, and necessary outgoings. One-half, at most, of the cost of such a re-valuation is to be borne by the Council (sec. 65, sub-sec. 1).

(c) When part of a union is within and part without a county borough, the amount to be raised for union charges is to be apportioned between the two parts according to the revised valuation of the former part; but the apportionment may be revised if, five years afterwards, no general revision has taken place, and if the Council of the borough, or the Guardians of that portion of the union outside the borough, or a majority of them, satisfy the Commissioner of Valuation that the existing apportionment has become inequitable by reason of changes in the value of any hereditaments in the union (sec. 65, sub-sec. 2).

(d) The provisions just noted regarding apportionment after re-valuation are to apply, *mutatis mutandis*, to the apportionment of police and bridge-tax charges between the municipal and extra-municipal parts of the Dublin Metropolitan Police District and the municipal and extra-municipal parts of the Dublin Bridge Area respectively (sec. 65, sub-sec. 2).

It may be mentioned that the Dublin Metropolitan Police District, exclusive of the City of Dublin, consists of the townships of Blackrock, Dalkey, Drumcondra, Killiney and Bally-brack, Kilmainham (New), Kingstown, and Rathmines, and a small portion of the County of Dublin. The Bridge Area consists of—(1) the whole Dublin Metropolitan Police District; (2) the portion of New Kilmainham not included in the Metropolitan Police District; (3) the Township of Clontarf, and (4) a portion of the County of Dublin lying between Clontarf and the boundaries of the Dublin Metropolitan Police District.

XV.—Rates in Dublin.

Hitherto—since the passing of the Dublin Improvement Act, 1890—the collection of the municipal rates in Dublin has been performed by the Corporation through its Rates Department; after the 1st October, 1899, the collection of the non-municipal rates—that is, the poor-rate, the police-rate, the bridge-tax, and the bridge-rate—will be transferred to the same body (sec. 66), and the offices of the Collector-General and his staff, who have up to the present collected these latter rates, will be abolished (sec. 66, (10)).

Special arrangements, however, are made as to each of the four rates mentioned.

1.—THE POOR-RATE.

The poor-rate is to be " levied in Dublin in like manner as in the rest of Ireland," and the enactments with respect to making, levying, collecting, and recovering the poor-rate shall apply accordingly (sec. 66 (1)). As in every other urban district in Ireland the authorities which are to make, levy, collect, and recover the poor-rate are the Urban District Councils or Corporations (where the latter exist), the authority in Dublin must, therefore, be the Corporation also; but, as has been already explained, not much discretion is left in the matter to the levying and collecting authorities in any case, because they must supply the money required by the Boards of Guardians on the demand of the latter (sec. 51, sub-sec. 1). As the Corporation of Dublin will not be a District Council, but a County

Council, it will pay the amount levied for poor-rate in the city to the two Dublin Boards of Guardians direct (sec. 51, sub-sec. 1, 2, & 9).

2. THE POLICE RATE.

(a) The amount required for police purposes in the Metro-politan Police District—(that is, in the city of Dublin, and in the townships of Pembroke, Blackrock, Kingstown, Dalkey,. and Rathmines, and in parts of the Township of Killiney and Ballybrack, New Kilmainham and Drumcondra, and in a por-tion of the County of Dublin)—is to be estimated by the Com-missioner of Police before the beginning of each local financial year, such amount not to exceed what he is entitled to raise under the Dublin Police Acts (for list of which see First Schedule, Part V.) (sec. 66 (2)); he is then to apportion the amount between the city and the portions of the County of Dublin within the Metropolitan Police District according to rateable value, and send a demand for each portion to the Cor-poration and the County Council of Dublin County, respectively; whereupon those two bodies are to pay the respective amounts by half-yearly payments, less five per cent. for cost of collection, irrecoverable rates, and office expenses, and also less such portion of the superannuation allowances and gratuities, payable, as hereafter mentioned, to the Collector-General and his staff (sec. 66 (4) (13)).

(b) The amount so payable to the Commissioner of Police may, in the case of the City of Dublin, be raised by the Cor-poration either by a separate rate on the same basis and in the same manner as the poor-rate or by means of the poor-rate itself, but, if by the poor-rate, as a separate item thereof (sec. 66 (5) (7)); in the County of Dublin, by either the poor-rate, but as a separate item thereof, like a railway or harbour charge (sec. 66 (6)), or by a separate rate raised like the poor-rate raised on the same basis and in the same manner as the poor-rate (sec. 66 (6) (7)). Payment of such a separate rate will not be necessary to qualify either for the Parliamentary or the Local Govern-ment Franchise (sec. 66 (7)); and any property which before the Act was liable to the police rate will also be liable now, no matter whether the rate be raised by means of the poor-rate or a separate rate (sec. 66 (8)).

This last-mentioned provision points to tenements and hereditaments of a " public nature " which, but for this provision, would be exempt from the rate, if they were raised as a poor-rate or as a separate rate, levied on the same basis as the poor-rate, but which were not exempt from the police rate

(Moylan *v.* Dublin Port and Docks Board, I. R. 6, C. L., 299, and I. R. 9, C. L., 457).

3.—THE BRIDGE TAX AND BRIDGE RATE.

The foregoing provisions relating to the Police Tax apply to those two rates, the Dublin Port and Docks Board being substituted for the Commissioner of Police, and "the Bridge Area" being substituted, in the case of the Bridge Rate, for the Dublin Metropolitan Police District. The Bridge Area is defined in the Dublin Port and Docks Board and Bridges Act, 1876, (39 & 40 Vic., c. lxxxv.) as (1) the Dublin Metropolitan Police District; (2) the portion of the township of New Kilmainham not included in that district; (3) the township of Clontarf; (4) so much of the County Dublin lying intermediately between Clontarf township and the boundaries of the police district. The area of the Bridge or Quay Wall Tax is the Metropolitan Police District.

4.—COST OF COMPENSATING COLLECTOR-GENERAL AND STAFF.

The amount required to pay the superannuation allowances to the Collector-General and his staff, which are referred to (*post*), must be raised as an addition to the Police Tax, the poor-rate, the Bridge Tax, and the Bridge Rate (sec. 66 (15)). It will be apportioned between the City of Dublin and the portions of the County of Dublin in which the rates mentioned are levied in the manner prescribed by the Dublin Corporation Act, 1890, sec. 71, sub-sec. 2 (sec. 66 (11)), and the amounts so apportioned will be paid by the Corporation and the Council of Dublin County, respectively, to the Local Government Board, and so will the similar sums payable by the Corporation under the Act of 1890, which have hitherto been payable to the Lord Lieutenant (sec. 66 (12) (13)); and, if there be a surplus on the occasion of any payment, it must be refunded to the body which has overpaid (sec. 66 (16)).

PART VII.

OFFICERS.

I.—Coroners.

(*a*) All Coroners are henceforth to be elected in counties by the County Councils; if a county has been divided into districts, a Coroner may be assigned a district by the Council, and any vacancy in the office of Coroner for a county must be filled

within one month after the vacancy, or within such further
time, not more than three months, as the Lord Chancellor may
allow (sec. 14, sub-sec. 1).

Coroners for any town which is not a borough will cease to
be appointed, the town being merged in the administrative
county of which it forms a part. The Council of a *borough* will
continue to elect its Coroner as heretofore (sec. 14, sub-sec. 1,
sec. 40, sub-sec. 1, 2, 3, and sec. 69, sub-sec. 1).

The rights of the existing Coroners for the towns of Galway
and Carrickfergus are preserved (sec. 117, sub-sec. 2).

(*b*) The County Council may alter Coroners' districts, and the
powers of the Lord Lieutenant and the Justices and Clerk of
the Peace in relation to that matter cease (sec. 14, sub-sec. 2).

(*c*) A Coroner cannot be removed except for proved inability
or misbehaviour in the discharge of his duty, and that only after
a public investigation (sec. 14, sub-sec. 3, 4 and 5, and s. 42 of 9
& 10 Vic., c. 37).

(*d*) The remuneration of every Coroner of a county and
borough, is to be by salary, which will be in lieu of all money,
for fees, mileage, and allowances, and that salary is to be fixed with
the approval of the Local Government Board, and shall not be
increased or diminished during his tenure of office (sec. 14,
sub-sec. 6); but a Coroner must still be repaid such expenses
and disbursements as may be lawfully paid by him on the holding of an inquest (sec. 14, sub-sec. 6 (*a*)). As to the salaries
of existing Coroners, see *post.*

(*e*) The property qualification required for the office of
Coroner for the City of Dublin, and other boroughs, is abolished
(sec. 14, sub-sec. 7, and sec. 21, sub-sec. 2 (*b*)).

(*f*) A *County* Coroner is not eligible for the office of county
or district Councillor in the county for which he is Coroner
(sec. 14, sub-sec. 5).

II.—Officers of Lunatic Asylums.

(*a*) As to the appointment, removal, and salaries of those
Officers, see *supra.*

(*b*) As to their superannuation, the Pauper Lunatic Asylums
(Ireland) Superanuation Act, 1890 (53 & 54 Vic., c. 31),
shall apply in every case, except that no grant of a superannuation allowance by the County Council shall require the approval
of the Inspectors of Lunatics, or of the Lord Lieutenant (sec.
84, sub-sec. 3). The enactment referred to empowered the
Board of Governors of Lunatic Asylums to give a superannuation allowance not exceeding two-thirds of his or her annual

salary and two-thirds of the annual value of his or her lodgings, rations, and other allowances to any servant of a District Asylum, and any officer of an Asylum coming within the definition of that word in the 30 & 31 Vic., c. 118, provided the following conditions were fulfilled, viz. : that

> (1) The officer or servant became incapable from sickness, age, or infirmity ; *or*
>
> (2) The officer or servant was not less than 50 years of age, *and* had served for not less than 15 years.

An exception as to the age limit was made in the case of a matron whose husband was a superintendent and was superannuated. It was competent for the Asylum Boards to give such a woman superannuation before she attained the age of fifty years, provided she had served twenty years. All this continues to apply to all officers and servants in the District Asylums.

If a resident medical superintendent or assistant medical officer of an asylum who is appointed by a County Council after the passing of this Act, holds at the time of the appointment a similar office in another asylum, he shall be entitled in calculating the amount of his superannuation on retirement to reckon his previous service in such other asylum (sec. 83, sub-sec. 13).

In addition to any qualifications which may be prescribed by the Local Government Board (sec. 84, sub-sec. 4, and sec. 109), a person to be qualified to hold the office of resident medical superintendent of an asylum must be a registered medical practitioner of not less than seven years' standing, *and* have served for not less than five years as a medical officer, or assistant medical officer, in a Lunatic Asylum (sec. 84, sub-sec. 2). In addition to any qualification that may be prescribed by the Local Government Board (sec. 84, sub-sec. 4), the qualification for an assistant medical officer in an asylum is that he shall be a registered medical practitioner (sec. 84, sub-sec. 2).

III.—Other County Officers.

(*a*) As to the appointment, salary, superannuation, and power of removal of County Officers, see *supra*, 12, *et seq.*, udder head of " Powers and Duties of County Councils."

(*b*) As to the first Secretaries, and other first Officers of the County Councils, see *post*, under head of " Existing Officers."

(*c*) The qualifications of County Surveyors may be certified by the Lord Lieutenant, who may also direct the Assistant Surveyors to be examined, and their qualifications to be certified by the Examiners (sec. 83, s.s. 4, 9).

(*d*) The Secretaries of the County Councils and of the Clerks of the Councils of county boroughs and Urban District Councils respectively are to discharge the duties hitherto imposed on the Clerks of Unions in relation to the registration of voters and the revision of the lists of jurors in rural districts and urban districts respectively (sec. 83, sub-sec. 7), except during the lives of existing Clerks of Unions who, however, may otherwise agree with the County Councils and the Urban District Councils concerned (sec. 121). The Secretaries of County Councils and the Town Clerks of County Boroughs, are also bound to send to the Lord Lieutenant or the Local Government Board such returns and information as may from time to time be required either by Parliament or that Board (sec. 83, sub-sec. 8).

(e) A paid officer, permanently employed by a County Council, and devoting his whole time to his duties, is not eligible to serve in Parliament (sec. 83, sub-sec. 10).

(f) The superannuation of all County and Rural District Officers, except the County Surveyor and *any* officer of a County Borough is to be regulated by the law relating to the superannuation of officers of Boards of Guardians (sec. 83, sub-sec. 11). The Act referred to is the 28 & 29 Vic., c. 26, under which an officer who is 60 years of age and has served 20 years in the Union, and has devoted his whole time to the service of the Union may be superannuated on the ground of old age, or, if he has devoted his whole time to the service of the Union, he may be superannuated on the ground only of being permanently disabled by reason of bodily or mental infirmity. The consent of the Local Government Board is necessary, and the superannuation allowance cannot exceed two-thirds of his salary at the time of his retirement.

County Surveyors stand in the same position as before the passing of the Act in respect of superannuation, as has been mentioned; but if a County Surveyor or a resident Medical Superintendent, or an assistant Medical Officer of a Lunatic Asylum is appointed by a County Council, and if he has previously held a similar office in another county or asylum, he will be entitled, for the purpose of superannuation, to reckon such previous service in estimating the amount of superannuation which he is to get (sec. 83, sub-sec. 13). This provision will probably prevent promotions from one county or asylum to another.

IV.—Officers of Rural District Councils and Guardians.

(a) Subject to the provisions to be noted, *post*, the same officers shall be appointed by a Rural District Council and the Guardians of the Union comprising the district, if the Local

G

Government Board make rules to that effect (sec. 85, sub-sec. 3); and, in so far as the Local Authorities to the whole or part of whose business the Rural District Councils will succeed have had the power of fixing and paying salaries, to that extent the Rural District Council will possess the same power (sec. 33, sub-sec. 1).

(*b*) Special provision is made as to clerks and treasurers of unions.

The clerk or treasurer of every Board of Guardians is to be the clerk or treasurer of the council of *every* rural district comprised in the Union, unless a District Council, with the authority of the Local Government Board, appoints a separate clerk or treasurer of its own. In case a separate clerk is so appointed, his salary must be fixed with the consent of the Local Government Board (sec. 85, sub-sec. 1). It would thus appear that, if there are two or more rural districts wholly comprised in one union—the clerk of the union may be clerk of two or more District Councils as well.

(*c*) The portion of the salary of any clerk of union which is to be paid by a District Council is to be determined by the Local Government Board, and the same provision applies to any other officer of a Board of Guardians who becomes also an officer of a Rural District Council (sec. 85, sub-sec. 2). If the Local Government Board directs that the same officers be employed by the District Council and the Guardians, this provision, it is submitted, will apply to all officers employed under such orders.

(*d*) The additional salary paid to a dispensary medical officer as Medical Officer of Health is to be paid by the new sanitary authority—that is, the proper District Council (sec. 85, sub-sec. 4).

(*e*) The law regarding the superannuation of the officers of Boards of Guardians is unchanged, and it applies to the officers of Rural District Councils (sec. 83, sub-sec. 11). As to what it provides, see *supra*.

V.—Officers under the Diseases of Animals Act.

The power of the Lord Lieutenant and Privy Council, or of the Lord Lieutenant alone, under the 68th and 69th sections of the Diseases of Animals Act, 1894, remain unaffected by the

Act (sec. 83, sub-sec. 14). Under these enactments the Lord Lieutenant and Privy Council are invested with power to

1. Define the number, qualifications, duties, powers` of remuneration, and period of service, of inspectors and valuers, and other officers of local authorities, and the terms and conditions of their appointment;

2. Unite two or more Poor Law Unions in a district for the purpose of inspection; and

3. Authorise or direct the local authorities of those Unions to appoint a veterinary inspector for the united district, and determine the mode of contribution of each Union to the cost.

As to an alternative to the power of the Lord Lieutenant and Privy Council to authorise or direct the appointment of an inspector over an area of two or more united districts, the Lord Lieutenant is himself empowered to appoint such an officer over such an area.

VI.—Officers of Urban Authorities.

Except as regards existing officers (as to whom, see *post*), the law regulating the appointment, removals, salaries, and super-annuation of the officers of the Councils of County Boroughs, Urban District Councils, and Town Boards, remains unchanged. The enactment regarding their superannuation is the Local Officers Superannuation (Ireland) Act, 1869. Under this Act any such officer who has devoted his whole time to his duties may, with the consent of the Lord Lieutenant, be granted a superannuation allowance not exceeding two-thirds of his salary, if he is suffering from permanent infirmity, or is 60 years of age and has served 20 years.

VII.—Miscellaneous Provisions as to Officers.

(*a*) A fine of 40s. or, in the case of a continuing offence, a fine of 40s. a day may be inflicted on any officer paid out of local rates for wilfully failing or refusing to do anything he is bound to do, and the fine may be recovered as a Crown debt; and, if it does not amount to more than £100, it may be recovered in a Court of Summary Jurisdiction (sec. 86).

(*b*) An officer holding any pensionable office (who is, of course, required to devote his whole time to his duties), is not to be disqualified for superannuation by reason only of having also acted, whether before or after the passing of the Act, as an officer of a School Attendance Committee under the Irish Education Act, 1892 (sec. 87).

(*c*) The secretary of every County Council and the clerk of every Urban District Council must send, within a time to be prescribed by the Local Government Board, to every Board of Guardians for a Union, wholly or partially in the county or district, a copy of so much of the poor rate book as relates to the county or district, and every ratepayer concerned shall have a right to take a copy of, or to make extracts from, such copy (sec. 96, sub-sec. 1).

(*d*) Clerks of the Peace shall be entitled to be paid for their work under the Act, and under the Registration (Ireland) Act, 1898, as for ordinary registration work (sec. 98, sub-sec. 8).

(*e*) If the Local Government Board amalgamate unions, and, as a consequential step, either amalgamate the rural districts in the same county which are comprised in the amalgamated unions, or direct that such districts shall remain separate rural districts, they may make, at the same time, arrangements for protecting the interests of the officers of the District Councils holding office at the time of the amalgamation, and for that purpose the Union Officers' (Ireland) Act, 1885, is to apply to such officers as if they were officers of Boards of Guardians (sec. 68, sub-sec. 5).

The enactment mentioned provides that a Board of Guardians may, with the consent of the Local Government Board, give to a person, retiring or removed from his office because of its abolition, an annual allowance, as if he were retiring through permanent ill-health or infirmity of mind or body, provided he be a person to whom such a superannuation might be granted under the 28 & 29 Vic., c. 26, Union Officers' Superannuation Act, 1865—that is, provided he (1) has given his whole time to the service of the Union, and (2) has either become incapable of discharging his duties through permanent infirmity of mind and body or (3) is sixty years of age, and has served for twenty years in the Union; the allowance not to exceed two-thirds of his salary at the time of retirement.

PART VIII.

TEMPORARY PROVISIONS.

I.—First Elections. Date of First Elections.

The first elections of

(1) County Councillors (except the Councillors of County Boroughs),
(2) Rural District Councillors, and
(3) Poor Law Guardians,

are to take place on the 25th March, 1899, or on such day within fourteen days before or after that day as the Local Government Board may determine (sec. 111, sub-sec. 1, 2); for the day actually appointed, see Local Government Board First Elections Order, Appendix III.

The first election of

(1) County Borough Aldermen and Councillors,
(2) Urban District Councillors, and
(3) Town Commissioners;

took place on the 15th January, 1899, and except in the cases of Belfast and Derry, the whole number of Aldermen, Councillors, and Town Commissioners were then elected, and the persons elected came into office on the day after, (sec. 112). The outgoing Aldermen, Councillors, and Town Commissioners remained in office till the 16th January, which is the ordinary day of retirement (sec. 94, sub-sec. 13).

II.—Additional Councillors and Committeemen.

(a) Additional Councillors may be chosen for the first County Councils (except the Councils of county boroughs), to the number of three for each, by the Grand Juries. Such choice must be made by the Grand Jury or by the Committee appointed by the Grand Jury at the Spring Assizes and, in the case of the County of Dublin, at the Easter presenting term of 1899, and the choice is limited to persons who either are then serving as Grand Jurors or have done so within the previous three years (sec. 113, sub-sec. 1);

(b) Three additional Councillors shall be chosen for each of the first rural district Councils by those Councils at their first meeting, or, if they fail so to choose, by the County Councils as soon as may be ; and in this case the choice is limited to persons who have actually served as *ex-officio* guardians at any time during the preceding three years (sec. 113, sub-sec. 3).

(*c*) Additional Committeemen may be nominated by the Lord Lieutenant for the first committees of management of lunatic asylums, the number so appointed not to exceed one-fourth of the committee (sec. 113, sub-sec. 2).

All such additional Councillors and Committeemen are to hold office for three years only (sec. 113, sub-sec. 4).

III.—Electoral Districts, Registers and Returning Officers.

(*a*) ELECTORAL DISTRICTS.

The poor law electoral divisions adopted for registration purposes in 1898 are to be the district electoral divisions for the first election of County Councillors, rural district Councillors, and guardians for urban districts, unless the Local Government Board otherwise direct (sec. 111, sub-sec. 4) ; and if that Board thinks that any such division ought to be divided, it may allow more than two Councillors to be elected for that division notwithstanding that no representation on the subject is made by a County Council (see *supra*), in which case each elector may give one vote for each Councillor to be elected (sec. 111, sub-sec. 3 (*b*)). For an Order under this provision, see p. 385.

(*b*) REGISTERS.

The registers made up in 1898 (which came into force on the 1st January, 1899), are not to be invalidated by reason of any error or omission, or by reason of anything relating to them not having been completed in time (sec. 114, sub-sec. 2), and the time for doing anything in relation thereto was extended for 1898 by one week in each case (sec. 114, sub-sec. 1).

(*c*) RETURNING OFFICERS.

The Local Government Board may appoint for the first elections the returning officers, where none such exist at the first elections, and do any other thing necessary for carrying out the first elections which is not otherwise provided for (Local Government (Application of Enactments) Order, 1898, Article 39).

For the Rules made by the Local Government Board, see Appendix III.

IV.—First Councils and Boards.

1. As to FIRST COUNTY COUNCILS:—

The first meeting of each Council is to be held on the twelfth day next after the day of the first elections (see *supra*, for day of first elections), and such first meeting is to be convened by the returning officer in the same manner as ordinary meetings (*supra*, p. 26), and as if the returning officer were the chairman of the Council (Local Government (Transitory Provisions) No. 2 Order, 1898, Article 9, sub-sec. 1). It may be held at the County Court-house or in such other place as the returning officer may fix.

The proceedings at such first meeting are regulated by the other sub-sections of the same Article and Order. The members of the Council are first to select a chairman *of the meeting*, the question to be determined, in the case of a tie, by lot; the choosing of additional councillors will be the next business, and the chairman *of the Council* is then to be elected, the chairman of the meeting having, in the case of a tie, a second or casting vote; the chairman so elected, if present, is to make the declaration accepting office, to take the chair immediately, and to continue to act as chairman till the day of the annual meeting in the year 1900.

2. As to FIRST RURAL DISTRICT COUNCILS:—

The first meeting of each such body is to be convened also by the returning officer, and held on the fifth day next after the day of the first election (as to which see *supra*, p. 85); and the proceedings thereat are to be the same as those at the first meetings of the County Councils which have just been mentioned (same Order, Article 6). The chairman and vice-chairman then elected are to hold office till the day of the annual meeting in the year 1900 (same Order, Article 10, sub-sec. 7).

2. As to FIRST GUARDIANS:—

The first meetings of the first Boards of Guardians are also to be convened by the returning officer, and are to be held on the same day as the first meeting of the Rural District Council in the Union, but after the conclusion of that meeting, or on such day not more than four days later, as may be fixed by the returning officer (Local Government Transitory Provisions (No. 2) Order, 1898, Article 11).

V.—Retirement of First Councillors.

1. As to COUNTY COUNCILS AND RURAL DISTRICT COUNCILS:—

In both cases the Councillors first elected will retire on the ordinary day of retirement in the year 1902, Local Government (Transitory Provisions) No. 2 Order, 1898, Article 15 (1).

The ordinary day of retirement for County Councillors and for Rural District Councillors is the day next after election—that is, the 1st June or such day seven days earlier or later as the County Council may fix (sec. 94, sub-sec. 7,8).

2. As to URBAN GUARDIANS :—

In this case the day of retirement shall be the same as for Rural District Councillors (*Ibid*).

3. As to URBAN DISTRICT COUNCILS AND TOWN COMMISSIONERS :

(*a*) Where the Urban District Councillors are all elected together, and all retire together, the first Councillors will retire on the ordinary day of retirement, in the year 1902 (same Order and Article, sub-sec. 4).

(*b*) Where the system continues of electing one-third annually, one-third of the Councillors are to retire on the ordinary day of retirement in the year 1900 ; one-third on the same day in the year 1901 ; and the remaining third on the same day in the year 1902 ; where a borough or district is divided into wards, those regulations will apply separately to each ward ; and the order in which the Councillors are to go out of office is to be determined, in the case of Councillors elected after a poll, by the number of votes they received, those receiving the smallest going first, and, in the case of those elected without a contest, the question being determined by the majority of the whole Council.

As to the aldermen in boroughs, except in Belfast and Londonderry, one half are to go out on the ordinary day of retirement in the year 1902, and the other half in the year 1905 (same Order and Article, sub-sec. 2).

4. As to the COUNCILS OF COUNTY BOROUGHS :—

The forgoing provisions regarding Urban District Councils for boroughs, apply in the case of the Councils for county boroughs (same Order and Article, sub-sec. 2).

VI.—Temporary Financial Arrangements and Adjustments.

1. The Grand Juries at Spring Assizes, 1899, and their officers are to proceed, as usual, to make arrangements for carrying on their business up to the 30th September, 1899, and they are not to take into account possible receipts from the agricultural grant (Local Government (Transitory Provisions) (No. 2) Order,

1898, Article 3); but after a day to be fixed by the County Councils, all receipts in respect of county cess applotted before the assizes of 1899 shall be paid into the county fund (same Order and Article, sub-sec. 7), and after that all sums required to meet payments for county purposes shall be raised by the councils (same Order and Article, sub-sec. 9).

2. The Boards of Guardians will continue to make and levy the poor rate, but only for a period ending the 31st March, 1899 (same Order, Article 4, sub-sec. 1); and this provision will apply to the parts of the two Dublin Unions which are outside the city (sub-sec. 2). As regards the portions of those unions within the city, the Boards will act as follows:—

(a) In the case of the sum required by them for the period ending the 31st March, 1899 (up to which they will retain all their powers), they will estimate it according to the law existing at the passing of the Act; and

(b) In the case of the amount required by them for the period from the 31st March, 1899 to the 30th September following, they will estimate it according to the law as altered by the Act (under which they will only have, after the 31st March, the expenditure of what is required for the relief of the poor).

Having so estimated those amounts, they will send their estimates to the Collector-General, who will make and levy the rates for those periods respectively (same Order and Article, sub-sec. 2).

3. Any adjustment of financial relations, consequent on alterations of boundaries, or on alterations in the method of assessing the poor-rate or of raising the charges heretofore levied off any area, or on other things done by virtue of the Act, may be made by the Local Government Board after communication with the various authorities concerned (same Order, Article 18); and the power of the Board in this matter extends to the adjustment of any guarantee affecting any barony or any other area, which is divided between two or more counties or districts (same Order and Article, sub-sec. 3), and to the transfer of any duties to be performed by any Council or Officer (same Order and Article, sub-sec. 5).

VII.—Existing Officers.

1. TRANSFER OF OFFICERS.

(a) The existing officers of any authority whose business is transferred to any County or District Council become the officers of the Council to which that business is transferred, provided they are employed in that business and not in any other business of the old authority, and for the purpose of this enactment, the following are deemed to be existing officers, viz.:—

(a) Grand Jury Secretaries;
(b) County Treasurers;
(c) County Surveyors;
(d) Assistant Surveyors;
(e) County Solicitors;
(f) County Analysts;
(g) Barony Constables or Cess Collectors;
(h) Deputy Cess Collectors duly appointed under sec. 148 of Grand Jury Act, 1836 (under which Deputies as well as principals were obliged to give security);
(i) Deputy County Treasurers and Secretaries who were appointed with the approval of the Lord Lieutenant and have devoted their whole time to their duties;
(j) Medical Superintendents and other officers in lunatic asylums;

all of whom but the last class are deemed to be existing officers of the Grand Jury, the last class being deemed to be existing officers of the Boards of Governors of the various asylums (sec. 115, sub-sec. 1); and all are transferred, accordingly to the County Councils, and that, too, in the case of the Grand Jury officers, whether they served in a county or in a county of a city or town (not a county borough), such counties of cities and towns being merged in thier respective counties (sec. 115, sub-sec. 2).

Poor-rate collectors in rural districts are transferred to the County Councils; poor-rate collectors in urban districts to the Urban District Councils (sec. 115, sub-sec. 1); and it is submitted that these latter officers do not come within the terms of sec. 115, sub-sec. 10, under which *County* Councils are to choose between poor rate collectors and cess collectors.

It will be seen that certain existing officers may be excluded from the benefits of this enactment—namely, all officers who have been employed by any of the old authorities in any business additional to that transferred. Dispensary doctors who will remain the medical officers of the Boards of Guardians, are not affected by this provision, in respect of their being also sanitary officers, because they must, in any case, be employed as sanitary officers in their respective districts (sec. 11, Public Health Act, 1878); but Clerks of Unions, who also are sanitary officers as well as Clerks of Unions, would not necessarily retain both positions. It is, however, expressly provided that those officers and the treasurers of unions shall be the clerks and treasurers respectively of the councils of the rural districts comprised in the respective unions, unless the Local Government Board authorise the appointment of separate clerks and treasurers by those Councils (sec. 85, sub-sec. 1).

(*b*) Existing Clerks of Unions are to continue to perform their work under the Registration Acts and Jurors' Acts, unless they otherwise arrange with the County Councils (sec. 121).

(*c*) Special provisions is made regarding existing secretaries of Grand Juries. Those officers, unless they resign or are removed with the concurrence of the Local Government Board, will be the secretaries of the County Councils till the 31st March, 1900, and any of them may then, if they have given three months' notice in writing, retire on an allowance as if his office were abolished (sec. 115, sub-sec. 4, and see *post*), or he may then be removed, on three months' notice beforehand, and if he is so removed without the concurrence of the Local Government Board, he will be entitled to a similar allowance (sec. 115, sub-sec. 5); and the secretary of the Grand Jury of Tipperary will become the secretary of the Council for each riding of that county, with the same right to retire on the 31st March, 1900, and the right to an allowance in the event of his being removed on or after that date as all other existing secretaries (sec. 115, sub-sec. 8).

(*d*) Special provision is also made for the existing Clerks of the Crown and Peace for Kilkenny city and Galway town, who are to continue to perform the same duties in the same areas as heretofore (sec. 117, sub-sec. 1).

(*e*) Special provision is also made for the Coroners for the borough of Galway and Carrickfergus. Those towns being merged in the counties of Galway and Antrim respectively, their existing Coroners will continue to act for the same districts as hitherto, as if their areas were districts of those counties (sec. 117, sub-sec. 2).

(*f*) County Cess Collectors are to continue the collection of the cess which they had in hand on the day when the Act came into operation, as respects their business (sec. 120, and see also sec. 124).

2. CONDITIONS OF SERVICE.

As to tenure and salary, every existing officer who is transferred from any local authority to any other will hold his office by the same tenure, and on the same terms and conditions as heretofore, and while he performs the same or analagous duties as heretofore will receive the same salary (sec. 115, sub-sec. 18), and this provision applies to all existing officers of any urban district Council, or town board, other than a town clerk (sec. 119), and any such officers as have hitherto been elected annually, need not be so elected in future (sec. 119).

Officers of Municipal Authorities, such as a Town Clerk of a Borough, or of a Town Board, and who have hitherto been permanent officers, remain permanent, and are to be paid as hitherto (sec. 116); and the same provision applies to all other existing officers of an Urban District Council or Town Board, even though they have been hitherto annually re-appointed (sec. 119).

The same provision as to salary applies to the Clerks of the Crown and Peace for Kilkenny and Galway (sec. 117, sub-sec. 1).

But, inasmuch as the areas, in which existing officers discharge their duties may be altered, and the duties of some existing officers will thus be increased, while those of others will be diminished, and inasmuch also as the County Councils must select between the cess collectors and the poor-rate collectors, as to whom they will in future employ as poor-rate collectors (sec. 115, sub-sec. 10), and as some officers will thus lose their employment, while others may have additional duties to discharge, it is provided, first, that the various officers must perform their duties in the altered areas (sec. 115, sub-sec. 16), and, second, must receive a proportionately increased or diminished remuneration (sec. 115, sub-sec. 18), it being in the power of the County Council, however, subject to the approval of the Local Government Board, to make a special agreement with any existing officer (sec. 115, sub-sec. 18). The obligation of choosing between the cess collectors and the poor-rate collectors, as the future poor-rate collectors, which is thrown on the County Councils (sec. 115, sub-sec. 10), does not seem to rest on the Urban District Councils, which are not mentioned in sec. 115, sub-sec. 10; and it would, therefore, seem to follow that poor-rate collectors in Urban Districts must continue to be employed by the Urban District Councils, concurrently with the cess collectors, subject to their remuneration being increased or diminished, according as their duties are increased or diminished, and to their being entitled, if those duties are diminished, to compensation.

The provision as to receiving the same remuneration for the performance of the same duties and increased remuneration for increased duties, applies to Town Clerks of boroughs and Commissioners (sec. 116). In regard to the Secretary of the two Councils of Tipperary, his remuneration is to be borne by the two Councils in proportions to be agreed upon, or in default of agreement, to be decided by the Local Government Board (sec. 115, sub-sec. 8).

3. SUPERANNUATION ALLOWANCES.

As to superannuation allowances and gratuities, the following are the provisions as regards existing officers:

(1) A Secretary of a County Council if he retires *after* 31st March, 1900, voluntarily, is to get a pension on the Civil Service scale (sec. 115, sub-sec. 6), if he retires on that day, after three months' notice, or if the County Council gets rid of him on that day by three months' notice given beforehand, or if before that day he satisfies the Local Government Board that he is unable, through age or infirmity, to discharge his duties and then retires, he will be entitled to an allowance as if his office were abolished (sec. 115, sub-sec. 4, 5, 6, 7, and see *post*, as to meaning of "abolition of office.")

(2) Town Clerks, if removed from office for any other cause than misconduct or incapacity, shall, in addition to any other rights they may have, be entitled to a superannuation on the Civil Service scale, if already qualified for a superannuation under the Local Officers' Superannuation (Ireland) Act, 1869; and if not so qualified, to a gratuity amounting to one year's net emoluments together with one quarter's net emoluments for each half-year served, the total amount, however, not to exceed *five* years' net emoluments (sec. 116, and 7th schedule, Part I).

(3) All other existing officers who are transferred to any county or district Council, or who are officers of any board of guardians, and who would be qualified for superannuation on the day the Act came into operation, shall be entitled on retirement at any time in the future, as a matter of right, to a superannuation on the Civil Service scale, without prejudice to any existing rights, which he may have, (sec. 118, sub-sec. 1); and the qualification for superannuation referred to means being of the necessary age where that is required, having served the necessary time, and (except in the case of medical officers) having devoted their whole time to their duties (sec. 118, sub-sec. 2). Those provisions, in other words, make it compulsory on the new authorities to grant pensions, on the Civil Service scale, to existing officers at any time they retire, provided they were qualified for pensions when the Act came into operation.

(4) The foregoing provision applies also to certain officers of Municipal Authorities—namely, to any existing officers of

any Urban District Council or Town Commissioners who could get superannuation if the authorities whom they served wished to give it to them, and provided they were qualified for super-annuation when the Act came into operation (sec. 119).

(5) In estimating the amount of superannuation to be given in any case, the service already given by any officer is to be taken into account, and this provision applies to the case of a secretary of a County Council who has served part of his time as assistant or deputy secretary (sec. 115, sub-sec. 3).

(6) Cess Collectors and deputy cess collectors are specially provided for, it being enacted that in case their services are dispensed with, they are to get compensation on the scale applying to Town Clerks not qualified for a superannuation allowance (sec. 120).

4. COMPENSATION AS FOR ABOLITION OF OFFICE.

(a) Any officer of a County or District Council such, for instance, as a poor-rate collector or cess collector, who is not continued in office, who could have got a pension, and who has expressed his willingness to continue to serve, is to receive compensation as if his office were abolished (sec. 115, sub-sec. 12).

(b) The same provision applies to any dispensary doctor, whose office is declared, by the Local Government Board, within six months after the passing of the Act to be unnecessary (sec. 115, sub-sec. 17).

(c) The same rule applies to any other officer, whether mentioned in sec. 115 or not, who is remunerated out of any cess or rate, and loses his employment or suffers any direct pecuniary loss in consequence of the Act, or who, on being transferred to a Council is dismissed within five years, from any other cause than misconduct or incapacity, provided he can be removed without the concurrence of the Lord Lieutenant or the Local Government Board, and is not a banking company (sec. 115, sub-sec. 19).

The compensation given "on abolition of office," or for loss or diminution of fees or salary, and the circumstances under which it is given are regulated by sec. 120 of the Local Government (England and Wales) Act, 1888 (sec. 115, sub-sec. 19). According to the provision of that enactment, compensation may be given to existing officers who suffer any direct pecuniary loss by either (1) abolition of office, or (2) diminution of fees or salary, but in estimating the amount of compensation to be given the following circumstances and matters are to be taken into account:—

1. The conditions of the appointment—that is, whether it was permanent or terminable at the discretion of the appointing body;

2. The nature of the office or employment—that is, whether it was an important office or the reverse;

3. The length of the service rendered;

4. Whether the officer has received any and, if any, what additional emoluments under or owing to the working of the Act, and what (if any) emoluments he might have obtained if he had not refused to accept office under any Council;

5. All the other circumstances of the case. (See Macmoran's " Local Government Act, 1888," p. 195.)

6. The compensation awarded is not to exceed the Civil Service scale allowed in the case of a person whose office is abolished.

5. GRATUITIES.

Gratuities may be given in the following cases:—

-(a) To existing Town Clerks who may not be entitled, in consequence of not having served a sufficiently long time, to superannuation, and who are removed from office for any other cause than misconduct or incapacity (sec. 116);

(b) To existing collectors who, if they hold a pensionable office, do not within the time prescribed by the Local Government Board, express their willingness to continue to serve, and are not continued in office (sec. 115, sub-sec. 12 (b)); and

(c) To existing officers who, do not hold a pensionable office, and express their unwillingness to serve, or are not continued in office (sec. 115, sub-sec. 12 (c)).

The scale on which gratuities may be calculated is that prescribed for high constables, and barony collectors, by Part I. of the 7th schedule of the Act.

6. THE CIVIL SERVICE SCALE.

The interpretation put by the Local Government Board upon the expression " Civil Service Scale," may be gathered from the following extract from a circular issued by the Board the 25th November, 1881 :—

" The Board, therefore, think it expedient to state, for the information of Boards of Guardians, that in giving their consent in future to Superannuation Allowances proposed to be granted to Union Officers they will be governed, as far as circumstances may permit, by the rules applicable to the Superannuation of the Civil Servants of the Crown under the Superannuation Act of 1859 : following, then, the scale of allowances prescribed by that Act, the amount which may, in the opinion of the Board, be properly awarded to an Officer who has served with efficiency for ten years and upwards, and under eleven years, will be an annual sum equal to ten-sixtieths of his salary and emoluments, and an addition of one-sixtieth in respect of each additional year of service until a maximum of forty-sixtieths, or two-thirds, be reached, which is the highest amount authorised by the Union Officers Super-annuation Acts. In cases where, for the due and efficient discharge of the duties of any office, professional or other special qualifications are required, a number of years not exceeding ten, may, for the purpose of the computation, be added to the number of years during which the Officer has served, provided such addition does not raise the amount to be awarded above the maximum amount of two-thirds of his salary and emoluments.'

7. Protection for Pensions and other Compensation.

No pension, allowance, or compensation granted to any exist-ing officer can be assigned, nor can it be changed with his debts (sec. 115, sub-sec. 23).

8. Salaries of Existing Coroners.

While the salary of every Coroner may be fixed at any sum, the County Council may fix and the Local Government Board may sanction, the salary of an *existing* Coroner shall not be less than his average annual net receipts as Coroner, during the five years next before the passing of the Act (sec. 14, sub-sec. 6 (*b*)).

9. Auditing of County Treasurer's Accounts.

The officers employed in auditing County Treasurer's ac-counts, who were formerly officers under the Receiver Master, and were subsequently transferred to the Local Government Board, are made officers of that Board at the same remunera-tion as heretofore. They are qualified to receive a superannua-tion, such as is provided under the Local Officers' (Ireland) Superannuation Act, 1869 ; in calculating the amount of the superannuation they are entitled to reckon their future service, as well as their past service ; and the superannuation is to be paid out of the Fee Fund mentioned in the said Act of 1869 (sec. 122, sub-sec. 2).

10. The Collector-General of Dublin and his Staff.

The Collector-General and such persons as were officers of his on the 31st March, 1898, are to hold their offices till the 1st October, 1899, and, unless they are then taken over by the Cor-poration, are to be entitled to superannuation allowance, in accordance with sec. 70 (A) of the Dublin Improvement Act, 1890 (sec. 66 (10)).

PART IX.
MISCELLANEOUS.
I.—The Appointed Day.

The Act comes into operation for:—

(a) Rural District Councils and Boards of Guardians on the 25th March, 1899;

(b) County Councils and Urban District Councils on the 1st April, 1899; and

(c) As to all other matters on the 1st April, 1899;

but, before the election of the County Councils, the Local Government Board may order that different dates be fixed, and then different days may be fixed for different purposes (sec. 124, sub-sec. 1), except that the provisions regarding the registration of electors, elections, and any matters that must be done to bring the Act into force, took effect on the passing of the Act (sec. 124, sub-sec. 2).

General Orders of the Local Government Board under this section will be found in Appendix III. After the election of the County Councils the dates can be fixed only on the application of those bodies (sec. 124, sub-sec. 1).

II.—Orders in Council and Rules.

(a) The Lord Lieutenant in Council may make orders applying to Ireland, for the purposes of the Act, certain provisions of the English and Scotch Local Government Acts (sec. 104); may adapt the Grand Jury Acts, the Valuation Acts, and other Irish Acts, to the new system of local government in Ireland (sec. 105); and may regulate the procedure of the County and District Councils in reference to the business transferred to them from the Grand Juries and Presentment Sessions and make all such transitary provisions regarding the business and officers of Councils and Guardians, first elections and retirement of Councillors, and other matters, as may be necessary for bringing the Act into operation (sec. 106). All such orders must be laid before Parliament and are subject to being annulled by a vote of either house within forty days after either house has begun to sit (sec. 107, sub-sec. 2).

(b) The Local Government Board may make rules for carrying into effect the financial provisions of the Act, and for regulating any matter authorised to be regulated by rules, and generally for carrying the Act into effect, so far as the Lord Lieutenant in Council is not invested with that power (sec. 108, sub-sec. 1). It may also make provisional orders for adapt-

H

ing any Local Act to the new state of things (sec. 108, sub-sec. 2); but such orders must be confirmed by Parliament and sections 214 and 215 of the Public Health (Ireland) Act, 1878, which provide for local inquiries being held before the orders are made, apply where they are applicable (sec. 101, sub-sec. 4)

III.—Existing Powers of Local Government Board.

The existing powers of the Local Government Board over the Boards of Guardians and their officers remain, and, if any of the new Councils so wish and apply, the Board may exercise in relation to that Council and its officers the powers of holding inquiries, and deputing inspectors to attend its meetings, as it possesses in the case of Boards of Guardians (sec. 101, sub-sec. 1). It may also decide any difference which under any applied enactment can be referred to the High Court, provided the parties differing agree to that course (sec. 101, sub-sec. 3).

IV.—Additional Members of Local Government Board.

The President of the Local Government—that is, the Chief Secretary for Ireland—may appoint an additional member of the Board to hold office for a term not exceeding five years, for the purpose of assisting in the work of bringing the Act into operation, at such salary as the Treasury fix (sec. 102, sub-sec. 5, 6).

V.—Imperative Presentments and Mandamus.

Where a judge orders a sum to be paid by any Council or by an officer of any Council under the Act—as, for instance, in an appeal in a case of compensation for malicious injuries; or where a judgment of a court has to be satisfied; or in the case of a fixed imperative presentment, such as that for extra police, the treasurer must pay the money required out of the first moneys coming to his hands and, if he fails, may be compelled to pay by *mandamus* (sec. 80, sub-sec. 1); and where a mandamus is issued by the High Court to any County or District

Council, and the Council fail to comply with it, the Court may appoint an officer with all the powers of the Council to carry the order into effect (sec. 81). Moreover, in the case of a debt due to the Crown, the amount may, in case of default, be deducted from the portion of the agricultural or other grant payable to the Council (sec. 80, sub-sec. 2).

VI.—Licensed Premises and Meetings of Councils.

If there is no other suitable place available, a County or District Council, or any committee thereof, may meet in licensed premises; but not otherwise, and in this connection licensed premises includes a club at which any intoxicating liquor is sold (sec. 77).

VII.—Registration of Electors.

(*a*) The register of electors for local government purposes is to be completed and on sale to the public, and is to come into operation, on the 1st January in each year, and is to continue in force for one year from that date (sec. 98, sub-sec. 1).

(*b*) Freeholders and leaseholders in a district electoral division which is now comprised in a Parliamentary borough, if before the Act they voted in a Parliamentary county and not in a Parliamentary borough, are to be entered in a separate list; but the entry of their names in a separate list will not alter the place where they may vote at a Parliamentary election (sec. 98, sub-sec. 2).

(*c*) Freemen, if resident in a Parliamentary borough, are to vote at local government elections in the electoral division in which they live; if non-resident, in the divisions to which they are allotted by the revising barrister, who will allot such freeman as they are at present allotted for Parliamentary purposes (sec. 98, sub-secs. 3, 4).

(*d*) For the purposes of the registration of voters in the year 1898, the time for doing anything in July or August, was extended by one week in each case (sec. 114, sub-sec. 1), and no election is to be questioned by reason of any error or informality in the lists in the year 1898 (sec. 114, sub-sec. 2).

VIII.—Ecclesiastial Dignitaries and County Infirmaries.

The right of any ecclesiastical person, by virtue of his dignity or office, to be a governor or trustee of any county infirmary or fever hospital is abolished (sec. 15, sub-sec. 11).

IX.—Future transfer of Additional Powers to County Councils.

If any drainage board or other public body, corporate or unincorporate (except a District Council, or a Town Board, or a Board of Guardians), consents, its business may be transferred to the County Council by a provisional order of the Local Government Board, and where a drainage board or other such body has ceased to exist, the transfer may be effected without the consent of the body effected (sec. 20, sub-sec. 1). The business so transferred, if it arises in two or more counties, may be transferred to the Councils of these counties jointly, and be managed by a joint Committee of these Councils (sec. 20, sub-sec. 2).

X.—Trackways in Navigable Rivers.

A trackway on the bank of any navigable river on which boats have been accustomed to be towed by horses, shall, while the canal continues to be used for navigation, be a public highway, and shall continue to be maintained as hitherto—that is, it may be kept in repair and widened, if necessary, to an extent not exceeding 15 feet, by the County Council, at the expense of the portion of the county through which it passes (sec. 78, and 36 & 37 Vic., c. 34, s. 1).

XI.—Amendment of Tramway Law

The requirement (23 & 24 Vic., c. 152, s. 38, (1)) that the approval or disapproval of a tramway undertaking by a municipal, corporate, or other municipal body shall be signified by a majority of two-thirds has been repealed. A mere majority will henceforth be sufficient '(sec. 93).

XII.—Leases of Dispensary Houses.

Hitherto such leases could not be made to a Board of Guardians for a longer period than 60 years (42 & 43 Vic., c. 25, s. 11). Henceforward they may be made for any term not less than 60 years which the owner has power to grant (sec. 91, and see Order of Local Government Board under this section, p. 276 *post*).

XIII.—Ballot Boxes and Fittings at Local and Parliamentary Elections.

Ballot-boxes, fittings, and compartments for voting at elections are to be provided and kept for each county, each urban and each rural district, and for each 'electoral division of a union in an urban district, at the expense of the county, the district and the union respectively, and they may be used free of charge at Parliamentary elections (sec. 99, sub-sec. 1); and if returning officers do not use such ballot-boxes, fittings and compartments at Parliamentary elections, they will not be allowed the cost of any others (sec. 99, sub-sec. 2).

XIV.—Contracts with County and District Councils.

Any two Councillors may make on behalf of any Council a contract by writing under their hands, (1) if the contract be one which need not, if made by a private person, be under seal; (2) if the subject matter does not exceed £50 in value, and (3) if they act by the direction of the Council (sec. 100).

XV.—The Ordnance Maps.

Changes necesary to be made in the Ordnance Maps in consequence of the Act, or of any Order in Council under the Act, are to be made by the Commissioner of Valuation in manner directed by Privy Council Order (sec. 68, sub-sec. 7).

XVI.—Existing Lunatic Asylum Regulations.

The existing rules regulating Lunatic Asylums are to continue in force until the first regulations respecting these instutions are made under the Act, and shall then cease to operate (sec. 110, 2 (*b*)).

APPENDIX I.

61 & 62 Vic.,
c. 37.
Local
Govern-
ment
(Ireland)
Act, 1898.

LOCAL GOVERNMENT (IRELAND) ACT, 1898.

[61 & 62 Vict. Ch. 37.]

ARRANGEMENT OF SECTIONS.

PART I.

County Councils.

Constitution.

61 & 62 VIC.,
c. 37.
LOCAL
GOVERN-
MENT
(IRELAND)
ACT, 1898.

PART II.

DISTRICT COUNCILS AND GUARDIANS.

Constitution.

PART VI.

ORDERS AND RULES.

PART VII.

DEFINITIONS, SHORT TITLE, AND REPEALS.

PART VIII.

TRANSITORY PROVISIONS.

First Elections and Councils.

Existing Officers.

Miscellaneous.

Commencement and Appointed Day.

SCHEDULES.

61 & 62 VIC.,
c. 37.
LOCAL
GOVERN-
MENT
(IRELAND)
ACT, 1898.

LOCAL GOVERNMENT (IRELAND) ACT, 1898.

(61 & 62 VICT. CH. 37.)

CHAPTER 37.

An Act for amending the Law relating to Local Government in Ireland, and for other purposes connected therewith.

[12th August, 1898.]

BE it enacted by the Queen's most Excellent Majesty, by and with the advice and consent of the Lords Spiritual and Temporal, and Commons, in this present Parliament assembled, and by the authority of the same, as follows :

PART I.

County Councils.

PART I.

COUNTY COUNCILS.

Constitution.

Establishment of county councils.

1. A council shall be established in every administrative county and be entrusted with the management of the administrative and financial business of that county, and shall consist of a chairman and councillors.

Election and qualification of councillors.

2.—(1.) The councillors of a county shall (subject to the provisions herein-after contained with respect to additional members) be elected by the local government electors for the county.

(2.) The councillors shall hold office for a term of three years, and shall then retire together, and their places shall be filled by a new election.

(3.) The number of councillors and the divisions in every county for their election (in this Act referred to as county electoral divisions) shall be thus provided by an order of the Local Government Board made before the first day of January next after the passing or this Act, subject after the first election to alteration in manner provided in pursuance of this Act :
Provided that—

(a) One councillor only shall be elected for each county electoral division except where an urban district forming one such division returns more than one councillor ; and

(b) The county electoral divisions shall be arranged with a view to the population of each division being, so nearly as conveniently may be, equal, regard being had to a proper representation both of the rural and urban population, and to the distribution and pursuits of such population, and to the last published census for the time being, and to evidence of any considerable change of population since such census.

(4.) At an election for a county, each elector may give in a county electoral division one vote and no more, or in case of an urban district forming one county electoral division and returning more than one councillor, one vote and no more for each of any number of persons not exceeding the number of councillors to be elected for that division, and shall not vote at the same election in more than one county electoral division of the county.

61 & 62 Vic., c. 37. LOCAL GOVERN- MENT (IRELAND) ACT, 1898.

PART I.

County Councils.

(5.) A person shall not be qualified to be elected or to be a councillor for a county, unless he is a local government elector for such county.

3.—(1.) The chairman of every rural district council (established under this Act) within the county shall, by virtue of his office, be an additional member of the county council, but if such chairman is otherwise a member, or is disqualified for election as a member, of the county council, the district council may assign one of their number who is not so disqualified to take during the term of office of that chairman the place of the chairman as additional member of the county council.

Additional members and chairman and vice-chairman of county council, and constitution of chairman as justice.

(2.) The county council may choose from persons qualified to be councillors one or two persons who shall be additional councillors during the term of office of the council by whom the choice is made. .

(3.) The first business of the council after any triennial election shall be the consideration of the question of choosing additional councillors. .

(4.) The county council may annually choose a chairman, and if they think fit a vice-chairman, from among the councillors, and the chairman, subject as hereafter provided by this Act, shall, during the term of and by virtue of his office, be a justice of the peace for the county. but before acting as such justice he shall, if he has not already done so, take the oaths required by law to be taken by a justice.

Powers of County Councils and County Courts.

4.—(1.) Subject to the provisions of this Act, there shall be transferred to the council of each county all the business of the grand jury not excepted by this section, and all the business of the county at large presentment sessions ; and the county council for the purpose of such business shall, save that any fiat or other sanction of a judge shall not be required, have the powers and duties of the grand jury and the said presentment sessions in connexion with the said business, and also such further powers and duties as are conferred on them by or in pursuance of this Act, or as may be necessary for conducting, as an administrative body, the powers hereby transferred.

Transfer to county council of business of grand jury and county at present-ment sessions.

(2.) Nothing in this Act shall transfer to a county council or a member thereof—

(a) any business relating to bills of indictment or any business of the grand jury at common law relating to crime ; or

(b) any business by this Act transferred to the county court ; or

(c) any power to appoint a visiting committee for a prison.

5.—(1.) There shall be transferred to the county court the business of any presentment sessions and grand jury in relation to compensation for criminal injuries, that is to say, compensation under the enactments mentioned in Part One of the First Schedule to this Act, and of those enactments section one hundred and thirty-five and the following sections of the Grand Juries Act, 1836, so far as unrepealed, shall extend to the case of maliciously setting fire to, destroying, or injuring property of any description, whether real, or personal, in like manner as they apply to the setting fire to, injuring, or destroying the particular descriptions of propery speci- fied in the first-mentioned section : Provided that this Act shall not extend the application of the said sections to any case except where the malicious act done was a crime punishable on indict- ment under the Malicious Damage Act, 1861.

(2.) Upon an application for such compensation, the county court may either refuse the application, or make a decree against the county council, and, if the decree is made, shall have the power of a judge of assize under section one hundred and forty of the Grand Juries Act, 1836, with respect to the apportionment of the com- pensation.

(3.) Any person claiming compensation in a county may apply to the county court, and the council for the county and the council for the district in or within one mile from the boundary of which county or district the injury is alleged to have been committed, and also any person paying poor rate in that county may, as well as the applicant, appear and be heard by the county court in relation to the application.

(4.) Any person or council who appeared, or though not actually appearing was entitled to appear, before the county court in rela- tion to such application, and also, where the area off which the compensation awarded is to be levied is less than the whole county, the council for any county district com- prising all or any part of that area, may, if aggrieved by the refusal or decree of the county court, appeal to the judge of assize, and, subject to this Act and to rules of court, the County Courts (Ireland) Acts, 1851 to 1889, shall, except in so far as they require security to be given, apply in like manner as in the case of any other appeal ; and the judge may vary the decree in respect of the area off which the compensation is levied as well as in respect of other matters.

(5.) The judge of assize upon any such appeal shall, in addition to any other power, have power if he thinks fit to empanel a jury to try any issue of fact arising on the appeal, and such jury shall, if any party to the proceedings so requires, be a special jury.

(6.) The county court and judge of assize respectively may award costs to or against any party to any proceedings under this section.

(7.) Rules of court may regulate the practice and procedure under this section, including costs, and the service of all preliminary notices, and the time within which any proceedings are to be had or taken ; and in particular such rules shall provide that non-compliance with any of the rules shall not render any proceedings void unless the court or judge of assize so direct, but the time may be extended and the proceedings may be set aside either wholly or in part, or be amended or otherwise dealt with, in such manner and upon such terms as the court or judge may think just.

(8.) Save so far as fees are taken by an existing clerk of the peace for his own use, court fees shall not be payable in any proceeding in the county court under this section.

(9.) The enactments mentioned in Part One of the First Schedule to this Act and this section shall extend to the whole of Ireland so far as they do not already so extend.

6. There shall be transferred to the council of each county—

(a) the business of the guardians with respect to making, levying, collecting and recovering the poor rate in so much of the county as is not comprised in an urban county district ;

(b) the business of the guardians as a local authority under the Diseases of Animals Act, 1894 ; and the Destructive Insect Act, 1877 ; and

(c) the business of the justices in petty sessions under the Explosives Act, 1875, except the power to appoint any officer, which power shall cease.

7. The council of a county shall be a local authority within the meaning of the Technical Instruction Acts, 1889 and 1891 ; but this section shall not prevent any other local authority under the said Acts from acting concurrently with the county council, if that authority act in accordance with any general scheme framed by the council, or otherwise with the consent of the council :
Provided that—

(a) The rate levied under the said Acts by such authority shall not, when combined with the rate levied thereunder by the county council, exceed the limit thereby authorised ; and

(b) Nothing in this section contained shall affect any scheme for technical or manual instruction instituted or made by any local authority before the passing of this Act, or the continued payment after the passing of this Act of any aid in pursuance of such scheme by such authority.

Marginal notes: 61 & 62 Vic., c. 37. LOCAL GOVERNMENT (IRELAND) ACT, 1898. PART I. *County Councils.* Transfer of county council of business of boards of guardians as to poor rate, cattle diseases, and explosives. 57 & 58 Vic., c. 57. 40 & 41 Vic., c. 68. 38 & 39 Vic., c. 17. Powers of county council as to technical instruction. 52 & 53 Vic., c. 57. 54 & 55 Vic., c. 4.

61 & 62 Vic.,
c. 37.
LOCAL
GOVERN-
MENT
(IRELAND)
ACT, 1898.

PART I.

*County
Councils*

Expenses
and deter-
mination
by county
council of
main roads

8.—(1.) One half of the expense of the maintenance of any main road shall be levied off the administrative county, and the other half off the county districts in which the road is situate.

(2.) Every road the expense of the maintenance of which at the passing of this Act is levied partly or wholly off the county at large shall be a main road until it ceases so to be as herein-after provided, and the enactments respecting main roads shall be repealed.

(3.) The council of each county may, upon the report of the county surveyor, make a general declaration declaring what roads in the county shall be main roads, and any road not mentioned in such declaration shall cease to be a main road; and at any time after the end of five years, the council may, if they think fit, reconsider the declaration and make a new declaration, and so on at intervals of not less than five years.

(4.) The county council may declare a proposed new road to be a main road, subject to reconsideration at any time at which the council reconsider any general declaration, and the cost of and incidental to the making of such road shall be levied in like manner as its maintenance.

(5.) A declaration, whether a general declaration or a declaration respecting a new road, shall at first be a provisional declaration, and shall be communicated by the county council to each district council in the count in the prescribed manner.

(6.) After the prescribed time, and after considering any representations which may meantime have been submitted either by any district council or by any person or persons claiming to be interested, the county council shall take the said provisional declaration into consideration, and may adopt the same, either in its original form or after modifying it either by way of exclusion or inclusion of roads.

(7.) The declaration, unless suspended as herein-after mentioned, shall come into operation at the date of its final adoption, or any later date specified in the declaration.

(8.) The county council shall forthwith communicate a declaration as finally adopted to every district council in the county; and any such district council if aggrieved by the declaration or by the omission therefrom of any road, may, within the prescribed time, appeal to the Local Government Board, and that Board, after communication with the county council, may dismiss the appeal, or make any declaration which the county council could have made, and that declaration shall operate as a declaration by the council.

(9.) In the event of such an appeal, the declaration shall be suspended while the appeal is pending. A county council may also suspend a declaration as regards a portion of an old road situate in any county district, until the council of the district have proposed the expenditure of sufficient money for placing that portion in proper repair and condition to the satisfaction of the county council.

(10.) A declaration, suspended while an appeal is pending, which afterwards becomes operative, shall operate as from the date when originally made, or any later date which may be fixed by the Local Government Board on the appeal.

(11.) This section shall apply to so much of any main or other road as is situate within an urban county district.

(12.) Nothing in this section shall be held to prevent the whole or a greater proportion than one-half of the expenses of the maintenance of any road heretofore leviable wholly off the county at large, or of the expenses of the maintenance or construction of any bridge, from being levied off the county at large.

9.—(1.) It shall be the duty of the council of every county to provide and maintain sufficient accommodation for the lunatic poor in that county in accordance with the Lunatic Asylum Acts, and if it appears to the Lord Lieutenant that any council fail to perform such duty, he may order that council to remedy the failure within the time and in the manner (if any) specified in the order.

(2.) The duties of the council under this section shall be exercised through a committee appointed by them, and if the Lord Lieutenant fixes a number of the number so fixed; and out of that committee a number not exceeding one-fourth may be persons not members of the councils.

(3.) There shall be transferred to the council, acting through that committee, the business of the governors and directors of the asylum under the Lunatic Asylum Acts, and the committee, subject to the general control of the council as respects finance, may act without their acts being confirmed by the council.

(4.) Plans or contracts for the purchase of land or buildings, or for the erection, restoration, or enlargement of buildings, shall not be carried into effect until approved by the Lord Lieutenant.

(5.) The county council, through the said committee, shall properly manage and maintain every lunatic asylum for their county; and, subject to the provisions of this Act, may appoint and remove the officers of the asylum and regulate the expenditure; and the powers under the Lunatic Asylum Acts of the Lord Lieutenant or the inspectors of lunatics, as to those matters, and as to land and buildings, and as to the appointment of governors or directors, shall cease, and also the Board of Control for lunatic asylums shall be abolished.

(6.) The county council, through the said committee, may, and if required by the Lord Lieutenant shall, make regulations respecting the government and management of every lunatic asylum for their county, and the admission, detention, and discharge of lunatics, and the conditions as to payment and accommodation under which private patients may be admitted into, and detained in the asylum, and the regulations when approved by the Lord Lieutenant with or without modification shall have full effect, and shall have the same effect for the purposes of the fourth section of the Lunatic Asylums (Ireland) Act, 1875, as if made by the Lord Lieutenant and Privy Council.

61 & 62 Vic., c. 37. LOCAL GOVERN- MENT (IRELAND) ACT, 1898.

PART I.

County Councils.

Provision and man- agement of lunatic asylums.

33 & 39 Vic., c. 67.

61 & 62 VIC.,
c. 37.
LOCAL
GOVERN-
MENT
(IRELAND)
ACT, 1898.

PART I.

*County
Councils.*

(7.) Where a district for a lunatic asylum comprises two or more counties, this section shall apply with the necessary modifications to those counties and to the councils thereof; and the expenses shall be defrayed by the several counties in proportion to the number of lunatics from each county according to the average of the three local financial years which ended next before the last triennial election of county councillors; and the committee for the asylum shall be a joint committee of the councils of the counties, with a representation of each council (determined in case of dispute by the Lord Lieutenant) in the same proportion as that in which the expenses are defrayed.

(8.) Where a county council fail or refuse to provide funds for any object approved by any such joint committee, the joint committee may, except where the majority of the county councils represented on such joint committee so fail or refuse, appeal to the Lord Lieutenant, and the said county council shall comply with any order made by the Lord Lieutenant upon that appeal.

(9.) Proceedings had or taken by any such joint committee shall be had or taken in the names of the said councils jointly, and proceedings had or taken against any such joint committee shall be had or taken against such councils jointly.

Powers of
county
council as to
acquisition
of land or
easements.

10.—(1.) A county council, for the purpose of any of their powers and duties, may acquire, purchase, take on lease or exchange any land or any easements or rights over or in land, whether within or without their county, including rights to water, and may acquire, hire, erect, and furnish such halls, buildings, and offices as they require, whether within or without their county, and for the purpose of this section section two 41 & 42 Vic.,
c. 52. hundred and three of the Public Health Act, 1878, shall apply with the necessary modifications, and in particular with the modification that the advertisements mentioned in sub-section two of the said section may be published in any month, and that the notice mentioned in the said sub-section shall be served in the next succeeding month.

(2.) A county council shall not take or use any such land, easements, or rights, without either the consent of the owner and occupier or the authority of a provisional order duly confirmed, and where the order does not affect demesne land, it may be confirmed without the authority of Parliament in manner 43 & 49 Vic.,
c. 77 provided by section twelve of the Labourers (Ireland) Act, 1885, and that section and any enactment amending the same shall apply, with the necessary modifications.

(3). Where a county council desire for the purpose of the work of widening an old road, or making a new road, to acquire otherwise than by agreement any land other than demesne land or pleasure ground or than land situate in a borough or town, they may, if they think fit, notwithstanding anything in the foregoing provisions of this section, proceed as follows, namely :—

(*a*) Publish such advertisement and serve such notice on the owner or reputed owner, lessee or reputed lessee, and

61 & 62 VIC.,
c. 37.
LOCAL
GOVERN-
MENT
(IRELAND)
ACT, 1898.

PART I.

County
Councils.

occupier, of the land as may be prescribed by the Local Government Board, and within the prescribed time petition the judge of assize for an order authorising the council to put into force with reference to such land the powers of the Land Clauses Acts with respect to the purchase and taking of land otherwise than by agreement ;

(*b*) The judge of assize, on due proof of the prescribed advertisements having been published and prescribed notices served, shall, unless there is an application as hereinafter mentioned, make an order in accordance with the prayer of the petition ;

(*c*) Any person interested in the said land on whom the said notice is required as aforesaid to be served and who objects to the land being acquired by the county council, and any owner or reputed owner, lessee or reputed lessee, or occupier, of any land who alleges that such land will be injuriously affected by the said work, and also any ratepayer in the county may within such time after the publication of the said notices as is fixed by rules of court, apply to the judge of assize to refuse the order upon the said petition, and the judge shall hear such application and determine all questions of law and fact arising thereon, and in particular the question whether the said work is of public utility, and of such importance to the public as to justify the compulsory acquisition of the land ;

(*d*) Any decision by the judge upon the hearing of such application, whether making or refusing the order, shall be subject to appeal by any party to the proceedings before the judge of assize to the Lord Lieutenant in Council within the time fixed by rules of court, and the appeal shall be heard by a committee of the Privy Council (which shall be styled the Judicial Committee), consisting of such members thereof as are or have been judges of the Supreme Court, who, or a quorum of whom consisting of not less than three, shall advise the Lord Lieutenant thereon ;

Provided that, with the consent of the parties, the judge of assize may state a case for the opinion of the Court of Appeal upon any question of law, and in such case no appeal shall lie to the Lord Lieutenant in Council.

(*e*) The judge of assize and Lord Lieutenant in Council and the Court of Appeal may respectively award such costs to be paid by or to parties to any proceedings under this section as appear just ;

(*f*) Rules of court regulating the practice and procedure and costs respecting the petitions to and proceedings before the judge of assize under this section, and appeals from such judge to the Lord Lieutenant in Council, and cases stated, may be made by the authority having power to make rules of court for the Supreme Court ;

(*g*) An order under this section granting in whole or in part the prayer of the petition, whether made by the judge of

61 & 62 VIC.,
c. 37.
LOCAL
GOVERN-
MENT
(IRELAND)
ACT, 1898.

PART I.

*County
Councils.*
41 & 42 VIC.,
c. 52.

assize or by the Lord Lieutenant in Council upon appeal from that judge, shall have effect as if it were a provisional order under section two hundred and three of the Public Health Act, 1878, duly confirmed, and upon any land being taken under the order, the compensation for the same to be paid by the county council shall, in the absence of agreement, be determined by an arbitrator appointed by the Local Government Board, or if the parties so agree, be determined by the judge of assize, either with or without a jury, according to the agreement ;

(*h*) The foregoing provisions with respect to the acquisition of any land for the purpose of widening an old road, or making a new road, shall apply to the acquisition of any easement or right over land in like manner as if it were land.

Powers of
county
council as
to sudden
damage
to public
works.

11.—(1.) The council of each county shall arrange for the immediate repair of sudden damage to any public work, maintained in whole or in part at the cost of the county or any rural district, but where the expense of the repair is wholly leviable off any district and not partly off the county at large, such expense shall not exceed fifty pounds if within the prescribed time the council of the district object to any larger expenditure.

(2.) For the purposes of this section "repair of sudden damage" means such repair of any sudden damage to any public work, and such erection of any temporary work in place of any public work suddenly carried away or destroyed, and such collection or preservation of the materials of any damaged public work, as, subject to the general directions of the county council, the county surveyor considers cannot, without prejudice to the public, be delayed until the ordinary procedure relating to the repair of public works can be followed.

(3.) The powers of any justices and of extraordinary presentment sessions in relation to the repair of sudden damage to public works shall cease.

Power of
county
council as
to purchase
of quarries
and
machinery
and
obtaining
materials.
6 & 7 Will. 4,
c. 116.

12.—(1.) The county council, without prejudice to the power under section one hundred and sixty-two of the Grand Juries Act, 1836, or any other enactment, may, for the purpose of the maintenance of the roads in their county, whether main or other roads, acquire, purchase, take on lease, or exchange any land from which materials may be got for the repair of such roads, and may purchase or hire any steam roller, scarifier, or other machine, and may place at the disposal of the persons contracting for the repair of the roads materials from the said land, and the use of the said steam roller, scarifier, or other machine, upon such reasonable terms as may be agreed upon.

(2.) Section one hundred and sixty-two of the Grand Juries Act, 1836 (which relates to the power to obtain gravel, stone, sand, or other materials), shall extend to authorise the digging for, raising, and carrying away of gravel, stone, sand, or other materials, out of any river or brook at a distance of at least a hundred and fifty feet above or below any bridge, dam, or weir, where the same can be taken away without diverting or interrupting the course of the river or brook, or prejudicing or damaging any building, highway, ford, or spawning-bed.

61 & 62 VIC., c. 37. LOCAL GOVERN-MENT (IRELAND) ACT, 1898.

13.—(1.) Where the guardians of any union satisfy the council of a county that exceptional distress exists in some district electoral division situate both in the union and in the county, and the council apply to the Local Government Board, that Board may, if they think fit, by order authorise the guardians, subject to the prescribed conditions, to administer relief out of the workhouse for any time not exceeding two months from the date of the order to poor persons of any description resident in the said electoral division, and may revoke any such order either wholly or partly or with reference to any particular class of persons.

PART I.

County Councils.

Powers of county council as to exceptional distress.

(2) Section two of the Poor Relief (Ireland) Act, 1862 (which excludes an occupier of more than a quarter of an acre from being relieved otherwise than in the workhouse), shall not apply as regards relief given under this section.

25 & 26 Vic., c. 83.

(3.) One half of any expenditure incurred in pursuance of an order under this section shall be levied off the county at large (so, however, that the total amount of such expenditure levied off the county at large in any one year shall not exceed a sum equal to threepence in the pound on the rateable value of the county), and the council of the county may nominate one of their members who shall be an additional member of the board of guardians for the period fixed by the order.

(4.) The guardians may, with the consent of the Local Government Board, obtain for the purpose of this section temporary advances of such amount and for such period and repayable in such manner as that Board may sanction, and may mortgage their property and funds to secure such advances.

14.—(1.) A coroner for a county shall not be elected as heretofore, and on a vacancy in the office of a coroner for a county the county council shall within one month after the vacancy, or such further time not exceeding three months after the vacancy as the Lord Chancellor may allow, appoint a qualified person to the office, and if the county is divided into coroner's districts assign him a district.

Powers of county council as to appointment of coroners and coroners districts, and provision as to removal, salary, and qualification of coroner.

(2) The county council may alter the coroners' districts, and the enactments respecting those districts shall apply as if the county council were the justices assembled in special sessions for that purpose under the direction of the Lord Lieutenant, and the secretary of the county council were the clerk of the peace, and the powers of the Lord Lieutenant and justices and the clerk of the peace in relation to coroners' districts shall cease.

(3.) The Lord Chancellor may, if he thinks fit, remove any coroner for a county from his office for inability or misbehaviour in the discharge of his duty.

(4.) The writ de coronatore eligendo need not be issued, but neither the omission to issue that writ nor anything else in this

61 & 62 Vic., section shall alter the jurisdiction of the Lord Chancellor, or the
c. 37. High Court or a judge of assize, in relation to the removal of a
LOCAL
GOVERN- coroner otherwise than in manner provided by this Act or in re-
MENT
(IRELAND) lation to ordering a new election of a coroner.
ACT, 1898.
    (5.) A person who is a coroner for a county shall not be
PART I. qualified to be elected, or to be, a county or district councillor in
—
County that county.
Councils.
    (6.) The salary of every coroner shall be in lieu of all sums
which otherwise would be payable to him for fees, mileage, and
allowances, and shall be fixed with the approval of the Local
Government Board by the county or borough council by whom
the salary is payable, or in default of the same being so fixed then
by the Local Government Board, and shall not be subject to
increase or diminution during his tenure of office.

Provided that—

    (a) nothing in this section shall deprive the coroner of the
        right to be repaid expenses and disbursements lawfully
        paid by him on the holding of any inquest ; and
    (b) the salary of any existing coroner shall not be less than the
        average annual net receipts of such coroner from his office
        of coroner during the five years next before the passing of
    this Act.

    (7.) So much of any Act as requires that a coroner shall possess
a property qualification shall be and the same is hereby repealed.

Power of   15.—(1.) A county council shall annually contribute towards
county any county infirmary or fever hospital which is situate in their
councils as
to county county or to which, though situate elsewhere, they are by statute
infirmaries empowered to contribute, and to any officer thereof, a sum not
and fever
hospitals. less than was so contributed out of the county cess in the standard
financial year, or any less minimum which the Local Government
Board sanction.

    (2.) Every such county infirmary shall be managed, and the
admission of patients thereto controlled, by a joint committee
appointed triennially, consisting of such number of members of the
corporation of the "governor or governesses of the infirmary"
appointed by the corporation, and of such number of members of
the county council or other persons appointed by the council, as
the Local Government Board from time to time fix in the case of
each infirmary, having regard as well as to the proportion of the
contribution out of the county cess or the poor rate towards the
building and maintenance of the infirmary as to all the other
circumstances of the case; and all powers vested in the corporation in relation to the infirmary shall be exercised only by the
said committee; and every member of the committee shall have
the same power of recommendation as a governor.

    (3.) Where the councils of two or more counties contribute to
the same county infirmary, each of those councils shall be
represented on the said committee.

61 & 62 Vic.,
c. 37.
LOCAL
GOVERN-
MENT
(IRELAND)
ACT, 1898.

PART I.

*County
Councils.*

(4.) The foregoing provisions with respect to the management of a county infirmary shall extend to every fever hospital which is vested in the corporation of the " president and assistants of the hospital."

(5.) Where a county infirmary or fever hospital is under the management of a governing body other than such corporation as above mentioned, the foregoing provisions of this section shall apply, with the necessary modifications, in like manner as if the governing body were the said corporation.

(6.) A county council may, if they think fit, contribute towards the rebuilding or enlargement or erection on a new site of any county infirmary (whether such rebuilding, enlargement, or erection takes place after the passing of this Act, or is in course of completion at that passing), or towards the re-opening of a closed county infirmary, a sum not exceeding in the whole one-third of the sum actually received from private donations or subscriptions for such rebuilding, enlargement, erection, or re-opening, and the foregoing provisions with respect to the management of the infirmary shall apply accordingly.

(7.) Where the boundary of a county for which an infirmary or hospital has been provided is altered by or in pursuance of this Act, or where part of any such county is constituted a county borough, the contribution to be made to such infirmary or hospital shall be a subject of adjustment, and the Local Government Board in making such adjustment may provide for the representation of the council of any contributing county upon the said committee.

(8.) Nothing in this Act shall deprive any existing officer of any infirmary or hospital to which this section applies of any privileges enjoyed by him under any Act, and such officer shall not be removed from his office except with the consent of the Local Government Board, but, subject as aforesaid, every officer of the hospital or infirmary may be appointed and removed by the committee appointed under this section.

(9.) Any county council may, notwithstanding anything in any other Act, contribute to any such county infirmary or fever hospital as above in this section mentioned any amount not exceeding the amount in that behalf mentioned in the Grand Juries Act, 1836.

6 & 7 Will. 1,
c. 116.

(10.) Any county councils may agree for the contribution by one council to the county infirmary or fever hospital of the other council, on such conditions as to the admission to the infirmary or hospital of patients from the county of the contributing council and the representation of that council on the committee for managing the infirmary or hospital, as may be agreed upon. And in the case of the county of Cork the county council may contribute a portion of the amount mentioned in sub-section nine of this section towards the maintenance of the North Cork Infirmary situate in the city of Cork upon such terms and

61 & 62 Vic.,
c. 37.
LOCAL
GOVERN-
MENT
(IRELAND)
ACT, 1898.

PART I.

*County
Councils.*

59 & 60 Vic.,
c. xxii.
2 & 3 Will. 4,
c. 85.
6 & 7 Will. 4,
c. 116.

conditions, and subject to such restrictions, as may be determined upon by the councils of the county of Cork and county borough of Cork.

(11.) No ecclesiastical person shall in right of his dignity or office be entitled to be a governor or trustee of any such infirmary or fever hospital as aforesaid.

(12.) This section shall not apply to the Waterford City and County Infirmary as regulated by the Waterford Infirmary Act, 1896.

(13.) The Charities (Ireland) Act, 1832, and section eighty-one of the Grand Juries Act, 1836, are hereby repealed.

Power of
county
council to
make
byelaws.

3 & 4 Vic.,
c. 108.
41 & 42 Vic.,
c. 52.

16.—(1.) A county council shall have the same power of making bye-laws in relation to their county, or to any specified part or parts thereof, as the council of a borough have of making bye-laws in relation to their borough under section one hundred and twenty-five to one hundred and twenty-seven of the Municipal Corporations (Ireland) Act, 1840, and section two hundred and twenty-four of the Public Health Act, 1878, shall apply to such bye-laws.

(2.) Provided that bye-laws made under this section shall not be of any force or effect within any borough.

Power of
county
council as
to opposing
Bills in
Parliament
and legal
proceed-
ings.
51 & 52 Vic.,
c. 53.

17. The council of a county shall have the same powers of opposing Bills in Parliament and of prosecuting and defending legal proceedings necessary for the promotion or protection of the interests of the inhabitants of the county, or any part thereof, as are conferred on the governing body in any district by the Borough Funds (Ireland) Act, 1888; and that Act shall extend to a county council as if they were a "governing body; and the county were their district: provided that—

(a) no approval of voters shall be required for any proceedings under this section; and

(b) this section shall not empower a county council to promote any Bill in Parliament, or to incur or raise any expenses in relation to such promotion.

As to
marine
works con-
structed by
Congested
Districts
Board of
Board of
Works or
at county
expense.
59 & 60 Vic.,
c. 34.

18.—(1) The council of any county may, if they think fit, agree with the Congested Districts Board for Ireland to take over from that board any marine work in the county constructed or acquired by such board, and agree with the Commissioners of Public Work in Ireland to take over any marine work constructed or acquired by those Commissioners under the Railways (Ireland) Act, 1896, and upon any such agreement the work shall become the public property of the county, subject nevertheless to the payment of compensation to any person other than the Congested Districts Board or the said Commissioners in like manner as if the same had been taken by the county council under the authority of a Provisional Order duly confirmed in pursuance of this Act.

(2.) Where any marine work becomes vested in a county council under this section, or is or becomes public property under section sixty-eight of the Grand Juries Act, 1836, the provisions of the Fisheries (Ireland) Act, 1846, and the Grand Juries Act, 1853, relative to maintenance and repair, and to tolls and rates, and to bye-laws, rates, orders, and regulations, and otherwise, shall apply to such work as if it had been constructed by the Commissioners of Public Works under the said Act of 1846, and become the public property of the county under the said Act of 1853.

(3.) The provisions of the said Acts and of this section respecting maintenance and repair shall extend to reconstruction according to the original of any new plan.

(4.) For the purposes of this section "marine work" means any harbour, dock, pier, quay, wharf, beacon, light, or other similar work, and includes the approaches to any marine work as above defined, and all land and property used in connexion therewith.

19.—(1.) Where any ancient monuments or remains within the meaning of this section are being dilapidated, injured, or endangered, the county surveyor of any county shall report the same to the county council, and a county council may prosecute for any penalty under section six of the Ancient Monuments Protection Act, 1882.

(2.) The provisions of section eleven of the said Act (defining "ancient monuments to which this Act applies") and section one of the Ancient Monuments Protection (Ireland) Act, 1892, shall have effect as if they were herein re-enacted, with the substitution of "county council" for "Commissioners of Works"; but this enactment shall be in addition to and not in derogation of the existing provisions of the said sections as respects the Commissioners of Works.

20.—(1) The Local Government Board may, with the consent of the board or body effected, make a provisional order for transferring to a county council business arising in their county under any Act of any drainage board, or other public body corporate or unincorporate (not being a district council or the commissioners of a town or a board of guardians), and where it appears to the Local Government Board that there are no persons capable of acting as such board or body, the order may be made without the consent of the board or body, and each order shall make such exceptions and modifications and also such provisions for carrying into effect the transfer as appear necessary or expedient.

(2.) Any such business, if arising within two or more counties, may be transferred to the councils of those counties jointly, and be administered by a joint committee with a representation of each council, to be determined in case of dispute by the Lord Lieutenant.

County Boroughs.

21.—(1.) Each of the boroughs mentioned in the Second Schedule to this Act shall be an administrative county of itself, and be called a county borough.

Margin notes

61 & 62 Vic., c. 37. LOCAL GOVERN-MENT (IRELAND) ACT, 1898.

PART I.

County Councils.
6 & 7 Will. 4, c. 116.
6 & 10 Vic., c. 3.
16 & 17 Vic., c. 136.

Powers of county council as to ancient monuments.

45 & 46 Vic., c. 73.

55 & 56 Vic., c. 46.

Power to transfer to county council powers of local bodies.

Constitution of and application of Act to county boroughs

61 & 62 Vic.,
c. 37.
LOCAL
GOVERN-
MENT
(IRELAND)
ACT, 1898.

PART I.

*County
Councils.*

(2.) The mayor, aldermen, and burgesses of each county borough acting by the council shall, subject as in this Act mentioned, have the powers and duties of a county council under this Act and the powers of baronial presentment sessions in so far as they have not the same already, and the provisions of this Act with respect to administrative counties shall, so far as circumstances admit, apply in the case of every such borough with the necessary modifications, subject as follows :—

(a) The local government register of electors shall be the burgess roll, and persons registered therein and no other shall be the burgesses, and the provisions made by or in pursuance of this Act respecting the qualification and mode of election of councillors shall extend as well to the aldermen as to the councillors of a county borough, but, save as aforesaid or as expressly provided by this Act, the provisions so made with respect to the constitution, number, duration of office, or chairman, of the county council shall not apply ;

Provided that the Local Government Board, on request made by a resolution of the council of any such borough passed by two-thirds of the members voting on such resolution, may by order apply to the borough the provisions of this Act with respect to the duration of office of councillors, and make such incidental provisions as appear to the Board necessary or expedient for bringing such application into full effect, and in particular for making the triennial election of councillors coincide with the triennial election of a portion of the aldermen ;

51 & 52 Vic.,
c. 53.

(b) The provisions of this Act relating to main roads, coroners (except as to property qualification), bye-laws, or the Borough Funds (Ireland) Act, 1888, shall not apply ;

(c) No approval of voters shall be necessary to enable the council of a county borough to oppose a Bill in Parliament pursuant to the provisions of the Borough Funds (Ireland) Act. 1888 ;

(d) The quorum of a council of a county borough shall be one-fourth of the total number of such council ;

(e) The provisions of this Act with respect to compensation for criminal injuries shall apply, although the business has before the passing of this Act, been vested in the council of a borough.

PART II.

*District
Councils
and
Guardians.*

PART II.

DISTRICT COUNCILS AND GUARDIANS.

Constitution.

County
districts
and district
councils.

22.—(1.) All urban sanitary authorities shall be called urban district councils and their districts shall be called urban districts, but nothing in this section shall alter the style or title of the corporation or council of a borough.

(2.) For every rural sanitary district there shall be a rural district council, whose district shall be called a rural district.

(3.) In this and every other Act, unless the context otherwise requires, the expression "district council" shall include the council of every urban district, whether a county or other borough or not, and of every rural district, and the expression "county district" shall include every urban district, whether a borough or not, which is not a county borough, and every rural district.

(4.) A poor law electoral division, that is to say, an electoral division within the meaning of the Poor Relief (Ireland) Acts, 1838 to 1892, shall be called a district electoral division.

23·—(1.) In an urban county district the members of the council of the district, other than the mayor or chairman, and if the district is divided into wards, he members for each ward, shall be elected by the local government electors for the district or ward, and in a borough those electors and no other persons shall be the burgesses, and the local government register of electors shall be the burgess rol¹ ; and the provisions made by or in pursuance of this Act respecting the qualification and mode of election of councillors shall extend as well to the aldermen as to the councillors of the urban district ; but, save as aforesaid or as expressly provided by this Act, there shall be no change in the constitution, number, duration of office, or chairman, of any such council :

Provided that where one-third of the councillors of any such district are elected annually, the Local Government Board, on request made by a resolution of the council passed by two-thirds of the members voting on such resolution, may by order apply to the district the provisions of this Act with respect to the duration of office of county councillors, and make such incidental provisions as appear to the Board necessary or expedient for bringing such application into full effect, and in particular, in the case of a borough, for making the triennial election of councillors coincide with the triennial election of a portion of the aldermen.

(2.) The quorum of an urban district council shall be one-fourth of the total number of such council.

(3.) In a rural district—

   (a) the district council shall consist of a chairman and councillors ;

   (b) two councillors shall be elected for each district electoral division, except where the Local Government Board assign more than two councillors to a town or part of a town forming one district electoral division, and the councillors for each district electoral division shall be elected by the local government electors for that division ;

   (c) at an election for the district council an elector may give in an electoral division one vote and no more for each of

---

Margin notes:

61 & 62 Vic., c. 37. LOCAL GOVERNMENT (IRELAND) ACT, 1898.

PART II.

District Councils and Guardians.

1 & 2 Vic., c. 56. 55 & 56 Vic., c. 41.

Constitution and election of district councils in county districts.

61 & 62 VIC.,
c. 37.
LOCAL
GOVERN-
MENT
(IRELAND)
ACT, 1898.

PART II.

*District
Councils
and
Guardians.*

any number of persons not exceeding the number of councillors to be elected for the division, and shall not vote at the same election in more than one district electoral division.

(*d*) the district councillors shall hold office for a term of three years, and shall then retire together, and their places shall be filled by a new election.

(4.) A person shall not be qualified to be elected, or to be, a councillor of the council of a county district, unless he is a local government elector for the district, or has during the whole of the twelve months preceding the election, resided, and continues to reside, in the district.

Constitu-
tion and
election of
guardians.

24. As from the appointed day in the year one thousand eight hundred and ninety-nine, there shall be no ex-officio guardians of a union, and—

(*a*) in a rural district the district councillors for every district electoral division shall be the guardians for that division ; and

(*b*) if an urban district the guardians for any district electoral division therein shall be elected by the local government electors for that division, subject to the like provisions in the like manner and at the like time as district councillors for a rural district, and shall be qualified in the like manner and hold office for the same term as such district councillors ; and

(*c*) where the Local Government Board constitute any urban county district, or pa·t thereof, or part of a county borough, a district electoral division, they may assign to that division two or more guardians ; and

(*d*) each elector may give in a district electoral division one vote and no more for each of any number of persons, not exceeding the number of guardians to be elected for that division ; and

(*e*) an elector shall not at the same election vote for the members, whether district councillors or guardians, of a board of guardians for a union in more than one district electoral division in that union.

Chairman
of rural
district
council or
guardians
and
additional
councillors
and
guardians.

25.—(1.) The district council of every rural district—

(*a*) may choose from persons qualified to be councillors of the district not more tha·n three persons, who shall be additional councillors during the term of office of the council by whom the choice is made ; and

(*b*) may annually choose a chairman, and if they think fit a vice-chairman, from among the councillors.

(2.) The first business of the Council after any triennial election shall be the consideration of the question of choosing additional councillors.

(3.) A person so chosen by a district council from outside their body as additional councillor shall be a member of the council, and also of the board of guardians of the union comprising the district.

(4.) Nothing in this section shall alter the power of guardians to choose their chairman and vice-chairman.

26.—(1.) Where an urban or rural county district in any county contains a population, according to the last published census for the time being, exceeding five thousand, the chairman of the council for the district shall, unless a woman or personally disqualified by any Act, but subject as hereafter provided by this Act, be during the term of and by virtue of his office a justice of the peace for the county, but, except when sitting in quarter or general sessions, shall act only within the petty sessional district or districts comprising the county district, or any part of the county district.

(2.) The chairman of the council of any urban county district who is not a justice of the peace under the foregoing provisions of this section, and also the chairman of the Commissioners of any town, shall, if not a woman or personally disqualified by any Act, but subject as hereafter provided by this Act, be a justice of the peace in like manner as if he had been appointed by the Lord Chancellor under section twenty-nine of the Towns Improvement (Ireland) Act, 1854.

(3.) A chairman before acting as justice under this section shall, if he has not already done so, take the oaths required by law to be taken by a justice of the peace.

(4.) The power of the Lord Chancellor under section twenty-nine of the Towns Improvement (Ireland) Act, 1854, to select a commissioner to act as justice of the peace shall cease.

(5.) This section shall apply to a borough not having a separate commission of the peace with the substitution of mayor for chairman, but shall not apply to any other borough.

Powers of District Councils and Guardians.

27.—(1.) Subject to the provisions of this Act there shall be transferred—

  (a) to the district council of every county district, the business of any baronial presentment sessions so far as respects their districts ; and

  (b) to the district council of every urban county district, so far as respects their district, the business of the grand jury of the county in relation to public works, the expense of the maintenance of which is not wholly or partly leviable off the county at large ;

but the said transfer shall only operate so far as the business is not already the business of the district council.

Marginal notes:

61 & 62 VIC., c. 37. LOCAL GOVERN-MENT (IRELAND) ACT, 1898. PART II.

District Councils and Guardians. Constitution of chairman of district council and of town commissioners as justice of the peace.

17 & 18 Vic. c. 103.

Transfer to district councils of business of baronial presentment sessions and grand jury and extension of powers of urban district councils as to roads.

61 & 62 Vic.,
c. 37.
LOCAL
GOVERN-
MENT
(IRELAND)
ACT, 1898.

PART II.

*District
Councils
and
Guardians.*

(2.) A county council shall not, without the consent of the Local Government Board, approve of any expenditure on roads proposed by the council of any rural district, which will cause the expenditure on the roads of the district to exceed by one-fourth the amount certified by the board to have been the average expenditure thereon during the three years next before the passing of this Act, and the Board may as respects each council consent either for a particular road or a particular year, or generally, and in the latter case may fix a new limit under this section.

(3.) An urban district council shall transact the business transferred to them by this section in the manner prescribed by general rules of the Local Government Board.

(4.) The council of every urban county district shall for the purpose of any business transferred to them from a grand jury, either by this or any other Act, or by any order made under the Public Health Act, 1878, have the same powers as respects land or easements or rights over land as a county council, and the provisions of Part I. of this Act with respect to the acquisition, purchase, taking on lease, or exchange of land, easements, or rights, or the taking or use of any land, easements, or rights by a county council, shall apply accordingly with the necessary modifications.

41 & 42 Vic.,
c. 52.

(5.) If the council of any urban county district, or the council of an adjoining rural district, consider that any contribution should be made by one council to the other in respect of a liability for maintaining any public work heretofore maintained out of money levied off an area comprising the whole or part of both such districts, the councils may agree upon such contribution, and in default of agreement either council may apply to the Local Government Board to order such contribution and that Board shall deal with the application as a matter of adjustment under this Act.

(6.) The council of any urban county district may undertake the entire maintenance of any road in the district, the expenses of the maintenance of which are leviable partly off the county at large, and may so undertake upon such terms as may be agreed upon, or in default of agreement be fixed by an order of the Local Government Board.

(7.) Where an order of the Local Government Board, under the foregoing provisions, deals with an application to order any contribution or fixes the terms of an undertaking, and within three months after the order the Board receive a petition against it from either council affected, or from at least one-fourth of the local government electors of any district or county affected, the order shall be provisional only, and a certificate of the Local Government Board that no such petition has been received, and that the order has taken effect, shall be conclusive evidence of those facts.

(8.) Nothing in this section or in the provisions of this Act with respect to main roads shall, save as respects the alteration of financial relations in Part Four of this Act mentioned, affect the provisions of any local Act, or any Provisional Order confirmed by an Act, respecting the maintenance of any road in an urban county district, or respecting the liability of the district to contribute towards any expenses of the maintenance of any road outside the district.

28. There shall be transferred, subject to the provisions of this Act, to the council of every urban district the business of the guardians as regards making, levying, collecting, and recovering the poor rate within the district.

29. There shall be transferred to the council of every urban district excepted from section one hundred and sixty of the Public Health Act, 1878 (by reason of being a town or township having commissioners under a local Act), the business of the board of guardians as burial board, and the said council shall be the burial board for the district.

30. There shall be transferred to the guardians the business of every committee of management of a dispensary district within their union, and those committees shall cease to be appointed.

31. The power conferred by section one hundred and four of the Public Health Act, 1878, upon an urban authority to purchase a market from a market company shall extend to authorise the purchase from any person of any franchise or right to hold a market or fair, whether under Act, letters patent, or otherwise, and the said section shall apply accordingly, with the necessary modifications.

32. There shall be transferred to every urban and rural district council the business of the board of guardians under section one hundred and fifty of the Public Health Act, 1878 (which relates to the execution of the regulations made when Ireland appears to be threatened by any formidable epidemic, endemic, or infectious disease), or under any enactment amending or extending that section, and section three of the Epidemic and Other Diseases Prevention Act, 1883, shall be repealed.

33.—(1.) There shall be transferred to the district council of every rural district the business of the rural sanitary authority in the district.

(2.) Rural district councils shall also have such powers and duties of urban sanitary authorities under the Public Health Acts or any other Act, and such provisions of any of those Acts relating to urban districts shall apply to rural districts as the Local Government Board by general order direct ; and every such order shall be forthwith laid before Parliament.

(3.) The power to make such general order shall be in addition to, and not in substitution for, the power conferred on the Board by section one of the Public Health Act, 1896 (which relates to investing rural authorities with the powers of urban authorities), and that power may be exercised by the Board on the application of a county council.

Side notes:

61 & 62 Vic., c. 37. LOCAL GOVERN- MENT (IRELAND) ACT, 1898.

PART II.

[District Council and Guardians.

Transfer to urban district councils of business of guardians as to poor rate.

Transfer of business of burial boards in certain towns. 41 & 42 Vic., c. 52, s. 160.

Transfer to guardians of business of dispensary com- mittees.

Extension of power of purchase of market under 41 & 42 Vic., c. 52, s. 104.

Transfer of sanitary powers of guardians under 41 & 42 Vic., c. 52. 46 & 47 Vic., c. 59.

Powers of rural district councils under Pub- lic Health Acts 41 & 42 Vic., c. 52

59 & 60 Vic., c. 54.

61 & 62 Vic.,
c. 37.
Local
Govern-
ment
(Ireland)
Act, 1898.

Part II.

*District
Councils
and
Guardians.*

34. Where a rural district council hold, under the Labourers. (Ireland) Acts, 1883 to 1896, any land on lease, they may by agreement purchase the interest of the lessor or any other superior interest in such land, and shall have the same power of borrowing the purchase money as they have of borrowing money for the purchase of land under the said Acts, and for the purpose of any such purchase an advance may be made under section eighteen of the Labourers (Ireland) Act, 1883, as amended by the Public Works Loans Act, 1897.

Power of
district
council to
purchase
lessor's
interest in
lands held
by them on
lease.
46 & 47 Vic.,
c. 60.

35. The provisions of the Towns Improvement (Ireland) Act, 1854, as amended by the Local Government Board (Ireland) Act, 1872, respecting byelaws in relation to boats plying for hire and the owners and boatmen thereof, shall apply to every rural district in like manner as if the council of the district were commissioners under the first-mentioned Act.

60 & 61 Vic.,
c. 51.

Bye-laws
in rural
district
regulating
boats plying
for hire.
17 & 18 Vic.,
c. 103.
35 & 36 Vic.,
c. 69, s. 2.

Powers of
district
council as to
recreation
ground
and public
walks.

36.—(1.) An urban district council, and if so authorised by order of the Local Government Board a rural district council, may—

(a) acquire, purchase, or take on lease, or lay out, plant, improve, and maintain land for a recreation ground or public walk ; and

(b) support or contribute to the support of a recreation ground or public walk, or contribute towards the purchase or cost of the laying out, planting, or improvement of any recreation ground or public walk, when provided by any person and permanently dedicated as such ; and

(c) make byelaws for the regulation of any such recreation ground or public walk, and by such byelaws provide for the removal from such recreation ground or public walk, by any officer of the said council or a constable, of any person infringing any such bye-law.

(2.) The recreation ground or public walk may be either within or without the district of the council, if it is convenient for the use of the inhabitants of such district.

41 & 42 Vic.,
c. 52.

(3.) Any expenses incurred under this section by a district council shall be defrayed as expenses under the Public Health Act, 1878.

(4.) The acquisition of land for the purpose of this section shall be deemed to be a purpose for which land may be acquired under the Public Health Act, 1878, and the provisions of that Act with respect to the acquisition of land shall apply accordingly.

(5.) Section two hundred and nineteen to two hundred and twenty-three of the Public Health Act, 1878, shall apply to the byelaws made under this section.

Provision
as to con-
tribution
by district
council to
fishery
district.
11 & 12 Vic.,
c. 92.

37.—(1.) The council of any county district comprising the whole or part of a fishery district under the Fisheries (Ireland) Act 1848, may, at the request of the board of conservators of such fishery district, made in pursuance of a resolution passed by such board at a meeting specially convened for the purpose of considering such resolution, make towards the expenses of that board a contribution not exceeding in any one local financial year a sum equal to a rate of one halfpenny in the pound on the rateable value of the county district at the beginning of the year.

(2.) Any such contribution shall be an annual contribution for a period of not less than three years, but (unless renewed) of not more than five years, and shall be a debt to the board of conservators, and the clerk of such board may sue for the same on behalf of the board.

(3.) A district council, upon paying in any year such contribution, may appoint such number of persons as the Lord Lieutenant may determine to act for that year as conservators of fisheries for that fishery district, in addition to and together with the Conservators under the said Act, but the total number of conservators appointed under this section shall always be less than the number of conservators under the said Act.

38. So much of the Municipal Corporations (Ireland) Act, 1840, as requires the approval of the Honourable Society of the Governor and Assistants of London of the new plantation in Ulster within the realm of Ireland to any bye-law made by the council of the boroughs of Coleraine and Londonderry shall be repealed.

District and Union Committees.

39.—(1.) A rural district council for any purpose of the Public Health Acts, and a board of guardians for the purpose of the admission of paupers to the union workhouse, may appoint for a dispensary district or other part of their district or union a local committee composed either wholly of members of their own body representing that dispensary, district or part, or partly of such members and partly of other persons, whether members of their own body or not, resident or interested in the said district or part.

(2.) The appointing body may authorise the committee to institute any proceedings or do any act which that body might have instituted or done for the said purpose, except that they shall not authorise the committee to raise any money, nor to expend any money beyond such limit as is fixed by the appointing body, nor to appoint, remove, or alter the remuneration of, any officer.

(3.) The same person may be appointed by any council and board to be a committee under this section of each appointing body in the same area.

(4.) A district council, on the application of a committee under the section for any area, may authorise any expenditure, which otherwise would be general expenses under the Public Health Acts, to be incurred by the committee, on condition that the cost of the same is levied as special expenses off such area.

(5.) The appointing body may revoke, in whole or in part, any appointment or authority made or given under this section.

Marginal notes:

61 & 62 Vic. c. 37. LOCAL GOVERNMENT (IRELAND) ACT, 1898.

PART II.

District Councils and Guardians.

Consent to bye-laws. 3 & 4 Vic., c. 108.

Appointment by district councils and guardians of committees, consisting partly of non-members.

K

61 & 62 Vic.,
c. 3².
Local
Govern-
ment
(Ireland)
Act, 1898.

Part II.

*District
Councils
and
Guardians.*

Application
of Act to
counties of
cities and
towns not
county
boroughs.

Counties of Cities and Towns.

40.—(1.) Any county of a city or town which does not become a county borough shall, for the purposes of this Act, be situated in and form part of the administrative county which it adjoins, or if it adjoins more than one such county, then such one of those counties as the Local Government Board order.

(2.) The council of the county of which it so forms part shall in relation thereto have all the powers and duties of a county council; and any urban district council within the area of such county of a city or town shall have all the powers and duties under this Act of an urban district council, and their urban district shall be a county district of the said county; and the provisions of this Act with respect to the business of the grand jury, and presentment sessions, shall apply accordingly.

(3.) Provided that nothing in this section shall deprive the council of a borough of the right to appoint as heretofore a coroner, and that coroner shall be subject in all respects to the law relating to borough coroners.

(4.) Such portion of the county of the town of Carrickfergus as is not at the passing of this Act comprised in an urban sanitary district shall form part of the rural sanitary district constituted by the union in which that portion is situate, and upon the election under this Act of a rural district council, the business of the Municipal Commissioners of Carrickfergus in relation to the said portion shall be transferred to that council, and any question as to the right of the said portion to share in the property vested in those Municipal Commissioners shall, on the application of the rural district council, be dealt with by the Local Government Board as a matter of adjustment under this Act.

Application
of 17 & 18
Vic., c. 103,
to certain
towns.

9 Geo. 4,
c. 82.

41.—(1.) The Towns Improvement (Ireland) Act, 1854, and the enactments amending the same, shall, subject to the exceptions and with the amendments made by this Act, apply to the town forming the urban sanitary district of Carrickfergus, and to every town having commissioners under the Lighting of Towns (Ireland) Act, 1828, and shall so apply in like manner as if it had been in whole adopted in the town, and the boundaries of each such town at the passing of this Act were the boundaries approved under the first-mentioned Act.

(2.) In each such town the number of councillors or commissioners, as the case may be, shall be the same as the existing number of commissioners: Provided that, if the Local Government Board think fit to divide the town into wards, the wards shall be determined and set out, and the commissioners apportioned among the wards, in manner provided by section fifteen of the said Act of 1854 for a town where there are municipal commissioners, and the number of commissioners may be varied so as to be in accordance with section sixteen of the said Act.

(3.) The urban district council of Carrickfergus shall, as successors of the municipal commissioners of Carrickfergus, be the Carrickfergus Harbour Commissioners, and the enactments relating to the transfer of property from the said municipal commissioners to the urban district council shall be subject to the provisions of this Act, with respect to such portion of the county of the town of Carrickfergus as forms part of the rural sanitary district.

Towns not Urban Sanitary Districts.

42.—(1.) Where a town has a population exceeding one thousand five hundred, according to the last published census for the time being, but is not an urban sanitary district, any order of the Local Government Board constituting such town an urban sanitary district shall, unless within three months after the order is published, the Board receive a petition against it,

    (*a*) if the petition is before the first election of rural district councils from at least one-fourth of the parliamentary electors registered in respect of qualifications within the town, or from the guardians of the union comprising the town or any part thereof ; or,

    (*b*) if the petition is after such first election, then, from at least one-fourth of the local government electors within the town, or from the guardians of the union, or council of the rural district, comprising the town or any part thereof,

take effect without the authority of Parliament ; and a certificate of the Board that no such petition has been received, and that the order has taken effect, shall be conclusive evidence of those facts.

(2.) An order of the Local Government Board under section seven of the Public Health Act, 1878, for adding any town having a population according to the last census of less than five thousand, and being an urban sanitary district to a rural sanitary district, if made before the end of six months after the passing of this Act, and if the powers of the grand jury in respect of roads have not been previously transferred to the sanitary authority of the district, shall, unless within three months after the order is published, the board receive a petition against it from at least one-fourth of the parliamentary electors registered in respect of qualifications within the town, or from the guardians of the union comprising the town or any part thereof, take effect without the authority of Parliament ; and a certificate of the board that no such petition has been received, and that the order has taken effect, shall be conclusive evidence of those facts ; provided that until the expiration of ten years from the said year, an order shall not be made constituting such town an urban sanitary district.

(3.) An order made after the passing of this Act for constituting a town an urban sanitary district, or for adding an urban sanitary district to a rural sanitary district, or for enlarging the boundaries of an urban county district, shall contain such provisions as may seem necessary or expedient for adapting the provisions of this Act in respect to public works, and making an adjustment of property, rights, and liabilities.

Margin notes:

61 & 62 Vic., c. 37., LOCAL GOVERN-MENT (IRELAND) ACT, 1898.

PART II.

District Councils and Guardians.

Orders as to making, dissolving, or extending urban sanitary districts.

41 & 42 Vic., c. 52.

61 & 62 VIC.,
c. 37.
LOCAL
GOVERN-
MENT
(IRELAND)
ACT, 1898.

[PART III.

Finance.

PART III.

FINANCE.

Incidence of Rates as regards Areas and establishment of County, etc., Funds.

Raising of
guardians'
expenses
equally
over union.

43. Notwithstanding anything in any Act, all expenses of the guardians of a union shall be raised equally over the whole union, and shall be called union charges, and where a union is divided between more than one county, the total amount to be raised over the union shall be apportioned between each divided part in proportion to rateable value, and the amount so apportioned to a divided part shall be raised equally over that part as if it were a separate union.

Raising of
road and
sanitary
expenses in
rural
districts
equally
over rural
district.

44. Notwithstanding anything in any Act, all expenses incurred in relation to the business of the council of a rural district, including those expenses connected with any public work in the district which are not leviable off the county at large, shall, subject to the provisions of this Act with respect to excluded charges, be raised equally over the whole district, and shall be called district charges.

Raising of
expenses of
county
council
equally
over
county or
district.

45.—(1.) The expenses incurred by the council of a county at large in the execution of this Act, or otherwise in relation to their business, which are not union or district charges, nor the excluded charges hereinafter mentioned, shall, where no provision is otherwise made by law, be raised equally over the whole county, and shall be called county at large charges.

(2.) Where any expenses so incurred by the council of a county may by virtue of any enactment, or any direction given thereunder, be levied off an urban district, they shall be called urban charges.

(3.) Where any expenses so incurred by the council of a county may, by virtue of any enactment, or any direction given thereunder, be levied off a barony or other portion of a county, they shall, according as the county council direct, be raised equally over the whole of the county district or districts comprising the barony or portion, or equally over the whole of the county, and shall be district charges or urban charges or county at large charges accordingly.

Raising of
expenses of
council of
urban
county
district and
county
borough.

46.—(1.) The expenses of the council of an urban county district, if incurred in meeting the demands of the county council, or in connection with the poor rate, shall be defrayed out of the poor rate.

(2.) The expenses not above mentioned, but incurred by the council of an urban county district in relation to the business transferred to the council by or in pursuance of this Act or otherwise in the execution of this Act, shall be defrayed out of the fund or rate out of which the cost of paving and cleansing the streets in such district are or can be defrayed, but shall be excluded in ascertaining any limit imposed by law upon any such rate.

(3.) The expenses incurred by the council of a county borough if incurred in meeting the expenses of guardians or in connection with the poor rate, shall be defrayed out of the poor rate, and if not so incurred and incurred in relation to the business transferred to the council by or in pursuance of this Act or otherwise in the execution of this Act, or as incidental to their powers and duties as a county council, shall, where the like expenses have hitherto been defrayed out of any rate levied by the council of the borough other than county cess, or than a rate levied under the enactments relating to county cess, continue to be so defrayed, but in any other case shall be defrayed out of the poor rate.

(4.) Provided that the foregoing provisions with respect to the expenses incurred by the council of an urban county district or county borough shall not extend to the expenses incurred under any provision of this Act amending or extending the Public Health Acts.

47.—(1.) All receipts of a district or county council, whether from rates levied off the whole or any part of the district or county, or from sources other than rates, shall be paid to the treasurer of such council, and the receipt alone of that treasurer shall be a good discharge to the person paying the same ; and, subject to the provisions of this Act, all such receipts shall be carried in a county or other borough to the borough fund, and in any other county or county district to the county or district fund, as the case requires, and all payments for any purpose out of any such fund shall be made by the treasurer ;

Provided that a receipt given by a collector of rates in the case of payment of rates, or, where the treasurer is a banking company, by the secretary or clerk of the council in the case of any payment unconnected with rates, shall be a good discharge to the person making the payment, but the amount of the payment shall be forthwith paid by such collector, secretary, or clerk to the treasurer.

(2.) A council shall not directly or indirectly apply any part of their county or district fund, or any moneys under their control, for any purpose not authorised by this or any other Act, or, in the case of money derived from trust funds, then by the specific trusts affecting those funds.

(3.) In the county fund separate accounts shall be kept of all receipts and payments in respect of county at large, union, urban, and district charges respectively ; and if the moneys standing to the county fund on account of any of those charges are insufficient to meet the sums payable in respect thereof, including the sums required to reimburse the treasurer for sums by law payable by him thereout, the county council shall raise the deficiency in manner provided by this Act by means of the poor rate ; and the poor rate shall be levied, where the deficiency is in respect of union, urban, or district charges, off the union or district as the case requires, and in any other case off the county at large.

Marginal notes:

61 & 62 Vic., c. 37. LOCAL GOVERN- MENT (IRELAND) ACT, 1898. PART III.

Finance.

County and borough and district fund and raising of deficiency in county fund.

61 & 62 Vic.,
c. 37.
LOCAL
GOVERN-
MENT
(IRELAND)
ACT, 1898.

PART III.

Finance.

Payment to
and out of
Local
Taxation
(Ireland)
Account of
agricultural
grant.
59 & 60 Vic.,
c. 41.

Agricultural Grant.

48.—(1.) As from the twenty-ninth day of September next after the passing of this Act, section one of the Local Taxation (Ireland) Estate Duty Act, 1896, shall be repealed, and there shall be annually paid out of the Consolidated Fund to the Local Taxation (Ireland) Account a sum (in this Act referred to as the agricultural grant) equal to half the amount certified under this Act to be taken for the purpose of this Act as having been raised in the whole of Ireland by poor rate and county cess off agricultural land, as herein-after defined, during the twelve months ending as regards poor rate on the twenty-ninth day of September, one thousand eight hundred and ninety-seven, and as regards county cess on the last day of June in the same year (which twelve months are respectively in this Act referred to as the standard financial year).

(2.) Such portion of the agricultural grant as is certified under the Act to be payable to each county council shall be issued by the Lord Lieutenant from the Local Taxation (Ireland) Account to that council half-yearly, subject nevertheless to such conditions and provisions as are contained in this Act.

(3.) The first payments under this section to the Local Taxation (Ireland) Account shall be made during the six months ending on the last day of March next after the passing of this Act, so as to make up the sum required to meet the half-yearly payments to the county councils on account of the six months next ensuing on such last day of March, but such half-yearly payments shall not be applied towards the cost of work done or expenses incurred before such six months.

(4.) The provisions of this Act with respect to agricultural land shall extend to every hereditament entered as land in the vuluation list within the meaning of the Valuation Acts which is not part of a railway or canal, but shall not extend to any hereditament situate within the boundary of any borough or of any town which is (for the time being) an urban sanitary district.

Certificates
by Local
Govern.
ment Board
as to poor
ra'e and
county cess
in standard
financial
year.

49.—(1.) Subject to the provisions herein-after contained with respect to excluded charges, the Local Government Board, on the report of the Commissioner of Valuation made in accordance with the prescribed rules, and on taking into account any exceptional circumstances which appear to the Board to have caused a variation from the average, shall, as soon as may be after the passing of this Act, certify as respects the standard financial year,—

(a) the amounts to be taken for the purpose of this Act as having been raised in the whole of Ireland by poor rate and county cess of Agricultural land and off any other hereditaments respectively ; and

61 & 62 Vic., c. 37. LOCAL GOVERN-MENT (IRELAND) ACT, 1898.

PART III.

Finance.

(*b*) the portion of each of those amounts which is to be taken for the purpose of this Act as having been raised in each administrative county—

    (i) in respect of county at large charges ; and
    (ii) in respect of union charges ; and
    (iii) in respect of urban charges ; and
    (iv) in respect of district charges ; and

(*c*) the rate in the pound (in this Act referred to as the standard rate) at which poor rate and at which county cess is respectively to be taken for the purpose of this Act as having been levied off agricultural land and off other hereditaments respectively, in each union or district, in respect of county at large and union and urban or district charges added together ; and

(*d*) any other matters in relation to the poor rate or county cess levied off agricultural land or other hereditaments that are required by this Act to be certified, or that may appear to the Board to be required for carrying this Act into effect.

(2.) In estimating the sums to be taken for the purpose of this Act as having been raised in any county, or district, or union, or in estimating the standard rate, all sums raised to meet expenses which, if this Act had been in force in the standard financial year would have been raised equally over the whole county or district or union, shall be treated as having been so raised ; and any town which is constituted an urban sanitary district or which being an urban sanitary district is added to a rural sanitary district shall, if the order for such constitution or addition was made before the end of six months after the passing of this Act, whether made before or after that passing, and whether confirmed or taking effect before or after the end of such six months, be treated as having been so constituted or added, as the case may be, during the standard year ; and where a union is divided between more than one administrative county, the amount which would have been apportioned to each divided part shall be ascertained, and treated as having been so raised over a separate union.

(3.) The sum payable to each county out of the agricultural grant shall be equal to half the amounts so certified as aforesaid to be taken as having been raised in the county off agricultural land in respect of county at large and union and district charges when added together, and shall be certified accordingly.

(4.) For the purpose of certificates under this section the Local Government Board, on the report of the Commissioner of Valuation shall determine, in the prescribed manner, the adjustments which are to be made in consequence of any difference between the authorities or the boundaries of counties, unions or other areas, as existing in the standard financial year, and as they will exist after the appointed day, or in consequence of other changes made by or in pursuance of this Act.

61 & 62 Vic.,
c. 37.
LOCAL
GOVERN-
MENT
(IRELAND)
ACT, 1898.

PART III.

Finance.

(5.) The Local Government Board and Commissioner of Valuation in acting under this section shall obtain such information and make such inquiries and in such manner as seems fit, and every officer of any local authority shall give the Board and Commissioner such information and reply to such inquiries and in such form as they or he may require.

(6.) The Local Government Board, on the report of the Commissioner of Valuation, may in case of error amend, or for the purpose of meeting any alteration in an area or authority to which a certificate relates vary, a certificate under this section, and any such amendment or variation shall have effect from the date of the original certificate, or any later date fixed by the amending or varying certificate ; but, save as aforesaid, a certificate under this section shall be final and binding on all persons.

(7.) Provisional certificates may, if it is thought necessary, be given for enabling the first payments under this Act to and out of the Local Taxation (Ireland) Account to be made before sufficient information has been obtained to enable final certificates to be given.

Disposal of
agricultural
grant in
case of
constitution
or extension
of urban
district.

50.—(1.) Where, by virtue of an order respecting the constitution of an urban county district, whether by the constitution of a new or the extension of the boundaries of an old urban county district, any agricultural land in a rural district becomes included within the boundaries of the said urban district, such portion of the agricultural grant payable to the council of the county comprising the district as is proportionate to the rateable value in the standard financial year of that agricultural land shall be applied by the county council in manner directed by the said order for the relief of the said land from rates, whether by the payment thereof to the council of the urban district in exchange for an adequate exemption from rates or otherwise.

(2.) This section shall apply to a county borough in like manner as to an urban county district, but in that case the said portion of the agricultural grant shall be paid direct to the council of the county borough instead of to the council of the county at large.

Method of raising Expenses.

Raising of
expenses
of district
councils,
guardians,
and county
councils by
poor rate,
and deduc-
tion of
agricultural
grant.

51.—(1.) The money required to meet the expenses of a rural district council or of a board of guardians shall be supplied by the county council upon the prescribed demand by the district council or board ; and the county council shall pay the money so demanded out of the county fund.

(2.) The county council shall apportion every amount to be raised for county at large charges, and every amount to be raised for union charges, between any urban district situate in the county or union, and the rest of the county or union in proportion to rateable value, and shall also apportion, in proportion to rateable·

value, every amount to be raised partly off any urban and partly off any rural district in the county, and any amount apportioned as aforesaid to an urban district, and also any urban charge leviable off an urban district shall be paid by the council of that district to the county council upon the prescribed demand.

61 & 62 VIC.,
c. 37.
LOCAL
GOVERN-
MENT
(IRELAND)
ACT, 1898.

PART III.

Finance.

(3.) The county council shall divide the amount which is not so apportioned to an urban district and is to be raised either for county at large or for union charges, and every amount which is to be raised for district charges, between the agricultural land in the county, union, or district and the other hereditaments therein in proportion to rateable value.

(4.) There shall be deducted from the amount assigned upon such division to the agricultural land the sum payable out of the agricultural grant to the council—

(a) where the amount is to be raised for county at large charges, then in respect of county at large charges ; and

(b) where the amount is to be raised for union or district charges, then in respect of union or district charges in that union or district ;

as certified for the standard financial year, and the balance remaining after that deduction shall be the amount to be levied off the agricultural land in respect of the amount so assigned thereto.

(5.) The council shall raise the several amounts apportioned as above-mentioned to any part of the county which is not an urban district by means of the poor rate, and shall make that poor rate twice a year, and every demand note in respect of that rate shall specify approximately the respective rates in the pound required to raise the several amounts above mentioned, and the rates in the pound to which the sums deducted in respect of the agricultural grant amount.

(6.) Such poor rate shall be made either immediately prior to, or at the beginning of, the first six months of the local financial year and the second six months of that year, and shall be made in respect of the service of such first six months or second six months as the case may be.

(7.) Every debt, claim, or demand which is directly or indirectly payable out of the poor rate, and becomes due after the passing of this Act, shall be paid within the half year (whether the first or the second six months of the local financial year), in which the same was incurred or became due, or within three months after the expiration of such half year, and not afterwards : Provided that the Local Government Board may, if they think fit, extend the time within which such payment may be made to a time not exceeding twelve months from the date at which the same was incurred or became due.

(8.) If any person claiming any such debt, claim, or demand commences any legal proceedings within the time herein-before limited, or the time to which the Local Government Board may grant extension, and with due diligence prosecute such proceedings

61 & 62 Vic., c. 37. LOCAL GOVERN- MENT (IRELAND) ACT, 1898.

PART III.

Finance.

to judgment or other final settlement of the question such judgment shall be satisfied notwithstanding that the judgment is recovered or the final settlement arrived at after the expiration of the said time, and all proceedings taken by mandamus or otherwise for enforcing such judgment without delay shall be deemed to be within the operation of this enactment.

(9.) This section shall apply with the necessary modifications—

    (a.) to the making of a poor rate by the council of a county borough or other urban district ; and

    (b.) to a county borough so far as regards the demands of a board of guardians, and the money required to meet those demands or to meet expenses of the council of the borough which under this Act are to be defrayed out of the poor rate : Provided that in a county borough the council may, if they think fit, either immediately prior to or at the beginning of each local financial year, make one poor rate for the whole financial year, and collect the same in equal moieties, one moiety for each half year.

Incidence of Rates.

Incidence of poor rate as between occupier and landlord. 6 & 7 Vic., c. 92.

52.—(1.) The poor rate shall be made upon the occupier and not the landlord of a hereditament, except where under section four of the Poor Relief (Ireland) Act, 1843, it is made on the landlord as the immediate lessor of a house let in separate apartments or lodgings, and except that if made heretofore in respect of a half rent under section sixty-three of the Poor Relief (Ireland) Act, 1838, and the enactments amending the same, it shall continue to be so made.

(2.) The occupier of a hereditament shall not be entitled to deduct from his rent any part of the poor rate, and any contract to the contrary respecting such deduction shall be void ; subject nevertheless to the exceptions in this Act and to the provisions herein-after contained respecting occupiers under existing tenancies.

Rates of urban district councils and towns, and power to consoli- date rates.

53.—(1.) Where the council of any borough or other urban district or the commissioners of any town independenly of this Act can make any rate in respect of any hereditament upon the landlord or immediate lessor, and not on the occupier of the hereditament, such rate shall be made on the occupier of the hereditament except where it is a house let in separate apartments or lodgings. and except that if made heretofore in respect of a half rent under section sixty-three of the Poor Relief (Ireland) Act, 1838, and the enactments amending the same, it shall continue to be so made : Provided that the foregoing provisions of this section shall not apply to a rate under a local Act in any county borongh, if the council of that borough by a majority of not less than two thirds of the members present at a meeting specially summoned for the purpose so resolve.

(2.) Where an urban district council independently of this Act—

(*a*.) can raise a sum by a rate upon the same basis as the poor rate, that sum may be raised by means of the poor rate, but as a separate item thereof, and any right to deduct any part of the said rate from rent shall continue as respects that item ; or

(*b*.) can make more than one rate upon the same basis, but on a basis different from that of the poor rate, such rates may be consolidated and made, levied, collected and recovered as one rate, and be made half-yearly, but the demand note shall specify the amount in the pound required for each such rate.

(3.) " The same basis " in this section means the same property, the same rateable value, and subject to the same exemptions.

54—(1.) Where the poor rate is made upon an occupier of any holding under an existing tenancy, then, until the tenancy is determined or a new statutory term in the tenancy begins, the following provisions shall have effect as from the gale day next after the appointed day :—

(*a*) Where the occupier is entitled to deduct from his rent one-half of the county cess, the rent shall be reduced by half the appropriate standard amount (herein-after defined) :

(*b*.) Where the occupier is entitled to deduct from his rent one-half of the poor rate, and the holding is not agricultural land, the rent shall be reduced by half the appropriate standard amount :

(*c*.) Where the occupier is entitled to deduct from his rent the whole of the county cess or poor rate, the rent shall be reduced, in the case of cess, by the whole of the appropriate standard amount, and in the case of poor rate, where the holding is agricultural land by half, and where it is not agricultural land by the whole, of the appropriate standard amount :

(*d*) Where the occupier is not entitled to make any deduction from his rent in respect of poor rate, and the holding is agricultural land, he shall be liable to pay annually to his landlord a sum equal to half the appropriate standard amount and such sum shall be recoverable as, and be deemed for all purposes to be, part of his rent.

(2.) Provided that where the occupier is entitled to deduct from his rent a sum less than one-half of the county cess or of the poor rate, as the case may be, the foregoing provisions shall apply, with the exception that a sum bearing such proportion to half the appropriate standard amount as the amount he was entitled to deduct bore to half the county cess or poor rate, shall be substituted for a sum equal to half the appropriate standard amount.

(3.) An occupier entitled, whether by law or contract, to deduct a sum from his rent shall be deemed entitled to deduct within the

Margin notes:

61 & 62 VIC, c. 37.

LOCAL GOVERNMENT (IRELAND) ACT, 1898.

PART III.

Finance.

Adjustment of rent as between occupier and landlord in consequence of agricultural grant, and change in incidence of rate.

61 & 62 Vic.,
c. 37.
LOCAL
GOVERN-
MENT
(IRELAND)
ACT, 1898.

PART III.

Finance.

meaning of this section ; and where a person under the law existing at the time of his contract of tenancy, or under his contract of tenancy, is not liable to any cess or rate, he shall be in. the same position under this section as if he were entitled to deduct the whole of that cess or rate from his rent.

(4.) Where a person receiving rent in respect of any holding which is not agricultural land also pays rent in respect of such holding, and the rent he receives is reduced by virtue of this section, the rent he pays shall, except where under the terms of his contract he is not entitled to make any deduction from his rent in respect of rates, be reduced by a sum bearing such proportion to the amount of the reduction as the rent he pays bears to the rent he receives.

(5.). Where part of a holding is agricultural land and part is not agricultural land, the foregoing provisions of this section shall apply separately to each part as if it were a separate holding.

(6.) The "standard amount " for the purposes of this section means, in relation to any holding a sum equal to what is produced by a rate on the rateable value of the holding in the standard financial year, according to the standard rate of poor rate or county cess, as the case requires.

(7.) Where any change of the rent of a holding, whether by way of reduction, payment or deduction, caused by the provisions of this section, would amount to less than sixpence, no such change shall be made ; and where though exceeding sixpence it would involve a fraction of sixpence, then, if the fraction amounts to threepence or upwards, the change shall include the full sixpence, and if the fraction amounts to less than threepence the change shall include the fraction.

(8.) Any difference which may arise as to the amount to be deducted or paid by occupiers under existing tenancies in pursuance of this section, shall be referred to the Commissioner of Valuation whose decision shall be final.

(9.) An occupier of any holding under an existing tenancy shall, until the tenancy is determined or a new statutory term in the tenancy begins, be entitled notwithstanding any provision of this Act, to deduct from his rent the like proportion of any sum paid by him for poor rate on account of any railway, harbour, navigation or public health charge, as he would have been entitled to deduct from his rent on account of any cess or rate to meet the charge, if the provisions of this Act with reference to the deduction of poor rate from his rent had not been enacted, and in the case of existing charges, as if the charge had continued to be raised by the same cess or rate as previously.

(10.) The secretary of the county council, including the town clerk of a county borough, shall, on the request of the landlord or occupier of any holding, give a certificate of the rateable value of the holding and of the standard rate in the pound under this Act for the union or district in which the holding is situate, and, where part of the holding is agricultural land and part is not agricultural land, shall distinguish the rateable value of each such part. The

said certificate shall be in such form, and contain such particulars,
and the said secretary shall be entitled to such payment for each
certificate as may be prescribed.

(11.) Where the existing tenancy of a holding in an urban
district is constituted by a lease for lives, or a lease of which not
less than five years are unexpired on the appointed day, then,
notwithstanding anything in the foregoing provisions of this
section, the rent of such holding shall be unaltered, but the
occupier shall be entitled to deduct from his rent such portion
of the amount of poor rate actually paid by him from time to
time in respect of such holding as he would have been entitled
to deduct if this Act had not passed, or, if he was entitled
before the passing of this Act to deduct all the poor rate and
county cess, then the whole of the poor rate so actually paid.

(12.) Where the occupier of a hereditament in an urban
district becomes, by reason of this Act, liable to pay all or part
of any rate made by the council of such urban district, other
than the poor rate, and such rate was previously made upon the
landlord, or immediate lessor, he shall, until his tenancy
determines, be entitled, save so far as his contract of tenancy
otherwise provides, to deduct the amount for which he so
becomes liable from his rent.

55. After the appointed day, a fair rent in a rural district
shall be fixed under the Land Law (Ireland) Acts on the
assumption that there has been no decrease or increase of the
rate in the pound of poor rate as compared with the total rate in
the pound to which the standard rate for poor rate and county
cess as certified under this Act, when added together, amount,
and that the tenant is to have any benefit from the agricultural
grant given in respect of the county cess, and that the landlord
is to have any benefit from the agricultural grant given in respect
of the poor rate ; and where after the appointed day any such
fair rent is fixed there shall be recorded in the schedule specified
in section one of the Land Law (Ireland) Act, 1896, the standard
amount as defined in the preceding section both for poor rate
and county cess, and the benefit in respect of the holding received
by the landlord and tenant respectively out of the agricultural
grant.

Excluded Charges.

56.—(1.) In estimating the sums raised by the county cess,
and estimating the standard rate, the Local Government Board
on the report of the Commissioner of Valuation shall exclude
such amount as they determine is to be taken as having been
raised during the standard financial year in any area for the
purpose—

> (a) of expenses in relation to additional constabulary under
> the Constabulary (Ireland) Acts, 1836 to 1897 ; or
> (b) of compensation for criminal injuries as before defined ;

and the amount so excluded is in this Act included in the
expression "excluded charges."

61 & 62 Vic.,
c. 37.
LOCAL
GOVERN-
MENT
(IRELAND)
ACT, 1898.

PART III.

Finance.

(2.) The amount required to meet any charge in connection with such expenses or compensation shall be separately estimated and raised by means of the poor rate, but as a separate item thereof, and the provisions of this Act with respect to raising expenses and to the poor rate shall apply with the necessary modifications; Provided that—

(*a*) the provisions with respect to the division between agricultural land and other hereditaments, and the deduction in respect of the amount assigned to agricultural land, shall not apply; and

(*b*) the amount may be raised as heretofore off any area though less than a district or union, and for that purpose there shall be a separate account in the county fund.

Special pro-
visions as to
charge⁸ fᵒʳ
ailways,
harbours,
navigations
and public
health and
labourers'
dwellings.

57.—(1.) In estimating the sums raised by poor rate and county cess, and in estimating the standard rate, the Local Government Board on the report of the Commissioner of Valuation shall exclude such amount as they determine is to be taken as having been raised during the standard financial year, in any area for the purpose—

(*a*) of any railway or harbour charge, that is to say, any charge in connection with—

46 & 47 Vic.,
c. 43.
52 & 53 Vic.,
c. 66.
53 & 54 Vic.,
c. 52.

    (i) any railway or tramway under the Tramways and Public Companies (Ireland) Act, 1883, the Light Railways (Ireland) Act, 1889, or the Railways (Ireland) Act, 1890, or any special Act, whether public or local; or

    (ii) any railway or means of communication under the Railways (Ireland) Act, 1896; or

9 & 10 Vic.,
c. 3.
29 & 30 Vic.,
c. 45.
45 & 46 Vic.,
c. 62.
46 & 47 Vic.,
c. 26.
50 & 51 Vic.,
c. 37.
43 Vic., c. 4.

    (iii) any harbour, pier, or quay, under the Fisheries (Ireland) Act, 1846, the Piers and Harbours (Ireland) Act, 1886, the Public Works Loans Act, 1882, the Sea Fisheries (Ireland) Act, 1883, or the Public Works Loans Act, 1887, or under any special Act whether public or local; or

    (iv) any work under the Relief of Distress (Ireland) Act, 1880, and the Acts amending the same; or

(*b*) of any navigation or public health charge, that is to say, any charge in connection with—

    (i) navigation works under the Drainage and Navigation (Ireland) Acts, 1842 to 1857, or any special Act whether public or local; or

    (ii) special expenses leviable off a contributory place in a rural sanitary district, either under the Public Health Acts or under any enactment directing expenses to be levied as expenses under those Acts;

and the amount so excluded is in this Act included in the expression " excluded charge "

(2.) The amount required to meet payments in respect of any railway or harbour charge, or any navigation or public health charge, shall be separately estimated and raised by means of the poor rate, but as a separate item thereof, and the provisions of this Act with respect to raising expenses and to the poor rate shall apply with the necessary modifications ;

Provided that—

(a) the provisions with respect to the division between agricultural land and other hereditaments and the deduction in respect of the amount assigned to agricultural land shall not apply ; and

(b) the amount may be raised as heretofore off any area though less than a district or union, and for that purpose there shall be a separate account in the county fund.

(3.) The provisions of this Act with reference to the fixing of fair rents shall not apply in the case of any item of the poor rate raised under this section.

(4.) The expenses incurred by a sanitary authority, in the execution of the Labourers Acts, 1883 to 1896, when incurred in the standard year, shall not be deemed to have been special expenses within the meaning of this section, and when hereafter incurred, whether in respect of transactions begun before or after the passing of this Act shall be expenses incurred in relation to the business of the council of a rural district, and be levied as district charges accordingly.

Licence Duties and Local Grants.

58.—(1.) After the thirty-first day of March next after the passing of this Act there shall be annually paid out of the Consolidated Fund to the Local Taxation (Ireland) Account—

(a) a sum equal to the amount which is ascertained in manner provided by the regulations of the Treasury to be the proceeds, in the previous financial year, of the duties collected in Ireland by the Commissioners of Inland Revenue on the local taxation licences specified in the Third Schedule to this Act, and such amount shall be ascertained in like manner as under section twenty of the Local Government Act, 1888 ; and

(b) an annual sum of seventy-nine thousand pounds.

(2.) Whereas by reason of this section certain grants heretofore made out of the Exchequer in aid of the rates will cease, the Lord Lieutenant shall cause to be paid in respect of every local financial year, out of the Local Taxation (Ireland) Account, at

Marginal notes:

61 & 62 Vic., c. 37. LOCAL GOVERNMENT (IRELAND) ACT, 1898.

PART III.

Finance.

46 & 47 Vic., c. 60. 59 & 60 Vic., c. 53.

Payment of proceeds of local taxation licences and of 79,000*l.* annually to Local Taxation (Ireland) Account and payments thereout in lieu of local grants. 51 & 52 Vic., c. 41.

61 & 62 Vic.,
c. 37.
LOCAL
GOVERN-
MENT
(IRELAND)
ACT, 1898.

PART III.

Finance.

such times and by such payments as he may direct, the following sums, namely :—

(a) to each county council, on behalf of the guardians of every union, the following amounts towards the salaries approved by the Local Government Board of the following officers, namely,

(i) one-half of the said salaries of the medical officers of the workhouse and dispensaries in respect of their duties under those guardians ; and

(ii) one-half of the said salary of one trained nurse in each workhouse, who is actually employed and possesses the prescribed qualifications ; and

(iii) the whole of the said salaries of schoolmasters and schoolmistresses in the workhouses ;

and also one-half of the cost of such medicines and medical and surgical appliances as are provided in accordance with the prescribed conditions ; and

(b) to each county council, on behalf of every rural district in the county, and to each urban district council, one-half of the salaries approved by the Local Government Board of sanitary officers in respect of their duties under the district council ; and

(c) to each county council who satisfy the Lord Lieutenant that they have fulfilled their duty in respect to accommodation and buildings for lunatic poor, and that their lunatic asylum is well managed and in good order and condition, and the lunatics therein properly maintained and cared for, sums at the rate for each lunatic in the asylum for whom the net charge upon the council (after deducting any amount received by them for his maintenance from any source other than poor rate) is equal to or exceeds four shillings a week throughout the period of maintenance for which the sum is calculated, of one-half of such net charge, or four shillings a week, whichever is least.

(3.) Where a union is situate in more counties than one, the amount payable as aforesaid on behalf of the guardians of the union shall be divided between the counties in the proportion in which the expenses of such guardians are divided.

(4.) Where the amount required to be raised in any area by a county council in any local financial year, in order to meet any railway or harbour charge connected with any guarantee given or transaction occurring before the passing of this Act, or to meet two or more such charges when added together, exceeds, or would but for the payments hereinafter mentioned exceed, a sum equal to sixpence in the pound on the rateable value of the area, the Lord Lieutenant on the report of the Commissioner of Valuation of those facts, may pay to the county council out of the sum paid under this section to the Local Taxation (Ireland) Account a sum equal to one-half of such excess to be applied by that council in reduction of the said amount.

(5.) If the amount paid under this section to the Local Taxation (Ireland) Account is insufficient to meet the sums payable thereout under this section those sums shall be proportionately abated as directed by the Lord Lieutenant, but, if the amount exceeds the sums so payable, the excess shall be accumulated and applied to meet any future deficiency, and subject thereto be applied in such manner as Parliament directs.

61 & 62 Vic
c. 37.
LOCAL
GOVERN-
MENT
(IRELAND)
ACT, 1898.

PART III.

Finance.

(6.) All sums paid to the Local Taxation (Ireland) Account under this section shall form part of the contingent portion of the guarantee fund under the Purchase of Land (Ireland) Act, 1891.

General.

59.—(1.) All sums directed by this Act to be paid out of the Consolidated Fund shall be charged on and paid out of the Consolidated Fund of the United Kingdom, or the growing produce thereof, at such times and by such instalments as the Treasury direct.

General
provisions
as to pay-
ments out
of Consoli-
dated Fund
and as to
Local
Taxation
(Ireland)
Account.

(2.) The Treasury may make regulations respecting the accounts of the receipts and expenditure of the Local Taxation (Ireland) Account, and for carrying into effect the provisions of this Act with respect to such Account, and in particular for carrying to separate credits the several sums payable under this or any other Act to that Account, and for the accumulation and investment of sums directed to be accumulated, and for the audit of the said accounts ; and such regulations shall be duly observed, and the regulations made under this section, and an annual return of the said accounts when audited, shall be laid before Parliament.

60. The term within which a loan borrowed by the county council is to be repaid shall be such period, not exceeding sixty years, as the council, with the consent of the Local Government Board, determine in each case, having regard to the duration of the work or object for which the loan is borrowed.

61.—(1.) A loan raised after the passing of this Act, under the Poor Relief (Ireland) Act, 1838, and any Acts amending that Act, including the Medical Charities Acts, shall be repaid within such period, not exceeding sixty years, as the guardians with the sanction of the Local Government Board may determine, either by equal yearly or half-yearly instalments of principal or principal and interest, or by means of a sinking fund.

(2.) The provisions of section two hundred and thirty-eight of the Public Health Act, 1878, respecting a sinking fund, shall apply to the said sinking fund.

(3.) Guardians may borrow money under the Poor Relief (Ireland) Act, 1838, and any Acts amending that Act, including the Medical Charities Acts, for the purpose of repaying any outstanding part of any loan raised by them under those Acts which they have power to repay.

(4.) Any money so borrowed shall be repaid in the manner directed by the section and within the same period as that

61 & 62 Vic.,
c. 37.
LOCAL
GOVERN-
MENT
(IRELAND)
ACT, 1898.

PART III.

Finance.

originally sanctioned for the repayment of the loan, unless the Local Government Board consent to the period for repayment being enlarged, but that period shall in no case exceed sixty years from the date of the original borrowing.

(5.) For the purpose of this section the expression "outstanding" means not repaid by instalments, or by means of a sinking fund, or out of capital money properly applicable for the purpose of repayment other than money borrowed for that purpose.

(6.) A loan raised by guardians shall not be of such amount as exceeds, or will make the total debt of the guardians under the Acts above in this section mentioned exceed, one-fourth of the total annual rateable value of the union : Provided that the Local Government Board by Provisional Order may extend the said maximum to double the amount above authorised, and the provisions of the Public Health Acts and this Act with respect to Provisional Orders shall apply with the necessary modifications.

(7.) In the Poor Relief (Ireland) Act, 1838, and any other enactment relating to borrowing by boards of guardians, the Commissioners of Public Works in Ireland shall, as respect any borrowing after the passing of this Act, be substituted for the Public Works Loan Commissioners, and the loan may be made for the period above mentioned.

Amend-
ment of
53 & 54 Vic.,
c. 30.

62. In the construction of the Poor Law Acts (Ireland) Amendment Act, 1890, sub-section two of section two of the said Act shall have effect only in cases in which the local authority have come to such determination as in the first sub-section of the said section is mentioned.

Amend-
ment of law
as to audit.
34 & 35 Vic.,
c 109.
35 & 36 Vic.,
c. 69.

1 & 2 Vic.,
c. 56.

63.—(1.) Sections twelve and thirteen of the Local Government (Ireland) Act, 1871, as amended by the Local Government Board (Ireland) Act, 1872, shall apply to the audit of the accounts of boards of guardians and their officers in like manner as it applies to the audit of accounts of governing bodies of towns and their officers ; and notwithstanding anything in section one hundred and fourteen of the Poor Relief (Ireland) Act, 1838, the legality of an order of the guardians may be questioned by the auditor in like manner as the legality of an order of the governing body of a town.

34 & 35 Vic.
c. 109.

(2.) Where an application, under this section or under the said section twelve of the Local Government (Ireland) Act, 1871, is made to the Local Government Board against any allowance, disallowance, or surcharge, made by any auditor of the Board—

(a) the Board may decide the application according to the merits of the case, and if the Board find that any disallowance or surcharge was lawfully made, but that the subject matter thereof was incurred under such circumstances as to make it fair and equitable that the disallowance or surcharge should be remitted, they may direct that the same shall be remitted upon payment of the costs (if any) which may have been incurred by the auditor or other competent authority in enforcing the disallowance or surcharge ; and *(b)* the decision of the Board shall be final ; and

(c) section thirteen of the Local Government (Ireland) Act, 1871, shall apply, as if the sum found by the decision of the Local Government Board to be due from any person were at the date of such decision certified by the auditor to be due, and there was no appeal.

64. The charge for auditing accounts of a county council in any year shall not exceed the sum of one hundred pounds.

65.—(1.) A general revaluation of rateable hereditaments under the Valuation Acts may be made, as respects a county borough, on the application of the council, and the council so applying shall pay such portion, not exceeding one-half, of the costs of the revaluation as the Treasury direct, and upon any such general revaluation the land in the borough shall be valued in the manner directed by section eleven of the Valuation (Ireland) Act, 1852, with respect to houses and buildings.

(2.) Where part of a union is within and part without any county borough in respect of which a valuation is made under this section, the total amount to be raised for union charges in that union shall be apportioned between each such part of the union in proportion to the rateable value of each part at the date when the revaluation under this section came into force : Provided that after the expiration of five years from that date, if no general revision has meantime been made, the Commissioner of Valuation, if satisfied by the council of the borough or the guardians representing the electoral divisions of the union situated outside the borough, or a majority of them, that the apportionment has become inequitable by reason of subsequent changes in the value of any hereditaments in the union, may revise the proportion in which the union charges are to be apportioned. This enactment shall apply to the police district of Dublin metropolis and to the Dublin bridge area within the meaning of the Dublin Port and Docks Board and Bridges Act, 1876, as if it were a union, but with the substitution of the county council of the county of Dublin, with respect to the revision of the apportionment, for the said guardians.

(3.) In this section the expression "general valuation" means a general revision under section thirty-four of the Valuation (Ireland) Act, 1852.

Collection of Rates and Duties in Dublin.

65. On and after the first day of October one thousand eight hundred and ninety-nine, or such other day not more than six months earlier or later as may be appointed under Part Eight of this Act by the Local Government Board, the following provisions

Margin notes:
61 & 62 Vic. c. 37.
LOCAL GOVERNMENT (IRELAND) ACT, 1898.
PART III
Finance.
34 & 35 Vic., c. 109. Charge for auditing accounts of county council.
Amendment of 15 & 16 Vic, c. 63, and 17 & 18 Vic., c. 8, as to general revaluation.
39 & 40 Vic., c. lxxxv.
15 & 16 Vic., c. 63.
Collector-General of Rates Dublin.

& 62 Vic.,
c. 37.
Local
Govern-
(Ireland)
Act, 1898.

Part III.

Finance.

shall apply with respect to the Dublin Collector-General of Rates and to the poor rate, police rate, bridge tax, and bridge rate :—

(1.) The poor rate shall be levied in the city of Dublin in like manner as in the rest of Ireland, and all enactments with respect to making, levying, collecting, and recovering the poor rate shall apply accordingly ;

(2.) The Commissioner of Police of Dublin Metropolis under the Dublin Metropolis Police Acts shall, at the prescribed time before the beginning of every local financial year, estimate the amount of money which he finds necessary for the maintenance of the police force, and for the several purposes of the said Acts during that year, not exceeding the amount which the Commissioner is, under the said Acts, or any of them, entitled to raise by a rate thereunder ;

(3.) The Dublin Port and Docks Board shall, at the prescribed time before the beginning of every local financial year, estimate the amount of money which they require to be raised in that year for the purpose of the bridge tax (if any) and bridge rate respectively ;

(4.) The Commissioner and Board respectively shall apportion each amount so estimated between the city of Dublin and the rest of the police district of Dublin Metropolis, or of the bridge area (as the case may be) which is outside the city of Dublin, and shall so apportion according to rateable value, and shall send to the council for the city of Dublin a demand for the amount apportioned to that city, and to the apportioned to the rest of the police district or bridge area ; and each council shall pay by equal half-yearly payments the amount specified in such demand, less five per cent. as and for the cost of collection and irrecoverable rates and office expenses, and also less such sum (if any) as the Local Government Board certify in each half-year to be the proportion of the Collector-General's annuity herein-after mentioned properly chargeable against any such payment ;

(5.) The council of the city of Dublin shall raise, either by council of the county of Dublin a demand for the amount means of a separate rate or by means of the poor rate but as a seperate item thereof, a sum equal to the amounts specified in such demand, but the demand note shall specify approximately the amount in the pound required for each amount ;

(6.) A sum equal to each of the amounts specified in such demand on the county council of the county of Dublin shall be raised in manner provided by this Act with respect to a railway or harbour charge ; but a council, in lieu of raising the amount required to meet the same by means of the poor rate, may, if they think fit, raise it by levying a separate rate ;

(7.) A council levying a separate rate for the purpose of this section shall make, levy, and collect the same upon the same basis and in like manner as the poor rate and all enactments relating to the poor rate shall apply accordingly, with the exception that a person shall not be disqualified for being registered as a parliamentary or local government elector by reason of the non-payment of any such separate rate ;

(8.) Where any property would but for this section be liable to be assessed for the purpose of raising any amount which under this section is to be raised by the poor rate, such property shall be liable for the purpose of that amount to be assessed to the poor rate and to the said separate rate ;

(9.) In this section the expression " bridge tax " means the quay wall tax and bridge tax leviable under the Dublin Bridge Act, 1854, and the expression " bridge rate " means the rate leviable under the Dublin Port and Docks Board and Bridges Act, 1876 ; and the expression "bridge area" has the same meaning as in the latter Act ;

(10.) The offices of the Collector-General of Rates under the Dublin Collection of Rates Act, 1849, and of his officers, shall be abolished, without prejudice to the provisions of the Dublin Corporation Act, 1890; and the persons who on the last day of March one thousand eight hundred and ninety-eight, held the said offices, and continue to hold them until abolition of their offices, shall be entitled to abolition superannuation allowance in accordance with section seventy (A) of the said Act of 1890, and that section shall apply, with the necessary modifications, and in particular with the substitution of the Local Government Board for the Lord Lieutenant ;

(11.) The compensation granted in pursuance of this section to the Collector-General, or any such officer, shall be apportioned in manner provided by sub-section two of section seventy-one of the Dublin Corporation Act, 1890, as if it were the abolition compensation mentioned in that section ;

(12.) Any sum which on such appointment is payable by the Corporation of the City of Dublin, and such portions of any superannuation allowances, abolition superannuation allowances, or abolition compensation, as under the said section seventy-one are payable by the said corporation shall be paid by the council of the city of Dublin to the Local Government Board ;

(13) Such portions of any compensation granted in pursuance of this section, or of any superannuation allowances, abolition superannuation allowances, or abolition compensation, under section seventy-one of the Dublin Corporation Act, 1890, as are payable otherwise than by the corporation of the city of Dublin (the total of which portions is in this Act referred to as the Collector-General's annuity) shall be obtained by the Local Government Board from, and be payable by, the county councils of the county at large, and the city of Dublin in the proportions ascertained as hereinafter mentioned ;

61 & 62 Vic. c. 37. LOCAL GOVERNMENT (IRELAND) ACT, 1898

PART III.

Finance.

17 & 18 Vic. c. 22. 39 & 40 Vic., c. lxxxv

12 & 13 Vic., c. 91. 53 & 54 Vic., c. ccxlvi.

61 & 62 Vic.,
c. 37.
LOCAL
GOVERN-
MENT
(IRELAND)
ACT, 1898.

PART III.

Finance.

(14.) The Local Government Board shall certify the amount raised during the twelve months ending the thirty-first day of December one thousand eight hundred and ninety-eight by the Collector-General of Rates in the police district of Dublin metropolis in respect of poor rate, police rate, bridge tax (if any), and bridge rate, distinguishing the total amount raised within and the total amount raised without the city of Dublin, and shall determine approximately, according to the proportions to each other other of the said totals, the proportion of the Collector-General's annuity which should be borne by the city and county of Dublin respectively ;

(15.) The council of the city of Dublin and the council of the county of Dublin respectively shall pay the proportion of the Collector-General's annuity to be borne by the city or county, as the case may be, and that proportion shall be raised as an addition to the several amounts to be raised by the council of the said city or county under this section ;

(16) Every sum to be paid to the Local Government Board in pursuance of this section shall be certified by the Board, and be paid to that Board by the council of the city or county of Dublin, as the ca e may be, and be a debt to the Crown from that council, and shall be applied by the Local Government Board in paying the allowances or compensation for the time being payable thereout, and so far as not required for that purpose shall be repaid to the council paying the same ;

(17.) The lists of voters and jurors shall be made out in the city of Dublin in like manner as in the rest of Ireland, and the Registration Acts and the Juries (Ireland) Acts, 1871 to 1894 shall apply accordingly ;

(18.) The Acts specified in Part Four of the First Schedule to this Act are in this section referred to by the short and collective titles therein mentioned.

Duties on
Dublin
pawn-
brokers'
licences
under
48 Geo. 3,
c. 140.
Geo. 3, xii.

67. The duties payable by pawnbrokers under section sixty-six of the Dublin Police Magistrates Act, 1808, and the Act therein mentioned, in any part of the police district of Dublin metropolis, shall be payable to and be collected by the council of the borough or county district where the place of business of the pawnbroker in respect of which the duties are paid is situate, and the amount so received by such council shall be applied in aid of their expenses in the execution of this Act, and the receiver mentioned in the said section shall cease to have any concern with the said duties.

PART IV.

*Boundaries
and
Adjustment.*

Boundaries
of counties,
unions,
rural dis-
tricts, and
district
electoral
divisions.

PART IV.

BOUNDARIES AND ADJUSTMENT.

68.—(1.) The first council elected under this Act for a county shall, subject as herein-after mentioned, be elected for the county as bounded at the passing of this Act for the purposes of the grand jury (in this Act referred to as the existing judicial county), or where such county is for those purposes divided into ridings, for the riding : Provided that the Local Government Board, by order made within six months after the passing of this Act, may alter for the purpose of the election of such council the boundaries of any existing judicial county, and if that order is made the first council shall be elected for the county as so altered.

(2.) The county council shall have for the purposes of this Act authority throughout the county for which it is elected (in this Act referred to as an administrative county), and that county as bounded for the purpose of the first election shall, subject to alterations made in pursuance of any Order in Council made under Part Six of this Act, be for all the purposes of this Act the county of such council.

(3.) In exercising their powers under this Act or any Order in Council made under Part Six of this Act, whether in making an order or in confirming an order made by a county council, and in the exercise of their existing powers to alter by order district electoral divisions or the boundaries of unions, the Local Government Board shall secure that—

(a) the boundaries of counties at large and unions as existing at the date of the order shall be preserved, except in any case where the preservation thereof would cause substantial inconvenience ; and

(b) a union shall not, if it is conveniently possible to avoid it, be divided between more than two counties, and shall not in any case be divided between more than three counties ; and

(c) where a union is divided between more than one county, the area of each divided part, so far as it is not contained in an urban sanitary district, shall be of sufficient size and rateable value to constitute a suitable rural district ; and

(d) a district electoral division shall be situate wholly in one county district ; and

(e) a county district shall be situate wholly in one county.

(4.) Where a union is divided between more than one county each divided part, so far as it is not contained in an urban sanitary district, shall be a separate rural sanitary district.

(5.) If the Local Government Board amalgamate two unions, they may, after communication with the county council and rural district councils concerned, either amalgamate the rural districts in the same county which are comprised in the amalgamated unions, or direct that those districts shall continue as separate rural districts, and in either case may make such arrangements as may be necessary for protecting the interests of the officers of the district councils holding office at the time of the amalgamation, and for that purpose the Union Officers (Ireland) Act, 1885, shall apply to officers of the district councils in like manner as it applies to the officers of boards of guardians.

61 & 62 VIC., c. 37.
LOCAL GOVERNMENT (IRELAND) ACT, 1898.

PART IV.

Boundaries and Adjustment..

43 & 49 Vic. c. 80.

61 & 62 VIC.,
c. 37.
LOCAL
GOVERN-
MENT
(IRELAND)
ACT, 1898.

PART IV.

Boundaries
and
Adjustment.
1 & 42 Vic.,
c. 52.

(6.) The power of the Local Government Board to divide a poor law electoral division into wards or to combine poor law electoral divisions for the purpose only of election shall cease, but nothing in this Act, nor in any Order made thereunder, shall affect—

(a) any power of the Local Government Board in relation to sanitary districts under section seven of the Public Health Act, 1878; or

(b) the general power of the Board to combine, divide, or otherwise alter district electoral divisions;

and the Board in the exercise of any such power may divide any townland;

Provided that any order of the Local Government Board combining, dividing, or otherwise altering district electoral divisions if made after the first day of May in any calendar year, shall apply to lists of electors in the next calendar year, and to any register of electors formed out of such lists, and to elections held after the time at which the register of electors so formed has come into force, and shall not apply previously.

(7.) Such changes in the Ordnance map as appear to the Lord Lieutenant in Council to be rendered necessary by this Act, or any Order in Council made thereunder, shall be made through the Commissioner of Valuation in manner directed by the Lord Lieutenant in Council.

Boundaries
of counties
for judicial,
militia,
jury, police,
and other
purposes,
and provi-
sion as to
revocation
of borough
commission
of the peace
and as to
certain
clerks o
crown and
peace.
39 & 40 Vic,
c. 76.

69.—(1.) A place which, for the purposes of this Act, is a part of an administrative county shall, subject as in this section mentioned, form part of that county for all other purposes, whether assizes, sheriff, lieutenant, custos rotulorum, justices, general quarter or petty sessions, jurors, militia, police, registration, coroner, clerk of the peace, or other county officers, or otherwise, and a sheriff and lieutenant for the counties of the cities of Belfast and Londonderry may accordingly be appointed in like manner as for any other county of a city named in section four of the Municipal Privilege (Ireland) Act, 1876, and as respects the sheriff in the manner in the said Act provided, and a sheriff and lieutenant shall cease to be appointed for those counties of cities and towns which under this Act do not become county boroughs.

(2.) Provided that—

(a) the entire county of Tipperary shall, subject to variation of boundaries, continue to be one county for the said purposes so far as it is one county at the passing of this Act; and

(b) nothing in this Act, nor anything done in pursuance of this Act, shall alter the limits of any parliamentary borough or parliamentary county within the meaning of the Redistribution of Seats Act, 1885, or confer any right to vote at the election of a member to serve in Parliament in any parliamentary borough where such right did not previously exist.

(3.) The court house of a county at large, when situate within a county of a city or town, shall, while it continues to be such court house, be deemed to form part of the body of such county at large; provided that if any court held for the county of the city or town is held in such court house, the court house shall then be deemed, for the purpose of the jurisdiction of that court, to be part of the body of the county of the city or town.

(4.) It shall be lawful for Her Majesty the Queen, on petition from the council of any borough other than a county borough, by letters patent, to revoke the grant of the commission of the peace for the borough, and to make such provision as to Her Majesty seems proper for the protection of interests existing at the date of the revocation.

(5.) Notwithstanding anything in this Act, the same officer shall continue to be clerk of the Crown, and when the offices of clerk of the Crown and clerk of the peace are amalgamated shall be clerk of the Crown and peace, for the county of Antrim and for the county of the city of Belfast constituted by this Act, and the same officer shall continue to be clerk of the Crown and peace for the county of Londonderry, and for the county of the city of Londonderry constituted by this Act.

(6.) Nothing in this Act shall affect the provisions of section twenty-five of the Municipal Corporations (Ireland) Act, 1843, nor those provisions of section one of the Quarter Sessions (Ireland) Act, 1845, which relate to the county of the city of Kilkenny.

(7.) The Juries (Ireland) Acts, 1871 to 1894, shall extend to any county of a city constituted by this Act, in like manner as if it were mentioned in the same class in the First and Second Schedules respectively to the Jurors' Qualification (Ireland) Act, 1876, as that in which the counties of the cities of Dublin and Cork are mentioned, and jurors' books shall be made for such county of a city accordingly.

70.—(1.) Where any county of a city or town becomes by virtue of this Act part of a county at large, then, on the application within the prescribed time of the council for any district, urban or rural, which comprises all or any part of the area of such county of a city or town, the Local Government Board shall make an adjustment as between that area and the rest of the said county at large respecting the contribution by the said area to the county at large charges (whether for the salaries of the county officers or main road or other purposes), and as respects the declaration o any roads within the said area to be main roads ; and any order made upon such application in respect of the main roa s shall have the same effect as if it were a declaration by the county council under this Act in respect of such roads

(2.) Any order for adjustment under this section shall be subject to appeal within the prescribed time to the Appeal Commission mentioned in this Act, and in the event of an appeal the order

Margin notes:

61 & 62 Vic., c. 37. LOCAL GOVERNMENT (IRELAND) ACT, 1898.

PART IV.

Boundaries and Adjustment.

6 & 7 Vic., c. 93. 8 & 9 Vic., c. 80.

34 & 35 Vic., c. 65. 37 & 38 Vic., c. 49. 39 & 40 Vic., c. 21.

Adjustment of financial relations between county at large and merged county of city or town.

61 & 62 VIC.,
c. 37.
LOCAL
GOVERN-
MENT
(IRELAND)
ACT, 1898.

PART IV.
――
*Boundaries
and
Adjustment.*

Periodical
revision of
financial
relations
between
county and
urban
district or
between
two county
districts.
shall be suspended, but shall afterwards operate as from the date at which it would but for the appeal have operated, or from any later date fixed by the Commission on the appeal.

71.—(1.) If, after the expiration of not less than fifteen years from the date heieinafter mentioned the co ncil either of a county or of an urban county district as respects the financial relations between such county and district, or the council of any county district as respects the financial relations between that district and any other county district, allege that the said financial relations are inequitable, and satisfy the Local Government Board that there is reasonable ground for that allegation, the Board may inquire into the circumstances, and, if they think it just so to do, may by order alter the financial relations. but such order where it alters the provisions of any local Act of Provisional Order shall be a Provisional Order.

(2.) "Financial relations" means the relations between the county and urban county district, or between the two county districts, as respects the burden of the expense of the maintenance or construction of any road or public work, or of the salaries of the county officers, or of any other county at large or district charges or as respects any contribution by the county or any district to such expenses, salaries, or charges, whether such relations are specified in any Act, or Provisional Order confirmed by an Act, or in any agreement or order made under Part Two of this Act in respect of any public work, or by any adjustment made in pursuance of this Act, or of an Order in Council under this Act, or are not so specified.

(3.) The date from which the said fifteen years are to be calculated shall be the passing of this Act, or in case of any Act Provisional Order, agreement, order or adjustment, made before or after the passing of this Act, then the date at which the Act, Provisional Order, agreement, order or adjustment came into operation, or in the case of an order under this section then the date of that order.

PART V

SUPPLEMENTAL.

As to the Powers of County and District Councils.

General
provisions
as to
transfer of
business to
county and
district
councils
and as to
use of court
house.
72.—(1.) Any council, board, or court shall, as respects the business by this Act transferred to them from any authority, be subject to the provisions and limitations affecting them, whether in this Act or in any Order in Council made under Part Six of this Act, but, save as aforesaid, shall have all the powers and duties of the authority in respect of the business transferred.

(2.) There shall be transferred to the county and district council respectively, in relation to any business transferred to that council, all the powers and duties under any Act of any officer of such council other than the treasurer in relation to that business.

(3.) Except so far as the sheriff or the justices may require for the administration of justice, or the discharge of his or their duties, the use of any court house, sessions house, or other county building under his or their custody or control, the county council may use the same for the purpose of the execution of their duties, and if any difference arises between the sheriff or justices and the county council as to such use, or as to the remuneration of any court keeper or other officer, such difference shall be determined by the Lord Lieutenant.

73. In the application of the Military Manœuvres Act, 1897, to Ireland, the council of each county, county borough, and district, shall be construed to mean the council elected in pursuance of this Act, and the references to the coun il of a parish shall not apply ; and sub-sections one and two of section nine of that Act (which substitute boards of guardians for county councils and exclude county boroughs) shall be repealed.

74.—(1.) In the Irish Education Act, 1892, the expression "baronial council" shall mean rural district council, and the expression "local rate" shall mean the rate out of which the expenses of the execution of this Act by a county or district council, as the case may be, are defrayed.

(2.) In the application of the Technical Instruction Acts, 1889 and 1891, to the council of a county other than a county borough the expression "local rate" shall mean the poor rate, and the expenses of a county council under those Acts shall be county at large or district charges according as that council direct.

75. Where the council of any county borough or any urban county district consider that it would be beneficial for the inhabitants of the borough or district that any post or telegraph office should be established within such borough or district or any additional facilities (postal or other) provided by the Postmaster General within such borough or district, the council may undertake to pay the Postmaster General any loss he may sustain by reason of the establishment or maintenance of the office, or the provision of the facilities, and any expenses incurred under this section may be paid in the case of a borough out of the borough fund or the borough rate, and in the case of any urban district not a borough out of the rate out of which the expenses of the council under the Public Health Act, 1878, are defrayed.

76.—(1.) The council for a county may, either by the exercise of their powers under this Act, or by taking over for the purpose any workhouse or other suitable building in possession of the guardians, provide an auxiliary lunatic asylum for the reception of chronic lunatics who, not being dangerous to themselves or others, are certified by the resident medical superintendent of an asylum of such council not to require special care and treatment in a fully equipped lunatic asylum ; and any such auxiliary

61 & 62 Vic., c. 37.
LOCAL GOVERNMENT (IRELAND) ACT, 1898.

PART V.

Supplemental.

Adaptation to county and district councils of 60 & 61 Vic., c. 43.

Adaptation of 55 & 56 Vic., c. 42; 52 & 53 Vic., c. 76, and 54 & 55 Vic., c. 4.

Establishment of post or telegraph offices in county boroughs or urban districts.

41 & 42 Vic., c. 52.

Provision for chronic and harmless lunatics.

61 & 62 Vic.,
c. 37.
LOCAL
GOVERN-
MENT
(IRELAND)
ACT, 1898.

PART V.

*Supple-
mental.*

lunatic asylum shall either be a separate asylum within the meaning of the Lunatic Asylum Acts, or if the Lord Lieutenant so directs, a department of such an asylum :

Provided that the sum payable out of the Local Taxation (Ireland) Account in respect of the net charge for any lunatic therein may be paid when the net charge equals or exceeds three shillings and sixpence a week, but that sum shall not exceed two shillings a week.

(2.) The Local Government Board, on the application of a county council and after communication with the guardians concerned, may by amalgamating unions provide for placing a workhouse at the disposal of the council for the above purpose, and may dispose of the workhouse for that purpose.

38 & 39 Vic.,
c. 67

(3.) Where an auxiliary asylum is so provided for any county, section nine of the Lunatic Asylums (Ireland) Act, 1875 (which relates to sending lunatics to a workhouse), shall cease to apply as respects that county.

(4.) This section shall apply with the necessary modifications to a lunatic asylum district comprising two or more counties.

Restriction
on use of
licensed
premises
for
meetings,
offices, &c

77. Except in cases where no other suitable room is available either free of charge or at a reasonable cost, a district or county council, or any committee thereof, shall not hold a m eting on any licensed premises, nor shall such premises be used as an office of the council, or for any purpose of or incidental to the business of the council or of any officer of the council ; and the expression "licensed premises" in this section means premises licensed for the sale of intoxicating liquor, and includes any club at which such liquor is sold.

As to
navigation
trackways.
36 & 37 Vic.,
c. 34.

78. A trackway on the bank of any navigable river within the meaning of the Grand Juries Act, 1873, shall, without prejudice to the reasonable use thereof for any purpose connected with navigation, be a public highway, and shall continue to be maintainable as provided by that Act.

Relative
position of
district
council and
guardians.

79.—(1.) Where a rural district is co-extensive with a union—

(a) the district councillors shall, when exercising the duties of guardians, continue to be a board of guardians under their existing name, and when exercising the duties of a district council shall be a district council under the name given by or in pursuance of this Act ; and

(b) matters affecting the board of guardians shall not by reason only of the members thereof forming also a district council affect that council, and matters affecting the district council shall not by reason only of the members thereof forming also a board of guardians affect that board ; and

(c) the meetings and business of the board and council may be held and transacted at the same place ; and

(d) subject to the express provisions of this section the Local Government Board may make regulations as to the property held jointly or severally by the council and the board.

(2.) Where a rural district is comprised in but not co-extensive with a union, the council for the district shall be entitled, under the prescribed conditions, to use the board-room and offices of the guardians of the union for their meetings and business, and if such board-room and offices are situate outside their district, to hire a board-room and offices.

61 & 62 Vic-
c. 37.
LOCAL
GOVERN-
MENT
(IRELAND)
ACT, 1898.

PART V.

Supple-
mental.

Imperative Presentments, Mandamus, and duty of maintaining Works.

80.—(1.) Where the payment of a sum by any county or district council, or by the treasurer of such council or other officer of the council on behalf of the council, is ordered by a judge of assize under this or any other Act, or is required, either to comply with any enactment, or to meet either a judgment or decree of any competent court, or an order for the payment or collection of any money made by the Lord Lieutenant in pursuance of any Act, the treasurer of the council shall pay the same out of moneys under his control as such treasurer, and, if those are insufficient, out of the first moneys coming under his control as treasurer, and such payment may, to the extent of any such moneys, be enforced against such treasurer in like manner as it might be enforced against the council.

Imperative
present-
ments.

(2.) Where any such sum is due to the Crown or any Government department the amount thereof may be deducted from any sums payable from the Local Taxation (Ireland) Account directly or indirectly to the council by whose treasurer the first mentioned sum is payable, and be paid into the Exchequer in discharge of that sum, and where the sum was due from a district council, the county council shall debit that district council with the amount so deducted: Provided that this enactment shall be without prejudice to the guarantee fund under the Purchase of Land (Ireland) Act, 1891

54 & 55 Vic.
c. 48.

81. Where a mandamus is issued by the High Court to any county or district council, and the council fail to comply therewith, the Court may appoint an officer, and confer on him all or any of the powers of the defaulting council which appear to the Court necessary for carrying into effect the mandamus.

As to
enforcing
mandamu-

82.—(1.) It shall be the duty of every county and district council, according to their respective powers, to keep all public works maintainable at the cost of their county or district in good condition and repair, and to take all steps necessary for that purpose.

Duty of
county and
district
council to
maintain
works.

(2.) The council of a county, upon a proposal made by the council of a district in which any old road or public work is situate, or where the expenses of the mainte nance of the road or work are levied wholly off the county then without such proposal, may, if the road or work appears to such county council to be useless, and they resolve so to do, stop up or abandon the road or work; but if an objection by any ratepayer is lodged in the manner and

61 & 62 Vic., *within the time determined by an Order in Council under Part VI.*
c. 37.
LOCAL of this Act, the said resolution shall be of no effect unless approved
GOVERN- by the Local Government Board.
MENT
(IRELAND) (3.) If any district council complain that a county council or
ACT, 1898. any county council complain that a district council, have failed to
PART V. perform any such duty as aforesaid, the complaining council
Supple- may, without prejudice to any other remedy, appeal to the Local
mental. Government Board, and section fifteen of the Public Health Act,
59 & 60 Vic., 1896, shall apply with necessary modifications, in like manner
c. 54. as where default is made by a sanitary authority.

(4.) Where a county council refuses at two successive quarterly
meetings to approve of any new public work submitted by a rural
district council, the cost of which is to be levied wholly off that
district, or fail to execute such work, the rural district council may
appeal to the Local Government Board, and if that Board consider
that such new work ought to be executed, they may order the
county council to execute the same, and, if the county council make
59 & 60 Vic., default in complying with the order, section fifteen of the Public
c. 54. Health Act, 1896. shall apply with the necessary modifications in
like manner as where default is made by a sanitary authority.

(5.) The provisions of the Grand Juries Acts with respect to
memorials, other than memorials by a grand jury, shall be repealed,
and the provisions of those and any other Acts with respect to
traverse shall be repealed, so far as they relate to business transferred by this Act to county or district councils or the county
court.

Officers.

Officers of   83.—(1) As respects the officers of the county council, the
county. council of a county other than a county borough, subject to the
provisions herein after contained—

    (a) shall appoint the secretary of the council (who shall act as
    the clerk of the council), the treasurer of the county (who
    shall be treasurer of the council), and the county surveyor
    or surveyors ; and

    (b) may appoint such assistant surveyors and such further
    officers as they think necessary for the performance of the
    duties of the council ;

and every officer so appointed shall perform such duties and,
subject (in the case of any officer whose salary can be fixed without the concurrence of the Local Government Board) to any
statutory limits, be paid such remuneration as the council may
assign to him.

(2.) A county council may provide for the performance by a
deputy of the duties of any officer in case of his illness, absence,
or incapacity, and anything required by law to be done by, to, or
before the officer may, subject to the directions of the council, be
done by, to, or before such deputy.

(3.) The county council may take from a treasurer, when a banking company, and shall t ke from any other officer who receives or pays any money on behalf of the council such security as may be approved by the Local Government Board.

(4.) Part of the payment to every county council out of the agricultural grant shall be deemed to be paid in respect of part of the salary of the secretary of the county council, and of the county surveyor, and of any assistant surveyor, and any such secretary or surveyor or assistant surveyor shall not be appointed or removed, nor shall his salary be fixed or altered, without the concurrence of the Local Government Board, and he shall have such qualifications (if any) as may be prescribed.

(5.) The Local Government Board shall also have the same power as regards collectors of the poor rate appointed by the county council and their accounts as they would have if those collectors had continued to be officers of the guardians.

(6.) Save as otherwise provided by this Act, the county council may remove any of their officers.

(7.) There shall be transferred from the clerk of the union to the secretary of the county council so far as respects rural districts, and to the clerk of the council of every county borough and urban county district so far as respects that borough or district, all powers and duties in relation to the registration of electors, or to jurors' lists.

(8.) The secretary of the county council (including in a county borough the town clerk), shall send to the Lord Lieutenant or the Local Government Board such returns and information as may from time to time be required by either House of Parliament or by that Board.

(9.) The Lord Lieutenant may, if he thinks fit, direct the assistant surveyors to be examined and their qualifications certified by the persons who examine, and certify the qualifications of, the county surveyor.

(10.) A paid officer in the permanent employment of a county council who is required to devote his whole time to such employment shall not be eligible to serve in Parliament.

(11.) The enactments relating to the superannuation of officers of boards of guardians shall, with the necessary modifications, apply to officers of county and rural district councils other than the county surveyor and any officer of a county borough, and the amount of any such superannuation shall be paid as expenses of the county or district council.

(12.) The law relating to the treasurers of counties and this section shall apply to the county of Dublin in like manner as to any other county.

(13.) Where a county surveyor, or any resident medical superintendent or assistant medical officer of a lunatic asylum, is appointed by a county council after the passing of this Act, and at the time of such appointment held a like office in another county or lunatic asylum, he shall, upon ceasing to hold office, be entitled, for the purpose of the enactments relating to super-

61 & 62 Vic.,
c. 37.
LOCAL
GOVERN-
MENT
(IRELAND)
ACT, 1898.

PART V.

Supple-
mental.

28 & 29 Vic.,
c. 26.

61 & 62 Vic.,
c. 37.
LOCAL
GOVERN-
MENT
(IRELAND)
ACT, 1898.

PART V.

*Supple-
mental*

57 & 58 Vic.,
c. 57.
Officers of
lunatic
asylum.

annuation, to reckon any previous service as county surveyor or as officer of a lunatic asylum which he might have reckoned if his service had been under the appointing council or committee.

(14.) This section shall be without prejudice to the provisions of this Act respecting existing officers, or to the powers of the Lord Lieutenant and Privy Council or the Lord Lieutenant under sections sixty-eight and sixty-nine of the Diseases of Animals Act, 1894.

84.—(1.) Subject to the provisions hereinafter contained, the county council acting through their committee—

(a) shall appoint for each lunatic asylum a resident medical superintendent and at least one assistant medical officer; and

(b) may appoint such other officers as they consider necessary for the performance of their duties in relation to lunatic asylums,

and every officer so appointed shall perform such duties and be paid such remuneration as the council may assign to him.

(2.) Every resident medical superintendent shall be a registered medical practitioner of not less than seven years standing, and shall have served for not less than five years as a medical officer or assistant medical officer in an asylum for the treatment of the insane, and every assistant medical officer shall be a registered medical practitioner.

53 & 54 Vic.
c. 31.

(3.) The Pauper Lunatic Asylums (Ireland) (Superannuation) Act, 1890, shall apply to every officer of a lunatic asylum, save that all reference in that Act to the approval of the inspectors of lunatics or of the Lord Lieutenant shall be repealed.

(4.) The grant paid out of the Local Taxation (Ireland) Account for lunatics shall be deemed to be paid in respect of a part of the salary of any resident medical superintendent and assistant medical officer, and any such superintendent or medical officer, shall not be appointed or removed, nor shall his salary be fixed or altered, without the concurrence of the Lord Lieutenant, and he shall have such qualifications (if any) as may be prescribed.

(5.) This section shall be without prejudice to the provisions of this Act respecting existing officers.

Officers of
rural
district
council and
guardians
and salary
of medical
officer of
urban or
rural
district.

85.—(1.) The clerk or treasurer of the union shall be the clerk or treasurer of the council of every rural district comprised in the union, except where the Local Government Board authorise such council to appoint a separate clerk or treasurer, in which case the council may appoint a clerk or treasurer, and in the case of the clerk with such salary as that Board approve.

(2.) The portion of the salary of the clerk of the union which is to be paid in respect of his duties as clerk of any rural district council shall be determined by the Local Government Board, and this sub-section shall apply with the necessary modifications to any other officer of a board of guardians who, by virtue of this Act, becomes also an officer of a rural district council.

(3.) Subject as aforesaid, the Local Government Board may make rules as to the employment of the same officers by the council of a rural district and the guardians of the union comprising that district.

(4.) The additional salary granted to the medical officer of a dispensary district by reason of his being (under section eleven of the Public Health Act, 1878) medical officer of health of any sanitary district shall be paid by the council of the latter district.

86. Where by or in pursuance of this Act, or any Order or rules made thereunder by the Lord Lieutenant in Council or the Local Government Board, any officer paid out of the poor rate or any other local rate or cess is required to perform any duty, make any return, give any information, or do any other thing, and wilfully fails or refuses so to do, he shall be liable, if sued by the county or district council or Local Government Board, to a fine not exceeding forty shillings, or, in the case of any continuing offence, not exceeding forty shillings a day during the continuance of the offence, and any such fine may be recovered as a Crown debt, or to an amount not exceeding one hundred pounds before a court of summary jurisdiction.

87. An officer holding a pensionable office, whether the superannuation allowance is payable out of the poor rate, or any town rate, or other local rate, shall not be disqualified for receiving such an allowance by reason only of his having acted, whether before or after the passing of this Act, as an officer of a school attendance committee under the Irish Education Act, 1892.

Amendments of Law.

88.—(1.) A council of a county borough may make regulations for regulating the use and speed of bicycles, tricycles, velocipedes, and other similar machines, in the streets and roads within the county borough, and the carrying of lights on such machines, and the warning of approach to be given by persons using the same, and for preventing any obstruction or danger being caused by the same, and the provisions of sections two hundred and nineteen to two hundred and twenty-three of the Public Health Act, 1878, with respect to byelaws, shall apply to all regulations made under this section as if the same were byelaws authorised by that Act.

(2.) Any person summarily convicted of offending against any regulations made under the powers by this section conferred shall, for each and every such offence, forfeit and pay any sum not exceeding forty shillings.

89.—(1.) Notwithstanding anything in the Act of the Parliament of Ireland of the twenty-sixth year of the reign of King George the Third, chapter fifty-seven, intituled An Act for regulating the stage in the city and county of Dublin, the Lord Lieutenant may, on the application of the council for the county of Dublin or the county borough of Dublin, or of any urban district within the county of Dublin, grant an occasional licence for the performance

---

Marginal notes:

61 & 62 Vic., c. 37. LOCAL GOVERNMENT (IRELAND) ACT, 1898.

PART V.

Supplemental.

41 & 42 Vic., c. 52. Obligation of county and other local officers, and their superannuation

Amendment of law as to superannuation of officers.

55 & 56 Vic., c. 42.

Power of county borough council as to bicycles and other machines.

41 & 42 Vic., c. 52.

Licensing in county or city of Dublin of theatrical performances for charitable objects.

61 & 62 Vic.,
c. 37.
LOCAL
GOVERN-
MENT
(IRELAND)
ACT, 1898.

of any stage play or other dramatic entertainment in any theatre, room, or building where the profits arising therefrom are to be applied for some charitable purpose or in aid of the funds of any society instituted for the purpose of science, literature, or the fine arts exclusively.

PART V.

*Supple-
mental.*

Conversion
of work-
house
hospital
into district
hospital.

(2.) The licence may contain such conditions and regulations as appear fit to the Lord Lieutenant, and may be revoked by him.

90.—(1.) A board of guardians, with the consent of the Local Government Board, may make regulations for—

(*a*) the conversion of their workhouse hospital into a district hospital ; and

(*b*) the transfer of the duties and powers of the guardians as regards such hospital and the administrative control thereof to a committee of hospital governors appointed by the guardians of whom two-thirds at least shall be members of the board ; and

(*c*) the payment and accommodation under which private patients may be admitted.

(2.) Subject to the regulations of the Local Government Board and to the powers of that Board with respect to guardians and their officers, the guardians, acting through the said committee, shall properly manage and maintain such district hospital, and may appoint and remove officers, and regulate expenditure, and may receive and apply for the benefit of such district hospital any endowments or subscriptions given by private persons for that purpose.

(3.) Subject to the general control of the guardians in respect of all moneys provided out of rates, the acts of the committee shall not require confirmation by the guardians.

(4.) The guardians shall have power to dissolve the committee at any time on giving six months notice of their intention so to do, but such dissolution shall not invalidate any act done by the committee before dissolution.

As to leases
to boards of
guardian's
for dispen-
sary houses.
42 & 43 Vic.,
c. 25.

91. Notwithstanding anything in the eleventh section of the Dispensary Houses (Ireland) Act, 1879, a lease to a board of guardians made thereunder may be for any term which the owner has power to grant, not being less than sixty years.

Amend-
ment of
46 & 47 Vic.,
c. 43, as to
manage-
ment of
tramway.

92. Where the undertaking of a company becomes or has become the property of a county council, pursuant to the provisions of the Tramways and Public Companies (Ireland) Act, 1883, or any Order in Council issued thereunder, the council may, with the approval of the Lord Lieutenant in Council, enter into an arrangement with any railway or tramway company with any of whose railways or tramways the said undertaking is connected, for the working of the said undertaking upon such terms as may be agreed upon.

Amend-
ment of
23 & 24 Vic.,
c. 152, s. 38,
as to tram-
ways.

93. Section thirty-eight of the Tramways (Ireland) Act, 1860, shall have effect as if the words " of not less than two-thirds " were omitted therefrom.

Miscellaneous.

61 & 62 Vic }
c. 37.
LOCAL
GOVERN-
MENT
(IRELAND)
ACT, 1898.

94.—(1.) A person being in holy orders or being a regular minister of any religious denomination shall not be eligible as a county or district councillor.

PART V.

*Supple-
mental.*

(2.) So much of any enactment, whether public or local, as requires a member of the council of a borough, or of an urban or rural sanitary authority, or board of guardians, or commissioners of a town, to have any property qualification or to have any other qualification than that of being a local government elector or resident as required by this Act, shall be repealed.

Special
provisions
as to quali-
fications,
elections,
and retire-
ment of
councillois,
guardiaus,
commis-
sioners, &c.,
day of
annual or
borough
quarterly
meeting,
and day for
electing
mayor or
chairman,
selecting
sheriffs, &c.

(3.) Any member of the council of a county or county district or board of guardians or commissioners of a town who, after the pasting of this Act is convicted of acting when disqualified, or of voting when prohibited, shall for a period of seven years after such conviction be disqualified for being elected or being a member of the same or any other such council, board, or commissioners.

(4.) Casual vacancies in the council of any county (not being a county borough) or in any rural district council shall be, as soon as may be, filled by the council.

(5.) Casual vacancies among the guardians elected for any electoral division in a county borough or urban county district may be filled by the board of guardians.

(6.) Outside a county borough the elections of county and rural district councillors shall be held together, and each district electoral division shall, unless the Local Government Board on the representation of the county council otherwise direct, be a polling district, and such direction, if given, may authorise the poll for a councillor for a district electoral division to be taken outside that division, if it is taken within the county electoral division comprising it.

(7.) The ordinary day of election of such councillors shall be the first day of June, or such day not more than seven days earlier or later than that day as may be fixed by the county council with respect to their county, and the day of the annual meeting and ordinary day of election of the chairman and vice-chairman of a rural district council shall be the fifth day, and of a county council the twelfth day, next after the said day of election of councillors.

(8.) Outside a county borough the old county and rural district councillors shall retire, and the newly elected councillors shall come into office, on the day next after the said day of election of councillors, which day shall be the ordinary day of retirement of councillors.

(9.) In the case of the council of an urban district other than a borough, and of the commissioners of a town, the ordinary day of election of councillors and commissioners shall be the fifteenth day of January, and the day of the annual meeting and ordinary day of election of the chairman and vice-chairman of the council or commissioners shall be the twenty-third day of January, and such chairman or vice-chairman shall come into office as soon as he has made the declaration accepting the office.

61 & 62 VIC.,
c. 37.
LOCAL
GOVERN-
MENT
(IRELAND)
ACT, 1898.

PART V.

Supple-
mental.

(10.) In the case of the council of a borough, the ordinary day of election of councillors and aldermen shall be the fifteenth day of January, and the quarterly meeting of the council shall be held at noon on the twenty-third day of January, and at such hour on such other three days before the fifteenth day of January then next following, as the council at the quarterly meeting in January decide.

(11.) The first business transacted at the said quarterly meeting in January shall be the election of the mayor, and the outgoing mayor shall retire and the newly elected mayor shall come into office on the ordinary day of retirement of the mayor, or as soon after as the new mayor has made a declaration accepting the office, and the ordinary day of retirement of the mayor shall be the day of the said quarterly meeting, or, if the council have by a general resolution so directed, the following twenty-third day of February.

(12.) In a county of a city or town, the selection of three persons qualified to fill the office of sheriff shall be part of the business transacted at the said quarterly meeting in January, and the day of that meeting and the twenty-third day of February shall respectively be substituted for the 1st day of December and the first day of January in sections three and four of the Municipal

Privilege (Ireland) Act, 1876, and the day next before the day of the said quarterly meeting shall be substituted for the thirtieth day of November in section five of the said Act.

(13.) In the case of the council of any borough or other urban district, or the commissioners of any town, the outgoing aldermen, councillors, and commissioners shall retire, and the newly elected aldermen, councillors, and commissioners shall come into office on the sixteenth day of January, and that day shall be the ordinary day of retirement of aldermen, councillors, and commissioners.

(14.) The fact that an outgoing mayor, chairman, alderman, councillor, or commissioner has ceased, upon the new register of local government electors coming into force on the previous first day of January, to be a local government elector shall not disqualify him for continuing in office until the above-mentioned ordinary day of retirement of mayor, chairman, alderman, councillor, or commissioner, as the case may be, and also, if he is a mayor or chairman, and a new mayor or chairman has been elected, until that new mayor or chairman has made a declaration accepting the office.

(15.) Where any members of a joint committee or joint board are appointed by any county or district council, whether under this or any other Act or an Order in Council, and the council are elected triennially, the members appointed by such council who are in office at the date of any triennial election shall continue to be members of such joint committee or board until the day after the first meeting of the newly elected council, and the consideration of the appointment of such members shall be part of the business at the said meeting after the election of mayor or chairman.

61 & 62 Vic.
c. 37.
LOCAL
GOVERN-
MENT
(IRELAND)
ACT, 1898.

PART V.

Supple-
mental.

(16.) The scale of expenses of any election shall require the approval of the Local Government Board.

95.—(1.) A chairman of any county or district council, or of any commissioners, who is by virtue of this Act a justice of the peace, and has been re-elected to the said office of chairman on the expiration or other determination of a previous term of office, may continue to act as a justice of the peace without again taking the oaths required by law to be taken by a justice of the peace.

Position of
chairman
as justice of
the peace.

(2.) Every such chairman who is by virtue of this Act a justice of the peace shall, in his capacity of justice but not otherwise, notwithstanding anything in the other provisions of this Act, be subject to the same restrictions, disqualifications, and power of removal by the Lord Chancellor, as any other justice of the peace,

96.- -(1.) The secretary of every county council and the clerk of every urban district council shall, within the prescribed time after making a poor rate, send, without payment, to every board of guardians for a union wholly or partly situate within the county or district, a copy, certified by such secretary or clerk to be a true copy, of so much of the rate book containing the said poor rate as relates to the union, and the Evidence Act, 1851, shall apply as if the copy were a certified copy within the meaning of that Act, and every person shall have the same right to inspect and take copies or extracts from the said copy as he would have if it were a poor rate, and section seventy of the Poor Relief (Ireland) Act, 1838, and any other enactment relating to such inspection, copies, or extracts, shall apply accordingly.

As to rate
books and
lists of
voters and
jurors.

14 & 15 Vic.,
c. 99.

1 & 2 Vic.,
c. 56.

(2.) Every county council shall arrange by contract for all printing, whether of lists, forms, registers, or otherwise, required in connexion with the Registration Acts, or with the Juries (Ireland) Acts, 1871 to 1894, whether such printing is required by the secretary of the council, or any clerk of the peace, clerk of a union, or town clerk, and the said printing shall be done in accordance with the contract so made, and not otherwise, unless in any exceptional case the county council for special reasons so permit.

34 & 35 Vic.,
c. 65.
57 & 58 Vic.,
c. 49.

(3.) Every such contract shall be made in like manner and the like tenders shall be obtained in like manner. so nearly as circumstances admit, as in the case of a public work the expenses of which are leviable off the county at large.

97.—(1.) The local government electors of any town or other area shall be the persons entitled to vote at the election of commissioners of the town, or to petition for a provisional or other order in relation to the government of the town or area, or for a charter, or to petition, present a memorial, or vote, respecting the adoption of any Act or enactment capable of being adopted for such town or area, and shall be so entitled in substitution for the persons who, under any enactment, are entitled so to petition or vote, except where the persons so entitled are a council elected under this Act.

Adaptation
of Acts as to
the persons
entitled to
petition for
charter, &c.
as to voting
on adop-
tion of
Act, and as
to qualifi-
cation of
town com-
missioner.

61 & 62 Vic.,
c. 37.
LOCAL
GOVERN-
MENT
(IRELAND)
ACT, 1898.

PART V

Supple-
mental.

Registra-
tion of
electors.

(2.) Where a poll is taken with reference to such adoption, it shall be taken by ballot, in accordance as near as may be with the ballot taken at the election of a council under this Act.

(3.) A person shall not be qualified to be elected or to be a commissioner of a town unless he is a local government elector for such town, or has during the whole twelve months preceding the election resided and continues to reside in the town.

98.—(1.) The local government register of electors shall be completed, and on sale to the public, and come into operation on the same day as the parliamentary register of electors, and shall continue in force for the same period.

(2.) In a district electoral division comprised in a parliamentary borough in which, prior to the passing of this Act, the freeholders voted for the parliamentary county and not for the parliamentary borough, the names of the freeholders, that is to say, the persons entitled in respect of a freehold, leasehold, or copyhold qualification within the parliamentary borough, shall be entered in a separate list, and that list shall form part of the local government supplement in the said division ; but nothing in this enactment shall alter the right of such freeholders to vote for the parliamentary county, or confer on them a right to vote at a parliamentary election for the parliamentary borough.

(3.) A person registered as a freeman in a parliamentary borough shall be entitled to vote as a local government elector--

(a) if his place of abode is in the borough, then in the electoral division in which that place of abode is situate ; and

(b) if his place of abode is not in the borough (in this Act referred to as a non-resident freeman), then in the electoral division to which he is allotted by the revising barrister ;

and shall not be entitled in respect of the qualification of freeman to vote elsewhere than in such electoral division, and the registration of electors shall be conducted, and the register arranged so as to give effect to this enactment.

(4.) The non-resident freemen shall be allotted among the several district electoral divisions of the borough in proportion, as nearly as may be, to the number of electors in each electoral division, and shall be so allotted in like manner as is provided

by section fourteen of the Redistribution of Seats Act, 1885, with respect to the allotment of non-resident freemen among the several divisions of a parliamentary borough.

(5.) Where an electoral division is situate partly within and partly without a parliamentary borough this section shall apply to each divided part as if it were an electoral division.

(6.) Where the non-resident freemen have been allotted among the divisions of a parliamentary borough in manner provided by

section fourteen of the Redistribution of Seats Act, 1885, the provisions of this section shall apply as if each such division were a parliamentary borough.

(7.) Rules under the Registration (Ireland) Act, 1898, may be made for carrying into effect the provisions of this Act with respect to local government electors, and in particular for adapting the Registration Acts to the provisions of this Act and Orders in Council made thereunder; and so much of the said Act of 1898 as requires the rules to be made before the end of the year one thousand eight hundred and ninety-eight, shall be repealed.

(8.) For the purpose of section twenty-one of the County Officers and Courts (Ireland) Act, 1877, the Registration (Ireland) Act, 1898, and this Act shall be deemed to be Acts relating to the registration of voters.

(9.) The sums payable to the Exchequer under the Registration (Ireland) Act, 1898, shall be paid by the several county councils in lieu of the guardians.

(10.) In this Act, and in every Act hereafter passed, the expression "local government register of electors" shall, unless the context otherwise requires, mean, as respects any county or borough, district, electoral division, ward, or other area in Ireland, the register of parliamentary electors, or the portion of that register which relates to such county or borough, district, electoral division, ward, or other area, together with the local government supplement.

99.—(1.) Ballot boxes, fittings, and compartments shall be provided and kept for each county and county district and for each electoral division of a union situate in an urban district, at the expense of the rates of such county, district, or union, and may be used free of charge at any parliamentary election for any county or parliamentary borough comprising the whole or any part of such county, district, or union, and any damage other than reasonable wear and tear caused to the same shall be paid as part of the expenses of the election in which they are so used.

(2.) It shall be the duty of the returning officer at any such parliamentary election to make use, so far as practicable, of the ballot boxes, fittings, and compartments provided in pursuance of this section, or otherwise the property of any county or district council, and the court upon taxation of his accounts shall have regard to the provisions of this section.

100. Any contract in writing, which if made by private persons would not by law be required to be made under seal, may, if made by a county or district council, and if the subject matter thereof does not exceed fifty pounds in value, be made under the hand of any two councillors acting by the direction and on behalf of the council.

101.—(1.) Nothing in this Act shall affect any powers of the Local Government Board with respect to guardians or the officers of guardians; and that Board may, on the application of any council, exercise in relation to the council and the officers of the council all such powers of holding inquiries on oath and deputing any officer of the Board to attend at the meetings of the council as they are by law empowered to exercise in the case of guardians and their officers.

Marginal notes:

61 & 62 Vic., c. 37.
LOCAL GOVERNMENT (IRELAND) ACT, 1898.

PART V.

Supplemental.

40 & 41 Vic., c. 37.
61 & 62 Vic., c. 2.

Provisions as to ballot boxes &c., at elections.

As to contracts in writing by county and district councils

Powers of Lord Lieutenant and Local Government Board

61 & 62 Vic., c. 37.
LOCAL GOVERN- MENT (IRELAND) ACT, 1898.

PART V.

Supple- mental.

(2.) Where the Lord Lieutenant or the Local Government Board is authorised to make an order under this Act, such order may be enforced by mandamus.

(3.) Any difference which under any enactment applied by an Order in Council under this Act can be referred to the High Court may, if the parties to such difference so agree, be referred to and decided by the Local Government Board.

(4.) A Provisional Order made under this Act shall be of no effect until confirmed, and, save as otherwise provided, until confirmed by Parliament, and sections two hundred and fourteen 41 & 42 Vic. and two hundred and fifteen of the Public Health Act, 1878, c. 52. shall, with the necessary modifications, apply for the purpose of any such Order.

102.—(1.) Any act to be done or instrument to be executed by or on behalf of the Local Government Board may be done or executed in the name of that Board by the president, or by the under secretary to the Lord Lieutenant, or by the vice-president, or by any person appointed by the president or vice-president to act on behalf of the vice-president.

(5.) A rule, order, or regulation made by the Local Govern- ment Board shall be valid if it is made under the seal of the Board and signed by any of the above-mentioned persons.

(3.) Every document purporting to be a rule, order, or regula- tion of the Local Government Board, and to be sealed and signed as above mentioned, shall be received in evidence, and be deemed to be a rule, order, or regulation duly made by the Board, unless the contrary is shown.

(4.) The Local Government Board may distribute the business of the Board among the several members thereof in such manner as the Board may think right.

(5) The President of the Local Government Board may appoint an inspector or auditor of the Board or other person to be tem- porarily a commissioner of the Board for the purpose of aiding in the additional work of the Board in bringing this Act into operation and in carrying it into effect and superintending the working thereof during a limited period. Such appointment shall be in the first instance for one year after the passing of this Act, but may, with the consent of the Treasury, be continued from year to year for a total term not exceeding five years after the passing of this Act.

(6.) There shall be paid to the temporary commissioner, out of moneys provided by Parliament, such sum as the Treasury may sanction, not exceeding together with any other remuneration received by him the remuneration paid to a commissioner of the Board.

103.—(1.) If within six months after an order of the Local Government Board is made under Part Four of this Act with respect to county boundaries a petition against the order, so far as it affects any county, is presented to the Local Government Board by the council or grand jury for the county, or by any sanitary authority, district council, or guardians, in the county, or by not less than one hundred parliamentary electors for the county, the order so far as it relates to that county shall be referred to the Appeal Commission in this Act mentioned, and after that Commission have held such inquiry as they think necessary, and given an opportunity of being heard to all parties concerned who apply within the prescribed time to be heard, may be annulled or varied by order of that Commission, and that order of the Commission shall after it comes into operation have effect as if made by the Local Government Board under this Act.

(2.) The order of the Commission shall not, unless it otherwise provides, come into operation until the second election of the county council, and if it so otherwise provides, the Commission shall by the same or any subsequent order make such arrangements respecting county and district councils and boards of guardians and the members thereof, and respecting all other matters, as appear necessary or expedient for bringing the order into operation at the earlier date, and for that purpose may make the like provisions as are authorised by or in pursuance of this Act to be made by the Local Government Board.

(3.) Where any other provision of this Act provides for an appeal to the Appeal Commission, the foregoing provisions of this section shall apply with the necessary modifications.

(4.) The Appeal Commission shall consist of the Vice-President of the Local Government Board and four other commissioners, of whom two at least shall be members of the Commons House of Parliament, appointed by the Lord Lieutenant.

(5.) Any vacancy arising among any such four commissioners, whether by death, resignation, incapacity, or otherwise, may be filled by the Lord Lieutenant; and the Lord Lieutenant may appoint any member of the Local Government Board to take the place of the Vice-President in case of his illness or unavoidable absence.

(6.) For the purpose of any inquiry, an Appeal Commissioner shall have the same powers as an inspector of the Local Government Board when holding an inquiry under the Public Health Act, 1878 ; and the Commission shall have the same power respecting costs as is given to the Local Government Board by section two hundred and ten of that Act.

(7.) Any expenses of the Appeal Commission and of any officer assigned by the Local Government Board to assist the Commission shall be defrayed in like manner as the remuneration of officers appointed by the Board for carrying this Act into effect is directed by Part Eight of this Act to be defrayed.

(8.) Any act of the Appeal Commission may be signified by any three of the commissioners under their hands.

61 & 62 Vic., c. 37. LOCAL GOVERNMENT (IRELAND) ACT, 1898.

PART V.

Supplemental.

41 & 42 Vic., c. 52.

61 & 62 VIC.,
c. 37.
LOCAL
GOVERN-
MENT
(IRELAND)
ACT, 1898.

PART VI.

*Orders
and Rules.*

Applica-
tion with
adaptations
by Order
in Council
of English
and Scotch
enactments
respecting
supple-
mental
provisions.

PART VI.

ORDERS AND RULES.

104.—(1.) There shall apply to Ireland so much as the Lord Lieutenant by Order in Council declares applicable of the English and Scotch enactments specified in the Fourth Schedule to this Act, and the enactments amending the same, being enactments relating among other matters to—

(a) the making of registers of electors according to street order ;

(b) elections of county and district councils and guardians ;

(c) acceptance of office, fine, resignation, casual vacancy, &c. ;

(d) disqualifications of persons for being members of a county or district council, or board of guardians, and of members of any such council or board, and their partners, for appointment to an office ;

(e) incorporation of county and district councils ;

(f) transfer of property and expenses of county and district councils ;

(g) accounts, audit, and annual budget ;

(h) borrowing by county councils ;

(i) transfer of powers of Treasury in relation to borrowing, and to the acquisition and disposition of land by councils of boroughs ;

(j) alteration of boundaries and adjustments of property and liabilities ;

(k) the division of a borough into wards or alteration of wards ;

(l) local inquiries and Provisional Orders by the Local Government Board ;

(m) construction of enactments relating to business transferred by this Act ;

(n) proceedings and committees of county and district councils, and chairman and vice-chairman of those councils ; and

(o) powers of the Local Government Board for the purpose of remedying defects and bringing the Act into full operation upon the commencement thereof, and transitional proceedings and savings.

(2.) An Order in Council under this section may—

(a) apply any of the said enactments to both county and district councils and guardians and town commissioners, and committees appointed by or comprising members of any of such councils, guardians, or commissioners, or to any of them, notwithstanding that they relate to county councils only or to district councils only or to guardians only ; and

(b) provide for the transfer to county councils of lunatic asylums and all property and liabilities connected therewith, and for the exception of any debt incurred (whether before or after the passing of this Act) on account of lunatic asylums from being reckoned in the limitation of amount imposed by any of the said enactments upon the borrowing by county councils, and for the joint committee of the counties comprised in a lunatic asylum district exercising jointly for the purpose of the lunatic asylum the powers of those councils relating to borrowing ; and

(c) make such adaptations of the said enactments as appear necessary or expedient for carrying into effect the application thereof to Ireland ; and

(d) make such adaptations of local Acts as appear required to bring them into conformity with any of the said enactments.

105. The Lord Lieutenant by Order in Council may make such adaptations of the Irish enactments specified in the Fifth Schedule to this Act, or of other enactments affected by this Act, as appear to him necessary or expedient for carrying into effect this Act or any Order in Council made thereunder ; and for that purpose may modify the provisions in the Valuation Acts as to dates and mode of procedure, and as to levying a rate pending an appeal.

106. The Lord Lieutenant by Order in Council may do all or any of the following things, that is to say—

(1.) Regulate the procedure of county and district councils in connection with the business transferred to them by this or any other Act from presentment sessions and grand juries :

(2.) Make such transitory provisions as appear to him necessary or expedient for bringing this Act into operation, and in particular—

(i) for regulating the actions of guardians and grand juries and presentment sessions and councils authorities and officers affected by this Act, during the period between the passing of this Act and the time at which this Act comes into full operation ;

(ii) for securing to existing officers until they begin to receive remuneration under the provisions of this Act the like remuneration as they would have received if this Act had not passed ;

(iii) for regulating the proceedings of the collector general of rates in Dublin until the abolition of his office, and for the estimating, raising, and collecting, until this Act comes into full operation, of the sums which but for such abolition would be raised by him ;

(iv) for the first elections, and for the retirement and first meetings and proceedings of councillors and aldermen and commissioners of a town elected at the first elections ;

(v) for regulating the continuance in or retirement from office of the members of any existing local authority affected by this Act ; and

61 & 62 VIC,.
c. 37.
LOCAL
GOVERN-
MENT
(IRELAND)
ACT, 1898.

PART VI.

*Orders
and Rules.*

Order in
Council for
adapting
Irish
enactments

Order in
Council for
regulating
procedure
of councils
and
making
transitory
provisions
for
bringing
Act into
operation.

61 & 62 VIC.
c. 37.
LOCAL
GOVERN-
MENT
(IRELAND)
ACT, 1898.

PART VI.

*Orders
and Rules.*

General
provisions
and
restrictions
as to Orders
in Council.

Rules and
Provisional
Orders by
Local
Govern-
ment
Board.

(vi) for enabling the Local Government Board to adjust any property, income, debts, liabilities, and expenses, of any area or local authority, or any other matter which requires adjustment in consequence of this Act, or any order made or thing done in pursuance of this Act within twelve months after the passing thereof.

107.—(1.) An Order of the Lord Lieutenant in Council under this Part of this Act, shall, save as herein-after mentioned, be made before the last day of January next after the passing of this Act, and unless annulled as herein-after mentioned shall be deemed to have been duly made and to be within the powers conferred by this Act, and no objection to the validity thereof shall be taken in any proceedings.

(2.) The Order shall be laid before both Houses of Parliament as soon as may be after it is made, and, if within the next subsequent forty days on which either House has sat, that House presents an address to Her Majesty praying that any such Order may either in whole or in part be annulled, Her Majesty in Council may annul the same either in whole or in part, as the case may require, and the Order or part so annulled shall thenceforth become void, without prejudice to the validity of any proceedings taken under the same in the meantime :

Provided that where any Order or any part thereof is so annulled the Lord Lieutenant in Council may, within six months thereafter make another Order in place of the Order or part so annulled, subject nevertheless to be laid before Parliament and to be annulled by Her Majesty in Council in manner above mentioned, and so on as often as occasion requires.

108.—(1.) The Local Government Board may make rules —

(a) for carrying into effect the provisions of Part Three of this Act so far as regards councils and guardians and their officers ; and in particular for regulating—

(i) the communication by rural district councils and guardians to county councils and by county councils to urban district councils, of the amounts respectively required to be raised in each local financial year or any part thereof ; and

(ii) the estimates to be made by district councils or guardians or their officers of their receipts and expenditure in each local financial year ; and

(b) for regulating any matter authorised by this Act to be prescribed or to be regulated by rules of the Local Government Board ; and

(c) generally for carrying into effect this Act, so far as the Lord Lieutenant in Council is not authorised to make provision for that purpose.

(2.) The Local Government Board may make Provisional Orders for adapting any local Act to the provisions of this Act and of any Order in Council made thereunder.

61 & 62 VIC.,
c. 37.
LOCAL
GOVERN-
MENT
(IRELAND)
ACT, 1898.
___
PART VII.

PART VII.

DEFINITIONS, SHORT TITLE, AND REPEALS.

109.—(1.) In this Act, unless the context otherwise requires :— *Definitions and Repeals.*

The expression " union " means a poor law union :

The expression "borough" means a municipal borough having *Interpretation of certain terms in the Act.* a town council :

The expression " town" means the area comprised in any town 9 Geo. IV. or township having commissioners under the Lighting of *c. 82.* Towns (Ireland) Act, 1828, or the Towns Improvement 17 & 18 Vic., (Ireland) Act, 1854, or under any local Act : *c. 103.*

The expression " mayor " includes a lord mayor :

The expression " guardians " means a board of guardians :

The expression "presentment sessions" includes road sessions and special road sessions :

The expressions "local authority" and "authority" respectively include a grand jury and presentment sessions :

The expression " Local Government Board " means the Local Government Board for Ireland :

The expression " Board of Control for lunatic asylums " means the Commissioners for General Control and Correspondence, and for the superintending and directing the erection, establishment, and regulation of asylums for the lunatic poor in Ireland :

The expression "Commissioner of Valuation" means the Commissioner of Valuation and Boundary Surveyor :

The expression "jud$_o$e of assize " shall, as respects the county of Dublin, or the county of the city of Dublin, mean the High Court or any judge thereof :

The expression " revising barrister " has the same meaning as in the Parliamentary Registration (Ireland) Act, 1885 : 48 & 49 Vic., c. 17.

The expression " high constable or collector of a barony " includes a collector for a district of a barony appointed under 11 & 12 Vic. the County Cess (Ireland) Act, 1848 : c. 32.

The expression " Local Taxation (Ireland) Account " has the same meaning as in the Probate Duties (Scotland and 51 & 52 Vic., Ireland) Act, 1868 : c. 60.

The expression " road " includes any bridge, pipe, arch, gullet, fence, railing, or wall forming part of such road :

The expression " public work " means any road or work in respect of which, under the Grand Juries Acts, a presentment might but for this Act be made by any presentment sessions for a barony or county at large or any grand jury :

The expression " maintenance " when used in relation to any road or public work, includes the reasonable improvement and enlargement of such road or work :

The expression " lunatic asylum " means an asylum for the lunatic poor under the Lunatic Asylum Acts :

61 & 62 VIC.,
c. 37.
LOCAL
GOVERN-
MENT
(IRELAND)
ACT, 1898.

PART VII.

*Definitions
and
Repeals.*

The expression "landlord," when used with reference to land or other hereditaments, means the immediate lessor or other person receiving rent in respect of such land or hereditaments :

The expression "holding" means any house or land or house and land held by a tenant of a landlord for the same term and under the same contract of tenancy :

The expression ' rateable value," when used in relation to any hereditament or area, means the annual rateable value under the Valuation Acts of such hereditament, or of all the hereditaments comprised in such area :

The expression "local government electors" means as respects any county or borough, district, electoral division, ward, or other area, the persons for the time being registered in the local government register of electors in respect of qualifications within such county, district, division, borough, ward, or other area :

The expression "prescribed" means prescribed by the Local Government Board :

The expression "existing" means, as respects any officer, an officer holding office on the last day March one thousand eight hundred and ninety-eight, and also on the appointed day, and in any other case existing at the time specified in the enactment in which the expression is used, and if no such time is expressed, then at the appointed day for the coming into operation of such enactment :

The expression "powers" includes rights, jurisdiction, capacities, privileges, and immunities :

The expression "duties" includes responsibilities and obligations :

The expression "powers and duties" includes all powers and duties conferred or imposed by or arising under any local Act :

The expression "office" includes any office, situation, or employment, and the expression "officer" shall be construed accordingly :

The expression "pensionable office" means an office coming within the provisions of any Act authorising the grant of a superannuation allowance :

The expression "local financial" means the twelve months ending the thirty-first day of March :

The expression "Registration Acts" means the Acts and enactments relating to the registration of parliamentary voters in Ireland :

The Grand Juries (Ireland) Acts, 1816 to 1895, are in this Act referred to as the Grand Juries Acts, and each of them is in this Act referred to as the Grand Juries Act of the year in which it was passed :

The expression "Lunatic Asylum Acts" means the Acts specified in Part Two of the First Schedule to this Act :

The Public Health (Ireland) Acts, 1878 to 1896, are in this Act referred to as the Public Health Acts, ánd each of them is in this Act referred to as the Public Health Act of the year in which it was passed : *61 & 62 Vic., c. 37. LOCAL GOVERN-MENT (IRELAND) ACT, 1898.*

The expression " Medical Charities Acts " means the Acts so defined by the Dispensary Houses (Ireland) Act, 1879, and includes the last-mentioned Act : *PART VII. Definitions and Repeals.*

The expression " Valuation Acts " means the Acts specified in Part Three of the First Schedule to this Act :

The expression " Dublin Metropolis Police Acts " means the Acts specified in Part Five of the First Schedule to this Act. *41 & 42 Vic., c. 52. 59 & 60 Vic., c. 54. 42 & 43 Vic., c. 25.*

Each of the Acts relating to the Dublin collection of rates specified in Part Four of the First Schedule to this Act is in this Act referred to by the short title in that schedule mentioned.

(2.) For the purposes of the Interpretation Act, 1889, this Act shall be deemed to be an Act amending the Poor Relief (Ireland) Act, 1838. *52 & 53 Vic., c. 63. 1 & 2 Vic., c. 56.*

110.—(1.) This Act shall extend to Ireland only, and may be cited as the Local Government (Ireland) Act, 1898. *Extent of Act, short titles, and repeal.*

(2.) The enactments specified in the Sixth Schedule to this Act are hereby repealed to the extent in the third column of that schedule mentioned.

Provided that—

(a) any enactment or document referring to any Act or enactment hereby repealed shall be construed to refer to this Act or to the corresponding enactments in this Act :

(b) the existing rules of the Lord Lieutenant in Council under the Lunatic Asylum Acts shall continue in force in every county and lunatic asylum district until the first regulations under this Act in respect of that county or district come into force, and upon any such regulations coming into force, the said rules shall cease as respects that county or district.

(3.) The order of the Lord Lieutenant in Council relating to the division of Tipperary may be varied by the Lord Lieutenant in Council, so as to bring the same into conformity with this Act and with the Orders in Council made in pursuance of this Act, but otherwise shall continue in force.

(4.) Any other enactments of any Act, whether general or local, touching any business tranferred to county or district councils or the county court by this Act, so far as they relate to any fiat or other sanction of a judge, court, or recorder, or relate to traverses or memorials other than memorials by a grand jury, shall be repealed.

61 & 62 Vic.,
c. 37.
LOCAL
GOVERN-
MENT
(IRELAND)
ACT, 1898.
_____
PART VIII.

PART VIII.

TRANSITORY PROVISIONS.

First Elections and Councils.

Transitory Provisions.

First elections of county and rural district councillors and urban guardians and first councils.

111.—(1.) The first election under this Act of county and rural district councillors and guardians in urban districts shall be held on the twenty-fifth day of March next after the passing of this Act, or on such day within fourteen days before or after that day as the Local Government Board may appoint.

(2.) The foregoing provisions of this section shall not apply to councillors of county boroughs.

(3.) The Local Government Board in the case of the first election—

(a) may give a direction under this Act with respect to a district electoral division not being a polling district, although there is no representation made by the county council; and

(b) if of opinion that any district electoral division ought to be divided, may allow more than two councillors to be elected for that division, and in that case each elector in that division may at the first election give one vote, and no more, for each of any number of persons not exceeding the number of councillors authorised by the Board to be elected for that division.

(4.) A poor law electoral division as adopted in fact for the purpose of registration in the year one thousand eight hundred and ninety-eight shall be deemed to have been legally so adopted, and shall, except so far as the Local Government Board otherwise direct, be a district electoral division for the purpose of the election of county and rural district councillors and guardians at the first election under this Act.

First election of aldermen and councillors in county boroughs and urban districts and of town commissioners.

112. The first election in accordance with this Act of aldermen and councillors of any county borough or any urban district and of town commissioners shall be held on the fifteenth day of January next after the passing of this Act, and except in the county boroughs of Belfast and Londonderry the whole number of aldermen and councillors of each borough or district and of commissioners of each town shall be then elected, and shall come into office on the day next after the day of election.

Additional councillors for first councils and additional members of first lunatic asylum committee.

113.—(1.) The grand jury of any county other than a county of a city or town at the spring assizes, or in the county of Dublin at the Easter presenting term, next after the passing of this Act, may choose or appoint a committee to choose from persons who are then serving, or have at any time during the previous three years served, as grand jurors, three persons who shall be additional councillors of the first council for that county.

(2.) The Lord Lieutenant may nominate persons to be additional members of the first committee of a county council (includ-

61 & 62 VIC.,
c. 37.
LOCAL .
GOVERN-
MENT
(IRELAND)
ACT. 1898.

PART VIII.

Transitory
Provisions.

ing the council of a county borough), or joint committee of such county councils, for any lunatic asylum district, but the number shall not exceed one-fourth of the whole number of the committee.

(3.) The first rural district council under this Act shall, at their first meeting, choose as additional councillors three persons from among the persons who have at any time during the preceding three years been ex-officio guardians of the union, co-extensive with, or comprising the whole or part of, their district, and have actually served as such guardians, and are willing to serve as district councillors, and, if they fail so to choose, the county council shall, as soon as may be, appoint from among those persons additional councillors, who shall be in the same position as if they had been so chosen ; and additional councillors so chosen or appointed shall also be additional guardians.

(4.) All additional councillors appointed or chosen under this part of this Act, and the additional members of the first committee for a lunatic asylum district, shall retire from office in the third year after the election of the council upon which, or upon the committee of which, they are appointed or chosen to serve, and shall so retire on the day fixed by this Act for the ordinary day of retirement of the councillors of such councils.

As to regis-
tration in
1898.

114.—(1.) In the year one thousand eight hundred and ninety-eight the Registration Acts shall have effect as if for every date therein mentioned in July or August in respect of any matter, other than one affecting qualification, there were substituted such day as is seven days later than that date.

(2.) As regards the registers of voters to be made in the year one thousand eight hundred and ninety-eight, no election shall be questioned by reason of any error or informality whatsoever in relation to the filling up the forms or lists, the forming, printing, publishing, revising, or completing the lists of voters, or the register of voters, for any county or borough, or by reason of any matter or thing not having been done within the time limited by law for that purpose. The signature of the chairman or revising barrister, or his deputy, to such register shall be conclusive evidence that such register has been in all repects duly made and revised at the time and in the manner prescribed by and in conformity with the Registration Acts and this Act and the rules made thereunder.

Existing Officers.

Provision
for interests
of existing
officers.

115.—(1.) Where the business of any authority is transferred by or in pursuance of this Act to any county or district council, the existing officers of that authority employed in that business, and not in any other business of that authority, shall become the officers of the council of that county or district in like manner, subject to the provisions of this section, as if they had been appointed by that council; and for the purpose of this section any secretary of the grand jury, county treasurer, county surveyor,

61 & 62 VIC.,
c. 37.
LOCAL
GOVERN-
MENT
(IRELAND)
ACT, 1898.

PART VIII

Transitory
Provisions.

assistant surveyor, county solicitor, public analyst for a county, and a high constable and collector or collector of a barony, and a deputy collector duly appointed under section one hundred and forty-eight of the Grand Juries Act, 1836, and also any deputy of the county treasurer or secretary of the Grand Jury, appointed with the approval of the Lord Lieutenant, who has devoted his whole time to his office, shall be deemed to be an officer of the grand jury, and the existing officers of every lunatic asylum shall be deemed to be existing officers of the governors and directors of that asylum ; and every existing officer of the grand jury of a county shall be transferred to the council of the county and not to the council of any urban county district.

(2.) The foregoing provisions of this section shall apply to a county of a city or town ; but, if it does not become a county borough, any existing officer of the grand jury shall become the officer of the council of the county at large of which such county of a city or town will by virtue of this Act form part.

(3.) For the purpose of the enactments relating to superannuation, the service of any existing officer of any authority before the transfer to a county or district council shall be reckoned as service under that council, and the service of any existing secretary as assistant or deputy secretary in the same county shall be reckoned as part of his service.

(4.) Any existing secretary of the grand jury, unless he dies or resigns, or is removed with the concurrence of the Local Government Board, shall become and continue the secretary of the county council up to the last day of March nineteen hundred, and may then, if he has given three months' previous notice in writing to the county council of his intention to retire, retire from office, and shall thereupon be entitled to receive an allowance under this Act of the same amount as if his office were abolished.

(5.) The county council may by notice given three months next before the said last day of March require such secretary to retire, and if they do so without the concurrence of the Local Government Board he shall be entitled to the same compensation under this Act as if his office were abolished.

(6.) If at any time after the said last day of March such secretary retires voluntarily, he shall be entitled to receive from the county council a superannuation allowance on the scale provided by the Acts and rules relating to Her Majesty's Civil Service, and the amount of such allowance in case of dispute shall be determined by the treasury.

(7.) If at any time before the said last day of March such secretary satisfies the Local Government Board that he is unable, through age or infirmity, to discharge the duties of his office under this Act, he may retire from office, and shall thereupon be entitled to receive an allowance under this Act of the same amount as if his office were abolished.

(8.) The secretary of the grand jury of the county of Tipperary shall become the secretary of the council of each riding of such county; and the foregoing provisions of this section shall apply as if he were separately the secretary of each such council, and the proportion of the remuneration, allowance, or compensation to be paid by each riding shall in default of agreement be determined by the Local Government Board.

(9.) An existing officer of the grand jury of any county of a city or town, who by this Act becomes the officer of the council of the county at large of which such county of a city or town will form part, shall perform under the like officer of the council of that county at large the like duties as he has hitherto performed as respects the county of a city or county of a town, but in other respects the foregoing provisions of this section with respect to the like officer of a grand jury of a county at large shall apply to him.

(10.) Every county council shall, within six weks after their first meeting, submit to the Local Government Board a scheme setting forth their arrangements for the collection of the poor rate and the officers they propose to employ for the purpose, and the names and descriptions of the existing officers transferred to the county council by this Act (whether high constables and collectors, or collectors of a barony, or deputy collectors, or poor rate collectors of the guardians, or deputy collectors of such poor rate collectors, where such deputy collectors devote their whole time to the work of rate collection) whom they propose to employ as officers under such scheme, and the scheme shall not authorise the employment of officers not transferred to or previously employed by the council if sufficient existing officers have expressed their willingness to serve.

(11.) The scheme shall provide for the existing officers employed under the scheme receiving remuneration substantially identical with that which they formerly received.

(12.) An existing officer who can be employed under the scheme—

(a) if he holds a pensionable office, and has within the prescribed time, notified his willingness to serve, shall, if he is not continued by the scheme as an officer of the county council, be entitled to receive from the county council the same compensation under this Act as if his office were abolished ; and

(b) if he holds a pensionable office, and has not within the prescribed time expressed his willingness to serve, and is not continued by the scheme as an officer of the county council shall be entitled to receive from the county council a gratuity ; and

(c) if he does not hold a pensionable office, and either within the prescribed time expresses his unwillingness to serve, or is not continued by the scheme as an officer of the county council. shall be entitled to receive from the county council a gratuity.

61 & 62 VIC.,
c. 37.
LOCAL
GOVERN-
MENT
(IRELAND)
ACT, 1898.

PART VIII.

*Transitory
Provisions.*

59 & 60 VIC.,
c. 41.

(13.) Every such gratuity shall be according to the scale in Part One of the Seventh Schedule to this Act: Provided that, until the expiration of not less than twelve months after receiving a gratuity under that schedule, an officer shall not be qualified to be appointed to any office under the county council, unless he refunds to the county council the gratuity. Of such gratuity, one-half shall be repaid to the county council out of the moneys standing to the Local Taxation (Ireland) Account by virtue of the Local Taxation (Ireland) Estate Duty Act, 1896, and the half of any gratuity so refunded shall be repaid by the council to that account.

(14.) For the purpose of the foregoing enactments a person appointed collector under the County Dublin Grand Jury Act, 1844, shall be deemed to hold a pensionable office.

(15.) The Local Government Board may approve any such scheme with or without modifications ; and all officers employed in pursuance of the scheme shall be deemed to be poor rate collectors appointed by the county council within the meaning of this Act.

(16.) If in the case of any officer the area in which his duties are required to be performed is, by reason of any alteration of any boundary by or in pursuance of or for the purposes of this Act, increased or diminished, the officer shall be bound to perform his duties in such altered area.

(17.) If, by reason of a change made within six months after the passing of this Act in the boundaries of a union or dispensary district, the office of any existing dispensary doctor becomes in the opinion of the Local Government Board unnecessary, that office shall be deemed to be abolished within the meaning of the enactment applied by this Act ; and any compensation payable to him shall be paid by the guardians of the unions which comprise his former district in such proportion as may be agreed upon, or in default of agreement be determined by the Local Government Board.

(18.) Subject to the provisions of this Act, every existing officer transferred under this section shall hold his office by the same tenure and upon the same terms and conditions as heretofore, and while performing the same or analogous duties shall receive not less remuneration than heretofore ; and if, by reason of any alteration of boundary or other thing done by or in pursuance of this Act, his duties are increased or diminished, the officer shall be bound to perform those duties, and shall receive such increase or diminution of remuneration in proportion to the increase or diminution of his duties as the Local Government Board may determine, subject nevertheless in case of diminution to such compensation as is provided by this Act ; provided that any county or district council may, subject to the approval of the Local Government Board, make a special agreement with any of such existing officers respecting the terms and conditions on which he may continue to hold his office, and the remuneration which he shall receive therefor.

(19.) Section one hundred and twenty of the Local Government Act, 1888, set out in Part Two of the Seventh Schedule to this Act (which relates to compensation to existing officers), shall apply in the case of existing officers affected by this Act, who are remunerated out of the cess or rate raised in any county or district, or in an urban district out of any borough or corporate fund, whether officers above in this section mentioned or not, and references in the said section one hundred and twenty to the county council shall include references to a district council ; and if any officer transferred by this Act to a council who can be removed without the concurrence of the Local Government Board or the Lord Lieutenant (and is not a banking company) is within five years from the date of the transfer removed from his office for any cause other than misconduct or incapacity, his office shall be deemed to have been abolished within the meaning of the said section.

(20.) Any difference as to the council to whom an officer is transferred by this Act shall, in the absence of agreement, be determined by the Local Government Board.

(21.) All expenses incurred by any council in pursuance of this section shall be paid as expenses of the execution of this Act, and in the case of a county council may, if the county council, with the consent of the Local Government Board, so direct, be defrayed as district charges.

(22.) The provision of a gratuity by a council to any existing officer under this Act shall be a purpose for which such council may borrow in accordance with the enactments relating to borrowing by such council.

(23.) Every pension, allowance, or other compensation, granted under this section shall be payable to or in trust for the officer to whom it is granted, and shall not be assignable for nor chargeable with his debts or other liabilities.

116. If any existing town clerk of a borough or clerk to the commissioners of any town is removed from his office for any cause other than misconduct or incapacity, he shall, without prejudice to any existing right, be entitled to receive from the council of such borough or district, if he is qualified for a superannuation allowance under the Local Officers Superannuation (Ireland) Act, 1869, a superannuation allowance on the scale provided by the Acts and rules relating to Her Majesty's civil service, and if he is not so qualified a gratuity according to the scale in Part One of the Seventh Schedule to this Act, and the amount of any such allowance or gratuity shall, in case of dispute, be determined by the Treasury, and while any such clerk remains in office he shall receive not less remuneration than heretofore, and shall, if his duties are increased, receive such increase of salary in proportion to that increase of duties as the Local Government Board may determine.

117.—(1.) Each of the following officers, namely, the existing clerk of the Crown and peace for the county of the city of

Marginal notes:

61 & 62 VIC. c. 37. LOCAL GOVERNMENT (IRELAND) ACT, 1898.

PART VIII.

Transitory Provisions.

51 & 52 Vic., c. 41.

Provision for existing town clerks

32 & 33 Vic. c. 79.

Existing clerks of Crown and Peace.

61 & 62 Vic.,
c. 37.
LOCAL
GOVERN-
MENT
(IRELAND)
ACT, 1898.
Kilkenny, and the existing clerk of the Crown and peace for the county of the town of Galway, shall continue to hold his office and to perform the duties thereof for the like area, and while performing the same shall be entitled to receive the same emoluments, as heretofore.

PART VIII.

Transitory Provisions.

coroners, and justices.

(2.) The existing coroner of the county of the town of Galway, and the existing coroner of the county of the town of Carrickfergus shall respectively continue to be coroner in like manner as if the county of the town were a coroner's district of the county of Galway or of Antrim, as the case requires.

(3.) Every existing justice of the county of the town of Galway, or the county of the town of Carrickfergus, shall be a justice of the county of Galway or of Antrim, as the case requires, in like manner as if he were named a justice in the commission of the peace for such county ; and the said county of the town shall, until any other district is made, form part of the county petty sessional district to which it adjoins, or, if it adjoins more than one such district, then of the district with which it has the longest common boundary, and any such existing justice shall, except when at quarter or general sessions, act only within the petty sessional district of which such county of a town forms part.

Super-
annuation
allowance
of existing
officers.

118.—(1.) Every existing officer who is by this Act transferred to any county or district council, or is an officer of any board of guardians, and would, if he were to retire on the appointed day, be qualified for a superannuation allowance, shall, without prejudice to any existing right, when he resigns or ceases to hold his office for some cause other than misconduct, be entitled to receive a superannuation allowance on the scale and according to the Acts and rules relating to Her Majesty's civil service.

(2.) For the purpose of the provisions of this Part of this Act with respect to existing officers, the expression "qualified for superannuation allowance" shall mean qualified as regards age and length of service, and except as respects a medical officer to whom the Medical Officers Superannuation Act (Ireland), 1869, applies, the devotion of his whole time to the service.

32 & 33 Vic.,
c. 50.

Provision
for existing
officers of
urban
authorities
other than
town
clerks.

119. The provisions of this Act with respect to officers transferred to a county council shall apply to all existing officers of any urban district council or town commissioners other than a town clerk or clerk to the commissioners, in like manner as if they were officers transferred by this Act to such council or commissioners, and an annual election or appointment shall not in future be necessary in the case of any such existing officer.

Provision
as to county
cess in
arrear.

120. Nothing in this Act shall prevent any high constable and collector, or collector of a barony, from collecting, in like manner as if this Act had not passed, any county cess comprised in any warrant held by him on the appointed day :

Provided that, if such constable or collector alleges that any portion of the said cess not recovered by him is irrecoverable, or that from sufficient cause he has been unable to collect the same before the appointed day, he may apply to the county council to ^{61 & 62 VIC.} relieve him from so paying that portion, or if he has paid it to the county treasurer, to repay him the sum paid ; and the county council, with the approval of the Local Government Board, if it seems, having regard to the diligence used by the high constable or collector, and to the poundage he received in respect of the collection, and to all the circumstances of the case, equitable to grant the application in whole or in part, may so grant the application and pay the necessary sum as part of their expenses in the execution of this Act ; provided always that, in the case of a high constable or collector who is not employed as a rate collector under a scheme made in pursuance of this Part of this Act, in the event of the refusal of such application by the county council, the high constable and collector or collector of a barony may appeal from such refusal to the Local Government Board, who shall entertain the subject matter of such appeal, and make such order thereon as to them seems just.

61 & 62 VIC. c. 37.
LOCAL GOVERN-MENT (IRELAND) ACT, 1898.

PART VIII.

Transitory Provisions.

121. Every existing clerk of a union shall, unless he otherwise agrees with the county council, or urban district council, as the case may be, continue to perform the duties of the clerk of a union under the Registration Acts and the Juries (Ireland) Acts, 1871 to 1894, and every collector of poor rate shall continue to give the same information and assistance as heretofore to that clerk in relation to the said duties.

Perfo-mance of duties under Registra-tion and Juries Acts by existing officers. 34 & 35 Vic., c. 65. 57 & 58 Vic., c. 49.

Miscellaneous.

122.—(1.) The Local Government Board and Commissioner of Valuation respectively may, with the consent of the Treasury, as to number and remuneration, appoint and remove such officers and other persons as they or he may think necessary for the purposes of any adjustment under this Part of this Act, or otherwise, for the purpose of any work to be done for carrying this Act into effect, if such adjustment is made or work is done within twelve months after the commencement thereof, and the remuneration and expenses of all officers and other persons so appointed shall be defrayed out of the money standing to the Local Taxation (Ireland) Account under the Local Taxation (Ireland) Estate Duty Act. 1896.

Employ-ment and payment of officers by Local Govern-ment Board

59 & 60 Vic. c. 41.

(2.) The officers employed in auditing county treasurers' accounts, who were formerly officers in the office of the Receiver Master and were subsequently transferred to the Local Govern-ment Board, shall become officers under that Board at the same remuneration as they have hitherto received ; and they shall be qualified to receive a grant of such superannuation allowance as is authorised by the Local Officers (Ireland) Superannuation Act, 1869 ; and their service as such officers after the transfer shall, as well as their past service, be reckoned as service for the purpose of such superannuation allowance, and any such allowance shall be paid out of the fee fund mentioned in the said Act ; and any surplus of that fee fund above what is required to meet such

32 & 33 Vic. c. 79.

61 & 62 Vic., c. 37. LOCAL GOVERN-MENT (IRELAND) ACT, 1898.

PART VIII,

Transitory Provisions.

Provisions consequential on change of boundaries of judicial county.

superannuation and other expenses payable thereout shall be paid to the Local Taxation (Ireland) Account, and be applied as if it had been paid under the said Act of 1896.

123.—(1.) Any change made by this Act, or by an order made within six months after the passing of this Act, as respects the boundary of a judicial county shall not take effect until the jurors' books which are revised in the year one thousand eight hundred and ninety-nine come into operation; Provided that in that year the jurors' lists and books shall be made out by the same officer and in the same manner as if the said order had taken effect.

(2.) Every matter, civil or criminal, arising before such change takes effect, which would have been heard, tried, determined, or otherwise dealt with, by any court or justices, may after such change takes effect be heard, tried, determined, and dealt with in like manner as if such change had taken effect before the said matter arose.

(3.) Provided that, where any proceeding in relation to any such matter had begun before the change took effect, the same may, if the court or justices so direct, be continued as if the change had not taken effect, and recognizances existing at the date of such change shall have effect and may be enforced in like manner, as nearly as circumstances admit, as they would have been if such change had not taken effect.

Commencement and Appointed Day.

Commencement of Act.

124.—(1.) Subject as in this Act mentioned, this Act shall, in each administrative county, come into operation as to rural district councils and guardians on the twenty-fifth day of March, and as to county councils and urban districts on the first day of April, and as to all other matters on the first day of April next after the passing thereof; or on such other day, not more than twelve months earlier or later, as in any case the Local Government Board (but after the election of county councillors for such county, on the application of the county council) may appoint, either generally or with reference to any particular provision of this Act, and different days may be appointed for different purposes and different provisions of this Act, whether contained in the same section or in different sections or for different counties, and where any particular day is appointed for any particular provision of this Act coming into operation, that provision shall not come into force until the day so appointed.

(2.) Provided that the enactments relating to the registration of local government electors, or to the elections, or to any matter required to be done for the purpose of bringing this Act into operation on the appointed day, shall come into effect on the passing of this Act.

(3.) A reference in any enactment of this Act to the appointed day shall mean the day upon which such enactment comes into operation.

SCHEDULES.

FIRST SCHEDULE.

ACTS REFERRED TO.

PART I.

Section 5.

Enactments relating to Compensation for Criminal Injury.

Session and Chapter.	Short Title.	Enactments referred to.
6 & 7 Will. 4, c. 116,	The Grand Jury (Ireland) Act, 1836.	Section one hundred and six ; sections one hundred and thirty-five to one hundred and forty so far as unrepealed.
11 & 12 Vict. c. 69, .	The Malicious Injuries (Ireland) Act, 1848.	The whole Act.
16 & 17 Vict. c. 38, .	The Malicious Injuries (Ireland) Act, 1853.	The whole Act.
57 & 58 Vict. c. 60, .	The Merchant Shipping Act, 1894.	Section five hundred and fifteen, so far as it relates to Ireland.

Also any enactment applying or amending any of the above enactments, or otherwise touching compensation thereunder.

PART II.

Section 109.

Lunatic Asylum Acts.

Session and Chapter.	Short Title.
1 & 2 Geo. 4, c. 33, . .	The Lunacy (Ireland) Act, 1821.
7 Geo. 4, c. 14, . . .	The Lunacy (Ireland) Act, 1826.
11 Geo. 4, and 1 Will. 4, c. 22.	The Richmond Lunatic Asylum Act, 1830.
8 & 9 Vict., c. 107, . .	The Central Criminal Lunatic Asylum (Ireland) Act, 1845.
9 & 10 Vict., c. 115, . .	The Lunatic Asylums (Ireland) Act, 1846.
18 & 19 Vict., c. 109, . .	The Lunatic Asylums Repayment of Advances (Ireland) Act, 1855.
30 & 31 Vict., c. 118, . .	The Lunacy (Ireland) Act, 1867.
31 & 32 Vict., c. 97, . .	The Lunatic Asylums (Ireland) Accounts Audit Act, 1868.
38 & 39 Vict., c. 67, . .	The Lunatic Asylums (Ireland Act, 1875.
53 & 54 Vict., c. 31, . .	The Pauper Lunatic Asylums (Ireland) (Superannuation) Act, 1890.
60 & 61 Vict., c. xxxvii, .	Richmond District Asylum Act, 1897.

Section 109.

PART III.

Valuation Acts.

Session and Chapter.		Short Title.
15 & 16 Vict., c. 63,	. .	The Valuation (Ireland) Act, 1852.
17 & 18 Vict., c. 8,	.	The Valuation (Ireland) Act, 1854.
19 & 20 Vict., c. 63,	.	The Grand Juries (Ireland) Act, 1856.
23 & 24 Vict., c. 4,	.	The Annual Revision of Rateable Property (Ireland) Amendment Act, 1860.
27 & 28 Vict., c. 52,	.	The Valuation (Ireland) Act, 1864.
37 & 38 Vict., c. 70,	.	The Valuation (Ireland) Amendment Act, 1874.
17 & 18 Vict., c. 17,	.	The Boundary Survey (Ireland) Act, 1854.
20 & 21 Vict., c. 45,	.	The Boundary Survey (Ireland) Act, 1857.
22 & 23 Vict., c. 8,	.	The Boundary Survey (Ireland) Act, 1859.

Sections 66, 109.

PART IV.

Dublin Collection of Rates Acts.

Session and Chapter.	Title.	Short Title.
12 & 13 Vict., c. 91,	An Act to provide for the collection of rates in the City of Dublin.	The Dublin Collection of Rates Act, 1849.
17 & 18 Vict., c. 22,	An Act to enable the Collector - General of Dublin to levy money to repay a certain outlay by the corporation for preserving and improving the port of Dublin in and about repairing the the quay wall of the River Liffey, and for future repairs thereof, and for repairing and rebuilding bridges over the said river.	The Dublin Bridge Act, 1854.

PART V.

Dublin Metropolis Police Acts.

Section 109.

Session and Chapter.	Title or Short Title.
6 & 7 Will. 4, c. 29,	The Dublin Police Act, 1836.
7 Will. 4 & 1 Vict. c. 25,	The Dublin Police Act, 1837.
2 & 3 Vict. c. 78,	The Dublin Police Act, 1839.
5 & 6 Vict. c. 24,	The Dublin Police Act, 1842.
12 & 13 Vict. c. 91,	An Act to provide for the collection of rates in the city of Dublin.
22 & 23 Vict. c. 52,	The Dublin Police Act, 1859.
31 & 32 Vict. c. 95,	The Dublin Police Act, 1867,.
37 & 38 Vict. c 23,	The Resident Magistrates and Police Commissioners Salaries Act, 1874.
46 & 47 Vict. c. 14,	The Constabulary and Police (Ireland) Act, 1883.

SECOND SCHEDULE.

Section 12.

COUNTY BOROUGHS.

Dublin.
Belfast.
Cork.

Limerick.
Londonderry.
Waterford.

THIRD SCHEDULE.

Local Taxation Licences.

Section 58.

Licences for the sale of intoxicating liquor for consumption on the premises :

Retailers of spirits (publicans).
Retailers of spirits, occasional licences.
Retailers of beer.
Retailers of beer and wine.

Retailers of wine.
Retailers of wine, occasional licences.
Retailers of sweets.

Licences for the sale of intoxicating liquor by retail, by persons not licensed to deal therein, for consumption off the premises :

Retailers of spirits (grocers).
Retailers of beer and wine.

Retailers of wine.
Retailers of table beer.

Licences to deal in game.

Licences for—

Beer dealers.
Spirit dealers.
Sweet dealers.
Wine dealers.
Refreshment house keepers.
Guns.
Appraisers.

Auctioneers.
Hawkers.
House agents
Pawnbrokers.
Plate dealers.
Tobacco dealers.

Certificates for killing game.

FOURTH SCHEDULE.

English and Scotch Enactments capable of being applied.

Session and Chapter.	Short Title.	Enactments capable of being applied.
38 & 39 Vict. c. 55,	The Public Health Act, 1875.	Section one hundred and ninety-nine, and sub-sections six and eleven of Schedule One.
41 & 42 Vict. c. 26,	The Parliamentary and Municipal Registration Act, 1878.	Section twenty-one.
45 & 46 Vict. c. 50,	The Municipal Corporations Act, 1882.	Section seven, sub-section one of section twelve, sub-section three of section fifteen, section twenty-two, sub-section one of section twenty-seven, sub-sections one and three to six of section twenty-eight, sections thirty, thirty-four, thirty-five, thirty-six, and thirty-seven, sub-section four of section thirty-nine, sections forty and forty-one, sub-section one of section forty-two, sections sixty-one and sixty-eight, Schedule Two, and Schedule Eight.
51 & 52 Vict. c. 10,	The County Electors Act, 1888.	Sub-section three of section four.
51 & 52 Vict. c. 41,	The Local Government Act, 1888.	Sub-section six of section two, sub-sections one, three, and four of section fifty-four, sub-sections one to six of section fifty-seven, sections fifty-nine, sixty, and sixty-three, sub-sections one, two, and three of section sixty-four, sub-section three of section sixty-five, sub-sections seven and eight of section sixty-eight, sections sixty-nine, seventy, seventy-two, seventy-four and seventy-five, sub-section two of section seventy-six, section seventy-eight, sub-section three of section seventy-nine, sub-sections one to three of section eighty, section eighty-one, sub-section

Session and Chapter.	Short Title.	Enactments capable of being applied.
51 & 52 Vict. c. 41 —*cont.*		three of section eighty-two, sub-sections one, two, and five of section eighty-seven, section one hundred, sub-sections one, three, and four of section one hundred and eight, section one hundred and ten (except sub-section three), section one hundred and eleven (except sub-section three), and sections one hundred and twenty-two, one hundred and twenty-three, and one hundred and twenty-four.
52 & 53 Vict. c. 50,	The Local Government (Scotland) Act, 1889.	Sub-section one of section nine, and sub-section five of section eighty-three.
54 & 55 Vict. c. 68,	The County Councils (Elections) Act, 1891.	Section five.
56 & 57 Vict. c. 9,	The Municipal Corporations Act, 1893.	The whole Act.
56 & 57 Vict. c. 73,	The Local Government Act, 1894.	Sub-section two (so far as relates to the qualification of women) and sub-section five of section twenty, sub-section two (so far as relates to the qualification of women) and sub-section five of section twenty three, sub-sections four and seven of section twenty-four, sections forty-three, forty-six, and forty-eight, sub-sections three, four, and five of section fifty-five, sub-sections one, two, and three of section fifty-eight, sub-sections one and five of section fifty-nine, sections sixty seven and sixty-eight sub-sections one and three of section seventy, sections seventy-three and seventy-five, sub-section five of section eighty-five, and Part Four of Schedule One.
59 & 60 Vict c. 1, . .	The Local Government (Elections) Act, 1896.	Section one.

FIFTH SCHEDULE.

IrIsh Enactments subject to Adaptation by Order in Council.

The Grand Juries Acts.·
The Municipal Corporations (Ireland) Act, 1840.
The Lighting of Towns (Ireland) Act, 1828.
The Towns Improvement (Ireland) Act, 1854.
The Public Health Acts, 1878 to 1896.
The Valuation Acts.
The Registration Acts.
The Lunatic Asylum Acts.
The Local Government (Ireland) Act, 1871.
The Local Government Board (Ireland) Act, 1872.
The Tramways (Ireland) Acts, 1860 to 1896.

SIXTH SCHEDULE

Acts repealed.

Part I.—Grand Juries Acts.

Session and Chapter.	Short Title.	Extent of Repeal.
4 Geo. 4, c. 33, .	The County Treasurers (Ireland) Act, 1823.	The whole Act so far as unrepealed.
3 & 4 Will. 4, c. 37,	An Act to alter and amend the laws relating to the temporalities of the church in Ireland.	Section seventy-two.
3 & 4 Will. 4, c. 78,	The Grand Juries (Ireland) Act, 1833.	Section seventy-four from "Provided always" to the end of the section.
6 & 7 Will. 4, c. 116.	The Grand Jury (Ireland) Act, 1836.	Sections four to twenty-eight. Section twenty-nine from "shall inspect the "schedules" to "the said "commission and such "sheriff," and the word "so" where the same next occurs, and from "and the clerk of the "Crown" to the end of the section. Section thirty. Section thirty-two from "or to act" to the end of the section. Section thirty-three from "and the assizes of each "county" to the end of

Session and Chapter.	Short Title.	Extent of Repeal.
6 & 7 Will. 4, c. 116 —*cont.*		the section, and so much of the rest of the section as relates to the powers and duties of the grand jury in relation to the business transferred by this Act.
		Section thirty-four from " other than those " to " concerns of the county," and from "and " the whole of such " fiscal " down to "here- " inafter provided and," and from " save the " making " to the end of the section.
		Section thirty-five to " provided further that."
		Section thirty-seven.
		Section thirty-eight from " which fact together " with the necessity " to the end of the section.
		Sections thirty-nine, and forty.
		Section forty-one.
		Section forty-two.
		Section forty-three from " and each such sur- veyor " down to "instal- " ments at each assizes,' and from " and every " such assistant " to the end of the section.
		Section forty five.
		Section forty-six from " and in .case " to the end of the section.
		Sections forty-seven to forty-nine.
		Section fifty from " pro- " vided always " to the end of the section.
		Section fifty-two from " provided always " to the end of the section.
		Section fifty-five from " unless such new " to the end of the section.
		Sections sixty to sixty- four.
		Sections sixty-nine from " and whenever any pre- " sentment " to the end of the section.
		Sections seventy - two, seventy-four, seventy- five, and eighty-one.
		Section eighty-four from " and to set forth " to " yearly instalments," and from " and the trea- " surer " to the end of the section.

Session and Chapter.	Short Title.	Extent of Repeal.
6 & 7 Will. 4. c. 116—*cont.*		Section eighty-seven from "and every person ap-" "pointed" to the end of the section. Sections ninety-one and ninety-two. Section ninety-three except as respects the repayment of advances made before the commencement of this Act. Sections ninety-four and ninety-six. Section one hundred and seven, from "and such "presentment" to the end of the section. In section one hundred and ten the words "secretaries to grand "juries," "medical "officers of prisons," and "payable half-yearly at "each assizes by equal "moieties," and from "and the grand jury at "any assizes," to the end of the section, so far as respects officers appointed under this Act. Section one hundred and eleven. In section one hundred and seventeen, the words "high constable" wherever they occur. Section one hundred and twenty-four. Section one hundred and twenty-six, except as respects the repayment of advances made before the commencement of this Act. Sections one hundred and twenty-seven to one hundred and thirty-four so far as unrepealed. Section one hundred and thirty-five, from "any "person or persons "injured" to "touching "the said offence and." Sections one hundred and thirty-six, one hundred and thirty-eight, one hundred and thirty-nine to "received to any such "presentment," one hundred and forty-two, and one hundred and forty-four. Sections one hundred and forty-five to one hundred and forty-nine.

Session and Chapter.	Short Title.	Extent of Repeal.
6 & 7 Will. 4, c. 116—*cont.*		Sections one hundred and fifty-two to one hundred and fifty-four. Section one hundred and fifty-five, from " sanc-" tioned" to " may be " made." Section one hundred and sixty-six. Sections one hundred and seventy - five to, one hundred and seventy-seven. Schedule Z, Form A, Form B, and Form C; Schedules X, Y, and T. In Schedule S, anything relating to medical officers of prisons and secretaries to grand jury.
7 Will. 4. & 1 Vict. c. 2.	The Grand Jury (Ireland) Act, 1837.	Section two, from " and " for the more speedy " to the end of section. Sections three, four, and eight. Sections twelve to sixteen.
7 Will. 4, and 1 Vict., c. 54.	The County Treasurers (Ireland) Act, 1837.	The whole Act so far as unrepealed, except section seven so far as that section relates to existing treasurers not banking companies.
1 & 2 Vict., c. 51,	The Grand Jury Cess (Dublin) Act, 1838.	Section two.
1 & 2 Vict., c. 53,	The County Treasurers (Ireland) Act, 1838.	The whole Act so far as unrepealed, except section one so far as that section relates to existing treasurers not banking companies.
1 & 2 Vict., c. 115,	The County Dublin Baronies Act, 1838,	The whole Act so far as unrepealed.
1 & 2 Vict., c. 116,	The County Institutions (Ireland) Act, 1838.	The whole Act so far as unrepealed.
2 & 3 Vict., c. 50,	The Public Works (Ireland) Act, 1839.	Sections eighteen and nineteen, except as respects the repayment of advances made before the commencement of this Act. Sections twenty-two to twenty-four.

Session and Chapter.	Short Title.	Extent of Repeal.
4 & 5 Vict., c 10,	An Act for extending to the county of the city of Dublin the provisions of an Act passed in the nineteenth and twentieth years of His late Majesty King George the Third, in Ireland, intituled " An Act to prevent " the detestable "practices of " houghing cattle, " burning of houses, " barns, haggards, "·and corn, and for " other purposes," so far as relates to burning of houses.	The whole Act.
6 & 7 Vict., c. 32,	The Grand Juries (Ireland) Act, 1843.	The whole Act, except sections fourteen, nineteen, twenty, and twenty-six.
7 & 8 Vict., c. 106,	The County Dublin Grand Jury Act, 1844.	Sections two to four. Section five from " and in "case" to end of section. Section six. Sections seven to twelve. Section thirteen from " and whenever any pre- "sentment " to the end of the section. Sections sixteen and eighteen Sections twenty-seven and twenty-eight. Section twenty-nine, except as respects the repayment of advances made before the commencement of this Act. Sections thirty and forty-one. Section forty-two from " and such presentment" to the end of the section. Section forty-five from " payable half-yearly " to "in the said schedule." Section forty-six. Section forty-seven from " subject nevertheless " to the end of the section. Section fifty-one, the words "the judges of the " Court of Queen's Bench " or," wherever those words occur, " or any " finance committee," and " or the finance " committee." Section fifty-eight from " provided always that " to the end of the section.

Session and Chapter.	Short Title.	Extent of Repeal.
7 & 8 Vict., c. 106 —*cont.*		Section sixty-one. Section sixty-two. Sections sixty-four to eighty-four. Section eighty-five from "which fact, together "with the necessity," to the end of the section. Sections eighty-six to one hundred and six. In section one hundred and eight, the words " or "any road warden" and " or road warden " wherever those words occur. Section one hundred and nine. Section one hundred and ten from "and every "person " to the end of the section. Sections one hundred and eleven and one hundred and twelve. Section one hundred and fourteen from " sanctioned " to " may be made." Sections one hundred and twenty-two to one hundred and twenty-eight. Sections one hundred and thirty-one, one hundred and thirty-four, and one hundred and thirty-five. Schedules Number One to Number Fourteen; Number Fifteen so far as it specifies the amount of any salary; Number Sixteen.
8 & 9 Vict. c. 81, .	The Grand Jury (Dublin) Act, 1845.	Sections two, three, eight, nine, and eleven.
11 & 12 Vict. c. 26,	The Grand Jury Cess (Ireland) Act, 1848.	The whole Act so far as unrepealed, except section six.
11 & 12 Vict. c. 32,	The County Cess (Ireland) Act, 1848.	The whole Act so far as unrepealed.
11 & 12 Vict c. 69,	The Malicious Injuries (Ireland) Act, 1848.	Section two from " Provided always that ' to the end of the section.
13 & 14 Vict. c 82,	The Grand Jury Cess (Ireland) Act, 1850.	The whole Act so far as unrepealed.
14 & 15 Vict. c. 65,	The Grand Jury Cess (Dublin) Act, 1851.	The whole Act so far as unrepealed.

Session and Chapter.	Short Title.	Extent of Repeal.
16 & 17 Vict. c. 38,	The Malicious Injuries (Ireland) Act, 1853.	Section one from " Pro-" vided always that " 1o the end of the section.
19 & 20 Vict. c. 63,	The Grand Jury (Ireland) Act, 1856.	The whole Act, so far as unrepealed, except sections thirteen, seventeen, eighteen, and twenty-one.
20 & 21 Vict. c. 7,	The Grand Jury Cess (Ireland) Act, 1857.	Sections one and two.
20 & 21 Vict. c. 15,	The Grand Jury (Ireland) Act, 1857.	The whole Act.
24 & 25 Vict. c, 63,	The County Surveyors, &c. (Ireland) Act, 1861.	The whole Act.
25 & 26 Vict. c. 106.	The County Surveyors (Ireland) Act, 1862.	In section two, the words " the Lord Lieutenant " subject to the appro-" val of."
30 & 31 Vict. c. 46,	The County Treasurers (Ireland) Act, 1867.	Sections four to nine. Section eleven from " to fix the nature " to " nominated or appointed treasurer." Sections twelve to fifteen. Section seventeen except as regards any existing treasurer. Sections nineteen and twenty.
30 & 31 Vict. c. 112.	The Public Works (Ireland) Act, 1867.	The whole Act.
32 & 33 Vict. c. 79,	The Local Officers Superannuation (Ireland) Act, 1869.	Section five save so far as relates to any existing officer.
34 & 35 Vict. c. 106.	The Detached Portions of Counties (Ireland) Act, 1871.	The whole Act except section four.
35 & 36 Vict. c. 48,	The County Boundaries (Ireland) Act, 1872.	Section five.
36 & 37 Vict. c. 65,	The County and City of Dublin Grand Jurors Act, 1873.	Section two.
38 & 39 Vict. c 56	The County Surveyors (Superannuation (Ireland) Act, 1875.	Section three.

Session and Chapter.	Short Title.	Extent of Repeal.
40 & 41 Vict. c. 57,	The Supreme Court of Judicature (Ireland) Act, 1877.	Section seventy-five from " the jurisdiction to "audit " to " jurisdic-" tions aforesaid," so far as relates to the auditors of county treasurers' accounts, and from " to " transfer and attach " to " prescribe and also."
58 & 59 Vict. c. 8,	The Grand Jury (Ireland) Act, 1895.	The whole Act.
60 & 61 Vict. c. 2,	The County Dublin Surveyors Act, 1897.	The whole Act.

PART II.—MUNICIPAL CORPORATIONS (IRELAND) ACTS.

Session and Chapter.	Short Title.	Extent of Repeal.
3 & 4 Vict. c. 108,	The Municipal Corporations (Ireland) Act, 1840.	Section fourteen from " and if the persons " to "and in every such " case." Section sixteen from " or " until there shall " to " Fourth," where that word next occurs, and from " or upon the elec-" tion" to " Fourth" where that word next occurs; and from " or " in the commissioners " down to " case may be"; section eighteen from " or until " down to " Fourth" where that word next occurs, and from " or upon the " election" down to " Fourth" where that word next occurs, and from " or in the com-" missioners" down to " case may be." In section thirty, the words " as herein-after " mentioned," from "if " duly enrolled" to " contained," and from "and in any borough " to the end of the section. Sections thirty-one to thirty-four. Sections thirty-six to forty-seven.

Session and Chapter.	Short Title.	Extent of Repeal.
3 & 4 Vict. c. 108 —*con.*		Sections forty-nine and fifty, section fifty-two from "but in case where" to " Monday following"; section fifty-three except as regards the mayor; section fifty-four.
		Section fifty-five, from " shall cause" to " year "and" and from " and " of the churchwardens" to " as aforesaid."
		Section fifty-six.
		Section fifty-seven, from "and in every such "borough" to the end of the section.
		Section fifty-eight from " nor shall any person "be qualified" to the end of the section.
		Section fifty-nine, from " delivered to the town " clerk" to the end of the section.
		Sections sixty-four to seventy.
		In section seventy-one the words "with respect " to the revision of the " lists of burgesses or."
		Section seventy-three.
		In section seventy-four the words " by the pro-"visions herein-before "contained," and from " except that every such " election " to the end of the section.
		In section eighty-one the words " municipal com-"missioner, auditor or " assessor," and " or " Commissioners," and from " and such election " shall be held" to " as " aforesaid."
		Section eighty-three from " and in like" to the end of the section.
		In section eighty-five " municipal commis-" sioner, auditor, or as-" sessor " wherever those words occur, and the words " alderman, " councillor, or assessor," and the words " or com-" missioners," and from "and in the case" to the end of the section.
		In section eighty-six the words " auditor or as-" sessor " and " assessors

Session and Chapter.	Short Title.	Extent of Repeal.
& 4 Vict., c. 108—con.		" or auditors," and from " and every municipal " to " his office." Section eighty–eight. In section eighty–nine the words "or municipal " commissioner or audi-" tor or assessor," " according to the pro-" visions of this Act," from " and every person" to " ward as the case " may be," and the words " commissioner, " auditor, or assessor," twice occurring, and the words " auditor or as-" sessor," and the words " or by a person ' qualified to vote for " the commissioners for " such borough," and " such person where those words next occur ; and the words " or town " fund." In section ninety-two the words " or board of " municipal commis-" sioners," " or commis-" sioners," and "or is " qualified to vote as " aforesaid," and the words " or board," " or " chairman," and " or " commissioner " where-ever they occur ; and from " the whole" to " whole council or board" and from " and the said "quarterly meetings" to the end of the section. In section ninety-three the words " or board of commissioners" and the words " or board " wherever they occur. In section ninety-five the words "or board" wher-ever they occur. Section ninety–eight. Section one hundred and twenty-five from " pro-" vided further " to the end of the section. In section one hundred and twenty-nine from " or on account " to " of " this Act," the words " or commissioners," and from " or person" to " such commissioners." In section one hundred and thirty the words "or " commissioners.'

Session and Chapter.	Short Title.	Extent of Repeal.
3 & 4 Vict., c, 108 —*con.*		Section one hundred and thirty-six from "and all "the accounts" to "sign "the same" and the words "or commis-"sioners," and "or com-"missioner" and "so "respectively examined "and and "in the "month of September." Sections one hundred and thirty-eight and one hundred and fifty. Section one hundred and fifty-three from "and "in such of the said "boroughs" to "office "of coroner," and from "provided always that "in every" to the end of the section.
5 & 6 Vict., c. 104,	The Municipal Corporations (Ireland) Act, 1842.	Section seven.
6 & 7 Vict., c. 93,	The Municipal Corporation (Ireland) Act, 18	Sections two and three. Section four. Section five from "and at "the like times" to the end of the section. Sections thirteen, fourteen, nineteen, and twenty. Section twenty-six except so far as it affects the title of any property real or personal. Sections twenty-seven and twenty-eight.
15 & 16 Vict. c. 5,	The Municipal Corporations Act, 1852.	The whole Act so far as unrepealed.
22 Vict., c. 35, .	The Municipal Corporations Act, 1859.	The whole Act so far as unrepealed.
23 & 24 Vict., c. 74,	The Borough Coroners (Ireland) Act, 1860.	Section one from "no "person shall be elected" to "said recited Act "and".
34 & 35 Vict., c. 109.	The Local Government (Ireland) Act, 1871.	In section eleven the words "except the "boroughs or munici-"palities of Cork, Kil-"kenny, and Water-"ford," and sections twenty, twenty-one, and twenty-seven.
35 & 36 Vict., c, 60,	The Corrupt Practices (Municipal Elections) Act, 1872.	The whole Act so far as unrepealed.
38 & 39 Vict., c. 40,	The Municipal Elections Act, 1875.	The whole Act so far as unrepealed.

Session and Chapter.	Short Title.	Extent of Repeal.
39 & 40 Vict., c. 76,	The Municipal Privilege Act, Ireland, 1876.	Section four, from "the "Council of the city of "Kilkenny" to "County "of the town of Drog-"heda."
42 & 43 Vict., c. 53,	The Municipal Elections (Ireland) Act, 1879.	The whole Act so far as unrepealed.
48 & 49 Vict., c. 9,	The Municipal Voters Relief Act, 1885.	The whole Act so far it relates to Ireland.

Part III.—Irish Town Acts.

Session and Chapter.	Short Title.	Extent of Repeal.
9 Geo. 4, c. 82, .	The Lighting of Towns (Ireland) Act, 1828.	The whole Act, except so far as it is applied by any Act or enactment.
17 & 18 Vict., c. 103,	The Towns Improvement (Ireland) Act, 1854.	Section four, from "each "of such" to "or up-"wards" and from "or "the chairman" down to "be in force." Section five, from "pro-"vided always" to the end of the section, so far as regards towns which are urban districts. Section seven, from "that "is to say" to the end of the section. Section ten, from "at "such polling place" to the end of the section. Sections eleven and twelve. In section fourteen, "qualified in each case "respectively as afore-"said" and "and occu-"piers" wherever those words occur respectively. Section seventeen. Section nineteen. Section twenty-one, from "qualified as next here-"inafter mentioned" to the end of the section ; section twenty-two,* so much of section twenty-four as incorporates sections twenty-one to twenty-three and sections twenty-six to

Session and Chapter.	Short Title.	Extent of Repeal.
17 & 18 Vict. c. 103—*con.*		thirty-one and section thirty-five of the Commissioners Clauses Act, 1847; section twenty-five; so much of section twenty-six as incorporates sections six to ten and twelve to sixteen of the Commissioners Clauses Act, 1847. Section sixty-four, from "provided that" to the end of the section, and the rest of the section except so far as it applies to any case where a rate can, under the provisions of this Act, be made on the immediate lessor. Section sixty-eight, so far as regards towns which are urban districts and Schedule B.

PART IV.—POOR RELIEF (IRELAND) ACTS.

Session and Chapter.	Short Title.	Extent of Repeal.
1 & 2 Vict. c. 56, .	The Poor Relief (Ireland) Act, 1838.	Section seventeen from "and the guardians "shall" to the end of the section. Section nineteen to "provided always that." Section twenty. Section twenty-one from "for the ensuing" to the end of the section. Sections twenty-three to twenty-five. Section thirty-one, from "for superintending" to "for the purposes of "this Act," so far as unrepealed. In section thirty-two the words "or of any electoral division comprised therein." Section forty-four from "and the board" to the end of the section. Sections sixty-two and seventy-four; section

Session and Chapter.	Short Title.	Extent of Repeal.
1 & 2 Vict., c. 56—con.		seventy-five except so far as it applies to any case where a rate can, under the provisions of this Act, be made on the immediate lessor. Section seventy-eight from "provided always" to the end of the section. Section seventy-nine from "that no deduction on "account of" down "to "provided also" and the rest of the section so far as regards rent except so far as it applies to any case where a rate can, under the provisions of this Act, be made on the immediate lessor. Section eighty, from "and not entitled"; "from the rent paid by "him." Sections eighty-one to eighty-six. Section eighty-eight.
2 & 3 Vict. c. 1, .	The Poor Relief (Ireland) Act, 1839.	Sections two and five.
6 & 7 Vict. c. 92, .	The Poor Relief (Ireland) Act, 1843.	Sections one to three except so far as they apply to any case where a rate can, under the provisions of this Act, be made on the immediate lessor. Section four from "pro- "vided always" where it last occurs to the end of the section. In section eleven the words "on any elec- "toral division." Sections twelve, thir- teen, nineteen, and twenty. Sections twenty-two to twenty-six.
10 & 11 Vict. c. 31,	The Poor Relief (Ireland) Act, 1847.	Section six, and section eleven from "which "determine" down to "provisions of the said "Acts" where those words next occur; and from "and all provisions "of the said Acts which "relate to the power" to the end of the section. Section twelve. In section thirteen the words "of the electoral "division in which such

Session and Chapter.	Short Title.	Extent of Repeal
10 & 11 Vict., c. 31 —*con.*		" person shall be resi- " dent," and from the first " notwithstanding" to " of such electoral " division and ". Section fifteen from " all " expenses" to " situ- " ated and"). Section sixteen.
11 & 12 Vict. c. 25,	The Poor Relief (Ireland) Act, 1848.	In section three the words " or any electoral " division therein" and from " at large" to the end of the section.
12 & 13 Vict. c. 91.	An Act to provide for the Collection of Rates in the City of Dublin.	In section twenty-nine the words " poor rates" and " grand jury cess." Section thirty-two. Section thirty-four. Section forty-one. In Schedule A. and Schedule B. the words " poor rate" and " grand "jury cess."
12 & 13 Vict. c. 104.	The Poor Relief (Ireland) Act, 1849.	Sections six to nine. Section eleven. Section twenty-five from " at large" to the end of the section. In section twenty-six the words "or electoral " division" " on any " electoral division or " divisions," " resident " therein respectively," " or of any electoral " division or divisions " thereof," and " of the " electoral division or " divisions." Section twenty - seven from " the sums or sum " of money" to " repay- ' ment thereof and that." Section twenty - eight from " resident or re- " lievable" to " shall " have been so charged " or."
14 & 15 Vict. c. 68,	The Poor Relief (Ireland) Act, 1851.	Section six from " and " from and after a day" to " force for the time " being," and from "and ' shall likewise declare" to the end of the section. Section seven. In section eleven the words " or member of " the committee of " management."

Session and Chapter.	Short Title.	Extent of Repeal.
14 & 15 Vict., c. 68 —con.		In section twelve the words " the committees " of management." In section eighteen the words " or dispensary " committee.
25 & 26 Vict. c. 83,	The Poor Relief (Ireland) Act, 1862.	In section three the words "electoral division or," and from " at large " to " Ireland." Section four from " to the " credit of the electoral" to " such poor person " or," and the words " as " the case may be." In section seven the words " or electoral division as " the case may be." Sections thirteen to twenty. Sections twenty-four and twenty-five.
1 & 30 Vict. c. 38,	The Poor Persons Burial (Ireland) Act, 1866.	In section one the words " the electoral division " or of " and from " in " like manner " to the end of the section.
39 & 40 Vict. c. 50.	The Poor Law Rating (Ireland) Act, 1876.	Sections three, five, and six.
42 & 43 Vict. c. 25,	The Dispensary Houses (Ireland) Act, 1879.	Section eleven the words " not being more than " sixty years" and from " of the electoral divi- "sion " to " dispensary ' district." Section twelve from " of " the electoral division" to " in relief " and from " of the same" to the end of the section. Section thirteen from " of " the electoral division" to " property in Ireland."
45 & 46 Vict. c. 61,	The Boards of Management of Poor Law District Schools (Ireland) Act, 1892.	Section two from " any " sum so paid" to the end of the section, being sub-section two.
53 & 54 Vict. c. 30,	The Poor Law Acts (Ireland) Amendment Act, 1890.	Section three.

PART V.—LUNATIC ASYLUM ACTS.

Session and Chapter.	Short Title.	Extent of Repeal.
1 & 2 Geo. 4, c. 33,	The Lunacy (Ireland) Act, 1821.	Section one. .. Section two from "and "that every such "asylum" to "Privy "Council," where those words lastly occur, and the rest of the section except so far as relates to districts. Sections four to thirteen so far as unrepealed.
7 Geo. 4, c. 14, .	The Lunacy (Ireland) land) Act, 1826.	Section one from "and "that every such "asylum" where those words first occur to "said "recited Act" where those words last occur, and the rest of the section except so far as it authorises the Lord Lieutenant to alter asylum districts.
11 Geo 4 & 1 Will. 4, c. 22.	The Richmond Lunatic Asylum Act, 1830.	Section two so far as it applies any enactments repealed by this Act. Sections three and five.
8 & 9 Vict., c. 107,	The Central Criminal Lunatic Asylum (Ireland) Act, 1845.	Sections thirteen to sixteen. Section nineteen so far as it applies any enactments repealed by this Act. Sections twenty to twenty-two. Section twenty-five from "in the forms" to the end of the section. The Schedules.
18 & 19 Vict., c. 109.	The Lunatic Asylums Repayment of Advances (Ireland) Act, 1855.	The whole Act, so far as unrepealed, except sections four and eight, and except so far as respects money expended or expenses incurred before the passing of this Act.
19 & 20 Vict., c. 99,	The Lunatic Asylums Superannuations (Ireland) Act, 1856.	The whole Act, except so far as it relates to existing officers or pensions.
30 & 31 Vict., c. 118,	The Lunacy (Ireland) Act, 1867.	Sections two to five; and sections one, six, and eight, except so far as they relate to existing officers or pensions.

Session and Chapter.	Short Title.	Extent of Repeal.
31 & 32 Vict., c. 97,	The Lunatic Asylums (Ireland) Accounts Audit Act, 1868.	The whole Act so far as unrepealed.
40 & 41 Vict , c. 27,	The Public Works Loans (Ireland) Act, 1877.	Section five, except as respects the repayment of advances made before the commencement of this Act.
41 & 42 Vict , c. 24,	The Lunatic Asylums Loans (Ireland) Act. 1878.	The whole Act.
53 & 54 Vict., c. 31,	The Pauper Lunatic Asylums (Ireland) Superannuation Act, 1890.	Section three, from "with- "in the meaning" down to " one hundred and eighteen," and the words " with the approval of " the inspectors of " lunatics, or one of " them " and the words " or servant " wherever they occur in that sec- tion ; and section four.

PART VI.—MISCELLANEOUS ACTS.

Session and Chapter.	Short Title.	Extent of Repeal.
55 Geo. 3, c. 89, .	The Court Houses (Ireland) Act, 1815.	Sections one and two.
2 & 3 Will. 4, c. 85,	The Charities (Ire- land) Act, 1832.	The whole Act.
3 & 4 Will. 4. c. 37,	An Act to alter and amend the laws relating to the temporalities of the Church in Ireland.	Section seventy-two from " at the next assizes " to the end of the section.
5 & 6 Will. 4, c. 26,	The Assizes (Ireland) Act, 1835.	Section two, from " and "to order" down to " such county " where those words next occur ; section three from " or " for dividing " to " this " Act " and the words " or division " ; and sec- tion four.
9 & 10 Vict., c. 37,	The Coroners (Ire- land) Act, 1846.	ction two. In section three the words " and they are hereby " required," from " and " to fix " to "shall be " taken," an l from " and

Session and Chapter.	Short Title.	Extent of Repeal.
9 & 10 Vic. c, 37— *con.*		"the said clerk" to "and "determined," and the words "riding or divi-"sion" wherever they occur. Section four, to "in man-"ner as aforesaid and ") In section five "riding or "division" wherever those words occur. Section six, from "as-"sembled at" to "special "sessions." Sections seven to seventeen so far as unrepealed. Section eighteen from "upon the receipt" to "this Act or," and from "any to direct a writ" to the end of the section. Section twenty. Section twenty-one from "and to order a writ' to the end of the section. In section twenty-four the words "riding or "division" wherever they occur. In section twenty-nine the words "at any "assizes or presenting "term," "for the board of superintendence of "the gaols of such 'county, city, or town," "until the next ensuing "assizes or presenting "term," "to such board "of superintendence" and "for the said Board "of superintendence if "they shall so think fit." Section forty-two, from "and thereupon a writ" to the end of the section. Section forty-three, from "nor shall it be lawful" to the end of the section. Schedule A. and Schedule B.
15 & 16 Vict. c. 63,	The Valuation (Ireland) Act, 1852.	Section twenty-six; in section thirty-one from "and to the town "council" to "county"; in section thirty-two the words "or town "council"; sections thirty-three and forty-seven.
17 & 18 Vict. c. 8,	The Valuation (Ireland) Act, 1854.	Section three.
20 & 21 Vict.c. 45,	The Boundary Lunacy (Ireland) Act, 1857.	Section three.

Session and Chapter.	Short Title.	Extent of Repeal.
23 & 24 Vict. c. 152.	The Tramways (Ireland) Act, 1860.	Section thirty-six and in section thirty-eight the words " of not less than " two-thirds."
24 & 25 Vict. c. 102.	The Tramways (Ireland) Amendment Act, 1861.	Section five.
31 & 32 Vict. c. 49.	The Representation of the People (Ireland) Act, 1868.	Section nineteen and sections twenty - one to twenty-three. Section twenty-four from " and in all towns " to " cleansing commis- " sioners." the words "or " municipal," and from " and in towns under " none " to the end of the section,
33 & 34 Vict. c. 46.	The Landlord and Tenant (Ireland) Act, 1870.	Sections sixty-five to sixty-seven.
35 & 36 Vict c. 69.	The Local Government Board (Ireland) Act, 1872.	Section four from " and " save as " to the end of the section.
37 & 38 Vict. c. 70.	The Valuation (Ireland) Amendment Act, 1874.	Section two from " in " equal moieties" to " assizes in each year."
38 & 39 Vict. c. 17.	The Explosives Act, 1875.	Section one hundred and eighteen from " includ- " ing" to " under this " Act" so far as relates to county councils other than the councils of county boroughs, and from " all expenses in- " curred in any petty " sessions district " to the end of the section.
39 & 40 Vict. c. 65.	The Tramways (Ireland) Amendment (Dublin) Act, 1876.	Section four.
39 & 40 Vict. c. xciii.	The Coroners(Dublin) Act, 1876.	Section three, from " in " addition" to " re- " quired" and the word " further."
41 & 42 Vict. c. 49.	The Weights and Measures Act, 1878.	Section seventy - nine, from " by inquiry " to "jury."
41 & 42 Vict. c. 52.	The Public Health (Ireland) Act, 1878.	Section six, from " and " the guardians " to the end of the section. Section two hundred and six. In section two hundred and thirty - two the words " the electoral " divisions or parts " thereof in " and from " according to the rate- " able " to " thereof."

Session and Chapter.	Short Title.	Extent of Repeal.
41 & 42 Vict., c. 52 —con.		Section two hundred and thirty-four, from " or of " any " to " case deter- " mine " and, so far as regards rural districts, from " Provided always'' to the end of the section.
42 & 43 Vict. c. 57.	The Public Health (Ireland) Amend- ment Act, 1879.	Section two. In section four the words " of the electoral divi- " sion or."
44 & 45 Vict. c. 35.	The Coroners (Ire- land) Act, 1881.	Section three, from " equal to" down to " said period " and from " provided always that " down to " hold such " inquest," and section four.
45 & 46 Vict. c. 49.	The Militia Act, 1882.	So much of subsection two of section fifty-three as relates to Galway; and so much of the first schedule as relates to Kilkenny, Drogheda, and Galway.
46 & 47 Vict c. 60.	The Labourers (Ire- land) Act, 1883.	Section five from " pro- " vided that" to "number " of twelve "; section six from " the scheme shall " also " to " charged "; in section seven the words "and the proposed " area of charge " and from " the provisional " order shall also " specify " down to " charged "; section seventeen, from the be- ginning down to " Part " Five of the Public " Health (Ireland) Act, " 1878," and the words " out of which special " expenses are payable."
47 & 48 Vict. c. 77.	The Public Health (Ireland) Amend- ment Act, 1884.	Sections two, three, and six.
48 & 49 Vict. c. 77.	The Labourers (Ire- land) Act, 1885.	In section twelve, the words " declared by such " order to be "; and section eighteen.
49 & 50 Vict. c. 59.	The Labourers (Ire- land) Act, 1886.	Section five.
60 & 61 Vict. c. 43.	The Military Man- œuvres Act, 1897.	Section nine from " persons not more " to " have effect," being sub-sections one and two.

SEVENTH SCHEDULE.

COMPENSATION.

PART I.

> *Scale of Compensation.*

The compensation payable to any high constable or collector of
a barony or to his deputy duly appointed under section one
hundred and forty-eight of the Grand Juries Act, 1836, shall be
according to the following scale :—

(*a*) If his service has not exceeded two grand jury half-years,
one year's net emoluments ;

(*b*) If his service has exceeded two grand jury half-years, one year's
net emoluments together with one quarter of one year's net
emoluments for each grand jury half-year which he has served
above the two first, but not exceeding in any case five years'
net emoluments ;

(*c*) The net emoluments shall be ascertained according to the
average for the six grand jury half-years next before the
summer assizes, 1898, or if the officer has served for less
than that period, then for the period of his service ;

(*d*) The gross emoluments of a deputy shall not exceed the sum
deducted in respect thereof in ascertaining the net emoluments
of the high constable or collector whose deputy he was ;

(*e*) The expression " grand jury half-year " means the period
between any assizes and the next assize.

In the Application of this Part of this Schedule to a person who
is not a high constable or collector of a barony or his deputy, the
necessary modifications shall be made, and in particular the first
half and the second half of each calendar year shall be substituted
for the " grand jury half-year."

PART II.

Section 120 (*omitting subs.* (8)) *of the Local Government Act*, 1888.

120.—(1.) Every existing officer declared by this Act to be
entitled to compensation, and every other existing officer, whether
before mentioned in this Act or not, who, by virtue of this Act
or anything done in pursuance of or in consequence of this Act,
suffers any direct pecuniary loss by abolition of office or by
diminution or loss of fees or salary, shall be entitled to have
compensation paid to him for such pecuniary loss by the county
council, to whom the powers of the authority, whose officer he
was are transferred under this Act, regard being had to the
conditions on which his appointment was made, to the nature
of his office or employment, to the duration of his service, to any
additional emoluments which he acquires by virtue of this Act, or
of anything done in pursuance of or in consequence of this Act,
and to the emoluments which he might have acquired if he had
not refused to accept any office offered by any council or other
body acting under this Act, and to all the other circumstances of
the case, and the compensation shall not exceed the amount which,

under the Acts and rules relating to Her Majesty's Civil Service, is paid to a person on abolition of office.

(2.) Every person who is entitled to compensation, as above mentioned, shall deliver to the county council a claim under his hand setting forth the whole amount received and expended by him or his predecessors in office, in every year during the period of five years next before the passing of this Act, on account of the emoluments for which he claims compensation, distinguishing the offices in respect of which the same have been received, and accompanied by a statutory declaration under the Statutory Declarations Act, 1835, that the same is a true statement according to the best of his knowledge, information, and belief.

(3.) Such statement shall be submitted to the county council, who shall forthwith take the same into consideration, and assess the just amount of compensation (if any), and shall forthwith inform the claimant of their decision.

(4.) If a claimant is aggrieved by the refusal of the county council to grant any compensation, or by the amount of compensation assessed, or if not less than one third of the members of such council subscribe a protest against the amount of the compensation as being excessive, the claimant or any subscriber to such protest (as the case may be), may, within three months after the decision of the council, appeal to the Treasury, who shall consider the case and determine whether any compensation, and if so, what amount, ought to be granted to the claimant, and such determination shall be final.

(5.) Any claimant under this section, if so required by any member of the county council, shall attend at a meeting of the council and answer upon oath, which any justice present may administer, all questions asked by any member of the council touching the matters set forth in his claim, and shall further produce all books, papers, and documents in his possession or under his control relating to such claim.

(6.) The sum payable as compensation to any person in pursuance of this section shall commence to be payable at the date fixed by the council on granting the compensation, or, in case of appeal, by the Treasury, and shall be a specialty debt due to him from the county council, and may be enforced accordingly in like manner as if the council had entered into a bond to pay the same.

(7.) If a person receiving compensation in pursuance of this section is appointed to any office under the same or any other county council, or by virtue of this Act, or anything done in pursuance of or in consequence of this Act, receives any increase of emoluments of the office held by him, he shall not, while receiving the emoluments of that office, receive any greater amount of his compensation, if any, than, with the emoluments of the said office is equal to the emoluments for which compensation was granted to him, and if the emoluments of the office he holds are equal to or greater than the emoluments for which compensation was granted, his compensation shall be suspended while he holds such office.

APPENDIX II.

ORDERS IN COUNCIL.

THE LOCAL GOVERNMENT (APPLICATION OF ENACTMENTS) ORDER, 1898.

By the LORD LIEUTENANT and Privy Council of Ireland.

CADOGAN,

WHEREAS it is enacted by section one hundred and four of the Local Government (Ireland) Act, 1898, that there shall apply to Ireland so much as the Lord Lieutenant, by Order in Council, declares applicable of the English and Scotch enactments specified in the Fourth Schedule to that Act, and the enactments amending the same, being enactments relating, among other matters, to matters in the said section mentioned, and that an Order in Council under the said section may—

(a) apply any of the said enactments to both county and district councils and guardians and town commissioners, and committees appointed by or comprising members of any of such councils, guardians, or commissioners, or to any of them, notwithstanding that they relate to county councils only or to district councils only or to guardians only ; and

(b) provide for the transfer to county councils of lunatic asylums and all property and liabilities connected therewith and for the exception of any debt incurred (whether before or after the passing of this Act) on account of lunatic asylums from being reckoned in the limitation of amount imposed by any of the said enactments upon the borrowing by county councils, and for the joint committee of the counties comprised in a lunatic asylum district exercising jointly for the purpose of the lunatic asylum the powers of those councils relating to borrowing ; and

(c) make such adaptations of the said enactments as appear necessary or expedient for carrying into effect the application thereof to Ireland ; and

(d) make such adaptations of local Acts as appear required to bring them into conformity with any of the said enactments.

And whereas it appears to us expedient that so much of the said enactments, as is set out in the schedule to this. Order with the adaptations and applications therein appearing should apply to Ireland, and that such provisions should be made with respect to lunatic asylums and the adaptation of local Acts as appear in the said Schedule.

Now therefore, We, the Lord Lieutenant-General and General Governor of Ireland, by virtue of the powers vested in us for that purpose as aforesaid, and of all other powers enabling us on that behalf, by and with the advice of Her Majesty's Privy Council in Ireland, do declare, and it is hereby declared that—

(1.) So much of each of the English and Scotch enactments specified in the Fourth Schedule to the Local Government (Ireland) Act, 1898, and the enactments amending the same, as is set out in the schedule to this Order, is applicable to Ireland and is hereby applied accordingly, with such adaptations and applications as appear in that schedule.

(2.) Such provisions shall be made with respect to lunatic asylums and the adaptation of local Acts as appear in the schedule to this Order.

(3.) The application of each of the said enactments to Ireland shall come into force on the day (if any) in that behalf mentioned, and subject thereto on the appointed day, as if this Order were part of the Local Goverhment (Ireland) Act, 1898.

(4.) This Order may be cited as the Local Government. (Application of Enactments) Order, 1898.

Given at the Council Chamber, Dublin Castle, the 22nd day of December, 1898.

ASHBOURNE, *C.*   WILLIAM O'BRIEN.

JOHN ATKINSON.   C. H. HEMPHILL.

W. J. PIRRIE.

SCHEDULE.

General.

1.—(1.) In this Schedule, unless the context otherwise requires :—

(*a.*) The expression "the Act" shall mean the Local Government (Ireland) Act, 1898, and includes any Order made under Part Six thereof; and expressions referring to the Act or to enactments in the Act, or to the passing of the Act, shall be construed to include a reference to such Order or to provisions of such Order, or to the making of such Order.

(*b.*) Other expressions shall, subject to the express provisions in this Schedule, have the same meaning as in the Act.

(*c.*) The expression "chairman" includes the mayor of a borough.

(*d.*) The expression "property" includes all property, real and personal, and all estates, interests, easements, and rights, whether equitable or legal, in, to, and out of property real and personal, including things in action, and registers, books, and documents; and when used in relation to any grand jury, board, sanitary authority, or other authority, includes any property which on the appointed day belongs to, or is vested in, or held in trust for, or would but for the Act have, on or after that day, belonged to, or been vested in, or held in trust for, such grand jury, board, sanitary authority, or other authority.

(*e.*) The expression "liabilities" includes liability to any proceeding for enforcing any duty, or for punishing the breach of any duty, and includes all debts and liabilities to which any authority are or would but for the Act be liable or subject to, whether accrued due at the date of the transfer or subsequently accruing, and includes any obligation to carry or apply any money to any sinking fund or to any particular purpose; and includes all liabilities imposed by or arising under any local and personal Act.

(*f.*) The expression "expenses" includes costs and charges.

(*g.*) The expression "costs" includes charges and expenses.

(*h.*) The expression "election" includes both the nomination and the poll.

(*i.*) The expression "local and personal Act" includes a Provisional Order confirmed by an Act and the Act confirming the Order.

General provisions as to adaptation and definitions

L. G. Act, 1888, s. 100.

L. G. Act, 1894, s. 75.

(2.) The Interpretation Act,.1889, applies for the purpose of the interpretation of this Order as it applies to the interpretation of an Act of Parliament.

Provision as to Sundays and Bank Holidays.
L. G. Act, 1894, s. 73.

2. When the day on which anything is required by or in pursuance of the Act to be done is Sunday, Christmas Day, or Good Friday, or a Bank Holiday, that thing shall be done on the next following day not being one of the days above mentioned.

Making of Registers by Street Order.

Lists and registers may be arranged according to streets.
41 & 42 Vict. c. 26, sec. 21.

3.—(1.) If and so far as the local authority so direct, the lists and registers of parliamentary voters and local government electors in parliamentary boroughs, and the lists of claimants and persons objected to in parliamentary boroughs, or any of those documents, shall so far as they relate to persons qualified in respect of the ownership or occupation of property (including persons qualified in respect of lodgings), be arranged in the same order in which the qualifying premises appear in the rate book relating to the poor rate in the district electoral division (or other area for which the lists are made up) in which those premises are situate, or as nearly thereto as will cause those lists and registers to record the qualifying premises in successive order in the street or other place in which they are situate.

(2.) " The local authority" in this Article means as regards a parliamentary borough the council of the municipal borough which comprises the whole or the larger part of the parliamentary borough.

51 & 52 Vict. c. 10, s. 4 (3).

48 & 49, Vict. c. 23.

(3.) Where a municipal borough or an urban county district is co-extensive with any parliamentary county within the meaning of the Redistribution of Seats Act, 1885, the lists and register of parliamentary voters and local government electors may be directed by the county council to be made out according to the order in which the qualifying premises appear in the said rate book, and the foregoing provisions of this Article shall apply to such borough or urban county district, and where lists of voters are so made out, nothing in this Act shall require such part of the county register as consists of those lists to be arranged alphabetically.

Elections.

Removal of disqualification of married women.
L. G. Act, 1894, s. 43.

4. For the purposes of the Act a woman shall not be disqualified by marriage for being on any local government register of electors, or for being an elector of any local authority, provided that a husband and wife shall not both be qualified in respect of the same property.

Elections, polls.
L. G. Act, 1894, ss. 20 (5), 23 (5), 24 (4).
L. G. Act, 1894, s. 48 (2) to (4).

5.—(1.) The election of county councillors and urban and rural district councillors and of aldermen in boroughs and of guardians in boroughs and urban county districts, and of commissioners of a town not being an urban district, shall, subject to the provisions of the Act, be conducted according to rules framed under this Order by the Local Government Board.

(2.) The Rules so framed shall, notwithstanding anything in any other Act, have effect as if enacted in the Act, and shall provide, amongst other things—

(*a*) for every candidate being nominated in writing by two local government electors as proposer and seconder and no more.

(*b*) for preventing an elector at an election of a council for a county, county borough, or district, or of guardians for an electoral division in an urban district, from subscribing a nomination paper or voting—

(i) in more than one county electoral division as respects the council for a county; or,

(ii) in more than one ward as respects the council for a county borough, or urban district, or commissioners of a town; or,

(iii) in more than one district electoral division as respects the council for a rural district; or,

(iv) in more than one district electoral division of a union for the members whether district councillors or guardians of the board of guardians for that union;

(*c*) for fixing or enabling the county council to fix the hours during which the poll is to be kept open, so, however, that the poll shall always be open between the hours of six or eight in the evening;

(*d*) for the polls at elections held at the same date and in the same area being taken together, except where this is impracticable;

(*e*) for the appointment of returning officers for the elections.

(3.) At every election regulated by rules framed under this Order, the poll shall be taken by ballot, and the Ballot Act, 1872, 35 & 36 Vict. and the Municipal Elections (Corrupt and Illegal Practices) Act, c. 33. 1884, and sections fifty-six, seventy-four and seventy-five and 47 & 48 Vict. Part IV. of the Municipal Corporations Act, 1882, as amended c. 70. 45 & 46 Vict. by the last-mentioned Act (including the penal provisions of those c. 50. Acts) shall, subject to adaptations, alterations, and exceptions made by such rules, apply in like manner as in the case of a municipal election. Provided that—

(*a*) section six of the Ballot Act, 1872, as modified by section seventeen of that Act, shall apply in the case of such elections, and the returning officer may, in addition to using the schools and public rooms therein referred to free of charge, for taking the poll, use the same, free of charge, for hearing objections to nomination papers and for counting votes; and

(*b*) section thirty-seven of the Municipal Elections (Corrupt and Illegal Practices) Act, 1884, shall apply as if the election were an election mentioned in the First Schedule to that Act.

(4.) The provisions of the Municipal Corporations Act, 1882, and the anactments amending the same with respect to the filling of casual vacancies, shall, subject to the adaptations, alterations, and exceptions made by the said rules, apply in the case of aldermen and councillors of a borough.

Munic. Corp.
Act, 1882, s. 68.

(5.) If a person is elected councillor or alderman or commissioner in more than one ward of a borough, urban district, or town or councillor in more than one county electoral division of a county or district electoral division of a rural district, or both district councillor and guardian in the same union, he shall within three days after notice of the election, choose by writing signed by him and delivered to the town clerk or secretary or clerk of the council or board of guardians or commissioners, or in his default the chairman of the council board or commissioners shall within three days after the time of choice has expired, declare for which of those wards or divisions he shall serve, and the choice or declaration shall be conclusive.

Costs of
elections.
L. G. Act, 1894,
s. 48 (7).

6.—(1.) The expenses of any election under the Act shall not exceed the scale fixed by the county council with the approval of the Local Government Board, and in the case of the first election under the Act the Local Government Board may frame a scale for the county, and the scale so framed shall apply to the first election, and shall have effect as if it had been made by the county council with the said approval.

L. G. Act, 1888,
s. 75 (17).

(2.) All costs properly incurred in relation to the holding of elections of councillors and aldermen of county or district councils, or of guardians in county boroughs and urban county districts or of commissioners of towns, so far as not otherwise provided for by law, shall be paid—

    (a) in the case of councillors of a county at large out of the county fund as county at large charges; and

    (b) in the case of councillors or aldermen of a county borough, or of any other borough, or of councillors of an urban or rural county district and of guardians in a county borough or an urban county district, out of the borough or district fund of the borough or district, as the case requires, and in the case of commissioners of a town not an urban district out of the funds or rates administered by the commissioners.

L. G. Act, 1888,
s. 75 (20).

(3.) A county council shall, on the request of the returning officer, prior to a poll being taken at any election of a councillor of such council, advance to him such sum not exceeding ten pounds for every thousand electors at the election as he may require.

L. G. Act, 1888.
s. 75 (19).
38 & 39 Vict.
c. 84, ss. 4-7.

(4.) Within twenty-one days after the day on which the return is made of the persons elected at an election under the Act, the returning officer shall transmit to the county or urban or rural district council or town commissioners as the case requires, a detailed account showing the amounts of all charges claimed by the returning officer, in respect of the election. He shall annex to the account a notice of the place where the vouchers relating to the account may be seen, and he shall at all reasonable times and without charge allow the council or commissioners or any agent of such council or commissioners, to inspect and take copies of the vouchers.

(5.) The returning officer shall not be entitled to any charges which are not duly included in his account.

(6.) If the council or commissioners object to any part of the claim, they may, at any time within one month from the time when the account is transmitted to them apply for a taxation of the account to the County Court having jurisdiction at the place of nomination for the election, and the court shall have jurisdiction to tax the account in such manner and at such time and place as the court thinks fit, and finally to determine the amount payable to the returning officer and to give and enforce judgment for the same as if such judgment were a judgment in an action in such court, and with or without costs at the discretion of the court.

(7.) The court may depute any of its powers or duties under this Article to the registrar or other principal officer of the court.

(8.) Every person having any claim against a returning officer for work, labour, materials, services, or expenses in respect of any contract made with him by or on behalf of the returning officer for the purposes of an election under the Act, shall, within fourteen days after the day on which the return is made of the person or persons elected at the election, transmit to the returning officer the detailed particulars of such claim in writing, and the returning officer shall not be liable in respect of anything which is not duly stated in such particulars. *L. G. Act, 1888, s. 75 (19). 38 & 39 Vict. c. 84, s. 5.*

(9.) There shall be added to every notice of election to be published under the provisions of the Ballot Act, 1872, the notification following with respect to claims against returning officers ; namely— *L. G. Act, 1888 s. 75 (19). 33 & 39 Vict c. 84, s. 7.*

Take notice that every person having any claim against a returning officer for work, labour, material, services, or expenses in respect of any contract made with him by or on behalf of the returning officer, for the purposes of an election shall, within fourteen days after the day on which the return is made of the person or persons elected at the election, transmit to the returning officer the detailed particulars of such claim in writing, and the returning officer shall not be liable in respect of anything which is not duly stated in such particulars.

(10.) Where application is made for taxation of the accounts of a returning officer, he may apply to the said County Court to examine any claim transmitted to him by any person in pursuance of this article, and the court after notice given to such person, and after hearing him, and any evidence tendered by him, may allow or disallow, or reduce the claim objected to, with or without *L. G. Act, 1888, s. 75 (19). 38 & 39 Vict. c. 84, s. 6.*

costs, and the determination of the court shall be final for all purposes, and as against all persons.

L. G. Act, 1888,
s. 75 (19).
49 & 50 Vict.
c. 57, s. 1.
(11.) The judge or officer by whom any account or claim is taxed or examined under this Article shall deliver to the return ing officer and to the other party to the taxation or examination, a certificate showing the items and amounts allowed or disallowed, with a copy of any order or judgment made thereon.

(12.) Either party may, within seven days of the delivery to him of such certificate, give notice in writing to the said judge or officer of intention to appeal, specifying in the notice the items and amounts in respect of which he intends to appeal.

(13.) The said judge or officer shall thereupon forthwith trans-mit to such taxing officer of the High Court as is directed by rules of court, the said account or claim, with any vouchers relating thereto, the certificate and the notice of appeal; and such taxing officer shall forthwith proceed to review the taxation or examination in the usual manner, or in such manner as may be directed by rules of court, and shall, if required, receive evidence in relation to the matters in dispute, and may confirm or vary the certificate, and direct by whom all or any part of the costs of review are to be paid, and shall return the certificate as confirmed or varied to the said judge or officer with any such direction, and effect shall be given to a certificate as so confirmed or varied, and to any such direction, as if the same had been a judgment of the County Court.

(14.) Any taxation or review of taxation under this Article shall be subject to appeal to the High Court in like manner as any ordinary taxation of costs is now subject.

Power of Local Government Board or county council to re-move difficulties as to elections or to order new election where council unable to act.
L. G. Act, 1894, s. 48 (5).
L. G. (Elections) Act, 1896, s. 1.
7.—(1.) If any difficulty arises as respects the election of any individual councillor, alderman, guardian, or town commissioner, and there is no provision for holding another election, then, in the case of a county councillor, or of an alderman of a county borough, the Local Government Board, and in any other case the county council, may order a new election to be held and give such directions as may be necessary for the purpose of holding the election.

(2.) If any difficulty arises with respect to any election of members of a county or district council or board of guardians, or town Commissioners, or to the first meeting after any ordinary triennial election of such members, if elected triennially, or if, from an election not being held, or being defective, or otherwise, any council or board, or town commissioners, have not been properly constituted, then in the case of a county council the Local Government Board, and in any other case the county council, may by order make any appointment or do anything which appears to them necessary or expedient for the proper holding of any such election or meeting, and properly constitut ing the council or board or commissioners, and may, if it appears to them necessary, direct the holding of an election or meeting, and fix the dates for any such election or meeting.

(3.) Any such order may modify the provisions of the Act, and the enactments applied by, or rule framed under, the Act, so far as may appear to the Local Government Board or county council necessary or expedient for carrying the order into effect.

(4.) A county council may delegate their powers under the foregoing provisions of this article to a committee. L. G. Act, 1891, s. 59 (5).

(5.) If any district or county council, other than a borough council, or any town commissioners, become unable to act, whether from failure to elect or otherwise, then in the case of a county council the Local Government Board, and in any other case the county council of the county in which the district or town is situate, may order elections to be held, and may appoint persons to form the district or county council or commissioners until the newly elected members come into office.

Acceptance of Office, Fine, Resignation, Casual Vacancy &c.

8. In this Order "corporate office in a county council" means the office of councillor of a council of a county at large, and "corporate office in a council or board," means a corporate office in a county council, and also the office of councillor of a council of an urban county district not a borough or of a rural district and the office of a guardian, and of the chairman or vice-chairman of any such county or district council or of a board of guardians. Definition of "corporate office." Munic. Corp. Act, 1882, s. 7. L. G. Act, 1888, s. 75.

9.—(1.) Every qualified person elected or chosen to a corporate office in a council or board, unless exempt under this Article, or otherwise by law, either shall accept the office by making and subscribing the declaration required by this Order within ten days, or in the case of a corporate office in a county council within three months, after notice of election, or shall in lieu thereof, be liable to pay to the council or board a fine of such amount not exceeding fifty pounds, and in case of a chairman or vice-chairman one hundred pounds, as the council or board by byelaw, made in accordance with the enactments relating to the making of byelaws by such council or board, or if there is no such enactment, made with the approval of the Local Government Board, determine. Obligation to accept office or pay fine, and declaration on acceptance of office. Munic. Corp. Act, 1882, s. 34 L. G. Act, 1888, s. 75 (14)

(2.) If there is no byelaw determining fines, the fine, in case of a councillor or guardian, shall be twenty-five pounds, and in case of a chairman or vice-chairman, fifty pounds.

(3.) The persons exempt under this section are—

(a.) any person disabled by lunacy or imbecility of mind, or by deafness, blindness, or other permanent infirmity of body; and

(b.) any person who, being above the age of sixty-five years, or having within five years before the day of his election either served the office or paid the fine for non-acceptance thereof, claims exemption within five days after notice of his election.

(4.) A fine payable under this Article shall be recoverable on conviction before a court of summary jurisdiction.

Munic. Corp. Act, 1882, s. 35. (5.) A person elected or chosen to a corporate office in a council or board shall not, until he has made and subscribed before two members or the secretary or clerk of the council or board, or in the case of a corporate office in a county council, either in that manner or before any justice of the peace or commissioner to administer oaths in the Supreme Court, a declaration as hereinafter mentioned, act in the office except in administering that declaration. The said declaration is as follows :—

Munic. Corp. Act, 1882, Sch. VIII. I, A.B., having been chosen chairman [or vice-chairman, or councillor] for the of , hereby declare that I take the said office upon myself, and will duly and faithfully fulfil the duties thereof according to the best of my judgment and ability.

County Councils (Elections) Act, 1891, s. 5. (6.) The said declaration by a person elected or chosen to a corporate office in a county council may be made at any time within three months after notice of the election, and may be made either in the manner above-mentioned or before any justice of the peace or commissioner to administer oaths in the Supreme Court of Judicature.

L. G. Act, 1888. s. 75 (16) (c). (7.) Nothing in this article shall render a person elected to a corporate office in a county council, without his consent to his nomination being previously obtained, liable to pay a fine on non-acceptance of office.

Fine on resignation, disqualification by absence, &c. Munic. Corp. Act, 1882, s. 36. L. G. Act, 1894, s. 48 (4) (a). **10.**—(1.) A person elected or chosen to a corporate office in a council or board may at any time by writing signed by him and delivered to the secretary or clerk of the council or board, resign the office, on payment of the fine provided for non-acceptance thereof :

Provided that this enactment shall not apply to guardians, and district councillors for a rural district shall be in the same position with respect to resignation as members of a board of guardians.

(2.) In any case of resignation under the foregoing power to resign, the council shall forthwith declare the office to be vacant, and signify the vacancy by notice in writing, signed by three members of the council and countersigned by the secretary or clerk of the council, and notified in such manner as the council direct, and the office shall thereupon become vacant.

Munic. Corp. Act, 1882, s. 39 (4). (3.) Where a person becomes disqualified by absence for holding a corporate office in a council or board, he shall be liable to the same fine as for non-acceptance of office, recoverable on conviction before a court of summary jurisdiction, but the disqualification shall, as regards subsequent elections, cease on his return.

Re-eligibility of office holders, casual vacancies and acting of unqualified person in office. Munic. Corp. Act, 1882, s. 37, s. 40 (1), (2). **11.**—(1.) A person ceasing to hold corporate office in a council or board, shall, unless disqualified to hold the office, be re-eligible.

(2.) The person elected or chosen to fill a casual vacancy in a corporate office in a council or board, shall hold the office until the time when the person in whose place he is elected would regularly have gone out of office, and he shall then go out of office.

(3.) In the case of every corporate office in a council or board, non-acceptance of office by a person elected or chosen creates a casual vacancy.

(4.) If any person acts in a corporate office in a council or board without having made the declaration by this Order required, or without being qualified at the time of making the declaration, or after ceasing to be qualified, he shall for each offence be liable to a fine not exceeding fifty pounds, recoverable by action. *Munic. Corp. Act, 1882, s. 41.*

(5.) A person being in fact registered in the local government register of electors shall not be liable to a fine for acting in a corporate office in a council or board on the ground only that he was not entitled to be registered therein.

(6.) The acts and proceedings of a person in possession of a corporate office in a council or board, and acting therein, shall, notwithstanding his disqualification or want of qualification, be as valid and effectual as if he had been qualified. *Munic. Corp. Act, 1882, s. 42 (1).*

Disqualifications.

12.—(1.) No woman shall be eligible for election or being chosen as a county councillor. *Disqualifications for being councillor,*

(2.) No person shall be disqualified by sex or marriage for being elected or chosen, or being, a guardian, or councillor of a rural or urban district other than a borough, or a town commissioner. *guardian, or town commissioner, and their partner for office. L. G. (Scot.) Act, 1889, s. 9 (1)*

(3.) It shall not be lawful to appoint any member of any county or district council or board of guardians or town commissioners or the partner in business of any such member, to any office or place of profit under the council, board or commissioners, and the disqualification shall apply to any person and his partner in business during six months next after such person has ceased to be such member.

(4.) A person shall be disqualified for being elected or chosen or being a member of a council of a county or of a district or of a board of guardians or of any town commissioners if he— *L. G. Act, 1894, ss. 20 (2), 23 (2), 24 (4). L. G. (Scot.) Act, 1889, s. 83 (5).*

(a) is an infant or an alien ; or

(b) has within twelve months before his election, or since his election, received union relief ; or *L. G. Act, 1894, s. 46.*

(c) has, within five years before his election, or since his election, been convicted either on indictment or summarily of any crime, and sentenced to imprisonment with hard labour without the option of a fine, or to any greater punishment, and has not received a free pardon, or has, within or during the time aforesaid, been adjudged bankrupt, or made a composition or arrangement with his creditors ; or

(d) holds any paid office or place of profit under or in the gift or disposal of the council, board or commissioners, as the case may be, other than that of mayor or sheriff ; or *Munic. Corp. Act, 1882, s. 12 (1) (a).*

(e) is concerned by himself or his partner in any bargain or contract entered into with the council, board or commis- *Munic. Corp. Act, 1882, s. 12 (1) (c).*

sioners, or participates by himself or his partner in the profit of any such bargain or contract or of any work done under the authority of the council or board, or commissioners, and for the purpose of this provision, any bargain or contract with a county council in respect of any public work in a district shall be deemed to be also a bargain or contract with the council of that district.

(5.) Provided that a person shall not be disqualified for being elected or chosen or being a member of any such council, board, or commissioners by reason of being, by himself or his partner, interested—

(a.) in the sale or lease of any lands or in any loan of money to the council, board, or commissioners, or in any contract with the council for the supply from land, of which he is owner or occupier, of stone, gravel, or other materials for making or repairing highways or bridges, or in the transport of materials for the repair of roads or bridges in his own immediate neighbourhood ; or

(b.) in any newspaper in which any advertisement relating to the affairs of the council, board, or commissioners is inserted ; or

(c.) in any contract with the council, board, or commissioners as a shareholder in any joint stock company.

(6.) Where a person is disqualified by being adjudged bankrupt or making a composition or arrangement with his creditors, the disqualification shall cease, in case of bankruptcy, when the adjudication is annulled, or when he obtains his discharge with a certificate that his bankruptcy was caused by misfortune without any misconduct on his part, and, in case of composition or arrangement, on payment of his debts in full.

(7.) A person disqualified for being a guardian shall also be disqualified for being a rural district councillor.

I. G. Act, 1883, s. 75 (14).

(8.) If a member of a council of a county or district, or of a board of guardians or of any town commissioners, is absent from meetings of the council, board, or commissioners for more in the case of a county council than twelve months, consecutively, and in the case of a district council, board, or commissioners than six months consecutively, except in case of illness or for some reason approved by the council, board, or commissioners, his office shall on the expiration of those months become vacant.

(9.) Where a member of a council or board of guardians or town commissioners becomes disqualified, for holding office, or vacates his seat for absence, the council, board, or commissioners shall forthwith declare the office to be vacant, and signify the vacancy by notice signed by three members and countersigned by the secretary or clerk of the council, board, or commissioners, and notified in such manner as the council, board, or commissioners direct, and the office shall thereupon become vacant.

(10.) If any person acts when disqualified, or votes when prohibited, under this Order, he shall for each offence be liable on summary conviction to a fine not exceeding twenty pounds, without prejudice to the disqualification enacted by sub-section three of section ninety-four of the Act.

Incorporation of County and District Councils.

13. (1.)—Every council for a county or urban or rural district, which is not the council of a borough, shall be a body corporate by the name of the county or urban or rural district council, with the addition of the name of the county or district, or if there is any doubt as to the latter name, of such name as the Local Government Board direct, and shall have perpetual succession and a common seal and may hold land for the purposes of their powers and duties without license in mortmain.

Incorporation of county and district councils. L. G. Act, 1894, s. 24 (7).

(2.) Where any enactment (whether relating to lunatic asylums or public works or other county purposes, or to grand juries), requires or authorises land to be conveyed or granted to, or any contract or agreement to be made in the name of the secretary of the grand jury, clerk of the peace, or any board, commissioners, or other person, on behalf of a county or any part thereof, such land shall be conveyed or granted to, and such contract and agreement shall be made with the council of the county concerned.

I. G. Act, 1888, s. 79 (3).

14.—(1.) Any district council may, with the sanction of the county council, change their name and the name of their district.

(2.) Every change of name so made shall be published in such manner as the authority authorising the change may direct, and shall be notified to the Local Government Board.

(3.) Any such change of name shall not affect any rights or obligations of any district council, authority, or person, or render defective any legal proceedings, and any legal proceedings may be continued or commenced as if there were no change of name.

Change of name of district council. L. G. Act, 1894, s. 55 (3) to (5).

Property and Expenses.

15.—(1.) On and after the appointed day all the property of the grand jury of a county, or held by the secretary to the grand jury, or any justices or treasurer of a county, or board, or commissioners, or otherwise for any public uses and purposes of a county or of any barony or other division thereof, shall pass to and vest in and be held in trust for the council of the county subject to all debts and liabilities affecting it, and shall be held by the county council for the same estate, interest, and purposes, and subject to the same covenants, conditions, and restrictions, for and subject to which that property is or would have been held if the Act had not passed, so far as those purposes are not modified by the Act. Provided that—

Transfer of county property and liabilities. L. G. Act, 1888, s. 64 (1) (2) (3).

(a) the existing records of or in the custody of the court of quarter sessions or county court, or, except so far as they relate to the business transferred by the Act to county councils, of the court of assize, shall, subject to any order of the court, remain in the same custody in which they would have been if the Act had not passed ; and

(*b*) the grand jury of any county may retain any pictures, chattels, or property on the ground that the same have been presented to them or purchased out of their own funds or otherwise belong to them, and are not held for public purposes of the county, and any difference arising between the county council and the grand jury with respect to any such retention shall be referred to and determined by the Local Government Board under the Act.

(2.) On and after the appointed day all debts and liabilities of the grand jury, or of the secretary to the grand jury, or of any justices, treasurer, board, or commissioners, incurred for county purposes, shall become debts and liabilities of the county council, and shall, subject to the provisions of the Act, be defrayed by them out of the like property and funds out of which they would have been defrayed if the Act had not passed.

(3.) The county council shall have full power to manage, alter, and enlarge, and, with the consent of the Local Government Board, to alienate any land or buildings transferred by virtue of the Act, or otherwise vested in the council, but shall provide such accommodation and rooms, and such furniture, books, and other things as may from time to time be determined by the Local Government Board to be necessary or proper for the due transaction of the business, and convenient keeping of the records and documents of quarter sessions, of the county court, of justices in petty and special sessions or out of session, or of any committee of such quarter sessions or justices.

L. G. Act, 1888, s. 65 (3).

(4.) Where the county council, with the consent of the Local Government Board, sell any land, the proceeds of such sale shall be applied in such manner as the said Board sanction towards the discharge of any loan of the council, or otherwise for any purpose for which capital may be applied by the council.

(5.) This article shall apply to property, debts, and liabilities in connexion with a lunatic asylum in like manner as if the property were held by commissioners for the public uses and purposes of a county, and the debts and liabilities were debts and liabilities of commissioners incurred for county purposes.

(6.) Where the district of a lunatic asylum comprises two or more counties, the foregoing provisions of this Article shall apply with the necessary modification to those counties and to the councils thereof, and the property, debts, and liabilities shall be the joint property, debts, and liabilities of those councils.

Transfer of property from one authority to another. L. G. Act, 1894, s. 67.

16.—In any case to which the last foregoing Article does not apply, where any powers and duties are transferred by the Act from one authority to another authority—

(1.) All property held by the first authority for the purpose or by virtue of such powers and duties shall pass to and vest in the other authority, subject to all debts and liabilities affecting the same; and

(2.) The latter authority shall hold the same for the estate, interest, and purposes, and subject to the covenants, conditions, and restrictions for and subject to which the property would have been held if the Act had not passed, so far as the same are not modified by or in pursuance of the Act; and

(3.) All debts and liabilities of the first authority incurred by virtue of such powers and duties shall become debts and liabilities of the latter authority, and be defrayed out of the like property and funds out of which they would have been defrayed if the Act had not passed.

17.—(1.) The county council shall keep such accounts as will prevent the whole county from being charged with expenditure properly payable by a portion only of the county, and will prevent any sums raised in a portion only of the county being applied in reduction of expenditure properly payable by the whole or a larger part of the county, and will prevent any sums by law specifically applicable to any particular purpose from being applied to any other purpose.

Keeping of county council accounts so as to charge expenditure to proper area. L. G. Act, 1888 s. 8 (7) (8).

(2.) In determining the amount of expenditure for any particular purpose, whether a county at large or district charge, a proper proportion of the cost of the officers and buildings and establishments of the county council may be added to the expenditure directly expended for that purpose.

(3.) This Article shall apply, with the necessary modifications, to a district council.

18.—(1.) All payments to and out of the county or rural district fund shall be made to and by the county or rural district treasurer, and all payments out of the fund shall, unless made in pursuance of the specific requirement of the Act or any other Act of Parliament or of an order of a competent court, be made in pursuance of an order of the council signed by three members present at the meeting of the council and countersigned by the secretary or clerk of the council, and the same order may include several payments.

Payment out of county or rural district fund and finance committee of county council. L. G. Act, 1888 s. 80 (1) to (3).

(2.) Any such order may be removed into the High Court of Justice by writ of certiorari, and may be wholly or partly disallowed or confirmed on motion and hearing, with or without costs, according to the judgment and discretion of the court.

(3.) Every county council shall from time to time appoint a finance committee for regulating and controlling the finance of their county, and an order for the payment of a sum out of the county fund, whether on account of capital or income, shall not be made by a county council, except in pursuance of a resolution of the council passed on the recommendation of the finance committee.

(4.) This article does not apply to the council of a county borough, except when acting as a county council.

Accounts, Audit, and Annual Budget.

Making up and audit of accounts under Act of county and district councils and inspection.
L. G. Act, 1894, s. 58.
L. G. Act, 1888, s. 73 (2).

19.—(1.) The accounts of the receipts and payments of county and district councils in respect of the poor rate or otherwise of their duties under the Act, and of the committees and officers of those councils, shall be made up yearly to the thirty-first day of March (in this Order referred to as the local financial year), or in the case of accounts which are required to be audited half-yearly, then half-yearly to the thirtieth day of September and the thirty-first day of March in each year, and in such form as the Local Government Board prescribe.

(2.) The accounts of all the receipts and payments of every county and district council, and their committtees and officers, shall be audited by an auditor of poor law unions, and sections eleven to eighteen of the Local Government (Ireland) Act, 1871, as amended by section six of the Local Government (Ireland)

34 & 35 Vict. c. 109.
35 & 36 Vict. c. 69.

Act, 1872, or any subsequent enactment (including the provisions of those sections which impose penalties, or provide for the recovery of sums) shall apply accordingly, except that in the case of the accounts of receipts or payments in respect of the poor rate, or money raised by the poor rate, and of all receipts and payments of the council of a county at large and their committees and officers, the audit shall be half yearly instead of yearly.

(3.) The Local Government Board may, with respect to any audit to which this article applies, make rules modifying the euactments as to publication of the audit and of the abstract of accounts and the report of the auditor.

(4.) Every local government elector in a county or county district may, at all reasonable times, without payment, inspect and take copies of and extracts from all books, accounts, and documents belonging to or under the control of the council of the county or district.

Munic. Corp. Act, 1882, s. 27 (1).

(5.) The treasurer, or where a banking company is treasurer, the secretary or other officer whose duty it is to keep the accounts of the council, shall within one month from the date to which he is required to make up his accounts in each year or half year, submit them with the necessary vouchers and papers to the auditors and they shall audit them.

Returns to Local Government Board.
Munic. Corp. Act, 1882, s. 28, subs. (1), (3) to (6).

20.—(1.) The secretary of the county council and the town clerk or clerk of every urban and rural district council shall make a return to the Local Government Board of the receipts and payments to which the preceding article applies for each local financial year.

(2.) The return shall be in such form and contain such particulars as the Local Government Board from time to time direct.

(3.) The return shall be sent to the Local Government Board
within one month after the completion of the audit, or if the
audit is half yearly, the audit for the second half of each financial year.

(4.) If the said secretary or town clerk or clerk fails to make
any return required under this Article, he shall for each offence
be liable to a fine not exceeding twenty pounds to be recovered
by action on behalf of the Crown in the High Court.

(5.) The Local Government Board shall in each year prepare
an abstract of the return made in pursuance of this Article,
under general heads, and it shall be laid before both houses of
Parliament.

21.—(1.) At the beginning of every local financial year, every Annual budget
county council shall cause to be submitted to them an estimate of county councils.
of the receipts and expenses of such council during that financial L. G. Act, 1888,
year, whether on account of property, rates, loans, or otherwise. s. 74.

(2.) The council shall estimate the amount which will require
to be raised in the first six months and in the second six months
of the said financial year by means of rates.

(3.) If at the expiration of the first six months of such financial
year it appears to the council that the amount of the rate estimated at the commencement of the year will be larger than is
necessary or will be insufficient, the council may revise the estimate and alter accordingly the amount of the rate.

(4.) This Article does not apply to the council of a county
borough except as regards their receipts and expenses as a county
council.

Borrowing by County Council.

22.—(1.) The county council may from time to time, with the Borrowing by
consent of the Local Government Board, borrow, on the security of county council
the county fund, and of any revenues of the council, or on either such L. G. Act, 1888
fund or revenues, or any part of the revenues, such sums as may s. 69 (1) to (9).
be required for the following purposes, or any of them; that is
to say,—

(a) for consolidating the debts of the county; and

(b) for purchasing any land or building any building which
the council are authorised by any Act to purchase or
build; and

(c) for any permanent work or other thing which the
county council are authorised to execute or do, and the cost
of which ought, in the opinion of the Local Government
Board, to be spread over a term of years; and

(d) for any purpose for which the county council are
authorised by any Act to borrow or the cost of which the
grand jury were authorised by any Act to spread over a
period of years;

but neither the transfer of powers by the Act, nor anything else in the Act shall confer on the county council any power to borrow without the consent above-mentioned, and that consent shall dispense with the necessity of obtaining any other consent which may be required by the Acts relating to such borrowing, and the Local Government Board, before giving their consent, shall take into consideration any representation made by any ratepayers or owner of property rated to the poor rate.

(2.) Provided that where the total debt of the county council, after deducting the amount of any sinking fund, and of any debt or capital liability incurred on account of lunatic asylums exceeds, or if the proposed loan is borrowed, will exceed the amount of one tenth of the annual rateable value of the rateable property in the county, the proposed loan shall not be borrowed, except where it is for the purpose of a lunatic asylum, or except in pursuance of a provisional order made by the Local Government Board and confirmed by Parliament.

(3.) A county council may also from time to time, without any consent of the Local Government Board, during the period which was fixed for the discharge of any loan raised by them under the Act or transferred to them by the Act, borrow on the like security such amount as may be required for the purpose of paying off the whole or any part of such loan, or if any part of such loan has been repaid otherwise than by capital money, for re-borrowing the amount so repaid, and for the purpose of this Article "capital money" includes any instalments, annual appropriations, and sinking fund and the proceeds of the sale of land or other property, but does not include money previously borrowed for the purpose of repaying a loan.

(4.) All money re-borrowed shall be repaid within the period fixed for the discharge of the original loan, and every loan for re-borrowing shall for the purpose of the ultimate discharge be deemed to form part of the same loan as the original loan, and the obligations of the council with respect to the discharge of the original loan shall not be in any way affected by means of the re-borrowing.

(5.) The foregoing provisions with respect to the discharge of a loan transferred to the council by the Act shall extend to any capital liability transferred to them by the Act in like manner as if it were a loan.

(6.) A loan under this Article shall be repaid within such period, not exceeding sixty years, as the county council, with the consent of the Local Government Board, determine in each case, having regard to the duration of the work or object for which the loan is borrowed.

(7.) The county council shall pay off every loan either by equal yearly or half-yearly instalments of principal, or of principal and interest combined, or by means of a sinking fund set apart, invested, and applied in accordance with regulations made by the Local Government Board.

(8.) Where a loan is raised for any purpose, the cost of which is not a county at large charge, the council shall take care that the sums payable in respect of the loan are charged to the account to which the expenditure for that purpose is chargeable.

(9.) Where the county council are authorised to borrow any money on loan, they may raise such money either as one loan or several loans, and either by stock issued under the Act, or if special reasons exist for so borrowing, by mortgage, in accordance with sections two hundred and forty and two hundred and forty-one of the Public Health (Ireland) Act, 1878.   41 & 42 Vict. s. 52.

(10.) Provided that where a county council have borrowed by means of stock they shall not borrow by way of mortgage except for a period not exceeding five years.

(11.) A joint committee of the councils of counties comprised in a lunatic asylum district may, in accordance with regulations of the Local Government Board, exercise jointly for the purpose of a lunatic asylum the powers of those councils relating to borrowing.

(12.) This Article shall not apply to county boroughs when acting otherwise than in their capacity as a county council, and shall not authorise the council of a county borough to raise any loan by stock issued under the Act.

23.—(1.) County stock may be created, issued, transferred, dealt with, and redeemed in such manner and in accordance with such regulations as the Local Government Board may from time to time prescribe.   Issue of county stock. L. G. Act, 1888 s. 70.

(2.) Without prejudice to the generality of the above power, such regulations may provide for the discharge of any loan raised by such stock, and in the case of consolidation of debt for extending or varying the times within which loans may be discharged, and may provide for the consent of limited owners, and for the application of the Acts relating to stamp duties and to cheques, and for the disposal of unclaimed dividends, and may apply for the purposes of this Article, with or without modifications, any enactments relating to stock issued by the corporation of any municipal borough in England or Ireland.

(3.) Such regulations shall be laid before each House of Parliament for not less than thirty days during which the House sits, and if either House during such thirty days resolves that such regulations ought not to be proceeded with, the same shall be of no effect, without prejudice nevertheless to the making of further regulations.

(4.) If no such resolution is passed it shall be lawful for the Lord Lieutenant in Council to confirm such regulations, and the same when so confirmed shall be deemed to have been duly made and to be within the powers of the Act, and shall be of the same force as if they were enacted in the Act.

Transfer of Powers from Treasury.

Adaptation of
3 & 4 Vict.
c. 108, &c., as
to corporate
property and
liabilities.
23 & 24 Vict.
c. 16.
L. G. Act, 1888,
s. 72.
24.—(1.) The Local Government Board shall exercise, as regards any county borough or other borough, the powers conferred by section one hundred and forty-one of the Municipal Corporations (Ireland) Act, 1840, section seven of the Municipal Corporations (Ireland) Act, 1843, and sections one to seven and nine to eleven of the Municipal Corporations (Mortgages, etc). Act, 1860, relating to corporate property and liabilities, as respects the approval of loans and of the alienation of property, and other matters therein mentioned, and those sections shall, as respects any transactions commenced after the appointed day, be construed as if "Local Government Board" were throughout those sections substituted for "Treasury."

(2.) Where a local Act contains any provisions relating to the corporate property and liabilities of a borough as respects the approval of loans and the alienation of property and other matters similar to those contained in the sections above mentioned in this Article, that Act shall, as respects any transaction commenced after the appointed day, be construed as if "Local Government Board" were throughout the said provisions substituted for "Treasury."

Boundaries and Adjustment.

Future altera-
tion of
boundaries.
L. G. Act, 1888,
s. 54, subs.
(1), (3), (4).
25.—(1.) Whenever it is represented by the council of any county or borough to the Local Government Board—

(a) that the alteration of the boundary of any county or borough is desirable ; or

(b) that the union, for the purposes of the Act, of a county borough with a county is desirable ; or

(c) that the union, for the purposes of the Act, of any counties or boroughs or the division of any county is desirable ; or

(d) that the alteration of the boundary of any county electoral division or of the number of county councillors and county electoral divisions is desirable ; or

(e) that the alteration of any area of local government partly situate in their county or borough is desirable ;
the Local Government Board shall, unless for special reasons they think that the representation ought not to be entertained, cause to be made a local inquiry, and may make an order for the proposal contained in such representation, or for such other proposal as they may deem expedient, or may refuse such order, and, if they make the order, may by such order divide or alter any county electoral division.

(2.) Provided that if the order alters the boundary of a county or borough, or provides for the union of a county borough with a county, or for the union of any counties or boroughs, or for the division of any county, it shall be provisional only, and shall not have effect unless confirmed by Parliament.

(3.) Where such order alters the boundary of a borough, it may, as consequential upon such alteration, do all or any of the following things :—Increase or decrease the number of the wards in the borough, and alter the boundaries of such wards, and alter the apportionment of the number of councillors among the wards, and alter the total number of councillors, and, in such case, make the proportionate alteration in the number of aldermen.

26.—(1.) Whenever a county council is satisfied that a *prima facie* case is made out as respects any urban county district not a borough, for a proposal for all or any of the following things ; that is to say—

Future altera-tion of urban county districts and wards. L. G. Act, 1888, s. 57.

     (*a*) the alteration or definition of the boundary thereof ;
     (*b*) the division of an urban county district into wards ;
and
     (*c*) the alteration of the number of wards, or of the boundaries of any ward, or of the number of members of any urban district council, or of the apportionment of such members among the wards,

the county council may cause such inquiry to be made in the locality, and such notice to be given, both in the locality and to the Local Government Board, or other Government department as may be prescribed, and such other inquiry and notices (if any) as they think fit, and if satisfied that such proposal is desirable, may make an order for the same accordingly.

(2.) Notice of the provisions of the order shall be given, and copies thereof shall be supplied in the prescribed manner, and otherwise as the county council think fit.

(3.) The order shall be submitted to the Local Government Board ; and if within three months after such notice of the provisions of the order as the Local Government Board determine to be the first notice, the council of any district affected by the order, or any number of local government electors registered in that district or in any ward of that district, not being less than one-sixth of the total number of such electors in that district or ward, petition the Local Government Board to disallow the order, the Local Government Board shall cause to be made a a local inquiry, and determine whether the order is to be confirmed or not.

(4.) If any such petition is not presented, or being presented is withdrawn, the Local Government Board shall confirm the order.

(5.) The Local Government Board, on confirming an order, may make such modifications therein as they consider necessary for carrying into effect the objects of the order.

(6.) An order under this Article when confirmed by the Local Government Board, shall be forthwith laid upon the table of both Houses of Parliament, if Parliament be then sitting, and, if not, forthwith after the then next meeting of Parliament.

Supplemental provisions as to alteration of areas.
L. G. Act, 1888, s. 59.

27.—(1.) An order under the Act may make such administrative and judicial arrangements incidental to or consequential on any alteration of boundaries, authorities, or other matters made by the order as may seem expedient.

(2.) A place which is part of an administrative county for the purposes of the Act shall, subject as in section sixty-nine of the Act mentioned, form part of that county for all purposes, whether sheriff, lieutenant, custos rotulorum, justices, police, militia, coroner, or other.

(3.) For the purposes of parliamentary elections, and of the registration of voters for such elections, the sheriff, clerk of the peace, council, and secretary of the council, of the county in which any place is comprised at the passing of the Act for the purpose of parliamentary elections shall, save as otherwise provided by the order, or by the Act, or by or in pursuance of the

61 & 62 Vict. c. 2.

Registration (Ireland) Act, 1898, continue to have the same powers, duties, and liabilities as they would have had if no alteration of boundary had taken place, and in the case of the said council and secretary of the council, they and he had had the said powers, duties, and liabilities before the passing of the Act.

(4.) Any order made in pursuance of the Act may, so far as may seem necessary or proper for the purposes of the order, provide for all or any of the following matters ; that is to say,—

(a) may provide for the abolition, restriction, or establishment, or extension of the jurisdiction of any local authority in or over any part of the area affected by the order, and for the adjustment or alteration of the boundaries of such area, and for the constitution of the local authorities therein, and may deal with the powers and duties of any council, local authorities, quarter sessions, justices of the peace, coroners, sheriff, lieutenant, custos rotulorum, clerk of the peace, and other office therein, and with the cost of any such authorities, sessions, persons, or officers as aforesaid, and may determine the status of any such area as a component part of any larger area, and provide for the election of representatives in such area, and may extend to any altered area the provisions of any local Act which were previously in force in a portion of the area ; and

(b) may make temporary provision for meeting the debts and liabilities of tl e various authorities affected by the order, for the management of their property, and for regulating the duties, position, and remuneration of officers affected by the order and applying to them the provisions of the Act as to existing officers ; and

(c) may provide for the transfer of any writs, process, records, and documents relating to or to be executed in any part of the area affected by the order and for determining questions arising from such transfer ; and

(d) may provide for all matters which appear necessary or

proper for bringing into operation and giving full effect
to the order ; and

(e) may adjust any property, debts, and liabilities affected
by the order.

(5.) Where an alteration of boundaries of a county is made by
the Act, and section seventy of the Act does not apply, and the
matter is not met by an adjustment order made in pursuance of
an order in council under section one hundred and six of the
Act making transitory provisions, an order for any of the above-
mentioned matters may, if it appears to the Local Government
Board desirable, be made by that Board, but such order, if
petitioned against by any council, grand jury, or local authority
affected thereby, within three months after notice of such order
is given in accordance with the Act, shall be provisional only,
unless the petition is withdrawn or the order is confirmed by
Parliament.

(6.) An order may be made for amending any order previously
made in pursuance of the Act, and may be made by the same
authority and after the same procedure as the original order.

(7.) Where a provision of the Act respecting an order
requires the order to be confirmed by Parliament, either in every
case or if it is petitioned against, such order may amend any local
and personal Act.

28. In every alteration of boundaries effected under the
authority of the Act, care shall be taken that, so far as practicable, the boundaries of an area of local government shall not
intersect the boundaries of any other area of local government.

General pro-
vision as to
alteration of
boundaries.
L. G. Act, 1888,
s. 60.

29. Where the Local Government Board are required in pursuance of the Act to determine or arbitrate on any difference,
the provisions of the Regulation of Railways Act, 1868, respecting arbitrations by the Board of Trade, and the enactments
amending those provisions, shall apply as if they were herein re-
enacted, and in terms made applicable to the Local Government
Board and the decision of differences and matters under the Act.

Determination
of difference by
Local Govern-
ment Board.
L. G. Act, 1888,
s. 63.
59 & 60 Vict.
c. 9.
31 & 32 Vict.
c. 119.

30.—(1.) Where any adjustment is required for the purpose
of the Act, or of any order or thing made or done under the Act,
then if the adjustment is not otherwise made, the authorities
interested may make agreements for the purpose, and may thereby
adjust any property, income, debts, liabilities and expenses, so far
s affected by the Act or such order or thing, of the parties to
the agreement.

Adjustment
of property and
liabilities.
L. G. Act, 1894,
s. 63.

(2.) The agreement may provide for the transfer or retention of
any property, debts, or liabilities, with or without any conditions,
and for the joint use of any property, and for payment by either
party to the agreement in respect of property, debts, and
liabilities so transferred or retained, or of such joint user, and in
respect of the salary or remuneration of any officer or person, and
that either by way of an annual payment or, except in the case

of a salary or remuneration, by way of a capital sum, or of a terminable annuity for a period not exceeding that allowed by the Local Government Board : Provided that where any of the authorities interested is a board of guardians, any such agreement, so far as it relates to the joint use of any property, shall be subject to the approval of the Local Goverment Board.

(3.) In default of an agreement, and as far as any such agreement does not extend, such adjustment shall be referred to arbitration in manner provided by the Common Law Procedure Amendment (Ireland) Act, 1853, as amended by any subsequent enactment, and the arbitrator shall have power to disallow as costs in the arbitration the costs of any witness whom he considers to have been called unnecessarily, and any other costs which he considers to have been incurred unnecessarily, and his award may provide for any matter for which an agreement might have provided.

16 & 17 Vict. c. 113.

(4.) Any sum required to be paid by any authority for the purpose of adjustment may be paid as part of the general expenses of exercising their duties under the Act, or out of such special fund as the authority, with the approval of the Local Government Board direct, and if it is a capital sum the payment thereof shall be a purpose for which the authority may borrow under the Acts relating to such authority, on the security of all or any of the funds, rates, and revenues of the authority and any such sum may be borrowed without the consent of any authority, so that it be repaid within such period as the Local Government Board may sanction.

(5.) Any capital sum paid to any authority for the purpose of any adjustment under the Act shall be treated as capital, and applied, with the sanction of the Local Government Board, either in the repayment of debt or for any other purpose for which capital money may be applied.

Division of Borough into Wards, or alteration of Wards.

Proceedings for division of borough into wards or alteration of wards. 45 & 46 Vict. c. 50, s. 30. 56 & 57 Vict. c. 9.

31.—(1.) If the council of a borough upon a resolution passed by a majority of the whole council agree to petition, and the council thereupon petition, the Lord Lieutenant for the division of the borough into wards, or for the alteration of the number and boundaries of its wards, or for the alteration of the boundaries of the wards of the borough without any alteration of their number, it shall be lawful for the Lord Lieutenant from time to time, by Order in Council, to fix the number of wards into which the borough shall be divided, or to order the boundaries of the wards to be altered as the case may be ; and the borough shall be divided into that number of wards, or the boundaries of the wards shall be altered as the case may be.

(2.) Notice of the petition, and of the time when it pleases the Lord Lieutenant to order that the same be taken into consideration by the Privy Council, shall be published in the *Dublin Gazette* one month at least before the petition is so considered.

(3.) Where an Order in Council has been so made, the Chief Secretary shall appoint a commissioner to prepare a scheme for determining the boundaries of the wards and apportioning the councillors and aldermen among them.

(4.) In case of division into wards, the commissioner shall apportion all the councillors and aldermen among the wards.

(5.) In case of alteration of wards, he shall so apportion among the altered wards the councillors and aldermen for those wards as to provide for their continuing to represent as large a number as possible of their former constituents.

(6.) In either case each councillor or alderman shall hold his office in the ward to which he is assigned for the same time that he would have held it had the borough remained undivided or the wards unaltered.

(7.) If by reason of any division or alteration under this Article any doubt arises as to which councillor or alderman should go out of office, the doubt may be determined by the council.

(8.) The number of councillors assigned to each ward shall be a number divisible by three; and in fixing their number the commissioner shall, as far as he deems it practicable, have regard as well to the number of persons rated in the ward as to the aggregate rating of the ward.

(9.) The commissioner shall make the scheme in duplicate, and shall deliver one of the duplicates to the town clerk, and shall send the other to the Chief Secretary, to be submitted by him to the Lord Lieutenant in council for approval.

(10.) The scheme shall be published in the *Dublin Gazette*, and shall come into operation at the date of that publication, and thenceforth the boundaries of wards and apportionment of councillors and aldermen determined and made by the scheme shall be observed and be in force.

(11.) If the Lord Lieutenant in Council does not approve the scheme as originally prepared by the commissioner, it shall nevertheless be published in the *Dublin Gazette*, and shall be in force for the purposes of any municipal election until the Lord Lieutenant in Council, on further information and report from the commissioner, definitely approves a scheme in that behalf.

(12.) The commissioner may administer oaths, and may require any person having the custody of any book containing a poor rate made for the borough or any part thereof to produce the book for his inspection; and every person required by the commissioner to answer any question put to him for the purposes of this section shall answer it.

(13.) The commissioner shall have remuneration at the rate of five guineas for every day he is employed over and above his travelling and other expenses, and that remuneration and also the expenses of and incidental to the division of the borough into wards, or the alteration of wards shall be paid out of the borough fund.

(14.) When the powers conferred by this Article have been exercised in pursuance of a petition by the council of any borough, a further petition from the council of the same borough shall not be presented before the expiration of seven years from the date of the previous Order in Council under this Article.

Local Inquiries and Provisional Orders by the Local Government Board.

Application of provisions of 38 & 39 Vict. c. 55, as to local inquiries and provisional orders. L. G. Act, 1888, s. 87 (1), (2), (5).

32 —(1.) Where the Local Government Board are authorised by the Act to make an inquiry, to determine any difference, to make or confirm any order, to frame any scheme, or to give any consent, sanction, or approval to any matter, or otherwise to act under the Act, they may cause to be made a local inquiry, and in that case, and also in a case where they are required by the Act to cause to be made a local inquiry, section two hundred and nine, two hundred and ten, two hundred and twelve, and two hundred and thirteen, of the Public Health (Ireland) Act, 1878, shall apply as if they were in terms made applicable to the Act.

(2.) Sections two hundred and fourteen and two hundred and fifteen of the Public Health (Ireland) Act, 1878 (which relate to the making of provisional orders by the Local Government Board), shall apply for the purposes of the Act as if they were in terms made applicable thereto.

(3.) Where the Board cause any local inquiry to be held under the Act, the costs incurred in relation to such inquiry, including the salary of any inspector or officer of the Board engaged in such inquiry, not exceeding three guineas a day, shall be paid by the councils and other authorities concerned in such inquiry, or by such of them and in such proportions as the Board may direct, and the Board may certify the amount of the costs incurred, and any sum so certified and directed by the Board to be paid by any council or authority shall be a debt to the Crown from such council or authority.

Construction of Enactments.

Construction of Acts referring to business transferred. L. G. Act, 1888, s. 78.

33.—(1.) All enactments in any Act, whether general or local and personal relating to any business, powers, duties, or liabilities transferred by or in pursuance of the Act from any authority to a county or district council, or guardians, or to any councils jointly, shall, subject to the provisions of the Act, and so far as circumstances admit, be construed as if—

(a) any reference therein to the said authority or to any committee or the foreman or a member thereof, or to any meeting thereof (so far as it relates to the business, powers, duties, or liabilities transferred) referred to the county or district council or guardians, or to a committee or the chair-

man or a member thereof, or to a meeting thereof, as the
the case requires, and as if

(*b*) a reference to any clerk or officer of such authority
referred to the secretary, clerk, or officer of a county or
district council or guardians or committee thereof, as the
case requires, and as if

(*c*) all reference to the fiat or other sanction of a judge of
assize or court or recorder were omitted ;

and all the said enactments shall be construed with such modifications as may be necessary for carrying the Act into effect.

(2.) Where under any such enactment as in this Article
mentioned any powers, duties, or liabilities are to be exercised
or discharged after any presentment, or in any particular manner
or at any particular assizes, sessions, or meeting, or subject to any
other conditions, the county or district council or guardians may
exercise and discharge those powers, duties, and liabilities without
any such prior presentment, or in a different manner, or at any
meeting of the council or board, or without such other conditions,
in manner provided by the Act, and any rules or regulations
made in pursuance of the Act ; and, subject thereto, shall exercise
and discharge them in accordance with the rules regulating the
proceedings of the council or guardians, but in the like manner,
and at the like time, and subject to the like conditions, so nearly
as circumstances admit ; and a presentment by a grand jury in
relation to any such powers, duties, or liabilities shall cease to be
made otherwise than by way of indictment.

(3.) For the purposes of this Article the expression "authority"
means any drainage board, commissioners, conservators, or public
body, corporate or unincorporate, specified in a Provisional Order
transferring any powers, duties, or liabilities to the county council,
also any board, grand jury, or other local authority mentioned in
the Act ; and the expression "member of an authority" includes,
where the authority are a grand jury, any member of a grand
jury ; and the expression "meeting of an authority" includes the
assembly of a grand jury at assizes and a meeting of presentment
sessions ; and the expression "clerk of an authority" includes, in
relation to any grand jury, the secretary of the grand jury.

34.—(1.) If any question arises, or is about to arise, as to
whether any power, duty, or liability is or is not transferred by
or under the Act to any county or district council, or guardians,
or any property is or is not vested in a county or district council
or guardians, that question, without prejudice to any other
mode of trying it, may, if the parties to the difference so agree,
be referred to and decided by the Local Government Board, but
in the absence of such agreement may, on the application of
the council, guardians, board, commissioners, or other authority
concerned, be submitted for decision to the High Court in such
summary manner as, subject to any rules of court, may be
directed by the Court : and the Court. after hearing such parties

Summary proceedings for determination of questions as to transfer of powers. L. G. Act, 1894, s. 70 (1), (3). 61 & 62 Vict. c. 37, s. 101 (3).

and taking such evidence (if any) as it thinks just, shall decide the question.

(2.) An appeal shall, with the leave of the High Court or Court of Appeal, but not otherwise, lie to the Court of Appeal against any decision under this Article.

Proceedings and Committees of County and District Councils, and Chairman and Vice-Chairman thereof.

Annual meeting of councils of county and districts not boroughs.
L. G. Acts, 1894, s. 59 (1).
38 & 39 Vict. c. 55, s. 199,
Sched. I. (11).
M. C. Act, 1882, s. 61 (2), (4).

35.—(1.) The council of every urban county district not a borough shall hold an annual meeting and other meetings for the transaction of business under the Act once at least in each month, and at such other times as may be necessary for properly executing their powers and duties under the Act.

(2.) The council of every county at large, and of every rural district, shall hold an annual meeting, and also meetings at such other times as may be necessary for properly executing their powers and duties under the Act.

(3.) The annual meeting of a rural district council shall be held in each year on the fifth day after the day which was the day of election at the last triennial election of the councillors.

(4.) The annual meeting of a county council shall be held in each year on the twelfth day next after the day which was the day of election at the last triennial election of the councillors.

(5.) At such annual meeting of a county or rural district council—

(*a*) if it is the first meeting after a triennial election, the first business transacted thereat shall be the consideration of the question of choosing, and if it is so determined the choice of, additional councillors, and the second business shall be the choice of a chairman and vice-chairman; and

(*b*) in the case of any other annual meeting, the first business shall be the choice of chairman and of vice-chairman; and

(*c*) in case of equality of votes, the chairman of the meeting, although not entitled to vote in the first instance, shall have the casting vote.

Meetings and proceedings of county and rural district councils, appointment of committees, minutes, &c.
L. G. Act, 1888, s. 75 (15), (21).
Munic. Corp. Act, 1882, s. 22.
L. G. Act, 1894, Sched. I., Part 4

36.—(1.) This Article and the rules hereinafter set out shall not extend to the council of a county borough, but shall extend to every other county council and to every rural district council.

(2.) The quorum of every such council shall be one-fourth of the whole number of the council.

(3.) The meeting of such council, or of any committee thereof, may be held at such place, either within or without their county or district, as the council from time to time direct.

(4.) Every such council may from time to time appoint, out of their own body, such and so many committees, either of a general or special nature, and consisting of such number of persons, as they think fit, for any purposes which, in the opinion of the council, would be better regulated and managed by means of such committees ; but the acts of every such committee shall be submitted to the council for their approval.

(5.) The quorum, proceedings, and place of meeting of a committee, whether within or without the county or district, and the area (if any) within which the committee are to exercise their authority, shall be such as may be determined by regulations of of the council appointing the committee, and, subject to those regulations, the quorum, proceedings, and place of meeting of a committee, whether within or without the county or district, shall be such as the committee direct, and the chairman at any meeting of the committee shall have a second or casting vote. Part 4 of First Schedule to L. G. Act, 1894.

(6.) A member of the council shall not vote, or take part in the discussion of any matter before the council, or a committee, in which he has, directly or indirectly, by himself or by his partner, any pecuniary interest. Munic. Corp. Act, 1882, s. 22.

(7.) No act or proceeding of the council, or of a committee, shall be questioned on account of any vacancy in their body.

(8.) A minute of proceedings at a meeting of the council, or of a committee, signed at the same or the next ensuing meeting, by the chairman, or by a member of the council or of the committee, describing himself as, or appearing to be, chairman of the meeting at which the minute is signed, shall be received in evidence without further proof.

(9.) Until the contrary is proved, every meeting of the council, or of a committee, in respect of the proceedings whereof a minute has been so made, shall be deemed to have been duly convened and held, and all the members of the meeting shall be deemed to have been duly qualified ; and where the proceedings are proceedings of a committee, the committee shall be deemed to have been duly constituted, and to have had power to deal with the matters referred to in the minutes.

(10.) The rules above mentioned are as follows :—

(I.) The council shall hold four quarterly meetings in every year for the transaction of general business.

(II.) The quarterly meeting shall be held at such hour on such days between the annual meeting and the first day of June then next following as, subject to the provisions of the Act—(a) in the case of the county council, the council at the annual meeting decide or afterwards from time to time by standing order determine ; and (b) in the case of a rural district council, the county council from time to time determine. Second Schedule of the Municipal Corporations Act, 1882.

(III.) The chairman may at any time call a meeting of the council.

(IV.) If the chairman refuses to call a meeting after a requisition for that purpose, signed by five members of the council, has been presented to him, any five members of the

R

council may forthwith, on that rafusal, call a meeting. If the chairman (without so refusing) does not within seven days after such presentation call a meeting, any five members of the council may, on the expiration of those seven days, call a meeting.

(V.) Three clear days at least before any meeting of the council, notice of the time and place of the intended meeting, signed by the chairman, or if the meeting is called by members of the council, by those members, shall be fixed on the hall or other place at which the council is accustomed to meet. Where the meeting is called by members of the council, the notice shall specify the business proposed to be transacted thereat.

(VI.) Three clear days at least before any meeting of the council, a summons to attend the meeting, specifying the business proposed to be transacted thereat, and signed by the secretary or clerk of the council, shall be left or delivered by post at the usual place of abode of every member of the council.

(VII.) Want of service of the summons on any member of the council shall not affect the validity of a meeting.

(VIII.) No business shall be transacted at a meeting other than that specified in the summons relating thereto, except in case of the annual meeting, business prescribed by the Act to be transacted thereat.

(IX.) At every meeting of the council, the chairman, if present, shall be chairman. If the chairman is absent, then the vice-chairman shall be chairman. If both the chairman and the vice-chairman are absent, then such councillor as the members of the council then present choose shall be chairman.

(X.) The names of the members present as well as of those voting on each question shall be recorded, so as to show whether each vote given was for or against the question.

ledule 1 (6)
38 & 39 Vict.
55, s. 59 (1) of
G. Act, 1894.

(XI.) All acts of the council, and all questions coming or arising before the council, may be done and decided by the majority of such members of the council as are present and vote at a meeting held in pursance of the Act, the whole number present at the meeting, whether voting or not, not being less than one-fourth of the number of the whole council.

(XII.) In case of equality of votes, the chairman of the meeting shall have a second or casting vote.

(XIII.) Minutes of the proceedings of every meeting shall be drawn up and fairly entered in a book kept for that purpose, and shall be signed in manner authorised by the Act.

(XIV.) Subject to an Order of the Lord Lieutenant in Council under Part Six of the Act, and to the foregoing provisions of these Rules, the council may from time to time make standing orders for the regulation of their proceedings and business, and vary or revoke the same.

37.—(1.) The term of office both of the chairman and of the vice-chairman of a county or rural district council shall be one year, but he shall continue in office until his successor has accepted office, and made and subscribed the required declaration. *Chairman and vice-chairman of county or rural district council. Munic. Corp. Act, 1882, s. 15 (3). L. G. Act, 1888, s. 2 (6).*

(2.) Subject to any rules made from time to time by the county or district council, anything authorised or required to be done by, to, or before the chairman may be done by, to, or before such vice-chairman.

38.—(1.) Any county councils, including councils of county boroughs, may from time to time join in appointing out of their respective bodies a joint committee for any purpose in respect of which they are jointly interested. *Appointment of joint committees. L. G. Act, 1888. ss. 81, 82 (3).*

(2.) Any council taking part in the appointment of any joint committee under this Article may from time to time delegate to the committee any power which such council might exercise for the purpose for which the committee is appointed.

(3.) Provided that nothing in this Article shall authorise a council to delegate to a committee any power of making a rate or borrowing any money.

(4.) Subject to the terms of delegation, any such joint committee shall, in respect of any matter delegated to it, have the same power in all respects as the councils appointing it, or any of them, as the case may be.

(5.) The members of a joint committee appointed under the Act shall be appointed at such times and in such manner as may be from time to time fixed by the councils who appointed them, and shall hold office for such time as may be fixed by those councils, so that such committee do not continue for more than three months after any triennial election of councillors of those councils.

(6.) The cost of a joint committee shall be defrayed by the councils by whom its members were appointed, in the proportion agreed to by them ; and the accounts of such joint committee and their officers shall, for the purposes of the provisions of the Act, be deemed to be accounts of the county councils and their officers.

(7.) In the case of a joint committee the councils appointing the joint committee shall jointly have the powers given by this Order to each council in respect of a committee appointed by that council. *s. 82 (3) of the L. G. Act, 1888.*

(8.) This Article shall apply to district councils *inter se* in like manner as to county councils.

Transitional Proceedings and Savings.

39.—(1.) If from any cause there is no returning officer able to act in any county, district, or town at the first election under *Power of Local Government Board to*

remedy defects.
L. G. Act, 1888,
s. 108 (1), (3), (4). the Act of a county or district council, or of guardians in a county borough or an urban county district or of commissioners of a town, or no register of electors properly made up or no proper election takes place, or an election of an insufficient number of persons takes place, or any difficulty arises as respects the holding of the first election of county or district councillors, or of guardians in a county borough or an urban county district or of commissioners of a town, or as to the first meeting of a county council, district council, board of guardians, or town commissioners first elected under the Act, the Local Government Board may by order appoint a returning officer or other officer, and do any matter or thing which appears to them necessary for the proper holding of the first election and for the proper holding of the first meeting of the said council or board or commissioners, and may, if it appears to them necessary, direct a new election to be held, and fix the dates requisite for such new election. Any such order may modify the provisions of the Act, and the enactments applied by the Act, so far as may appear to the Board necessary for the proper holding of the first election and first meeting of the council, board or commissioners.

(2.) The Local Government Board, on the application of any county or district council, or board of guardians, or town commissioners, may within six months after the day fixed for the first election of the councillors of such council, or board or commissioners, from time to time, make such orders as appear to them necessary for bringing the Act into full operation as respects the council, board or commissioners so applying, and such orders may modify any enactment in the Act or in any other Act, whether general or local and personal, so far as may appear to the Board necessary for the said purpose.

(3.) The Local Government Board may also, if satisfied that an election cannot properly be held for any county or district council, or of guardians in a county borough or an urban county district or of commissioners of a town, not an urban district, by reason of the electoral divisions not having been duly made, cause such steps to be taken as they consider necessary for constituting such electoral divisions and making up the registers of electors.

Current rates,
jury lists, &c.
L. G. Act, 1888,
s. 110. **40.**—(1.) Every rate and cess made or applotted before the appointed day may be assessed, levied and collected, and proceedings for the enforcement thereof taken, in like manner as nearly as may be as if the Act had not passed.

(2.) The accounts of all receipts and expenditure before the appointed day shall be audited, and allowances, surcharges, and penalties recovered and enforced, and other consequential proceedings had, in like manner as nearly as may be as if the Act had not passed but as soon as practicable after the appointed day ; and every authority, committee, or officer whose duty it is to make up any accounts, or to account for any portion of the receipts or expenditure in any account, shall, until the audit is completed, be deemed for the purpose of such audit to continue in office, and be bound to perform the same duties and render the same accounts and be subject to the same liabilities as before the appointed day.

(3.) All proceedings, legal and other, commenced before the appointed day, may be carried on in like manner, as nearly as may be, as if the Act had not passed, and any such legal proceeding may be amended in such manner as may appear necessary or proper in order to bring it into conformity with the provisions of the Act.

(4.) Every militiaman enlisted before the appointed day shall continue liable to serve in the same corps as if the Act had not passed.

41. The change of name of an urban or rural sanitary authority shall not affect their identity as a corporate body or derogate from their powers, and any enactment in any Act, whether public or local and personal, referring to the members of such authority, shall, unless inconsistent with the Act, continue to refer to the members of such authority under its new name.

Change of name of authority. L. G. Act, 1894, s. 85 (5).

42.—(1.) The governors or directors of an asylum for pauper lunatics holding office on the day fixed for the first election of county councillors under the Act, shall continue to hold office until the expiration of one week after the county council have elected a committee for the like purpose and no longer.

Transitory provisions as to lunatic asylums. L. G. Act, 1888, s. 111 (1), (2), (4), (5).

(2.) Any committee elected by the county council shall come into office at the expiration of the said week, and shall be deemed to be a continuance of the said governors or directors.

(3.) Anything done in pursuance of the enactments relating to pauper lunatics by the said governors or directors before the appointment of any committee by the county council shall have effect as if it had been done by the county council or by a committee elected by the county council.

(4.) Where a lunatic asylum district comprises two or more counties, this Article shall apply in like manner as if the joint committee appointed by councils of such counties were the committee above mentioned.

43.—(1.) Nothing in the Act shall prejudicially affect any securities granted before the passing of the Act on the credit of any rate cess or property transferred to a council by the Act, and all such securities, as well as all unsecured debts, liabilities, and obligations incurred by any author ty in the exercise of any powers or in relation to any property transferred from them to a council shall be discharged, paid and satisfied by that council, and where for that purpose it is necessary to continue the levy of any rate or cess or the exercise of any power which would have existed but for the Act, that rate or cess may continue to be levied and that power to be exercised either by the authority who otherwise would have levied or exercised the same, or by the council as the case may require.

Saving for existing securities and discharge of debts. L. G. Act, 1888. s. 122.

(2.) It shall be the duty of every authority whose powers, duties, and liabilities are transferred by the Act to liquidate, so far as practicable before the appointed day, all current debts and liabilities incurred by such authority.

Saving for existing byelaws.
L. G. Act, 1888, s. 123.

44. All such byelaws, orders, and regulations of any authority, whose powers and duties are transferred by or in pursuance of the Act to any council, as are in force at the time of the transfer, shall, so far as they relate to or are in pursuance of the powers and duties transferred, continue in force as if made by that council, and may be revoked or altered accordingly.

Saving for pending actions, contracts, &c.
L. G. Act, 1888, s. 124.

45.—(1.) If at the time when any powers, duties, liabilities, debts or property are, by or in pursuance of the Act, transferred to a council, any action or proceeding or any cause of action or proceeding is pending or existing by or against any authority in relation thereto, the same shall not be in any wise prejudicially affected by the passing of the Act, but may be continued, prosecuted, and enforced by or against the council as successors of the said authority in like manner as if the Act had not been passed.

(2.) All contracts, deeds, bonds, agreements, and other instruments subsisting at the time of the transfer in this Article mentioned, and affecting any of such powers, duties, liabilities, debts, or property, shall be of as full force and effect against or in favour of the council, and may be enforced as fully and effectually as if, instead of the authority, the council had been a party thereto.

(3.) All contracts or agreements which prior to the appointed day have been made by the secretary of the grand jury or any grand juror or commissioners or otherwise, on behalf of a county or any barony or part of a county, including contracts or agreements relating to lunatic asylums, shall have effect as if the council of that county had been named therein instead of the secretary, grand juror, or commissioner or other person acting on behalf of the county, and may be enforced by or against the county council accordingly.

(4.) This Article shall apply in the case of a committee of any authority in like manner as if the committee were such authority, and the committee of a county council were that council, and as if contracts and agreements by any such committee appointed by a grand jury were contracts or agreements on behalf of a county.

Adaptation of Local Acts.

Adaptation of Local Acts,
60 & 61 Vict.
c. 37, s. 104 (2) (d).

46. There shall be made in every local and personal Act such adaptations as appear requied to bring it into conformity with the enactments applied by this order.

LOCAL GOVERNMENT (TRANSITORY PROVISIONS) (No. 2) ORDER, 1898.

By the LORD LIEUTENANT and Privy Council of Ireland.

CADOGAN :

WHEREAS it is enacted by section one hundred and six of the Local Government (Ireland) Act, 1898, that the Lord Lieutenant by Order in Council may (among other matters) make such transitory provisions as appear to him necessary or expedient for bringing the said Act into operation, and in particular for the various matters in the said section mentioned. 61 & 62 Vict. c. 37.

And whereas it appears to Us necessary or expedient for the above purposes that the provisions herein-after contained should have full effect;

Now, therefore, We, the Lord Lieutenant-General and General Governor of Ireland, by virtue of the powers vested in Us for that purpose as aforesaid, and of all other powers enabling Us in that behalf, by and with the advice of Her Majesty's Privy Council in Ireland, do order and it is hereby ordered as follows :—

Short Title and Interpretation.

1. This Order may be cited as the Local Government (Transitory Provisions) (No. 2) Order, 1898. Short Title.

2.—(1.) In this Order, unless the context otherwise requires— Definitions.

(*a*) The expression "the Act" shall mean the Local Government (Ireland) Act, 1898, and includes any Order made under Part Six thereof, and expressions referring to the Act or to enactments in the Act or to the passing of the Act shall be construed to include a reference to any such Order, or to the provisions of any such Order, or to the making of any such Order.

(*b*) Other expressions shall, subject to the express provisions in this Order, have the same meaning as in the Act.

(*c*) Any reference in any provision to the appointed day shall mean such day as under the Act may be the appointed day for the purpose of that provision.

(*d*) The expression "local Act" includes a Provisional Order confirmed by an Act, and the Act confirming the Order.

(2.) The Interpretation Act, 1889, applies for the purpose of the interpretation of this Order as it applies for the interpretation of an Act of Parliament.

Action of Grand Juries, Presentment Sessions, Guardians,
Councils, Authorities, and Officers affected by the Act.

As to present-
ments and
county cess
before 30th
September,
1899.

3.—(1.) It shall be the duty of every grand jury and presentment sessions to provide for liquidating so far as practicable,
before the appointed day, all current debts and liabilities incurred
in respect of their county or barony.

(2.) The grand jury of each county at the spring assizes next
after the date of this Order and the presentment sessions held
next after the sixteenth day of August one thousand eight
hundred and ninety-eight shall proceed in like manner as if the
Act had not passed, subject as follows :

(*a*) they shall not take into account possible receipts from
the agricultural grant ; and

(*b*) they shall not make a presentment for any new work
unless it was certified by the foreman of the grand jury at
the previous assizes, but they shall make such presentments
in respect of works to be executed, salaries to be paid, and
matters to be done subsequent to the spring assizes as will
meet everything required up to the last day of September
next following, and as appear necessary to comply with the
provisions of this Order with respect to the liquidation of
current debts and liabilities ; and

(*c*) they may arrange for the continuance up to the said
last day of September of contracts expiring before that day,
and for any other matter required up to that day for the
maintenance of works ; and

(*d*) they may make presentments provisional upon a
certificate by the county surveyor before the assizes, and if
such certificate is given, such provisional presentment shall
have the effect of a presentment.

(3.) The grand jury shall, notwithstanding the absence of a
presentment by presentment sessions, or any disallowance by
presentment sessions, make such presentments and arrangements
as appear to them necessary or proper for carrying into effect
this Article, and for that purpose may vary any presentment by
presentment sessions.

(4.) Every grand jury may at the said spring assizes re-appoint
for a term not exceeding three months any high constable and
collector, or collector of a barony, or deputy-collector under
section one hundred and forty-eight of the Grand Juries Act,
1836, who was appointed at the summer assizes in the year one
thousand eight hundred and ninety-eight, and may also re-present
any arrears of county cess applotted at any assizes before the said
spring assizes.

(5.) Receipts in respect of the county cess applotted before the
said spring assizes shall, subject to the provisions of this Article,
be paid to the county treasurer in like manner as if the Act had
not passed.

(6.) Such payments out of the county cess applotted before the said spring assizes as are required to be made in pursuance of the presentments at those or former assizes shall, subject to the provisions of this Article, be paid by the county treasurer in like manner as if the Act had not passed.

(7.) After the day fixed by the county council or, if any adjustment is required, by the Local Government Board, all receipts and payments in respect of any county cess applotted before the said spring assizes shall be paid into and out of the county fund as if they were receipts and payments in respect of the poor rate levied under the Act, but until the day so fixed, the payments made to and by the county treasurer shall be made in accordance with the directions (if any) given by or on behalf of the Local Government Board.

(8.) The county treasurer shall pay such fee for the audit of the county treasurer's accounts after the spring assizes as would have been payable if the Act had not passed.

(9.) As respects payments out of money to be raised after the said spring assizes to meet presentments at those assizes, no county cess shall be applotted to meet the same, but the money required for those payments shall be raised by the county council.

(10.) In the construction of this Article with respect to the county of Dublin—

(a.) " presenting term ' shall be substituted for "assizes," and " Easter presenting term" for " spring assizes," and " finance committee " for " county treasurer "; and

(b.) presentments shall be made for the period ending the last day of September next following, and not for the whole year ; and

(c.) adjourned sessions shall not be held after the Easter presenting term in the year one thousand eight hundred and ninety-nine, but the grand jury at that term shall have all the powers of such adjourned presentment sessions, with the exception that they shall not continue the contracts expiring on the first day of June one thousand eight hundred and ninety-nine up to the following last day of September, but shall place all the works to which such contracts relate in the charge of the county surveyor ; and

(d.) the grand jury at the said presenting term shall provide that all works then in the charge of the county surveyor shall continue in that charge up to the last day of September, one thousand eight hundred and ninety-nine.

4.—(1.) Every board of guardians, as regards the first poor rate made after the sixteenth day of August one thousand eight hundred and ninety-eight, shall make the same only for the service of the period ending on the last day of March, one thousand eight hundred and ninety-nine ; but otherwise every

As to guardians and district councils before 30th September, 1899.

board of guardians shall make, levy, collect, and recover the poor rate in like manner as if the Act had not passed.

(2.) In the case of a union part of which is within and part without the city of Dublin, the foregoing provision shall apply as respects that portion of the union which is without the city ; but as respects that portion of the union which is within the city, the board of guardians shall estimate the amount required by them, according to the law existing at the passing of the Act, for the service of the period ending on the last day of March, one thousand eight hundred and ninety-nine, and estimate the amount required by them according to the law as altered by the Act, for the service of the period between the said last day of March and the first day of October following, and shall send the estimate of those amounts to the Collector-General of Rates under the Dublin Collection of Rates Act, 1849, and that Collector-General shall make, levy, collect, and recover the rate for the total of the two amounts in like manner as if the Act had not passed.

12 & 13 Vict. c. 91.

(3.) A county council may, with the approval of the Local Government Board, temporarily advance, out of the money received by the council from the agricultural grant, such sums to any rural district council or board of guardians as that council or board require to meet their expenses, until the full demand of such council or board can be met out of the poor rate ; and if and so far as any such advance is not made or is insufficient, the county council or the rural district council or board of guardians may, with the approval of the Local Government Board, borrow temporarily the required amount.

As to Dublin Collector-General of Rates and police and bridge rate.

5.—(1.) The Commissioner of Police of Dublin Metropolis and the Dublin Port and Docks Board respectively, shall estimate the amount required by him or them according to the law existing at the passing of the Act for the service of the period ending on the last day of September, one thousand eight hundred and ninety-nine, and shall send the estimate of those amounts to the Collector-General of Rates under the Dublin Collection of Rates Act, 1849, and that Collector-General shall make, levy, collect, and recover the rates for the said amounts in like manner as if the Act had not passed.

12 & 13 Vict. c. 91.

(2.) The Commissioner of Police of Dublin Metropolis and the Dublin Port and Docks Board respectively, shall estimate the amount required by him or them according to the law as altered by the Act for the service of the period between the last day of September, one thousand eight hundred and ninety-nine, and the first day of April, nineteen hundred, and shall send the estimate of those amounts to the county councils for the county and the city of Dublin, and those county councils shall pay and raise the amounts in accordance with the Act in like manner as if they were estimates for the second half of the local financial year.

6. Any sum due on account of a rate assessed upon any premises by the Collector-General of Rates under the Dublin Collection of Rates Act, 1849, which has not been collected at the time when the Collector-General ceases to hold office, may be collected by the county council of the county in which the said premises are situate, and for the purpose of collecting and recovering such sum the powers of the Collector-General of Rates shall be transferred to the said county council.

Collection of arrears of rates made by Dublin Collector-General of Rates.

7. Notwithstanding anything in any general or local Act, the council of any borough or town during the period between the passing of the Act and the time at which the Act comes into full operation may, for the purpose of raising money required to meet their expenses, make any rate or assessment either—

As to rates of urban authorities before the Act comes into full operation.

(*a*) for the service of the period ending on the thirtieth day of September, one thousand eight hundred and ninety-nine ; or

(*b*) for the service of the period ending on the thirty-first day of March, nineteen hundred ;

and in either case the making of such rate or assessment shall not, if the Local Government Board so authorise, prevent the making of any further rate or assessment during the same year, for the service of some period ending on the thirty-first day of March, nineteen hundred ; and where any rate or assessment is made as mentioned in this Article, enactments relating to the year's rates shall apply thereto with such modifications as may be prescribed by the Local Government Board.

8. Any rate made in the year one thousand eight hundred and ninety-nine after the first day of April shall be made according to the revised valuation list prepared by the Commissioner of Valuation, and sent by him to the authority making the rate ; and the said authority, if necessary, shall postpone the making of the rate until the list is so received, and, with the approval of the Local Government Board, may, during such postponement, borrow temporarily any sum required to meet their current expenses.

As to rates made in 1899 after 1st April.

First Meeting of County Councillors.

First county council. Cf. 51 & 52 Vict. c. 41. ss. 105, 107.

9.—(1.) The first meeting of the county council shall be held on the twelfth day next after the day of the first election at the court house of the county or other place fixed by the returning officer, and shall be convened by the returning officer in like manner as meetings of the council are required by the Act to be convened, and as if the person convening the same were the chairman of the council·

(2.) At the first meeting the council shall first choose one of their number to be chairman of the meeting, and if an equal number of votes is given for two or more persons for such chairman, the meeting shall determine by lot which of those persons shall be the chairman of the meeting.

(3.) The meeting shall then proceed as their first business to consider the question of choosing additional councillors, and, if it is so determined, to choose those councillors ; and those councillors, if in attendance, shall be entitled to make the declaration of office, and take their seats and vote in the choosing of the chairman.

(4.) The council shall then proceed as their second business to choose the chairman of the council for the year, and the chairman so chosen, if present, shall on making the declaration accepting office, take the chair in place of the chairman of the meeting.

(5.) In case of equality of votes at the choice of the chairman of the council, the chairman of the meeting shall have a second or casting vote.

(6.) If any members of a joint committee or joint board are appointed by the county council, the consideration of the appointment of such members shall be part of the business at the first meeting after the election of chairman.

(7.) The Council may also at their first meeting, if they think fit, choose a vice-chairman.

(8.) The term of office of the first chairman and vice-chairman of the county council shall end on the day of the annual meeting in the year nineteen hundred.

(9.) A county council need not hold an annual meeting in the year one thousand eight hundred and ninety-nine, and the annual meeting of the first county council in any subsequent year shall be held at the time it would be held if the election had been on the first day of June, one thousand eight hundred and ninety-nine.

(10.) This article shall apply to the county of Dublin in like manner as to any other county, except that the first meeting of the county council shall be held on the second day of May next after the day of the first election.

(11.) This Article shall not apply to a county boroughs.

First Rural District Councillors and Guardians.

First rural district councillors.

10.—(1.) The rural district councillors elected at the first election under the Act shall come into office in their capacity as rural district councillors on the day next after the day of election.

(2.) The first meeting of the rural district council shall be held on the fifth day next after the day of the first election at the board room of the guardians of the union or other place fixed by the returning officer, and shall be convened by the returning officer in like manner as the meetings of the ceuncil are required by the Act to be convened, and as if the person convening the same were the chairman of the council.

(3.) At the first meeting the council shall first choose one of their number to be chairman of the meeting, and if an equal number of votes is given for two or more persons for such chairman, the meeting shall determine by lot which of those persons shall be the chairman of the meeting.

(4.) The meeting shall then proceed as their first business to choose additional councillors, as required by section one hundred and thirteen of the Act, and the councillors then chosen, if in attendance, shall be entitled to make the declaration of office and take their seats and vote at the subsequent proceedings of the meeting.

(5.) The meeting shall then proceed as their second business, to consider the question of choosing additional councillors under section twenty-five of the Act, and if it is so determined to choose those councillors, and any additional councillors then chosen, if in attendance, shall be entitled to make the declaration of office and take their seats and vote in the choosing of the chairman.

(6.) The meeting shall then proceed, as their third business, to choose the chairman of the council for the year, and the chairman so chosen, if present, shall, on making the declaration accepting office, take the chair in place of the chairman of the meeting.

(7.) In case of equality of votes at the choosing of additional councillors or the choosing of the chairman of the council, the chairman of the meeting shall have a second or casting vote.

(8.) If any members of a joint committee or joint board are appointed by the rural district council, the consideration of the appointment of such members shall be part of the business of the first meeting after the election of chairman.

(9.) The council may also at their first meeting, if they think fit, choose a vice-chairman.

(10.) The term of office of the first chairman and vice-chairman of the rural district council shall end on the day oi the anuual meeting in the year nineteen hundred.

(11.) A rural district council need not hold an annual meeting in the year one thousand eight hundred and ninety-nine, and the annual meeting of the first rural district council in any subsequent year shall be held at the time it would be held if the election had been on the first day of June, one thousand eight hundred and ninety-nine.

11.—(1.) The rural district councillors elected at the first First election under the Act shall come into office in their capacity as guardians. guardians on the day of the meeting of the board of guardians next after the first meeting of the rural district council, and the guardians of a union elected at the first election under the Act for an electoral division in a county borough or urban county district shall come into office on the same day.

(2.) The first meeting of the board of guardians of a union after the first election under the Act of rural district councillors shall be held on the same day as the first meeting of the rural district council in the union, but after the conclusion of the first meeting of that council, or on such day not more than four days later as may be fixed by the returning officer, and shall be convened by the returning officer in like manner as meetings of the council are required by the Act to be convened, and as if the person convening the same were the chairman of the council.

(3.) On the day of such first meeting all persons who are then guardians shall retire from office, but until that day the persons who are guardians at the date of this Order shall continue in office, notwithstanding any want of qualification, as if the term of office for which they were elected expired on that day, and until the election under the Act no further election shall be held except for filling casual vacancies.

First County Borough and Urban County District Councillors and Continuance in Office of existing Councillors, &c.

First county borough and urban district councillors and aldermen and continuance in office of existing councillors, &c.

12.—(1.) Upon the day next after the day of election all the persons who are then members of the council of any borough or commissioners of a town shall cease to hold office, but until that day the term of office of any such members who were in office on the sixteenth day of August one thousand eight hundred and ninety eight shall continue, notwithstanding any want of qualification ; and until the first election under the Act no further election shall, after the said sixteenth day of August, be held except for filling casual vacancies ;

Provided that in the case of Belfast and Londonderry, this provision shall apply only to those persons who, but for the Act, would have retired in November one thousand eight hundred and ninety-eight, instead of applying to all the members of the council, and the other members of the council shall continue in office until the ordinary day of retirement of councillors and alderman next following the month of November in which but for the Act such members would have retired.

(2.) The first meeting of each council for a county borough or urban county district or of the commissioners of a town held after the first election under the Act, shall be convened by the mayor or chairman of the commissioners, as the case may be, to meet on the day on which the first meeting of the council or commissioners after the ordinary annual or triennial elections of councillors or commissioners are required by law to be held.

(3.) The term of office of the mayor of a borough or chairman of the commissioners of a town, who was in office on the sixteenth day of August one thousand eight hundred and ninety-eight, shall continue, notwithstanding any want of qualification, until a mayor or chairman has been chosen by the council or commissioners elected at the first election under the Act for that borough or town, and has made a declaration accepting office, and shall then cease, and until then such mayor or chairman may, notwithstanding any want of qualification, preside at the meetings of the council or commissioners in like manner as if there had been no new election under the Act of the members thereof.

(4.) In any town not a borough the council or commissioners at their first meeting shall, as their first business, choose the chairman for the year of the council or commissioners; and the chairman so chosen shall, upon making the declaration, come into office immediately.

(5.) In the case of equality of votes at the first meeting of the council of any county borough or urban county district, or of the commissioners of any town not an urban county district, the chairman of the meeting, whether entitled or not to vote in the first instance, shall have a casting vote, and if on the choice of the chairman of the meeting in the absence of the mayor or chairman, an equal number of votes is given to two or more persons, the meeting shall determine by lot which of those persons shall be the chairman.

(6.) Where a member of a joint board is appointed by the council of a borough or any urban sanitary authority all the members of which council or authority are re-elected under the Act, the term of office of a member of such joint board holding office at the date of this Order shall continue until the first meeting of the newly elected council, and shall then cease, and except for filling casual vacancies, no further appointment shall be made before that meeting.

(7.) The term of office of the municipal commissioners of Carrickfergus who were in office on sixteenth day of August one thousand eight hundred and ninety-eight shall continue, notwithstanding any want of qualification, until the day next following the day of the first election under the Act of a council—

(a) so far as the commissioners are an urban sanitary authority, then for the urban district of Carrickfergus; and

(b) so far as those commissioners are a rural sanitary authority, then for the rural district comprising the portion of Carrickfergus, which is a rural sanitary district;

and until the said elections no further election shall after the said sixteenth day of August be held except for filling casual vacancies. After the term of office of the Municipal Commissioners ceases under this provision, those commissioners shall finally cease to hold office

(8.) The term of office of the chairman of the municipal commissioners of Carrickfergus shall continue, notwithstanding any want of qualification, until the day above-named for the continuance in office of the municipal commissioners.

(9.) The term of office of any sheriff for a county of a city or county of a town, other than Galway and Carrickfergus, who was in office on sixteenth day of August one thousand eight hundred and ninety-eight shall continue until the twenty-third day of February next after the first election of councillors under the Act, and except for the purpose of filling a casual vacancy in the office of sheriff, no further selection of sheriff shall be made by the council of the city or town until after the first election under the Act.

(10.) Until the jurors' books, which are revised in the year one thousand eight hundred and ninety-nine, come into operation—

> (a) the sheriffs for the county of the city of Kilkenny and for the county of the town of Drogheda, shall continue to be selected and appointed in like manner as heretofore (but at the dates fixed by the Act as respects rheriffs of other counties of cities and towns), but upon the said jurors books coming into operation the sheriffs so appointed shall cease to hold office;
>
> (b) the sheriffs for the counties of the towns of Galway and Carrickfergus shall continue to be appointed as heretofore, but upon the said jurors books coming into operation, shall cease to hold office.

First Elections.

Arrangements for election by existing urban and rural sanitary authorities.

13. The existing urban and rural sanitary authorities, as respects district councillors, the existing commissioners of a town not an urban district as respects the commissioners of the town, and the council or commissioners for a county borough or urban county district, as respects the guardians for electoral divisions in such borough or district, shall take the necessary measures for the conduct of the first elections of district councillors, commissioners, or guardians, as the case may be, under the Act, including anything required by any Order in Council or rules made thereunder.

Relief of sureties under existing contracts from disqualification.

14.—The fact that a person is a surety for any contractor under a contract transferred to a county council by the virtue of the Act shall not disqualify that person from being elected or chosen or being a member of that council, or of any district council.

Retirement of First Councillors, &c.

Retirement of first councillors, guardians, &c.

15.—(1.) The councillors of a council for a county at large or a rural district who are elected at the first election under the

Act, shall retire from office on the ordinary day of retirement of such councillors in the year nineteen hundred and two, and the guardians of a union elected for electoral divisions in a county borough or urban county district shall retire from office on the ordinary day of retirement of rural district councillors in such union.

(2.) In the case of a county borough and every urban county district and every town not an urban district, the councillors, aldermen,· and commissioners elected at the first election under the Act shall, save as hereafter mentioned, retire as follows, that is to say :—

(a) One-third, as nearly as may be, of the councillors or commissioners shall continue in office until the ordinary day of retirement of such councillors or commissioners in the year one thousand nine hundred, and shall then retire.

(b) One-third, as nearly as may be, shall continue in office until the said day in the year nineteen hundred and one, and shall then retire.

(c) The remainder shall continue in office until the same day in the year nineteen hundred and two, and shall then retire.

(d) The councillors or commissioners who shall first go out of office shall be the councillors or commissioners who were elected by the smallest number of votes at the first election, and in the next year those who shall go out of office shall be the councillors or commissioners who were elected by the next smallest number of votes at the first election, the majority of the whole council or commissioners always determining, when the votes for any such persons have been equal, or when there has been no contest, who shall be the persons to go out of office. *See 3 & 4 Vict. c 108, s. 61.*

(e) Section sixty-two of the Municipal Corporations (Ireland) Act, 1840, shall, except in the case of Belfast and Londonderry, apply in like manner as if the year nineteen hundred and two were the third year after the Act came into operation in any borough. *3 & 4 Vict. c 108.*

(3.) In the case of a county borough or an urban county district or a town not an urban district divided into wards, the foregoing provisions with respect to the retirement of councillors or commissioners shall apply separately to each ward.

(4.) Where the councillors of an urban county district or commissioners of a town not an urban county district serve for three years and then retire together, the first councillors elected under the Act shall retire on the ordinary day of retirement of councillors in the year nineteen hundred and two.

Transfer of Property held under the Lighting of Towns (Ireland) Act, 1828.

16.—(1.) Where the Towns Improvement (Ireland) Act, 1854, and the Acts amending the same apply by virtue of section forty-one of the Act to a town having commissioners under the Lighting of Towns (Ireland) Act, 1828, then, on the first election of a council or commissioners for that town after the application takes effect, the powers, duties, and authorities conferred upon or vested in the old commissioners, whether by statute or otherwise, other than those conferred by the said Act of 1828, and all property of those commissioners (including all property vested in them under the Municipal Corporations (Ireland) Act, 1840, and all claims, demands, and liabilities or engagements of those commissioners), shall be transferred to and vested in the new council or commissioners constituted in pursuance of the Act.

(2.) On the first election of a council for the urban district of Carrickfergus, all claims, demands, liabilities, or engagements of the Municipal Commissioners of Carrickfergus shall be transferred to and vested in the council, but any liability of the portion of Carrickfergus which is not part of the urban district to meet such claims, demands, liabilities, and engagements, shall, on the application of the urban district council, be dealt with by the Local Government Board as a matter of adjustment under the Act.

Existing Officers' Remuneration.

17.—(1.) There shall be paid out of the county fund to any county or union officer such reasonable remuneration, not exceeding the scale approved by the Local Government Board, as the county council, or, in case of the officer being dissatisfied by the amount awarded by the county council, the Local Government Board, may award for expenses incurred or extra services rendered by him in bringing the Act into operation.

(2.) Every county council shall pay to the secretary of the grand jury, and any other officers transferred to that council, such sums as are necessary in order to give to such secretary or other officer until he begins to receive remuneration under the Act, the like remuneration as he would have received if the Act had not passed, and if any question arises as to what sums are so necessary, that question shall be referred to the Local Government Board, whose decision shall be final.

Adjustment by Local Government Board.

18.—(1.) Where, under the provisions of the Act, or any order made or thing done in pursuance of the Act within twelve months after the passing thereof, whether by reason of an alteration in the boundaries of any county or any district union or part of a county, or by reason of any alteration in the method of assessing the poor rate, or of raising the charges heretofore levied off any area, or of any transfer of business by or in pursuance of the Act, or otherwise by reason of anything contained in the Act, any change is caused in the area which is to bear any particular charge or expense, or where any matter is declared by the Act to be the subject or a matter of adjustment, the Local Government Board, as soon as may be after the passing of the Act, or the making of such order or the doing of such thing, but after due inquiry and communication with the various authorities concerned, shall by an order or orders apportion and adjust any property, income, debts, liabilities, and expenses of any area or local authority affected by such alteration.

(2.) Any such order may be varied by the Local Government Board if satisfied that any error has been made therein, but unless so varied shall be final, and all the provisions of the Act respecting adjustments and sums payable therefor and matters which may be done by such adjustment or by an order altering boundaries shall apply for the purposes of this Article.

(3.) Where a barony or any other area liable under any guarantee or other liability is divided between two or more counties or county districts the foregoing provisions shall apply to the adjustment of any guarantee, or other liability between the divided parts of the barony or area affected as the case may be, and such adjustment may be made to vary in any manner in which the amount of the guarantee or liability may vary.

(4.) Any balance in the hands of the treasurer of a board of guardians on the appointed day shall not, until an adjustment has been made between that board and the rural district council, be dealt with except to the extent and in the manner authorised by the Local Government Board.

(5.) An order under this Article shall contain such consequential provisions as the Local Government Board may deem necessary with respect to the transfer or retention of any property, duties, and liabilities with or without any conditions, and for the joint use of any property, and, for the transfer of any duties, whether of any council or officer, and for the payment of any sums by any authorities affected by any adjustment under this section, and for the funds out of which the same are to be paid.

19. In any union in which by reason of the adjustment made by an order under the preceding Article in relation to the balances, whether to debit or credit, as between electoral divisions and the union, any sum appears to the Local Government Board to be due from any electoral division to the union, or from the union to any electoral division, the Local Government Board shall, by the adjustment order or any other order, make such provisions as appear to them necessary. on the next practicable

levy of poor rate, to obtain such balance from the electoral
division, or to give to the electoral division the benefit of the
balance due to it ; and may for that purpose suspend or adapt
the provisions of the Act with respect to union rating, and the
agricultural grant in such manner, and make such supplemental
provisions respecting the demands made by the guardians on the
county council, or by the county council on urban district
councils, or otherwise as may appear to them necessary for carrying into effect this Article.

Given at Dublin Castle this 22nd day of December, 1898.

ASHBOURNE, *C*.   WILLIAM O'BRIEN.

JOHN ATKINSON.   C. H. HEMPHILL.

W. J. PIRRIE.

THE LOCAL GOVERNMENT (PROCEDURE OF COUNCILS) ORDER, 1899.

By the LORD LIEUTENANT and Privy Council of Ireland.

CADOGAN,

WHEREAS it is enacted by section one hundred and six of the Local Government (Ireland) Act, 1898, that the Lord Lieutenant by Order in Council may regulate the procedure of county and district councils in connexion with the business transferred to them by that or any other Act from presentment sessions and grand juries. 60 & 61 Vict.
c. 37.

Now, therefore, We, the Lord Lieutenant-General and General Governor of Ireland, by virtue of the powers vested in us for that purpose as aforesaid, and of all other powers enabling us on that behalf, by and with the advice of Her Majesty's Privy Council in Ireland, do order, and it is hereby ordered as follows:—

Short Title and Interpretation.

1. This Order may be cited as the Local Government (Procedure of Councils) Order, 1899. Short Title.

2.—(1.) The Interpretation Act, 1889, applies for the purpose of the interpretation of this Order, as it applies for the purpose of the interpretation of an Act of Parliament. Interpretation.

(2.) In this Order, unless the context otherwise requires, the expression "the Act" means the Local Government (Ireland) Act, 1898, and other expressions have the same meaning as in the Act.

Method of exercising Powers of making Presentments.

3. A rural district council shall exercise or perform any power or duty transferred to them from baronial presentment sessions of making any presentment by making a proposal under this order to the county council. Proposals of
rural district
council in place
of presentments

4.—(1.) A county council shall exercise or perform any power or duty transferred to them from a grand jury of making any presentment by passing a resolution at a quarterly meeting. Resolutions of
county council
in place of
presentments.

(2.) Where previously to the passing of the Act an application made and approved at baronial or county at large presentment sessions was required before the making of a presentment by the grand jury, a proposal made in accordance with this Order either by a district council or a proposal committee (hereinafter mentioned) of the county council, as the case requires, shall be required before the passing of the resolution of the county council which takes the place of the presentment of the grand jury.

(3.) A single resolution of the county council approving a proposal of a proposal committee shall be a sufficient exercise or performance of the power or duty transferred to the council both from the grand jury and the county at large presentment sessions.

Applications.

Applications necessary.

5. A proposal under this Order shall not be made except upon an application made in accordance with this Order.

Making of applications for proposals according to the area off which the cost is intended to be levied.

6. Applications shall be made—

(a) if it is intended that the cost of the work, or the payment, specified in the application is to be a county at large charge, to the county council ; and

(b) if it is intended that the cost of the work, or the payment, specified in the application is to be a district charge, then

(i.) where it is intended that the charge is to be levied off a single district, to the district council of that district; and

(ii.) where it is intended that the charge is to be levied off two or more districts, to the district council of the district off which the larger portion of the charge is intended to be levied, or if the charge is to be levied equally off two or more districts, to the district council of any of those districts ; and

(c) if the application relates to a public work, and it is intended that the cost of the work is to be half a county at large charge and half a district charge, to the council of the district in which the work or the greater portion thereof is locally situate ;

6 & 7 Will. 4, c. 116. 7 & 8 Vict. c. 106.

Provided that an application relating to any of the works specified in section fifty-six of the Grand Juries (Ireland) Act, 1836 (or, as respects the county of Dublin, section fifty-three of the County Dublin Grand Jury Act, 1844), shall, notwithstanding that the cost of the work is intended to be a county at large charge, be made to the council of the district in which the work is locally situate.

Mode of making applications.

7.—(1.) Application to a council may be made by any member of the council by means of notice of motion, and also, in the case of public works, by the county surveyor by means of the recommendations in the report hereinafter mentioned, and in the case of a payment, by the person claiming the payment by means of a notice in writing.

(2.) The notice of motion by a member of the council must be given as respects any quarter

(a) if the application is to a rural district council, at least ten days before the day fixed by the county council for the first quarterly meeting in that quarter of any rural district council in the county ; and

(b) if the application is to a county council, at least thirty days before the quarterly meeting of the council in that quarter ;

and where the application is to a rural district council, a duplicate of the notice of motion must be sent to the county council at the same time as the notice is given to the district council, and where it is intended that the charge for the ward is to be levied off two or more districts, then to the district council of each of those districts to which the application has not been made.

(3.) A notice of application by a person claiming payment must be sent to the council at least the same period before the quarterly meeting as a notice of motion by a member of the council.

(4.). Every application must be accompanied by the following particulars :—

(a) the matter in relation to which the application is made, specifying if it is a work, or a payment, or any other matter ; and

(b) where the application relates to a work or a payment, the probable expenditure required for the purpose of the application ; and

(c) whether it is intended that the expenditure is to be raised as a county at large charge, or as a district charge, and in the latter case the district or districts off which it is to be raised.

8.—(1.) The county surveyor shall, not less than ten days County before each quarterly meeting of the rural district council, make surveyor's report and a written report to that council as to the condition of the public recommenda- works in the district, the execution of the contracts respecting tions. those works, and such further matters as appear to him desirable with a view to maintaining the public works in good condition and repair ; and shall add to such report recommendations setting forth the proposals which he considers should be made by the district council at the said quarterly meeting, either for payments or otherwise, in respect of the maintenance of the public works in the district, and any such recommendation shall be accompanied by the same particulars as an application, and shall be deemed for the purpose of this Order to be an application.

(2.) The county surveyor shall, as soon as may be after the applications to be considered at any quarterly meeting of the rural district council are made, examine the applications, and before the meeting inform that council of his opinion with regard to such applications.

Publication of applications for new works or involving new contracts.

9. The county council and rural district council respectively shall cause to be published within their county or district a list of all applications made by notice of motion for new public works or involving new contracts as soon as may be after the last day for sending any such notice of motion to the council.

Consideration of Applications.

Proposal committee.

10.—(1.) The proposal committee may be either a committee specially appointed by the county council for the purpose of considering applications and formulating and submitting proposals thereon, or any other committee to whom any application is referred by the council, and may be a committee of the whole council.

(2.) A proposal committee to whom any application is referred shall hold a meeting for the purpose of considering that application on such day as may be fixed by the county council, not more than twenty and not less than fifteen days before each quarterly meeting of the council, and any such meeting is in this Order included in the expression a quarterly meeting of the proposal committee.

Consideration of applications at quarterly meetings.

11.—(1.) A rural district council and a proposal committee respectively shall at a quarterly meeting take into consideration all such applications as may be made to the rural district council or the county council, as the case may be, in accordance with this Order, and shall not formulate a proposal on any such application except at such a meeting.

(2.) The summons to attend a quarterly meeting of a rural district council or of a proposal committee shall comprise a list of all applications to be considered at the meeting which are for new public works or involve new contracts.

Day for quarterly meetings of district council.

12.—(1.) The rural district council shall hold their quarterly meetings on such days as the county council may determine.

(2.) The county council shall fix such days for the quarterly meetings of the rural district councils, and the rural district councils shall fix such days for any adjournments of those meetings, as will make it possible for the county surveyor or an assistant surveyor to be present at each such meeting or adjourned meeting.

Proposals formulated on consideration of applications.

13.—(1.) The district council and the proposal committee, on the consideration of applications at each quarterly meeting, may reject any application or adopt it, either wholly or in part, or subject to any limit of expenditure, or other conditions or modifications, as they may think fit.

(2.) Where at any such meeting the rural district council or proposal committee decide to adopt any application, either in whole or in part, they shall cause a proposal to be formulated in accordance with their decision, and if the proposal is for the execution of a public work—

(a) shall decide whether the expense of executing the work should be defrayed by means of borrowing, and, if it is so decided, the number of years within which the money borrowed should be paid off, and shall cause their decision to be embodied as part of the formulated proposal; and

(b) shall cause the county surveyor to prepare plans and specifications, expressing the nature and extent of the work, the time within which the work is to be completed, and if the council or committee think fit the quantity and description of materials proper to be employed upon it, and such other particulars as the council or committee direct.

14.—(1.) Where any proposal formulated by the rural district council or proposal committee is for the execution of any new public work, the probable expense of which, in the opinion of the county surveyor, will exceed fifty pounds, that council or committee shall adjourn the consideration of the proposal to a quarterly meeting held in the next quarter. *Provisional proposals for new works where expense exceeds fifty pounds.*

(2.) Any proposal, the consideration of which is so adjourned, is in this Order referred to as a provisional proposal.

(3.) The rural district council and the proposal committee, as the case may be, shall, at the meeting to which the consideration of any such provisional proposal has been adjourned, consider the plans and specifications prepared by the county surveyor, and also any other plans and specifications submitted to them for carrying out the work with regard to which the proposal is made, and may adopt any of those plans and specifications with such modifications as they think fit.

(4.) When the plans and specifications have been approved by the council or committee, the proposal shall cease to be a provisional proposal, and shall be dealt with as an ordinary proposal.

15.—(1.) In the first quarter of every local financial year, the county surveyor shall add to his report to each district council an estimate of the current road expenditure of the year—that is to say, of the amount which will be required during the year for the maintenance of the roads in the district in good condition and repair, including any amount to be levied off the district in respect of main roads, or in respect of any road the cost of which is levied partly off any other district. *Provision as to limit of expenditure on roads.*

(2.) The rural district council shall, at their quarterly meeting in the first quarter of the local financial year, consider such estimate, and cause their own estimate of such current road expenditure, to be made out and submitted to the county council together with their list of proposals.

(3.) The county council, before approving any proposals made in respect of roads by a rural district council, shall compare the cost, as estimated by the county surveyor, of carrying into effect such proposals with the estimate so submitted by the rural district council, with the object of ascertaining that the approval of such proposals will not, having regard to the estimate, cause any excess of expenditure on roads above the limit allowed by section twenty-seven of the Act.

(4.) The county council, before approving a proposal by the rural district council for any new road, shall be satisfied by the certificate of the county surveyor that the estimate submitted by the rural district council is reasonably sufficient to maintain the roads in the district in good condition and repair, and that the probable cost of such new road will not, when added to the cost of the said maintenance, cause any excess of expenditure on roads above the limit allowed by section twenty-seven of the Act.

(5.) For the purpose of this article, a new road includes any new bridge pipe, arch, gullet, fence, railing, or wall forming part of a road.

Tenders.

Preparation of forms of tender

16.—(1.) Where a proposal (other than a provisional proposal) is formulated by a rural district council or a proposal committee for the execution of any public work, that council or committee shall take steps for obtaining tenders for the work, and shall adjourn their meeting for the purpose to a day fixed by them, not being more than thirty or less than seven days after the day on which the adjournment is made.

(2.) The rural district council, so far as regards proposals formulated by them, and the county council, so far as regards proposals formulated by the proposal committee, shall, as soon as may be, cause notice to be published within their district or county of their readiness to receive tenders, and also of the manner in which tenders must be made, and of the day by which they must be received, that day being some day previous to the day fixed for the adjourned quarterly meeting.

(3.) The rural district council or the county council, as the case may be, shall cause forms of tender to be prepared in accordance with the plans and specifications of the county surveyor, and kept at the offices of the council for delivery to any person wishing to send in a tender, and shall also cause the plans, specifications, and particulars prepared by the county surveyor with regard to the work to be open for inspection gratis at all reasonable hours at the offices of the council.

Particulars to be contained in tenders.

17.—(1.) Every tender must be signed by the person making the tender, and enclosed in a sealed envelope, and must state

(a) the lowest sum for which the person tendering is willing to contract for the performance of the work; and (*b*) the description and address of the person tendering; and

(*c*) the name of the guarantor for the performance of the contract.

(2.) The guarantor shall be some sufficient company or society willing to guarantee the performance of the contract, or if it is a case in which the council or proposal committee have in their notice of tender stated that sureties may be accepted, then either such company or society or two sufficient persons who are willing to be bound as sureties for the performance of the contract.

18.—(1.) The rural district council or the proposal committee shall, at their adjourned quarterly meeting, open and consider the tenders received in respect of proposals formulated by them. *Opening of tenders.*

(2.) The council or committee shall not accept any tender, unless—

(*a*) the person tendering appears and satisfies the council or committee of the sufficiency of the guarantor and the willingness of the guarantor to give the guarantee; and

(*b*) the person tendering satisfies the council or committee that the tender has not been made for any unfair or fraudulent purpose; and

(*c*) the person tendering and the guarantor enter into security in accordance with this Order for the due performance of the contract;

(3.) The security for the due performance of the contract shall be—

(*a*) Where the guarantor is a company or society, an instrument executed by the person tendering and by the company or society, securing in case of non-performance of the contract payment to the county council of such sum as the county council direct, not being less than the total sum payable under the contract; and

(*b*) In a case where sureties are accepted, the joint and several bond of the person tendering and his sureties, conditioned in a penalty of double the sum mentioned in the tender as the sum for which the person tendering is willing to contract, or, if that sum exceeds one thousand pounds, of the sum so mentioned in the tender, with an addition of one thousand pounds.

(4.) Subject to compliance with the provisions of this article the council or committee may, at their discretion, accept the lowest or any other tender, or reject every tender.

(5.) The acceptance of any tender shall be provisional on the approval by the county council of the tender, as herein-after mentioned.

Consideration of Proposals.

List and particulars of proposals.   **19.**—(1.) The rural district council and the proposal committee respectively shall, as soon as may be, cause a list of the proposals formulated by them to be made out and submitted to the county council.

(2.) The list of proposals shall give as regards each proposal particulars :—

(*a*) respecting the matter for which the proposal is made (specifying whether it is for a work or for a payment or for any other matter) ; and

(*b*) if the proposal involves the expenditure of money, respecting the sum authorised to be expended and any decision of the council or committee as to borrowing to meet the expenditure ; and

(*c*) if the proposal is for the execution of any work—

(i) where a tender has been accepted, respecting the proposed contractor and and the terms of the contract, including the name and description of the guarantor ; and

(ii) where a tender has not been accepted, respecting the reason for no tender being accepted.

3.) Proposals for new works, proposals for the maintenance of works, proposals for payment, and provisional proposals shall be placed in separate parts in the list of proposals ; and proposals relating to roads or payments in respect of roads shall be distinguished from proposals relating to other works or payments.

Consideration of proposals by county council.   **20.**—(1.) The county council shall at each quarterly meeting consider all proposals (other than provisional proposals) which have been formulated either by the rural district council or by a proposal committee, but shall not formally consider any provisional proposals.

(2.) Subject to the provisions of this Order the functions of the county council in considering the proposals of a rural district council shall be limited to the approval or rejection of the proposals, and on the approval of any proposal the county council shall pass a resolution to the effect of the proposal.

(3.) Where the county council are willing to approve of any proposal of the rural district council if the proposal is modified but not otherwise, they may if they think fit instead of finally approving or rejecting the proposal, refer the proposal back to the rural district council with a statement of the modifications required.

(4.) The county council may approve, reject, or modify as they think fit any proposal of their proposal committee, so that the modification does not cause any increase of expenditure, or may refer the proposal back to the same or any other proposal committee.

(5.) When a proposal is so referred back to a rural district council or proposal committee, they shall reconsider it at a quarterly meeting held in the next quarter, and may make in the proposal such modifications, if any, as they think fit.

(6.) Proposals so reconsidered shall be included in a separate part in the list of proposals with a statement of the modifications (if any) made in the original proposal.

(7.) Where the county council reject or refer back a proposal of the rural district council, they shall send to that council a statement giving the reasons for that rejection or reference.

(8.) The county council may adjourn the consideration of a proposal for a new work to the next quarterly meeting for the purpose of the preparation of plans or of further enquiry, or other special reason, but an adjournment under this provision shall not be made more than once.

21. The county council shall, as respects each half-year, cause to be made out, and as soon as may be publish within their county a statement showing separately— *Half yearly statement by county council of business transacted.*

(a) the proposals considered by them during the half-year and the manner in which they have been dealt with ; and

(b) all resolutions in relation to business transferred to them from the grand jury passed by them during the half-year otherwise than on proposals, distinguishing the resolutions which under the laws for the time being in force it is imperative on them to pass.

Contracts.

22. All public works executed in pursuance of a proposal of the rural district council or proposal committee approved under this Order by the county council shall be executed by contract, except in cases where under the provisions of any Act or this Order works are given into the charge of or can be executed by the county surveyor. *Works to be executed by contract.*

23. Where an application is made for a proposal with regard to the repair of any road, the rural district council, or the proposal committee, as the case may be, shall consider whether it is not expedient to contract for that repair for a term of years, and may, if they think fit, make a proposal for such a contract for a period not exceeding seven years, and if such a proposal is made the form of tender shall be prepared in accordance therewith. *Contracts for repair for term of years.*

24.—(1.) Where at any adjourned quarterly meeting no tenders are received or accepted in the case of any work, a proposal for which has been formulated by the rural district council or proposal committee, that fact shall be noted in the list of proposals *Provision for case where no tender is received.*

sent by the council or committee to the county council, and the county council may, if they approve the proposal, enter into a contract for the execution of the work proposed, or, if no sufficient contractor can be found, give the work into the charge of the county surveyor.

(2.) The county council shall not, under this Article, authorise the expenditure of any larger sum on the work than that pro_posed by the rural district council or proposal committee, as the case may be.

Contracts in accordance with tenders.

25.—(1.) Where the county council approve any proposal of a rural district council or proposal committee for any work, and the rural district council or committee have accepted a tender for the work, the county council shall, subject to the provisions of this Article, enter into a contract for the execution of the work, in accordance with the tender accepted.

(2.) Where the county council have referred a proposal for the maintenance of any work back to the rural district council, on the ground only that they are dissatisfied with the tender accepted by the rural district council (including dissatisfaction with the guarantor), they may, if they think fit, proceed with the execution of the work as if the proposal had been approved, and for that purpose may put the work into the charge of the county surveyor until the proposal is ultimately approved.

(3.) Where the county council have referred any proposal back to the rural district council, on the ground that the county council are dissatisfied with the tender accepted by the rural district council (including dissatisfaction with the guarantor), the rural district council shall, on the re-consideration of the proposal, take steps for obtaining fresh tenders for the work, and for that purpose proceed in the matter as in the case of an original proposal.

(4.) Where, in consequence of the modifications made by the county council in any proposal of a proposal committee, it is found impossible to enter into a contract in accordance with the tender accepted by the committee, or where the county council approve of the proposed work, but not of the tender accepted by the proposal committee, the county council shall refer the proposal back to a proposal committee, and that committee, on the re-consideration of the proposal, shall take steps for obtaining fresh tenders in manner provided by this Order with respect to an original proposal.

(5.) If the proposal is for a work of maintenance, the county council may, if they think fit, put the work in the charge of the county surveyor until the proposal is ultimately approved.

(6.) The county council shall not, under this Article, authorise the expenditure by the county surveyor of any larger sum on any work than that proposed by the rural district council or proposal committee, as the case may be.

(7.) Where any proposal for a work approved by the county council involves the borrowing of money, the county council shall not enter into any contract for, or otherwise proceed with the execution of the work, until the Local Government Board have sanctioned the borrowing of that money.

(8.) Where any proposal approved by the county council relates to any work to which section fifty-seven of the Grand Juries (Ireland) Act, 1836 (or as respects the county of Dublin, section fifty-four of the County Dublin, Grand Jury Act, 1844) (which relates to works on the boundary of two counties), applies, the county council shall not enter into any contract for, or otherwise proceed with the execution of the work, until they are satisfied that the provisions of the said section with regard to raising one-half the expense of the work off the adjoining county or some district thereof, have been complied with.

26. A payment shall not be made to a contractor in respect of any public work unless the county surveyor certifies— *Payments on contract.*

(a) if the payment is to be made before the completion of the contract, that the payment may be so made under the terms of the contract ; and

(b) in any case that the work in respect of which the payment is to be made, has been executed in accordance with the contract ;

and an application on the part of a contractor for such a payment shall not be considered unless the certificate of the county surveyor to that effect is produced to the rural district council or proposal committee, as the case may be.

27.—(1.) Contracts may provide for payments to a contractor—- *Time for payments on contract.*

(a) where the contract is for a work of maintenance and for a term of years, at any period not exceeding a quarter of a year, for work executed during that period ; and

(b) in the case of any other contract, for the payment to the contractor of such proportion, not being more than eighty-five per cent., of the sum expended by him on the contract, as may be specified in the contract.

(2.) Where no special provision is made by the contract in accordance with this Article, a payment shall not be made to a contractor, until the completion of the contract.

Application of Order to County Boroughs and Urban Districts.

28. This Order (with the exception of the provisions thereof relating to the execution of public works by contract and the making of contracts and obtaining tenders therefor) shall apply *Application to county boroughs.*

within a county borough so far as respects any powers or duties in relation to any business transferred from a grand jury or presentment sessions to the council of the borough, either by the Act or by any previous Act, for which the fiat or sanction of any court, judge, or recorder is required, and shall so apply as if the cost of the execution or performance of those powers and duties were a county at large charge.

Application to urban districts.   **29.** This Order shall apply within an urban county district so far as respects any works the maintenance of which is partly leviable off the county at large and partly off the urban district (with the exception of roads the entire maintenance of which is undertaken by the urban district council under sub-section six of section twenty-seven of the Act), and shall so apply as if the urban district council were a rural district council.

Procedure under s. 82 (2) of the Act.

As to stopping up or abandoning an old road or public work.   **30.**—(1.) The provisions of this Order with respect to a new work shall, so far as circumstances admit, apply to the stopping up or abandonment of an old road or public work.

(2.) The manner in which an objection by a ratepayer to a resolution of the county council to stop up or abandon an old road or public work is to be lodged shall be the sending of a written notice of objection to the county council and to the Local Government Board.

(3.) The time within which any such objection by a ratepayer is to be lodged shall be any time not later than the end of six months after notice of the said resolution of the county council has been published within the county.

General.

Meetings.   **31.**—(1.) Every meeting of the county council during the consideration of proposals under this Order, and of the rural district council or proposal committee during the consideration of applications under this Order, shall be open to the public.

(2.) A reference to any quarterly or other meeting includes a reference to any adjournment of any such meeting.

(3.) Any power given by this Order to a county council to fix any meeting either of the district council or of a proposal committee, or to refer an application to a proposal committee, may be exercised by either a general or a special direction of the council.

Duties of county surveyor.   **32.**—(1.) The county surveyor in the exercise of any powers or duties given by this Order shall conform with any directions that may be given him by the county council for carrying the order into effect.

(2.) When the office of county surveyor is vacant, anything authorised or required by this Order to be done by, to, or before the county surveyor may be done by, to, or before any assistant surveyor of the county council, or if there is no such assistant surveyor, any person appointed by the county council for the purpose.

33.—(1.) The rural district council may make such arrange- Printing. ments as they think fit with respect to such printing as is required in connection with the business transferred to them from presentment sessions.

(2.) All printing required in connection with the business transferred to the county council from the grand jury or county at large presentment sessions shall be executed by contract, and tenders shall be obtained for such contract in like manner, so nearly as circumstances admit, as in the case of a public work ;

Provided that if such printing is required in any exceptional case which is not comprised in any contract, and is outside the ordinary current business of the year, and is estimated not to amount to more than ten pounds, the printing may be done without such contract, but the total cost of the printing so done in any one year shall not exceed twenty pounds.

34.—(1.) Where any notice or document is to be published Publication of under this Order, by any council— notices and documents.

(a) that notice or document shall be published by fixing copies of it in some conspicuous place on or near the outer door of the office of that council, and of every police station in the area within which it is to be published, and also at such other places (if any) as the council direct, and if the council think fit also by advertising it in any newspaper circulating within the said area, and

(b) that notice or document shall be open for inspection gratis, at all reasonable hours, at the office of the council.

35.—(1.) This Order shall not apply to any business of the Savings. county council other than the business transferred from the grand jury or county at large presentment sessions, as the case may be, except so far as any provisions thereof may be applied to such business by the standing orders of the county council.

2. Where the payment of a sum by any county council, or by the treasurer of such council or other officer of a council on behalf of the council, is ordered by a judge of assize, or is required either to comply with any enactment, or to meet either a judgment or decree of any competent court, or an order for the payment or collection

T

of any money made by the Lord Lieutenant in pursuance of any Act, nothing in this Order shall prevent the county council, if they think fit, from passing a resolution and ordering the payment of the sum of money at any meeting not a quarterly meeting, and without any proposal of a district council or proposal committee.

Given at the Council Chamber, Dublin Castle, this 30th day of January, 1899.

ASHBOURNE, C.	MORRIS.
WILLIAM O'BRIEN.	JOHN ATKINSON.
RICHARD MARTIN.	W. J. PIRRIE.

APPENDIX III.

ORDERS OF LOCAL GOVERNMENT BOARD.

In exercise of the power given to us by the Local Government (Ireland) Act, 1898, section 124, We, the Local Government Board for Ireland, order and appoint that the provisions of the said Act which repeal the enactments in the schedule hereto, shall come into operation on the First day of September, 1898.

SCHEDULE.

Section and Chapter.	Short Title.	Enactment.
3 and 4 Vic., c. 108.	The Municipal Corporations (Ireland) Act, 1840.	Sections thirty-nine to forty-seven, sections forty-nine and fifty, so much of section fifty-five as is specified in the 6th Schedule to the Local Government (Ireland) Act, 1898.
6 and 7 Vic., c. 93.	The Municipal Corporations (Ireland) Act, 1843	Section two, section four, except the enactment therein that the burgess roll completed on the 20th November in each year shall be the burgess roll from the 25th November following until a new burgess roll shall have been made.

Given under our Hands and Seal of Office, this Twenty-second day of August, in the year of Our Lord One Thousand Eight Hundred and Ninety-eight.

(Signed),

H. A. ROBINSON.

In exercise of the power given to us by the Local Government (Ireland) Act, 1898, section 124, We, the Local Government Board for Ireland, hereby order and appoint that the provision of the said Act repealing section 27 of the Local Government (Ireland) Act, 1871, shall come into operation on the 30th September, 1898.

> Given under our Hands and Seal of Office, this Thirteenth day of September, in the Year of Our Lord One Thousand Eight Hundred and Ninety-eight.

> (Signed),

> > Wm. L. Micks.
> > T. J. Stafford.

In exercise of the power given to us by the Local Government (Ireland) Act, 1898, section 124, We, the Local Government Board for Ireland, hereby order and appoint that the provision in section 91 of the said Act as to leases to boards of guardians for the purposes of the Dispensary Houses (Ireland) Act, 1879, shall come into operation on the 1st October, 1898.

> Given under our Hands and Seal of Office, this Twenty-ninth day of September, in the Year of Our Lord One Thousand Eight Hundred and Ninety-eight.

> (Signed),

> > Wm. L. Micks.
> > T. J. Stafford.

In exercise of the power given to us by the Local Government (Ireland) Act, 1898, section 124, We, the Local Government Board for Ireland, hereby order and appoint that the provision in section 68 of the said Act enabling Us to divide any townland, shall come into operation on the 19th October, 1898.

> Given under our Hands and Seal of Office, this Eighteenth day of October, in the Year of Our Lord One Thousand Eight Hundred and Ninety-eight.

> (Signed),

> > H. A. Robinson.
> > Wm. L. Micks.
> > T. J. Stafford.

In exercise of the power given to us by the Local Government (Ireland) Act, 1898, section 124, We, the Local Government Board for Ireland, hereby order and appoint that the provisions of sub-sections (1) and (2) of section 41 of the said Act shall come into operation on the 7th November, 1898.

Given under our Hands and Seal of Office, this Thirty-first day of October, in the Year of Our Lord, One Thousand Eight Hundred and Ninety-eight.

(Signed),

H. A. ROBINSON.
WM. L. MICKS.
T. J. STAFFORD.
R. BAGWELL.

WHEREAS, by Section 2 of the Local Government (Ireland) Act, 1898, it is enacted that the Local Government Board for Ireland may provide that more than one county councillor may be returned for a county electoral division where an urban district forms such a division:

AND WHEREAS by Orders bearing date the 1st day of November, 1898, We, the Local Government Board for Ireland, did provide that the urban districts mentioned in the schedule to this Order should each form one county electoral division:

NOW THEREFORE, We, the Local Government Board for Ireland, do hereby order and declare, that the number of county councillors to be returned for the several county electoral divisions mentioned in the first column of the said schedule to this Order shall be the number set out opposite to their respective names in the second column of the schedule.

AND We do further declare that this Order shall be in force and take effect at such time as may be necessary for the purposes of the first election of county councillors.

[SCHEDULE

SCHEDULE.

Name of County Electoral Division and Urban District.	Number of County Councillors to be returned.
Athlone	Two
Bray	Two
Carlow	Three
Clonmel	Two
Drogheda ...	Five
Dundalk (Urban)	Five
Kilkenny (Urban)	Two
Lurgan	Two
Sligo	Two
Wexford	Two

Given under our Hands and Seal of Office, this Twenty-eighth day of November, in the Year of Our Lord One Thousand Eight Hundred and Ninety-eight.

(Signed),

H. A. ROBINSON.
T. J. STAFFORD.
R. BAGWELL.

LOCAL GOVERNMENT BOARD, DUBLIN,

1st December, 1898.

The Local Government Board for Ireland, with the concurrence of the Lords Commissioners of Her Majesty's Treasury, hereby give notice that the appointment of Commissioner of the Board authorized to be made by the President of the Board under Section 102, sub-section 5, of the Local Government (Ireland) Act, 1898 (61 and 62 Vic., chap. 37), is to be added to Schedule B of the Order in Council of the 4th of June, 1870.

BY THE LOCAL GOVERNMENT BOARD FOR IRELAND.

WHEREAS, by Sub-sections 1 and 2 of Section 41 of the Local Government (Ireland) Act, 1898 (hereinafter referred to as the principal Act), it is enacted as follows :—

"41.—(1.) The Towns Improvement (Ireland) Act, 1854, and the "enactments amending the same, shall, subject to the exceptions "and with the amendments made by this Act, apply to the town "forming the urban sanitary district of Carrickfergus, and to "every town having Commissioners under the Lighting of Towns "(Ireland) Act, 1828, and shall so apply in like manner as if it "had been in whole adopted in the town, and the boundaries of "each such town at the passing of this Act were the boundaries "approved under the first-mentioned Act.

"(2.) In each such town the number of Councillors or Com-"missioners, as the case may be, shall be the same as the existing "number of Commissioners : Provided that if the Local Govern-"ment Board think fit to divide the town into Wards, the "Wards shall be determined and set out and the Commissoners "apportioned among the Wards, in manner provided by section "fifteen of the said Act of 1854 for a town where there are "Municipal Commissioners, and the number of Commissioners "may be varied so as to be in accordance with section sixteen of "the said Act."

And whereas, by an Order under our Seal bearing date the 31st October, 1898, We, the Local Government Board for Ireland, in exercise of the power given to us by section 124 of the principal Act, did order and appoint that the provisions of the said Sub-sections (1) and (2) of Section 41 should come into operation on the 7th November, 1898.

And whereas, the town of Dungannon, in the county of Tyrone, is a town having Commissioners, whereof the existing number is twenty-one, under the Lighting of Towns (Ireland) Act, 1828 ; and We think fit to divide the said town into Wards.

Now, therefore, in exercise of the powers vested in us in this behalf, We, the Local Government Board for Ireland, do, by this our Order, determine as follows :—

1. The said town of Dungannon shall be divided into three Wards, which shall be named, respectively, West Ward, East Ward, and Central Ward.

2. The boundaries of the three Wards into which the said town of Dungannon shall be divided shall be the limits or boundaries respectively set forth in the Schedule to this Order.

3. The number of Commissioners to be elected for the said town of Dungannon shall be twenty-one, whereof seven shall be elected for each Ward.

And We do further declare that this Order shall be in force and take effect at such time as may be necessary for the purposes of the first elections to be held under the principal Act.

SCHEDULE.

Town of Dungannon.

West Ward.

The boundary of West Ward shall commence at a point in the town boundary opposite the entrance gate to the union workhouse and thence running down the centre of the road to Thomas-street and the centre of Thomas-street to centre line of Market-square thence south to the south side of said Square thence along the centre line of Irish-street as far as William street thence south along the centre of William-street to and along the road south of John-street to the south end of Scotch-street thence south to the town boundary and thence following said boundary west and north to the point first described.

East Ward.

The boundary of East Ward shall commence at a point in the town boundary opposite the entrance gate to the union workhouse and follow the boundary of the West Ward as far as the south side of Market-square thence turning in an eastern direction along the centre lines of Church-street and Perry-street till it meets Park-road thence along the centre line of Park-road to Milltown-road thence along the centre line of Milltown-road in an easterly direction to the town boundary and thence northerly along said town boundary and following said town boundary until it reaches the point first described.

Central Ward.

Central Ward shall include all that part of the town not comprised in West Ward and East Ward.

Sealed with our Seal this Eight day of December, in the Year of our Lord One Thousand Eight Hundred and Ninety-eight.

H. A. ROBINSON.
WM. L. MICKS.
R. BAGWELL.

ORDERS

AS TO

COUNTY BOUNDARIES

AND

COUNTY ELECTORAL DIVISIONS.

The following Summaries show the Boundaries of the Administrative Counties, the County Electoral Divisions, and the District Electoral (or Poor Law Electoral Divisions) of which the County Electoral Divisions are composed in each case. The order relating to the County of Antrim only is given in full, the orders relating to the other Counties being similar in every respect, except as to the details in regard to each County.

ANTRIM.

WHEREAS it is enacted by Section 68 of the Local Government (Ireland) Act, 1898, that the first council elected under the Act shall be elected for the county as bounded at the passing of the Act for the purposes of the grand jury (referred to as the existing judicial county), provided that the Local Government Board for Ireland, by order made within six months after the passing of the Act, may, for the purpose of the election of such council, alter the boundaries of any existing judicial county; and that if such order is made the first council shall be elected for the county as so altered (referred to as an administrative county), and the county so altered shall, subject to alterations made in pursuance of any Order in Council under Part Six of the Act, be for all the purposes of the Act the county of such council:

AND WHEREAS it is enacted by Section 2 of the same Act that the administrative divisions of every county for the election of county councillors shall be provided by an order of the Local Government Board for Ireland made before the first day of January next after the passing of the Act:

NOW THEREFORE, WE, the Local Government Board for Ireland, do hereby order and declare:—

1. That the boundaries of the administrative County of

U

Antrim shall be those mentioned in Schedule A to
this Order.

2. That the several divisions in the said County of Antrim
for the election of County Councillors shall be the
several county electoral divisions defined in the
Schedule B to this Order.

AND WE do further declare that this Order shall be in force
and take effect at such time as may be necessary for the purposes of the first election of county councillors, and on and after
the first day of April, 1899, for all other purposes.

SCHEDULE A.

Name of Administrative County and Contents.

COUNTY OF ANTRIM—The existing judicial county of
Antrim (except the portion of the city of Belfast
situated therein);

The existing judicial county of the town of Carrickfergus; and

So much of the existing judicial county of Down as
comprises the portion of the town of Lisburn situated
therein.

SCHEDULE B.

County Electoral Divisions and Contents.

AHOGHILL—THE DISTRICT ELECTORAL DIVISIONS OF—
Ahoghill, Ballyconnelly, Ballyscullion, Portglenone.

ANTRIM—THE DISTRICT ELECTORAL DIVISIONS OF—
Antrim Rural, Antrim Urban, Ballyrobin, Craiga-
rogan, Carnmoney, Templepatrick.

BALLINDERRY—THE DISTRICT ELECTORAL DIVISIONS OF—
Aghagallon, Aghalee, Ballinderry, Ballyscolly, Knock-
nadona, Legatirriff, Lissue, Magheragall, Maghera-
mesk.

BALLYCASTLE—THE DISTRICT ELECTORAL DIVISIONS OF—
Armoy, Ballintoy, Ballycastle, Ballycregagh, Ballyhoe,
Castle Quarter, Glenmakeeran, Glenshesk, Rathlin,
Ramoan, The Fair Head.

BALLYCLARE—THE DISTRICT ELECTORAL DIVISIONS OF—
Ballyclare, Connor, Donegore, Kilbride, Rashee.

BALLYMENA—THE DISTRICT ELECTORAL DIVISION OF—
Ballymena.

BALLYMONEY—THE DISTRICT ELECTORAL DIVISIONS OF—
Ballymoney, Dirraw, Dunloy, Enagh, Kilraghts, The
Vow.

CARRICKFERGUS—THE DISTRICT ELECTORAL DIVISIONS OF
Ballylinny, Carrickfergus Rural, Carrickfergus Urban.

CRUMLIN—THE DISTRICT ELECTORAL DIVISIONS OF—
Ballygomartin, Crumlin, Derryaghy, Glenavy, Island
Kelly, Malone, Tullyrusk.

CUSHENDALL—THE DISTRICT ELECTORAL DIVISIONS OF—
Ardclinis, Corkey, Cushendall, Cushleake, Glencoy,
Glendun, Killagan, Newtown Crommelin, Redbay.

DERVOCK—THE DISTRICT ELECTORAL DIVISIONS OF—
Benvardin, Carnmoon, Croagh, Dervock, Drumtullagh,
Seacon, Stranocum.

GALGORM—THE DISTRICT ELECTORAL DIVISIONS OF—
Clogh, Dundermot, Galgorm, Glenravill, Kirkinriola.

GLENARM—THE DISTRICT ELECTORAL DIVISIONS OF—
Broughshane, Glenarm, Longmore, Slemish.

ISLAND MAGEE—THE DISTRICT ELECTORAL DIVISIONS OF—
Ballycor, Ballynure, Glynn, Island Magee, Raloo,
Templecorran.

KELLS—THE DISTRICT ELECTORAL DIVISIONS OF—
Ballyclug, Cloghogue, Kells, Shilvodan.

KILLOQUIN—THE DISTRICT ELECTORAL DIVISIONS OF—
Dunminning, Glenbuck, Killoquin Lower, Killoquin
Upper, Lisnagarran.

LARNE—THE DISTRICT ELECTORAL DIVISIONS OF—
Carncastle, Glenwhirry, Kilwaughter, Larne.

LISBURN—THE DISTRICT ELECTORAL DIVISION OF—
Lisburn.

PORTRUSH—THE DISTRICT ELECTORAL DIVISIONS OF—
Beardiville, Bushmills, Dunseverick, Portrush Rural,
Portrush Urban.

RANDALSTOWN—THE DISTRICT ELECTORAL DIVISIONS OF—
Cargin, Cranfield, Drumanaway, Randalstown, Shar-
voges, Toome.

WHITEHOUSE—THE DISTRICT ELECTORAL DIVISIONS OF—
Ballynadrentagh, Ballysillan, Dundesert, Sea Cash,
Whitehouse.

Note.—In the above schedule, District Electoral Divisions mean
the existing Poor Law Electoral Divisions having the same name.

Given under our Hands and Seal of Office, this First
day of November, in the year of Our Lord, One
Thousand Eight Hundred and Ninety-eight.

(Signed),

H. A. ROBINSON.
WM. L. MICKS.
T. J. STAFFORD.
R. BAGWELL.

ARMAGH.

SCHEDULE A.

Name of Administrative County and Contents.

COUNTY OF ARMAGH—The existing judicial county of Armagh (except the portion of the town of Newry situated therein).

SCHEDULE B.

County Electoral Divisions and Contents.

ANNAGHMORE—THE DISTRICT ELECTORAL DIVISIONS OF— Annaghmore, Breagh, Killyman, Tullyroan.

ARMAGH—THE DISTRICT ELECTORAL DIVISIONS OF— Armagh East Urban, Armagh North Urban, Armagh South Urban.

CAMLOUGH—THE DISTRICT ELECTORAL DIVISIONS OF— Ballybot, Camlough.

CHARLEMONT—THE DISTRICT ELECTORAL DIVISIONS OF— Charlemont, Grange, Kilmore, Loughgall.

CROSSMAGLEN—THE DISTRICT ELECTORAL DIVISIONS OF— Cloghoge, Crossmaglen, Cullyhanna, Lisleitrim, Moybane.

CROSSMORE—THE DISTRICT ELECTORAL DIVISIONS OF— Ballyards, Brootally, Crossmore.

DRUMCREE—THE DISTRICT ELECTORAL DIVISIONS OF— Drumcree, Tartaraghan.

FORKHILL—THE DISTRICT ELECTORAL DIVISIONS OF— Forkhill, Jonesborough, Lower Creggan.

HAMILTONS BAWN—DISTRICT ELECTORAL DIVISIONS OF— Armagh Rural, Hamiltons Bawn, Killeen, Mullaghbrack.

KEADY—THE DISTRICT ELECTORAL DIVISIONS OF— Derrynoose, Keady Rural, Keady Urban.

KERNAN—THE DISTRICT ELECTORAL DIVISIONS OF— Carrowbrack, Kernan, Lurgan Rural.

KILLEVY—THE DISTRICT ELECTORAL DIVISIONS OF— Dorsy, Killevy, Latbirget.

LURGAN—THE DISTRICT ELECTORAL DIVISION OF— Lurgan Urban.

MARKETHILL—THE DISTRICT ELECTORAL DIVISIONS OF— Clady, Lisnadill, Markethill, Mountnorris.

MIDDLETOWN—The District Electoral Divisions of—
Ballymartrim, Glenaul, Middletown, Tynan.

MONTIAGHS—The District Electoral Divisions of—
Brownlows Derry, Cornakinnegar, Montiaghs.

NEWTOWN HAMILTON—The District E. Divisions of
Armaghbrague, Ballymyre, Camly, Newtown Hamilton

POINTZPASS—The District Electoral Divisions of—
Belleek, Mullaghglass, Pointzpass, Tullyhappy.

PORTADOWN—The District Electoral Division of—
Portadown Urban.

RICH HILL—The District Electoral Divisions of—
Hockley, Portadown Rural, Rich Hill.

TANDERAGEE—The District Electoral Divisions of—
Ballysheil, Mullahead, Tanderagee Rural, Tanderagee
Urban

Note.—In the above schedule, District Electoral Divisions mean
the existing Poor Law Electoral Divisions having the same name.

CARLOW.

SCHEDULE A.

Name of Administrative County and Contents.

COUNTY OF CARLOW—The existing judicial county of
Carlow; and
So much of the existing judicial county named Queen's
County as comprises the portion of the town of Car-
low situated therein.

SCHEDULE B.

County Electoral Divisions and Contents.

BAGENALSTOWN—The District Electoral Divisions of
Bagenalstown Rural, Bagenalstown Urban.

BALLON—The District Electoral Divisions of—
Ballon, Fennagh, Rathrush, Templepeter.

BALLYMURPHY—The District Electoral Divisions of—
Ballymurphy, Coonogue, Kyle, Rathanna.

BORRIS—The District Electoral Divisions of—
Borris, Killedmond.

BURTON HALL—The District Electoral Divisions of—
Burton Hall, Carlow Rural, Johnstown, Killerrig.

CARLOW—THE DISTRICT ELECTORAL DIVISIONS OF—
Carlow Urban, Graigue Urban.

CLONEGALL—THE DISTRICT ELECTORAL DIVISIONS OF—
Clonegall, Cranemore.

CORRIES—THE DISTRICT ELECTORAL DIVISIONS OF—
Ballyellin, Ballymoon, Corries, Sliguff.

GLYNN—THE DISTRICT ELECTORAL DIVISIONS OF—
Glynn, Tinnahinch.

GRANGEFORD—THE DISTRICT ELECTORAL DIVISIONS OF—
Grangeford, Kineagh, Tankardstown, Williamstown.

HACKETSTOWN—THE DISTRICT ELECTORAL DIVISIONS OF—
Clonmore, Hacketstown.

LEIGHLINBRIDGE—THE DISTRICT ELECTORAL DIVISIONS OF
Agha, Leighlinbridge.

MYSHALL—THE DISTRICT ELECTORAL DIVISIONS OF—
Garryhill, Myshall, Shangarry.

NURNEY—THE DISTRICT ELECTORAL DIVISIONS OF—
Ballinacarrig, Clogrenan, Kellistown, Nurney.

OLDLEIGHLIN—THE DISTRICT ELECTORAL DIVISIONS OF—
Oldleighlin, Rathornan, Ridge.

RATHVILLY—THE DISTRICT ELECTORAL DIVISIONS OF—
Haroldstown, Rahill, Rathvilly, Ticknock.

TULLOW—THE DISTRICT ELECTORAL DIVISION OF—
Tullow.

TULLOWBEG—THE DISTRICT ELECTORAL DIVISIONS OF—
Ballintemple, Kilbride, Tullowbeg.

Note.—In the above schedule, District Electoral Divisions mean
the existing Poor Law Electoral Divisions having the same name.

CAVAN.

SCHEDULE A.

Name of Administrative County and Contents.

COUNTY OF CAVAN—The existing judicial county of
Cavan.

SCHEDULE B.

County Electoral Divisions and Contents.

ARVAGH—THE DISTRICT ELECTORAL DIVISIONS OF—
Arvagh, Brucehall, Drumcarban, Scrabby.

BAILIEBOROUGH—THE DISTRICT ELECTORAL DIVISIONS OF
Bailieborough, Drumanespick, Skeagh.

BALLYCONNELL—THE DISTRICT ELECTORAL DIVISIONS OF—
Ballyconnell, Ballymagauran, Bawnboy, Bilberry,
Carn, Doogary, Lissanover.

BALLYJAMESDUFF—DISTRICT ELECTORAL DIVISIONS OF—
Ballyjamesduff, Castlerahan, Kilbride.

BALLYHAISE—THE DISTRICT ELECTORAL DIVISIONS OF—
Ballyhaise, Butlersbridge, Drumcarn, Rakenny, Red-
hill.

BALLYMACHUGH—THE DISTRICT ELECTORAL DIVISIONS OF
Ballymachugh, Drumlumman, Kilcogy, Kilgolagh,
Lough Dawan.

BELLANANAGH—THE DISTRICT ELECTORAL DIVISIONS OF—
Bellananagh, Crossdoney, Denn, Killykeen, Moynehall.

BELTURBET—THE DISTRICT ELECTORAL DIVISIONS OF—
Ardue, Belturbet, Castlesaunderson, Grilly, Kilconny.

CAVAN—THE DISTRICT ELECTORAL DIVISIONS OF—
Cavan Rural, Cavan Urban, Clonervy.

COOTEHILL—THE DISTRICT ELECTORAL DIVISIONS OF—
Ashfield, Cootehill Rural, Cootehill Urban, Tullyvin
East

DOWRA—THE DISTRICT ELECTORAL DIVISIONS OF—
Derrylahan, Dowra, Dunmakeever, Eskey, Killinagh,
Teebane, Tuam.

KILLESHANDRA—THE DISTRICT ELECTORAL DIVISIONS OF—
Carrafin, Corr, Diamond, Killeshandra, Milltown,
Springfield.

KILLINKERE—THE DISTRICT ELECTORAL DIVISIONS OF—
Carnagrave, Crossbane, Killinkere, Lurgan, Termon.

KILNALECK—THE DISTRICT ELECTORAL DIVISIONS OF—
Ballintemple, Derrin, Graddum, Kill, Kilnaleck.

KINGSCOURT—THE DISTRICT ELECTORAL DIVISIONS OF—
Enniskeen, Kingscourt, Lisagoan, Taghart.

LARAH—THE DISTRICT ELECTORAL DIVISIONS OF—
Drung, Larah North, Larah South, Tullyvin West.

SHERCOCK—THE DISTRICT ELECTORAL DIVISIONS OF—
Canningstown, Corraneary, Knappagh, Shercock.

STRADONE—THE DISTRICT ELECTORAL DIVISIONS OF—
Crosskeys, Cuttragh, Stradone, Waterloo.

SWANLINBAR—THE DISTRICT ELECTORAL DIVISIONS OF—
Benbrack, Derrynananta, Kilawley, Pedara, Vohers,
Swanlinbar, Templeport, Tircahan.

VIRGINIA—The District Electoral Divisions of—
    Mullagh, Munterconnaught, Virginia.

Note.—In the above schedule, District Electoral Divisions mean the existing Poor Law Electoral Divisions having the same name.

CLARE.

SCHEDULE A.

Name of Administrative County and Contents.

COUNTY OF CLARE—The existing judicial county of Clare; and

So much of the existing judicial county of Galway as comprises the district electoral divisions of Drummaan, Inishcaltra North, and Mountshannon.

SCHEDULE B.

County Electoral Divisions and Contents.

BALLYNACALLY—The District Electoral Divisions of—
    Ballynacally, Clondagad, Furroor, Glenmore, Kilcloher, Liscasey, Lisheen.

CLAREABBEY—The District Electoral Divisions of—
    Clareabbey, Doora, Ennis Rural, Killone, Newmarket.

COOLREAGH—The District Electoral Divisions of—
    Ayle, Ballynahinch, Boherglass, Caherhurly, Coolreagh, Glendree, Inishcaltra South, Ogonnelloe, Scariff, Tulla.

COORACLARE—The District Electoral Divisions of—
    Cooraclare, Killimer, Kilmihil, Kilmurry, (Killadysert), Knock, Tullycreen.

CORROFIN—The District Electoral Divisions of—
    Ballagh, Ballyeighter, Boston, Clooney, Corrofin, Glenroe, Kilfenora, Killinaboy, Kiltoraght, Rath.

CRUSHEEN—The District Electoral Divisions of—
    Caher, Clooney, Crusheen, Kilraghtis, Kiltamon, Muckanagh, Newgrove, Rathclooney, Ruan, Spaicelhill, Templemaley, Toberbreeda.

DOONBEG—The District Electoral Divisions of—
    Cahermurphy (Kilrush), Cloonadrum, Creagh, Doonbeg, Knocknaboley, Mullagh.

DYSERT—The District Electoral Divisions of—
Ballyea, Cloonanaha, Dysert, Formoyle, Killanniv, Kilnamona, Kinturk, Magherareagh.

ENNIS—The District Electoral Divisions of—
Ennis No. 1 Urban, Ennis No. 2 Urban, Ennis No. 3 Urban, Ennis No. 4 Urban.

ENNISTYMON—The District Electoral Divisions of—
Ballysteen, Ennistymon, Killaspugloane, Kilshanny, Liscannor, Smithstown.

FEAKLE—The District Electoral Divisions of—
Cahermurphy (Scariff), Cappaghbaun, Cloonusker, Corlea, Derrynagittagh, Drummaan, Feakle, Inishcaltra North, Killanena, Loughea, Mountshannon.

KILKEE—The District Electoral Divisions of—
Kilballyowen, Kilkee, Moveen, Rahona, Tullig.

KILKISHEN—The District Electoral Divisions of—
Ballyblood, Ballycannan, Ballyglass, Cappavilla, Castlecrine, Cloghera, Cloontra, Dangan, Kilkishen, Kiltenanlea, Kyle.

KILLADYSERT—The District Electoral Divisions of—
Coolmeen, Kilchreest, Kilfiddane, Killadysert, Killofin, Rinealon.

KILLALOE—The District Electoral Divisions of—
Carrowbaun, Fahymore, Killaloe, Killokennedy, Killuran, Kilseily, Lackareagh, O'Briensbridge.

KILRUSH—The District Electoral Divisions of—
Clooncoorha, Kilrush Rural, Kilrush Urban.

LISDOONVARNA—The District Electoral Divisions of—
Abbey, Carran, Castletown, Cloghaun, Derreen, Drumcreehy, Gleninagh, Killilagh, Lisdoonvarna, Lurraga, Mount Elva, Noughaval, Oughtmama, Rathborney.

MILTOWN MALBAY—District Electoral Divisions of—
Annagh, Ballyvaskin, Kilmurry (Kilrush), Miltown Malbay, Moy.

MOYARTA—The District Electoral Divisions of—
Drumellihy, Einagh, Killard, Knocknagore, Moyarta, Querrin, St. Martin's.

QUIN—The District Electoral Divisions of—
Clenagh, Cratloe, Drumline, Killeely, Mountievers, Quin, Rossroe, Sixmilebridge, Tomfinlough, Urlan.

Note.—In the above schedule, District Electoral Divisions mean the existing Poor Law Electoral Divisions having the same name.

CORK.

SCHEDULE A.

Name of Administrative County and Contents.

COUNTY OF CORK—The existing judicial county of Cork.

SCHEDULE B.

County Electoral Divisions and Contents.

BALLINCOLLIG—THE DISTRICT ELECTORAL DIVISIONS OF—
Ballincollig, Ballygarvan, Ballygorman, Carrigrohane-
beg, Inishkenny, Lehenagh, Ovens, St. Mary's.

BALLYDEHOB—THE DISTRICT ELECTORAL DIVISIONS OF—
Aghadown North, Aghadown South, Ballybane, Ballydehob, Caheragh, Cloghdonnell, Dromdaleague Nth.,
Dromdaleague South, Gortnescreeny, Kilcoe, Killeen-
leagh, Mealagh.

BALLYHOOLY—THE DISTRICT ELECTORAL DIVISIONS OF—
Ballyhooly, Castle Hyde, Castletownroche, Derryvil-
lane, Farahy, Glanworth West, Kilcummer, Kil-
dinan, Kildorrey, Killathy, Rathcormack, Shanbally-
more, Skahanagh, Wallstown

BANDON—THE DISTRICT ELECTORAL DIVISIONS OF—
Ballinadee, Ballinspittle, Ballymackean, Ballymodan,
Bandon, Coolmain, Inishannon, Kilbrittain, Knock-
roe, Laherne.

BANTEER—THE DISTRICT ELECTORAL DIVISIONS OF—
Banteer, Caherbarnagh, Clonmeen, Coomlogane,
Crinnaloo, Drishane, Gortmore, Keale, Kilcorney,
Nad, Rathcool, Rossnalee, Tincoora.

BANTRY—THE DISTRICT ELECTORAL DIVISIONS OF—
Adrigole, Ahil, Bantry Rural, Bantry Urban, Douce,
Glengarriff, Kealkill, Kilcaskan, Whiddy.

BERE—THE DISTRICT ELECTORAL DIVISIONS OF—
Bere, Coulagh, Curryglass, Kilcatherine, Killacone-
nagh, Kilnamanagh.

BLACKROCK—THE DISTRICT ELECTORAL DIVISIONS OF—
Bishopstown, Blackrock, Douglas.

BLARNEY—THE DISTRICT ELECTORAL DIVISIONS OF—
Ballynamona, Blackpool, Blarney, Dripsey, Firmount,
Gowlane, Gre rt, Kilcullen, Knockantota,
Matehy, Mour ..vers.

BOHERBOY—THE DISTRICT ELECTORAL DIVISIONS OF—
Ballyhoolahan, Barnacurra, Boherboy, Coolclogh, Cullen, Derragh, Doonasleen, Kilmeen, King Williamstown, Knocknagree, Meens, Skagh.

CHARLEVILLE—THE DISTRICT ELECTORAL DIVISIONS OF—
Ardskeagh, Buttevant, Charleville, Churchtown, Doneraile, Imphrick, Milltown, Newtown, Springfort, Streamhill.

CLONAKILTY—THE DISTRICT ELECTORAL DIVISIONS OF—
Ardfield, Argideen, Castleventry, Clonakilty Rural, Clonakilty Urban, Coolcraheen, Kilkerranmore, Rathbarry, Rossmore, Templeomallus.

CLOYNE—THE DISTRICT ELECTORAL DIVISIONS OF—
Ballintemple, Ballycottin, Castlemartyr, Cloyne, Corkbeg, Garryvoe, Inch, Rostellan.

DUNMANWAY—THE DISTRICT ELECTORAL DIVISIONS OF—
Aultagh, Ballingurteen, Coolmountain, Drinagh (Dunmanway), Drinagh, (Skibbereen), Dunmanway, Garranes, Garrowen, Kinneigh, Manch, Milane.

FERMOY—THE DISTRICT ELECTORAL DIVISIONS OF—
Aghern, Castlelyons, Coole, Fermoy Rural, Fermoy Urban, Kilcor, Knockmourne.

INCHIGEELAGH—THE DISTRICT ELECTORAL DIVISIONS OF—
Bealanagarry, Bealanageary, Bealock, Candroma, Carrigboy, Cleanrath, Clondrohid, Derryfineen, Gortnatubbrid, Inchigeelagh, Kilnamartery, Slievereagh, Ullanes.

KANTURK—THE DISTRICT ELECTORAL DIVISIONS OF—
Ballyclogh, Castlecor, Castlemagner, Greenane, Kanturk, Kilbrin, Kilmaclenine, Kilshannig, Liscarroll, Roskeen, Templemary.

KINSALE—THE DISTRICT ELECTORAL DIVISIONS OF—
Ballymurphy, Ballymartle, Dunderrow, Kinsale Rural, Kinsale Urban, Leighmoney, Templemichael.

MACROOM—THE DISTRICT ELECTORAL DIVISIONS OF—
Aghinagh, Clonmoyle, Kilberrihert, Macloneigh, Macroom, Magourney, Mashanaglass, Rahalisk, Teerelton.

MALLOW—THE DISTRICT ELECTORAL DIVISIONS OF—
Ballynaglogh, Caherduggan, Carrig (Fermoy), Carrig (Mallow), Carrignavar, Clenor, Glenville, Killeagh, Mallow Rural, Mallow North Urban, Mallow South Urban, Monanimy, Rahan.

MIDLETON—THE DISTRICT ELECTORAL DIVISIONS OF—
Ardagh, Ballynoe, Ballyspillane, Clonmult, Curraglass, Dangan, Dungourney, Kilcronat, Midleton Rural, Midleton Urban, Mogeely, Templebodan, Templenacarriga.

MITCHELSTOWN—THE DISTRICT ELECTORAL DIVISIONS OF
Ballyarthur, Castlecooke, Glanworth E., Gortnaskehy, Kilgullane, Kilphelan, Kilworth, Leitrim, Marshalstown, Mitchelstown, Templemolaga.

MONKSTOWN—THE DISTRICT ELECTORAL DIVISIONS OF—
Ballyfeard, Ballyfoyle, Carrigaline (Cork), Carrigaline (Kinsale), Cullen, Farranbrien, Kilmonoge, Kilpatrick, Kinure, Liscleary, Monkstown, Nohaval, Templebreedy.

NEWMARKET—THE DISTRICT ELECTORAL DIVISIONS OF—
Allow, Barleyhill, Bawncross, Clonfert East, Clonfert West, Dromina, Glenlara, Knockatooan, Knocktemple, Milford, Newmarket, Rowls, Tullylease.

QUEENSTOWN—THE DISTRICT ELECTORAL DIVISIONS OF—
Queenstown Rural, Queenstown Urban.

ROSSCARBERY—THE DISTRICT ELECTORAL DIVISIONS OF—
Bredagh, Cahermore, Carrigbaun, Cloonkeen, Kilfaughnabeg, Knockskagh, Myross, Rosscarbery, Shreelane, Woodfort.

SKIBBEREEN—THE DISTRICT ELECTORAL DIVISIONS OF—
Cape Clear, Castlehaven North, Castlehaven South, Skibbereen Rural, Skibbereen Urban, Tullagh.

SKULL—THE DISTRICT ELECTORAL DIVISIONS OF—
Coolagh, Crookhaven, Dunbeacon, Dunmanus, Durrus East, Durrus West, Glanlough, Goleen, Lowertown, Scart, Seefin, Sheepshead, Skull, Toormore.

TIMOLEAGUE—THE DISTRICT ELECTORAL DIVISIONS OF—
Abbeymahon, Ballymoney, Baurleigh, Boulteen, Butlerstown, Cashel, Courtmacsherry, Kilmaloda East, Kilmaloda West, Kilmoylerane, Kilnagross, Knock, Rathclarin, Timoleague.

WARRENSCOURT—THE DISTRICT ELECTORAL DIVISIONS OF
Aglish, Bengour, Brinny, Cannaway, Castletown, Greenville, Kilbonane, Kilbrogan, Knockavilly, Moviddy, Murragh, Teadies, Templemartin, Warrenscourt.

WATERGRASSHILL—DISTRICT ELECTORAL DIVISIONS OF—
Caherlag, Carrigtohill, Gortroe, Knockraha, Lisgoold, Rathcooney, Riverstown, Watergrasshill, Whitechurch.

YOUGHAL—THE DISTRICT ELECTORAL DIVISIONS OF—
Clonpriest, Ightermurragh, Killeagh, Kilmacdonogh,
Youghal Rural, Youghal Urban.

Note.—In the above schedule, District Electoral Divisions mean
the existing Poor Law Electoral Divisions having the same name.

DONEGAL.

SCHEDULE A.

Name of Administrative County and Contents.

COUNTY OF DONEGAL—The existing judicial county of
Donegal.

SCHEDULE B.

County Electoral Divisions and Contents.

ANNAGARRY—THE DISTRICT ELECTORAL DIVISIONS OF—
Annagarry, Arran, Magheraclogher, Rutland.

BALLYSHANNON—THE DISTRICT ELECTORAL DIVISIONS OF
Ballyshannon Rural, Ballyshannon Urban, Bundoran,
Carrickboy, Cliff.

BUNCRANA—THE DISTRICT ELECTORAL DIVISIONS OF—
Ballyliffin. Buncrana, Desertegny, Dunaff, Illies,
Mintiaghs, Straid.

BURT—THE DISTRICT ELECTORAL DIVISIONS OF—
Birdstown, Burt, Castle Forward, Fahan, Inch Island,
Kilderry, Killea, Newtown Cunningham, Three
Trees.

CARNDONAGH—THE DISTRICT ELECTORAL DIVISIONS OF—
Ardmalin, Carndonagh, Carthage, Culdaff, Glene-
gauon, Glentoher, Malin.

CASTLE FINN—THE DISTRICT ELECTORAL DIVISIONS OF—
Castle Finn, Cloghard, Clonleigh North, Clonleigh
South, Gleneely (Stranorlar), Killygordon, West
Urney.

CHURCH HILL—THE DISTRICT ELECTORAL DIVISIONS OF—
Ards, Church Hill, Creanasmear, Creeslough, Doe
Castle Edenacarnan, Gartan, Killymasny, Seacor,
Temple Douglas, Termon.

DONEGAL—THE DISTRICT ELECTORAL DIVISIONS OF—
Clogher, Donegal, Eanymore, Haugh, Lough Eask,
Townawully, Tullynaught.

DUNFANAGHY—THE DISTRICT ELECTORAL DIVISIONS OF—
Crossroads, Dunfanaghy, Dunlewy, Gortahork, Meena-
aclady.

DUNGLOW—THE DISTRICT ELECTORAL DIVISIONS OF—
Crovehy, Doocharry, Dunglow, Fintown, Glenleheen,
Lettermacaward, Maghery.

DUNKINEELY—THE DISTRICT ELECTORAL DIVISIONS OF—
Binbane, Bonnyglen, Corkermore, Dunkineely, Inver,
Mountcharles.

GLENTIES—THE DISTRICT ELECTORAL DIVISIONS OF—
Ardara, Dawros, Glengesh, Glenties, Graffy, Inish-
Keel, Maas, Mulmosog.

KILLYBEGS—THE DISTRICT ELECTORAL DIVISIONS OF—
Crowkeeragh, Crownarad, Glencolumbkille, Kilcar,
Kilgoly, Killybegs, Largymore, Malinbeg, Tieves-
keelta.

LETTERKENNY—THE DISTRICT ELECTORAL DIVISIONS OF
Ballymacool, Castlewray, Corravaddy, Letterkenny
Rural, Letterkenny Urban, Magheraboy, Rath-
melton.

MILFORD—THE DISTRICT ELECTORAL DIVISIONS OF—
Ballyarr, Carrigart, Cranford, Glen, Gortnavern,
Kilmacrenan, Loughkeel, Milford, Rosguill.

MOVILLE—THE DISTRICT ELECTORAL DIVISIONS OF—
Castle Cary, Gleneely (Inishowen), Green Castle,
Moville, Red Castle, Turmone, White Castle.

PETTIGO—THE DISTRICT ELECTORAL DIVISIONS OF—
Ballintra (Ballyshannon), Ballintra (Donegal), Cavan
Garden, Grousehall, Laghy, Pettigo, Templecarne.

RAPHOE—THE DISTRICT ELECTORAL DIVISIONS OF—
Convoy, Feddyglass, Figart, Kincraigy, Manorcun-
ningham, Raphoe, St. Johnstown, Treantaghmuck-
lagh.

RATHMULLAN—THE DISTRICT ELECTORAL DIVISIONS OF—
Carrowkeel, Fanad North, Fanad West, Glenalla,
Greenfort, Killygarvan, Knockalla, Rathmullan,
Rosnakill.

STRANORLAR—THE DISTRICT ELECTORAL DIVISIONS OF—
Altnapaste, Cloghan, Dooish, Goland, Knock, Lettermore, Meencargagh, Stranorlar,

Note.—In the above schedule, District Electoral Divisions mean
the existing Poor Law Electoral Divisions having the same name.

DOWN.

SCHEDULE A.

Name of Administrative County and Contents.

COUNTY OF DOWN—The existing judicial county of Down (except the portion of the city of Belfast and of the town of Lisburn, situated therein); and

So much of the existing judicial county of Armagh as comprises the portion of the town of Newry situated therein.

SCHEDULE B.

County Electoral Divisions and Contents.

BALLYNAHINCH—THE DISTRICT ELECTORAL DIVISIONS OF Ardtanagh, Ballynahinch, Crosgar (Banbridge), Dromara, Dunmore, Rossconor.

BANBRIDGE—THE DISTRICT ELECTORAL DIVISIONS OF— Annaclone, Banbridge Rural, Banbridge East Urban, Banbridge West Urban, Loughbrickland, Scarva.

BANGOR—THE DISTRICT ELECTORAL DIVISIONS OF— Bangor Rural, Bangor Urban, Carrowdore, Donaghadee.

BRYANSFORD—THE DISTRICT ELECTORAL DIVISIONS OF— Ballyward, Bryansford, Clonduff, Fofanny, Leitrim, Maghera, Moneyslane.

CASTLEWELLAN—THE DISTRICT ELECTORAL DIVISIONS OF Castlewellan, Clough, Dundrum, Hollymount, Killough, Seaforde, Tyrella.

COMBER—THE DISTRICT ELECTORAL DIVISIONS OF— Breda, Comber, Kilmood, Moneyreagh, Tullynakill.

DOWNPATRICK—THE DISTRICT ELECTORAL DIVISIONS OF Ardglass, Downpatrick Rural, Downpatrick Urban, Dunsfort, Inch, Raholp, Strangford.

DROMORE—THE DISTRICT ELECTORAL DIVISIONS OF— Ballykeel (Lisburn), Dromore Rural, Dromore Urban, Kilmore, Magheralin, Moira.

GARVAGHY—THE DISTRICT ELECTORAL DIVISIONS OF— Balloolymore, Ballyleny, Donaghcloney, Garvaghy, Magherally, Quilly, Skeagh.

GILFORD—THE DISTRICT ELECTORAL DIVISIONS OF— Gilford, Tullylish (Banbridge), Tullylish (Lurgan), Waringstown.

HILLSBOROUGH—THE DISTRICT ELECTORAL DIVISIONS OF Annahilt, Ballymacbrennan, Ballyworfy, Glasdrumman, Hillsborough, Killany, Maze.

HOLYWOOD—THE DISTRICT ELECTORAL DIVISIONS OF— Ballyhackamore, Ballymaglaff, Castlereagh, Dundonald, Holywood Rural, Holywood Urban, Newtownards South.

KILKEEL—THE DISTRICT ELECTORAL DIVISIONS OF— Ballykeel (Kilkeel), Greencastle, Kilkeel, Kilowen, Mourne Park, Mullartown.

KILLYLEAGH—THE DISTRICT ELECTORAL DIVISIONS OF— Crossgar (Downpatrick), Killinchy, Killyleagh, Kilmore, Leggygowan.

NEWRY—THE DISTRICT ELECTORAL DIVISIONS OF— Newry North Urban, Newry South Urban, Newry West Urban.

NEWTOWNARDS—THE DISTRICT ELECTORAL DIVISIONS OF Mount Stewart, Newtownards North, Newtownards Urban.

PORTAFERRY—THE DISTRICT ELECTORAL DIVISIONS OF— Ardkeen, Ballyhalbert, Ballywalter, Grey Abbey, Kircubbin, Portaferry, Quintin.

RATHFRILAND—THE DISTRICT ELECTORAL DIVISIONS OF— Ballybrick, Donaghmore, Drumgath, Glaskermore, Glen, Ouley (Newry), Rathfriland, Tirkelly.

SAINTFIELD—THE DISTRICT ELECTORAL DIVISIONS OF— Ballygowan, Blaris, Drumbeg, Drumbo, Ouley (Lisburn), Saintfield.

WARRENPOINT—THE DISTRICT ELECTORAL DIVISIONS OF Crobane, Hilltown, Newry Rural, Rostrevor, Upper Cionallan, Warrenpoint Rural, Warrenpoint Urban.

Note.—In the above schedule, District Electoral Divisions mean the existing Poor Law Electoral Divisions having the same name.

DUBLIN.

SCHEDULE A.

Name of Administrative County and Contents.

COUNTY OF DUBLIN—The existing judicial county of Dublin (except the portion of the township of Bray situated therein).

SCHEDULE B.

County Electoral Divisions and Contents.

BALBRIGGAN—THE DISTRICT ELECTORAL DIVISIONS OF—
Balbriggan Rural, Balbriggan, Urban, Balscadden,
Garristown, Hollywood.

BLACKROCK—THE DISTRICT ELECTORAL DIVISIONS OF—
Blackrock No. 1, Blackrock No. 2, Blackrock No. 3,
Kingstown No. 1.

CASTLEKNOCK—THE DISTRICT ELECTORAL DIVISION OF—
Castleknock.

COOLOCK —THE DISTRICT ELECTORAL DIVISIONS OF—
Coolock, Finglas, Glasnevin.

DALKEY—THE DISTRICT ELECTORAL DIVISIONS OF—
Dalkey, Killiney, Kingstown No. 4.

DONNYBROOK—THE DISTRICT ELECTORAL DIVISIONS OF—
Donnybrook, Pembroke. East.

DRUMCONDRA—THE DISTRICT ELECTORAL DIVISIONS OF—
Drumcondra Rural, Drumcondra No. 1 Urban, Drumcondra No. 2 Urban, Drumcondra No. 3 Urban.

DUNDRUM—THE DISTRICT ELECTORAL DIVISIONS OF—
Dundrum, Glencullen.

HOWTH—THE DISTRICT ELECTORAL DIVISIONS OF—
Clontarf, Howth.

KINGSTOWN—THE DISTRICT ELECTORAL DIVISIONS OF—
Kingstown No. 2, Kingstown No. 3.

LUCAN—THE DISTRICT ELECTORAL DIVISIONS OF—
Blanchardstown, Clonsilla, Lucan, Palmerstown.

LUSK—THE DISTRICT ELECTORAL DIVISIONS OF—
Holmpatrick, Lusk.

NEW KILMAINHAM—DISTRICT ELECTORAL DIVISIONS OF
Clondalkin, New Kilmainham.

PEMBROKE WEST—THE DISTRICT ELECTORAL DIVISION OF
Pembroke West

RATHCOOLE—THE DISTRICT ELECTORAL DIVISIONS OF—
Newcastle, Rathcoole, Saggart, Tallaght.

RATHFARNHAM—THE DISTRICT ELECTORAL DIVISIONS OF—
Rathfarnham, Whitechurch.

RATHMINES EAST—DISTRICT ELECTORAL DIVISIONS OF—
Rathmines and Rathgar East

RATHMINES WEST—DISTRICT ELECTORAL DIVISIONS OF—
Rathmines and Rathgar West.

STILLORGAN—The District Electoral Divisions of—
　　Ballybrack, Rathmichael, Stillorgan.

SWORDS—The District Electoral Divisions of—
　　Ballyboghill, Clonmethan, Donabate, Kilsallaghan,
　　Kinsaley, Malahide, Swords.

Note.—In the above schedule, District Electoral Divisions mean
the existing Poor Law Electoral Divisions having the same name.

FERMANAGH.

SCHEDULE A.

Name of Administrative County and Contents.

COUNTY OF FERMANAGH—The existing judicial county
of Fermanagh.

SCHEDULE B.

County Electoral Divisions and Contents.

BELLEEK—The District Electoral Divisions of—
　　Belleek, Brookhill, Castlecaldwell, Clonelly, Drum-
　　rush, Mullybreen.

CROSS—The District Electoral Divisions of—
　　Clabby, Corralongford, Cross, Imeroo.

CRUM—The District Electoral Divisions of—
　　Aghyoule, Crum, Doon.

DERRYLEA—The District Electoral Divisions of—
　　Armagh Manor, Belleisle, Carrickmacosker, Derrylea,
　　Inismore, Kilmore.

DERRYLESTER—The District Electoral Divisions of—
　　Aghakillymaud, Derrylester, Drummully, Kinawley,
　　Kinglass, Springtown.

ENNISKILLEN—The District Electoral Division of—
　　Enniskillen Urban.

FLORENCECOURT—District Electoral Divisions of—
　　Cuilcagh, Drumane, Florencecourt, Gortahurk,
　　Killesher.

GARRISON—The District Electoral Divisions of—
　　Aghanaglack, Gardenhill, Garrison, Glenkeel, Holy-
　　well, Lattone, Oldbarr, Roogagh.

INISHMACSAINT—The District Electoral Divisions of
　　Church Hill, Inishmacsaint.

IRVINESTOWN—The District Electoral Divisions of—
Bellanamallard, Irvinestown, Newporton.

KESH—The District Electoral Divisions of—
Ballycassidy, Ederny, Kesh, Killadeas, Lisnarrick,
Milltown.

LACK—The District Electoral Divisions of—
Drumkeeran, Glenvannan, Lack, Magheraculmoney,
Tirmacspird.

LARAGH—The District Electoral Divisions of—
Coolyermer, Enniskillen Rural, Laragh, Lisbofin.

LISBELLAW—The District Electoral Divisions of—
Ballydoolagh, Ballyreagh, Lisbellaw, Tempo.

LISNASKEA—The District Electoral Divisions of—
Deerpark, Lisnaskea.

MAGHERAVEELY—The District Electoral Divisions of
Carnmore, Coolnamarrow, Grogey, Magheraveely,
Mullaghfad.

MAGUIRESBRIDGE—District Electoral Divisions of—
Brookeborough, Castlecoole, Derrybrusk, Greenhill,
Maguiresbridge.

MONEA—The District Electoral Divisions of—
Doagh, Ely, Monea, Rahalton, Ross.

NEWTOWNBUTLER—District Electoral Divisions of
Clonkeelan, Derrysteaton, Kilturk, Mullynagowan,
Newtownbutler.

ROSSLEA—The District Electoral Divisions of—
Dresternan, Rosslea.

Note.—In the above schedule, District Electoral Divisions mean
the existing Poor Law Electoral Divisions having the same name.

GALWAY.

SCHEDULE A.

Name of Administrative County and Contents.

COUNTY OF GALWAY—The existing judicial county of
Galway (except the district electoral divisions of
Ballinchalla, Drummaan, Inishcaltra North, Mount-
shannon, Owenbrin, and Rosmoylan);
So much of the existing judicial county of Roscommon
as comprises the portion of the town of Ballinasloe
situated therein ; and
The existing judicial county of the town of Galway.

SCHEDULE B.
County Electoral Divisions and Contents.

AHASCRAGH—The District Electoral Divisions of—
Ahascragh, Annagh, Ballymacward, Caltra, Castle-blakeney, Castleffrench, Clonbrock, Derryglassaun, Kilconnell, Killure, Mounthazel, Taghboy.

ATHENRY—The District Electoral Divisions of—
Athenry, Aughrim (Ballinasloe), Bullaun, Cappalusk, Cloonkeen (Loughrea), Graigabbey, Grange, Greet-hill, Kilconierin, Killallaghtan, Killimor, Killaan, Killoran, Kilreekill, Kiltullagh (Loughrea), Oatfield, Raford.

BALLINASLOE—The District Electoral Divisions of—
Ballinasloe Rural, Ballinasloe Urban, Clonfert, Clontuskert, Eyrecourt, Kellysgrove, Kilmacshane, Kiltormer, Kylemore, Laurencetown, Lismanny, Meelick.

CLIFDEN—The District Electoral Divisions of—
Ballynakill, Cleggan, Clifden, Cushkillary, Derrylea, Inishboffin, Rinvyle, Silerna.

DUNMORE—The District Electoral Divisions of—
Addergoole, Carrownagur, Clonbern, Cloonkeen (Glennamaddy), Cooloo, Dunmore, Kiltullagh (Glennamaddy), Raheen, Scregg.

GALWAY RURAL—The District Electoral Divisions of
Aughrim (Galway), Ballintemple, Belleville, Carnmore, Barrowbrowne, Colmanstown, Deerpark, Galway Rural, Inishmore, Lackaghbeg, Lisheenavalla, Monivea, Ryehill, Tiaquin.

GALWAY URBAN—The District Electoral Divisions of
Galway East Urban, Galway North Urban, Galway South Urban, Galway West Urban.

GLENNAMADDY—The District Electoral Divisions of—
Ballinastack, Ballymoe, Ballynakill (Glennamaddy), Boyounagh, Glennamaddy, Island, Kilcoran, Templetogher, Toberadosh, Toberroe.

GORT—The District Electoral Divisions of—
Ardamullivan, Ballycahalan, Beagh, Cahermore, Cappard, Doorus, Gort, Kilbeacanty, Killinny, Kiltartan, Kinvarra.

HEADFORD—The District Electoral Divisions of—
Annaghdown (Galway), Annaghdown (Tuam), Ballinderry, Ballinduff, Claregalway, Cummer, Headford, Killeany, Killower, Killursa, Kilmoylan, Liscannanaun.

LETTERMORE—The District Electoral Divisions of—
Camus, Crumpaun, Gorumna, Kilcummin (Galway),
Lettermore, Turlough.

LOUGHREA—The District Electoral Divisions of—
Ballynagar, Bracklagh, Derrylaur, Drumkeary, Kil-
meen, Kilteskill, Lackalea, Leitrim, Loughatorick,
Loughrea Rural, Loughrea Urban, Marblehill,
Mountain, Tynagh.

MILLTOWN—The District Electoral Divisions of—
Beaghmore, Belclare, Claretuam, Donaghpatrick,
Doonbally, Foxhall, Kilbennan, Kilcoona, Killeen,
Kilshanvy, Milltown.

MOUNT BELLEW—The District Electoral Divisions of
Ballynakill (Mount Bellew), Cloonkeen (Mount Bellew),
Creggs, Curraghmore, Killeroran, Killian, Mount
Bellew, Shankill.

ORANMORE—The District Electoral Divisions of—
Aille, Ardrahan, Ballynacourty, Castleboy, Castle-
taylor, Clairnbridge, Craughwell, Drumacoo,
Kilchreest, Kilconickny, Killeely, Killeenavarra,
Killogillen, Kilthomas, Moyode, Oranmore, Raha-
sane, Skehanagh, Stradbally.

OUGHTERARD—The District Electoral Divisions of—
Cloonbur, Cong, Cur, Illion, Kilcummin (Oughterard),
Letterbrickaun, Letterfore, Oughterard, Ross,

PORTUMNA—The District Electoral Divisions of—
Abbeygormacan, Abbeyville, Ballyglass, Coos, Derrew,
Drummin, Killimor, Kilmalinoge, Kilquain, Moat,
Pallas, Portumna, Tiranascragh, Woodford.

ROUNDSTONE—The District Electoral Divisions of—
Bencorr, Bunowen, Derrycunlagh, Doonloughan, Erris-
lannon, Knockboy, Moyrus, Roundstone, Owen-
gowla, Skannive.

SPIDDLE—The District Electoral Divisions of—
Barna, Furbogh, Killannin, Moycullen, Selerna,
Slieveaneena, Spiddle, Tullokyne, Wormhole.

TUAM—The District Electoral Divisions of—
Abbey East, Abbey West, Ballynapark, Carrowrevagh,
Hillsbrook, Killererin, Levally, Moyne, Tuam Rural,
Tuam Urban.

Note.—In the above schedule, District Electoral Divisions mean
the existing Poor Law Electoral Divisions having the same name.

KERRY.

SCHEDULE A.

Name of Administrative County and Contents.

COUNTY OF KERRY—The existing judicial county of Kerry.

SCHEDULE B.

County Electoral Divisions and Contents.

AGHADOE—The District Electoral Divisions of—
Aghadoe, Aglish, Ballyhar, Dunloe, Kilbonane, Kilcumin, Killeentierna, Lahard, Molahiffe, Muskross, Rockfield.

ARDFERT—The District Electoral Divisions of—
Abbeydorney, Ardfert, Ballynahaglish, Clogherbrien, Doon, Kilflyn, Kilshenane, Nohaval, O'Brennan, Ratass.

BALLYHEIGE—The District Electoral Divisions of—
Ballyheige, Ballynorig, Banna, Causeway, Kerryhead, Killahan, Killury, Tubrid.

CAHER—The District Electoral Divisions of—
Bahaghs, Caher, Castlequin, Cloon, Derriana, Killinane.

CASTLEGREGORY—The District Electoral Divisions of
Ballyduff, Ballynacourty, Brandon, Castlegregory, Cloghane, Kilquane, Kinard, Minard, Stradbally.

CASTLEISLAND—The District Electoral Divisions of—
Ballyegan, Brosna, Castleisland, Gneeves, Knocknagashel, Lackabaun.

DINGLE—The District Electoral Divisions of—
Dingle, Dunquin, Dunurlin, Kilmalkedar, Marhin, Ventry.

GLANBEHY—The District Electoral Divisions of—
Churchtown, Curraghbeg, Curraghmore, Dromore, Glanbehy, Greenane, Lickeen, Loughbrin, Maum, Reen.

HEADFORT—The District Electoral Divisions of—
Brewsterfield, Clydagh, Coolies, Doocarrig, Flesk, Headfort, Kilgarvan, Rathmore.

KENMARE—The District Electoral Divisions of—
Ardea, Banawn, Cappagh, Dawros, Glanlee, Glenlough, Glanmore, Kenmare.

KILGOBBAN—THE DISTRICT ELECTORAL DIVISIONS OF—
Ballinvoher, Baurtregaum, Blennerville, Boolteens, Deelis, Inch, Kilgarrylander, Kilgobban, Knockglass, Lack, Tralee Rural.

KILLARNEY—THE DISTRICT ELECTORAL DIVISIONS OF—
Killarney Rural, Killarney Urban, Knocknahore.

KILLORGLIN—THE DISTRICT ELECTORAL DIVISIONS OF—
Caragh, Dromin, Kilgobnet, Killorglin.

LISSELTON—THE DISTRICT ELECTORAL DIVISIONS OF—
Astee, Ballinconry, Beal, Carrig, Gullane, Gunsborough, Killehenny, Lisselton, Shronowen,. Urlee.

LISTOWEL—THE DISTRICT ELECTORAL DIVISIONS OF—
Duahg, Listowel Rural, Listowel Urban, Moynsha, Rathea, Trienearagh.

LIXNAW—THE DISTRICT ELECTORAL DIVISIONS OF—
Ardagh, Ballincloher, Ballyduff, Ballyegan, Ballyhorgan, Drommartin, Ennismore, Kilfeighny, Kiltorny, Lixnaw.

MILLTOWN—THE DISTRICT ELECTORAL DIVISIONS OF—
Arabela, Ballyseedy, Currans, Kilfelim, Kilnanare, Kiltallagh, Milltown.

SCARTAGLIN—THE DISTRICT ELECTORAL DIVISIONS OF—
Carker, Coom, Cordal, Crinny, Derreen, Kilmurry, Millbrook, Mount Eagle, Scartaglin.

SNEEM—THE DISTRICT ELECTORAL DIVISIONS OF—
Ballybrack, Caherdaniel, Castlecove, Darrynane, Loughcurrane, Mastergeehy, Sneem, Tahilla.

TARBERT—THE DISTRICT ELECTORAL DIVISIONS OF—
Cloontubbrid, Kilmeany, Leitrim, Lislaughtin, Newtownsandes, Tarbert, Tarmon.

TRALEE—THE DISTRICT ELECTORAL DIVISION OF—
Tralee Urban.

VALENTIA—THE DISTRICT ELECTORAL DIVISIONS OF—
Ballinskelligs, Canuig, Emlagh, Portmagee, St. Finan's, Teeranearagh, Valentia.

Note.—In the above schedule, District Electoral Divisions mean the existing Poor Law Electoral Divisions having the same name.

KILDARE.

SCHEDULE A.
Name of Administrative County and Contents.

COUNTY OF KILDARE—, e existing judicial county of Kildare.

SCHEDULE B.

County Electoral Divisions and Contents.

ATHY—The District Electoral Divisions of—
Athy East Urban, Athy West Urban.

BALLITORE—The District Electoral Divisions of—
Ballitore, Burtown, Grangemellon, Kilkea, Moone, Narraghmore.

BALLYMORE EUSTACE—District Electoral Divs. of
Ballymore Eustace, Carnalway, Killashee, Newtown.

CARBURY—The District Electoral Divisions of—
Ballynadrumny, Cadamstown, Carbury, Carrick, Kilrainy, Windmill Cross.

CASTLEDERMOT—The District Electoral Divisions of
Ballaghmoon, Belan, Carrigeen, Castledermot, Dunmanoge, Graney, Johnstown.

CELBRIDGE—The District Electoral Divisions of—
Bodenstown, Celbridge, Donagheumper.

CHURCHTOWN—The District Electoral Divisions of—
Athy Rural, Bert, Churchtown, Fontstown, Kilberry, Skerries.

CLANE—The District Electoral Divisions of—
Clane, Donore, Downings, Robertstown.

HARRISTOWN—The District Electoral Divisions of—
Ballysax West, Ballyshannon, Harristown, Kildangan, Kilrush, Nurney.

KILCOCK—The District Electoral Divisions of—
Balraheen, Kilcock, Straffan.

KILCULLEN—The District Electoral Divisions of—
Gilltown, Inchaquire, Kilcullen, Usk.

KILDARE—The District Electoral Divisions of—
Ballysax East, Kildare.

KILMEAGE—The District Electoral Divisions of—
Cloncurry (Edenderry), Kilmeage North, Kilmeage South, Kilpatrick, Lullymore, Rathernan.

KILTEEL—The District Electoral Divisions of—
Carragh, Kill, Kilteel, Naas Rural, Oughterard, Rathmore.

MAYNOOTH—The District Electoral Divisions of—
Leixlip, Maynooth.

MONASTEREVIN—The District Electoral Divisions of
Ballybruckan, Monasterevin.

MORRISTOWNBILLER—District Electoral Divisions of Feighcullen, Ladytown, Morristownbiller, Newbridge Rural, Oldconnell, Pollardstown.

NAAS—The District Electoral Division of— Naas Urban.

NEWBRIDGE—The District Electoral Division of— Newbridge Urban.

RATHANGAN—The District Electoral Divisions of— Dunmurry, Killinthomas, Lackagh, Quinsborough, Rathangan, Thomastown.

TIMAHOE—The District Electoral Divisions of— Cloncurry (Celbridge), Donadea, Drehid, Dunfierth, Timahoe North, Timahoe South.

Note.—In the above schedule, District Electoral Divisions mean the existing Poor Law Electoral Divisions having the same name.

KILKENNY.

SCHEDULE A.

Name of Adminstrative County and Contents.

COUNTY OF KILKENNY—The existing judicial county of Kilkenny (except the portion of the town of New Ross, situated therein);

The existing judicial county of the city of Kilkenny; and

So much of the existing judicial county of Waterford as comprises the district electoral division of Kilculliheen.

SCHEDULE B.

County Electoral Divisions and Contents.

BALLYRAGGET—The District Electoral Divisions of— Attanagh, Balleen, Ballyconra, Ballyragget, Clomantagh, Lisdowney, Rathbeagh.

CALLAN—The District Electoral Divisions of— Callan Rural, Callan Urban, Coolaghmore, Kilmanagh, Scotsborough, Tullaghanbrogue.

CASTLECOMER—The District Electoral Division of— Castlecomer.

DUNKITT—The District Electoral Divisions of— Ballincrea, Dunkitt, Farnoge, Kilculliheen, Rathpatrick, Rossinan.

FIDDOWN—The District Electoral Divisions of—
Castlegannon, Fiddown, Kilbeacon, Kilkeasy, Killahy, Muckalee, Tubbrid.

FRESHFORD—The District Electoral Divisions of—
Ballinamara, Ballybeagh, Ballycallan, Freshford, Odagh, Rathealy, St. Canice, Tullaroan.

GOWRAN—The District Electoral Divisions of—
Gowran, Paulstown, Rathcoole, Shankill, Tiscoffin.

GRAIGUENAMANAGH—District Electoral Divis. of—
Bramblestown, Freaghana, Goresbridge, Graiguenamanagh, Powerstown, Ullard.

INISTIOGE—The District Electoral Divisions of—
Ballyvool, Brownsford, Castlebanny, Coolhill, Inistioge, Pleberstown, The Rower.

KILKENNY RURAL—District Electoral Divisions of—
Clara, Dunbell, Dunmore, Grange, Kilkenny Rural, Outrath.

KILKENNY URBAN—District Electoral Divisions of—
Kilkenny No. 1 Urban, Kilkenny No. 2 Urban.

KNOCKTOPHER—The District Electoral Divisions of—
Ballylehale, Burnchurch, Danesfort, Dunnamaggan, Earlstown, Ennisnag, Kells, Knocktopher, Mallardstown, Stonyford.

LISTERLIN—The District Electoral Divisions of—
Dysartmoon, Jerpoint West, Kilbride, Kilcolumb, Kilmakevoge, Listerlin, Rosbercon Rural, Shanbogh.

MOTHELL—The District Electoral Divisions of—
Clogharinka, Coolcraheen, Kilkieran, Kilmacar, Mothell, Muckalee.

PILLTOWN—The District Electoral Divisions of—
Aghaviller, Boolyglass, Killamery, Kilmaganny, Pilltown, Templeorum, Tullahought, Whitechurch.

POLLRONE—The District Electoral Divisions of—
Aglish, Pollrone, Portnascully, Ullid.

THOMASTOWN—The District Electoral Divisions of—
Bennetsbridge, Famna, Jerpoint Church, Kilfane, Kiltorcan, Thomastown, Tullaherin, Woolengrange.

URLINGFORD—The District Electoral Divisions of—
Baunmore, Galmoy, Glashare, Johnstown, Tubbridbrittain, Urlingford.

Note.—In the above schedule, District Electoral Divisions mean the existing Poor Law Electoral Divisions having the same name.

KING'S COUNTY.

SCHEDULE A.

Name of Administrative County and Contents.

KING'S COUNTY—The existing judicial county named King's County.

SCHEDULE B.

County Electoral Divisions and Contents.

BALLYBURLEY—The District Electoral Divisions of— Ballyburley, Ballymacwilliam, Clonmore, Croghan, Knockdrin.

BALLYCUMBER—The District Electoral Divisions of Ballycumber, Bawn, Gorteen, Kilcumreragh, Tinamuck.

BANAGHER—The District Electoral Divisions of— Banagher, Derryad, Lusmagh, Mounterin.

CLARA—The District Electoral Division of— Clara.

CLONBULLOGE—The District Electoral Divisions of— Ballaghassaan, Bracknagh, Clonbulloge, Raheenakeeran, Rathfeston.

CLONMACNOISE—The District Electoral Divisions of Clonmacnoise, Doon, Hinds, Moyclare.

DUNKERRIN—The District Electoral Divisions of— Barna, Cullenwaine, Dunkerrin, Mountheaton, Templeharry.

EDENDERRY—The District Electoral Divisions of— Edenderry, Monasteroris.

EGLISH—The District Electoral Divisions of— Eglish, Killyon, Parsonstown Rural.

FERBANE—The District Electoral Divisions of— Broughal, Derrycooly, Ferbane, Gallen, Lea, Srah.

FRANKFORD—The District Electoral Divisions of— Derrinboy, Drumcullen, Frankford, Killooly, Knockbarron, Letter.

GEASHILL—The District Electoral Divisions of— Ballycommon, Cappancur, Geashill, Tinnycross.

KILLEIGH—The District Electoral Divisions of— Killeigh, Killoughy, Rathrobin, Screggan.

KINNITTY—The District Electoral Divisions of- -
    Aghancon, Dromoyle, Gorteen, Kinnitty, Roscomroe,
    Seirkieran, Tulla.

PARSONSTOWN—The District Electoral Division of—
    Parsonstown Urban.

PHILIPSTOWN—The District Electoral Divisions of—
    Esker, Kilclonfert, Mountbriscoe, Philipstown.

PORTARLINGTON NORTH—Dist. Electoral Divs. of
    Ballyshear, Clonygowan, Hammerlane, O'Dempsy,
    Portarlington North.

RAHAN—The District Electoral Divisions of—
    Durrow, Rahan, Silverbrook, Tullamore Rural.

SHANNONBRIDGE--The District Electoral Divisions of
    Cloghan, Huntston, Lumcloon, Shannonbridge, Shan-
    nonharbour.

SHINRONE—The District Electoral Divisions of—
    Ballincor, Cangort, Ettagh, Kilcolman, Shinrone.

TULLAMORE—The District Electoral Division of—
    Tullamore Urban.

Note.—In the above schedule, District Electoral Divisions mean
the existing Poor Law Electoral Divisions having the same name.

LEITRIM.

SCHEDULE A.

Name of Administrative County and Contents.

COUNTY OF LEITRIM—The existing judicial county of
    Leitrim.

SCHEDULE B.

County Electoral Divisions and Contents.

AGHACASHEL—The District Electoral Divisions of—
    Aghacashel, Barnameenagh, Drumreilly East, Drum-
    reilly West, Stralongford, Yugan.

BALLINAMORE—The District Electoral Divisions of—
    Ballinamore, Castlefore, Fenagh, Greaghglass, Rowan.

CARRICK-ON-SHANNON—Dist. Electoral Divisions of
    Carrick-on-Shannon, Gowel.

CARRIGALLEN—The District Electoral Divisions of—
    Carrigallen East, Carrigallen West, Corrala, Gorter-
    mone, Killygar.

CLOONE—The District Electoral Divisions of—
Cattan, Cloone, Corriga, Keeldra.

DRUMAHAIRE—The District Electoral Divisions of—
Belhavel, Drumahaire, Killanummery.

DRUMKEERAN—The District Electoral Divisions of—
Argina, Drumkeeran, Garvagh, St. Patrick's.

DRUMSHANBO—The District Electoral Divisions of—
Drumshanbo, Gortnagullion, Keshcarrigan, Kiltubbrid, Leitrim, Moher.

DRUMSNA—The District Electoral Divisions of—
Annaduff, Breandrum, Bunnybeg, Drumdoo, Drumsna.

KILTYCLOGHER—The District Electoral Divisions of—
Glenboy, Glenfarn, Kiltyclogher, Munakill.

KINLOUGH—The District Electoral Divisions of—
Gubacreeny, Kinlough, Tullaghan.

LURGANBOY—The District Electoral Divisions of—
Glenade, Glencar, Lurganboy, Sramore.

MAHANAGH—The District Electoral Divisions of—
Cloonclare, Killarga, Mahanagh.

MANORHAMILTON—District Electoral Divisions of—
Cloonclogher, Manorhamilton.

MELVIN—The District Electoral Divisions of—
Aghalateeve, Aghanlish, Aghavoghil, Ballaghameehan, Glenariff, Melvin. .

MOHILL—The District Electoral Divisions of—
Drumard, Drumod, Mohill.

NEWTOWNGORE—The District Electoral Divisions of
Cloverhill, Garadice, Newtowngore, Oughteragh.

RIVERSTOWN—The District Electoral Divisions of—
Aghavas, Drumreilly North, Drumreilly South,

ROOSKY—The District Electoral Divisions of—
Beihy, Cashel, Rinn, Roosky.

Note.—In the above schedule, District Electoral Divisions mean the existing Poor Law Electoral Divisions having the same name.

LIMERICK.

SCHEDULE A.

Name of Administrative County and Contents.

COUNTY OF LIMERICK—The existing judicial county of Limerick.

SCHEDULE B.

County Electoral Divisions and Contents.

ABBEYFEALE—THE DISTRICT ELECTORAL DIVISIONS OF—
Abbeyfeale, Caher, Dromtrasna, Glengort, Mount-collins, Port.

ASKEATON—THE DISTRICT ELECTORAL DIVISIONS OF—
Askeaton East, Askeaton West, Aughinish, Craggs, Dunmoylan East, Lissmakeery, Loghill, Shana-golden, Shanid.

BALLINGARRY—THE DISTRICT ELECTORAL DIVISIONS OF—
Ballingarry, Ballyallinan, Ballygrennan, Ballynoe, Ballynoe West, Cloncagh, Dromard, Kilfinny, Kilscannell, Riddlestown.

BALLYLANDERS—THE DISTRICT ELECTORAL DIVISIONS OF—
Anglesborough, Ballylanders, Cullane, Duntryleague, Galbally, Kilbeheny, Kilglass, Knocknascrow, Riversdale.

BRUFF—THE DISTRICT ELECTORAL DIVISIONS OF—
Ballybricken, Bruff, Caherelly, Crean, Crecora, Fedamore, Grange, Kilpeacon, Rathmore.

BRUREE—THE DISTRICT ELECTORAL DIVISIONS OF—
Athlacca, Ballyagran, Bruree, Castletown, Colmans-well, Coolrus, Dromin, Rockhill, Tobernea.

CAPPAMORE—THE DISTRICT ELECTORAL DIVISIONS OF—
Bilboa, Caherconlish East, Cappamore, Doon South, Doon West.

CASTLECONNELL—THE DISTRICT ELECTORAL DIVISIONS OF
Abington, Ballyvarra, Castleconnell, Clonkeen, Glenstal.

CROOM—THE DISTRICT ELECTORAL DIVISIONS OF—
Abbeyville, Adare North, Adare South, Ballyna-banoge, Croagh, Croom, Dunnaman, Garrane, Kildimo.

DROMCOLLIHER—THE DISTRICT ELECTORAL DIVISIONS OF
Ballintober, Boola, Broadford, Cleanglass, Dromcol-liher, Feenagh, Kilmeedy, Mountplummer.

GLIN—THE DISTRICT ELECTORAL DIVISIONS OF—
Dunmoylan West, Fleanmore, Glensharrold, Glin, Kilfergus, Kilmoylan, Mohernagh.

HOSPITAL—THE DISTRICT ELECTORAL. DIVISIONS OF—
Cahercorney, Hospital, Kilteely, Knockainy, Uregare.

KILFINNANE—THE DISTRICT ELECTORAL DIVISIONS OF—
Ardpatrick, Ballymacshaneboy, Darragh, Griston, Kil-finnane, Kilflyn, Particles.

KILMALLOCK—The District Electoral Divisions of—
Bulgaden, Emlygrennan, Glenbrohane, Kilmallock, Knocklong.

NEWCASTLE—The District Electoral Divisions of—
Ardagh, Danganbeg, Knockaderry, Mahoonagh, New-castle.

MONAGAY—The District Electoral Divisions of—
Garryduff, Glenagower, Monagay, Rathronan, Rooskagh, Templeglentan.

OOLA—The District Electoral Divisions of—
Grean, Kilmurry, Oola, Templebredon.

PATRICKSWELL—The District Electoral Divisions of
Ballycummin, Ballynacarriga, Carrig, Clarina, Limerick North Rural, Patrickswell.

RATHKEALE—The District Electoral Divisions of—
Castletown, Iveruss, Kilcornan, Nantinan, Pallaskenry, Rathkeale Rural, Rathkeale Urban.

ROXBOROUGH—The District Electoral Divisions of—
Ballysimon, Caherconlish West, Limerick South Rural, Roxborough.

Note.—In the above schedule, District Electoral Divisions mean the existing Poor Law Electoral Divisions having the same name.

LONDONDERRY.

SCHEDULE A.

Name of Administrative County and Contents.

COUNTY OF LONDONDERRY—The existing judicial county of Londonderry (except the city of Londonderry).

SCHEDULE B.

County Electoral Divisions and Contents.

AGHADOWEY—The District Electoral Divisions of—
Aghadowey, Gelvin, Glenkeen, Lislane, Ringsend, Slaght.

ARTICLAVE—The District Electoral Divisions of—
Articlave, Benone, Downhill, Drumcroon, Keady, Letterloan.

BALLYKELLY—THE DISTRICT ELECTORAL DIVISIONS OF—
    Ballykelly, Faughanvale, Myroe, Straw, The Highlands.

BELLAGHY—THE DISTRICT ELECTORAL DIVISIONS OF—
    Bellaghy, Gulladuff, Rocktown.

CASTLE DAWSON—THE DISTRICT ELECTORAL DIVISIONS OF
    Ballyronan, Castle Dawson, Salterstown.

COLERAINE—THE DISTRICT ELECTORAL DIVISION OF—
    Coleraine.

DRAPERSTOWN—THE DISTRICT ELECTORAL DIVISIONS OF—
    Banoran, Carnamoney, Draperstown, The Six Towns.

DUNGIVEN—THE DISTRICT ELECTORAL DIVISIONS OF—
    Claudy (Londonderry), Drum, Dungiven, Foreglen.

FEENY—THE DISTRICT ELECTORAL DIVISIONS OF—
    Ballymullins, Banagher, Feeny, Glenshane, Owenreagh.

GARVAGH—THE DISTRICT ELECTORAL DIVISIONS OF—
    Agivey, Bovagh, Garvagh, Hervey Hill.

GLENDERMOT—THE DISTRICT ELECTORAL DIVISIONS OF—
    Ardmore, Bonds Glen, Glendermot, Tamnaherin, Waterside.

KILREA—THE DISTRICT ELECTORAL DIVISIONS OF—
    Claudy (Magherafelt), Kilrea, Tamlaght.

LIBERTIES—THE DISTRICT ELECTORAL DIVISIONS OF—
    Eglinton, Lough Enagh, Lower Liberties, Upper Liberties.

LIMAVADY—THE DISTRICT ELECTORAL DIVISIONS OF—
    Aghanloo, Bellarena, Fruithill, Limavady.

MAGHERA—THE DISTRICT ELECTORAL DIVISIONS OF—
    Maghera, Swatragh, The Grove.

MAGHERAFELT—THE DISTRICT ELECTORAL DIVISIONS OF
    Ballymoghan, Magherafelt, The Loop.

MONEYMORE—THE DISTRICT ELECTORAL DIVISIONS OF—
    Brackagh-Slievegallion, Lissan Upper, Moneyhaw, Moneymore, Springhill.

PORTSTEWART—THE DISTRICT ELECTORAL DIVISIONS OF
    Ballylagan, Bannbrook, Knockantern, Portstewart, Somerset.

TOBERMORE—THE DISTRICT ELECTORAL DIVISIONS OF—
    Desertmartin, Iniscarn, Tobermore, Tullykeeran.

Note.—In the above schedule, District Electoral Divisions mean the existing Poor Law Electoral Divisions having the same name.

LONGFORD.

SCHEDULE A.

Name of Administrative County and Contents.

COUNTY OF LONGFORD—The existing judicial county of Longford.

SCHEDULE B.

County Electoral Divisions and Contents.

ABBEYLARA—THE DISTRICT ELECTORAL DIVISIONS OF—
Abbeylara, Coolamber, Firry, Milltown, Newgrove.

ARDAGH WEST—THE DISTRICT ELECTORAL DIVISIONS OF—
Ardagh West, Kilglass.

BALLINALEE—THE DISTRICT ELECTORAL DIVISIONS OF—
Ballinalee, Corboy, Crosagstown, Currygrane, Drummeel, Knockanbaun, Moatfarrell.

BALLINAMUCK—THE DISTRICT ELECTORAL DIVISIONS OF
Ballinamuck East, Ballinamuck West.

BALLYMAHON—THE DISTRICT ELECTORAL DIVISION OF—
Ballymahon.

BUNLAHY—THE DISTRICT ELECTORAL DIVISIONS OF—
Bunlahy, Gelshagh, Lislea.

CLOONDARA—THE DISTRICT ELECTORAL DIVISIONS OF—
Caldragh, Cloondara, Killashee, Longford Rural.

CLOONEE—THE DISTRICT ELECTORAL DIVISIONS OF—
Aghaboy, Cloonee.

COLUMBKILLE—THE DISTRICT ELECTORAL DIVISIONS OF—
Columbkille, Sonnagh.

DALYSTOWN—THE DISTRICT ELECTORAL DIVISIONS OF—
Creevy, Dalystown, Mullanalaghta.

DRUMLISH—THE DISTRICT ELECTORAL DIVISIONS OF—
Drumlish, Killoe.

EDGEWORTHSTOWN—DISTRICT ELECTORAL DIVISIONS OF
Ardagh East, Ballymuigh, Edgeworthstown.

FORGNEY—THE DISTRICT ELECTORAL DIVISIONS OF—
Agharra, Forgney, Foxhall.

GRANARD—THE DISTRICT ELECTORAL DIVISIONS OF—
Granard Rural, Granard Urban.

LEDWITHSTOWN—THE DISTRICT ELECTORAL DIVISIONS OF
Cashel West, Ledwithstown.

LONGFORD—The District Electoral Divisions of—
Longford No. 1 Urban, Longford No. 2 Urban.

MOYDOW—The District Electoral Divisions of—
Doory, Kilcommock, Moydow.

MOYNE—The District Electoral Divisions of—
Drumgort, Moyne.

NEWTOWN FORBES—District Electoral Divisions of
Breanrisk, Newtown Forbes.

RATHCLINE—The District Electoral Divisions of—
Cashel East, Mountdavis, Rathcline.

Note.—In the above schedule, District Electoral Divisions mean the existing Poor Law Electoral Divisions having the same name.

LOUTH.

SCHEDULE A.

Name of Administrative County and Contents.

COUNTY OF LOUTH—The existing judicial county of Louth; and
The existing judicial county of the town of Drogheda.

SCHEDULE B.

County Electoral Divisions and Contents.

ARDEE—The District Electoral Divisions of—
Ardee Rural, Ardee Urban.

BARRONSTOWN—The District Electoral Divisions of
Barronstown, Castlering.

CARLINGFORD—The District Electoral Division of—
Carlingford.

CASTLEBELLINGHAM—District Electoral Divisions of
Castlebellingham, Drumcar.

CASTLETOWN—The District Electoral Divisions of—
Castletown, Haggardstown.

CLOGHER—The District Electoral Divisions of—
Clogher, Dysart.

CLONKEEN—The District Electoral Divisions of—
Clonkeen, Mansfieldstown, Talanstown.

DROGHEDA—The District Electoral Divisions of—
Fair Gate, St. Lawrence Gate, West Gate.

DROMISKIN—The District Electoral Divisions of— Darver, Dromiskin.

DRUMMULLAGH—The District Electoral Division of— Drummullagh.

DUNDALK RURAL—The District Electoral Division of Dundalk Rural.

DUNDALK URBAN—The District Electoral Divisions of Dundalk No. 1 Urban, Dundalk No. 2 Urban, Dundalk No. 3 Urban, Dundalk No. 4 Urban.

DUNLEER—The District Electoral Divisions of— Dromin, Dunleer, Stabannan.

FOUGHART—The District Electoral Divisions of— Foughart, Upper Creggan.

LOUTH—The District Electoral Divisions of— Killanny, Louth.

MONASTERBOICE—The District Electoral Divisions of Collon, Monasterboice.

MULLARY—The District Electoral Divisions of— Mullary, St. Peter's.

RATHCORR—The District Electoral Divisions of— Jenkinstown, Rathcorr.

RAVENSDALE—The District Electoral Divisions of— Ballymascanlan, Ravensdale.

TERMONFECKEN—The District Electoral Division of Termonfecken.

Note.—In the above schedule, District Electoral Divisions mean the existing Poor Law Electoral Divisions having the same name.

MAYO.

SCHEDULE A.

Name of Administrative County and Contents.

COUNTY OF MAYO—The existing judicial county of Mayo (except the district electoral divisions of Ballaghaderreen and Edmondstown);

So much of the existing judicial county of Galway as comprises the district electoral divisions of Ballinchalla and Owenbrin; and

So much of the existing judicial county of Sligo as comprises the district electoral divisions of Ardnaree North, Ardnaree South Rural, and Ardnaree South Urban.

SCHEDULE B.

County Electoral Divisions and Contents.

ACHILL—THE DISTRICT ELECTORAL DIVISIONS OF—
Achill, Ballycroy North, Ballycroy South, Corraun, Achill, Dooega, Slievemore.

ARDNAREE—THE DISTRICT ELECTORAL DIVISIONS OF—
Ardnaree North, Ardnaree South Rural, Ardnaree South Urban, Attymass East, Kilgarvan, Sallymount

BALLA—THE DISTRICT ELECTORAL DIVISIONS OF—
Balla, Ballinafad, Ballyhean, Clogher (Castlebar), Cloonkeen, Killavally, Mayo, Roslee.

BALLINA—THE DISTRICT ELECTORAL DIVISIONS OF—
Ardagh, Ballina Rural, Ballina Urban, Ballysakeery, Carrowmore, Fortland, Rathoma.

BALLINROBE—THE DISTRICT ELECTORAL DIVISIONS OF—
Ballinrobe, Hollymount, Neale, Newbrook.

BALLYHAUNIS—THE DISTRICT ELECTORAL DIVISIONS OF—
Ballindine, Ballyhaunis, Course, Culnacleha, Kilvine.

BANGOR—THE DISTRICT ELECTORAL DIVISIONS OF—
Bangor, Barroosky, Glenamoy, Glenco, Goolamore, Knockaduff, Knocknalower, Muingnabo, Muings, Sheskin.

BELLAVARY—THE DISTRICT ELECTORAL DIVISIONS OF—
Bellavary, Bohola, Killedan, Strade, Toocananagh.

BELMULLET—THE DISTRICT ELECTORAL DIVISIONS OF—
Belmullet, Binghamstown North, Binghamstown Sth., Glencastle, Rathhill.

CASTLEBAR—THE DISTRICT ELECTORAL DIVISIONS OF—
Breaghwy, Castlebar Rural, Castlebar Urban, Manulla, Turlough.

CLAREMORRIS—THE DISTRICT ELECTORAL DIVISIONS OF—
Claremorris, Cloghermore, Coonard, Crossboyne, Kilcolman, Murneen, Tagheen.

CONG—THE DISTRICT ELECTORAL DIVISIONS OF—
Cong, Dalgan, Garrymore, Houndswood, Kilcommon, Kilmaine, Shrule.

CROSSMOLINA—THE DISTRICT ELECTORAL DIVISIONS OF—
Addergoole, Ballynagoraher, Bunaveela, Crossmolina North, Crossmolina South, Deel, Derry, Letterbrick, Pontoon.

KILBEAGH—THE DISTRICT ELECTORAL DIVISIONS OF—
Cloonmore, Doocastle, Kilbeagh, Kilmovee.

KILKELLY—The District Electoral Divisions of—
Aghamore, Bekan, Coolnaha, Kilkelly, Loughanboy.

KILLALA—The District Electoral Divisions of—
Ballycastle, Beldergmore, Kilfian East, Kilfian South, Kilfian West, Killala, Lackan North, Lackan South.

KILTAMAGH—The District Electoral Divisions of—
Ballinamore, Ballyhowly, Caraun, Kiltamagh, Knock North, Knock South.

LOUISBURGH—The District Electoral Divisions of—
Aghagower South, Aillemore,, Bundorragha, Clare Island, Croaghpatrick, Drummin, Emlagh, Erriff, Kilgeever, Kilsallagh, Louisburgh, Owennadornaun, Slievemahanagh.

MOUNTFALCON—The District Electoral Divisions of
Attymass West, Meelick, Mountfalcon, Sraheen, Toomore.

NEWPORT—The District Electoral Divisions .of—
Burren, Croaghmoyle, Derryloughan, Glenhest, Islandeady, Kilmaclasser, Newport East, Newport West, Srahmore.

PORTROYAL—The District Electoral Divisions of—
Ballinchalla, Ballyovey, Burriscarragh, Cappaduff, Owenbrin, Portroyal, Tawnynagry.

SWINEFORD—The District Electoral Divisions of—
Callow, Cuildoo, Swineford, Tumgesh.

URLAUR—The District Electoral Divisions of—
Brackloon, Sonnagh, Urlaur.

WESTPORT—The District Electoral Divisions of—
Aghagower North, Clogher (Westport), Knappagh, Kilmeena, Westport Rural, Westport Urban.

Note.—In the above schedule, District Electoral Divisions mean the existing Poor Law Electoral Divisions having the same name.

MEATH.

SCHEDULE A.

Name of Administrative County and Contents.

COUNTY OF MEATH.—The existing judicial county of Meath.

SCHEDULE B.

County Electoral Divisions and Contents.

ARDBRACCAN—THE DISTRICT ELECTORAL DIVISIONS OF—
Ardbraccan, Balrathboyne, Clonmacduff, Kilbride, Martry, Rathmore.

ATHBOY—THE DISTRICT ELECTORAL DIVISIONS OF—
Athboy, Burry, Girley, Grennanstown, Kilskeer.

BALLYBOGGAN—THE DISTRICT ELECTORAL DIVISIONS OF—
Ardnamullan, Ballyboggan, Castlejordan, Castlerickard, Hill of Down, Killyon.

BECTIVE—THE DISTRICT ELECTORAL DIVISIONS OF—
Ardmulchan, Bective, Navan Rural.

CROSSAKEEL—THE DISTRICT ELECTORAL DIVISIONS OF—
Ballinlough, Crossakeel, Crosskeys, Killallon, Knocklough, Stonefield.

DONAGHPATRICK—DISTRICT ELECTORAL DIVISIONS OF—
Castletown, Donaghpatrick, Rathkenny, Staholmog, Teltown.

DRUMCONDRA—THE DISTRICT ELECTORAL DIVISIONS OF—
Ardagh, Drumcondra, Killary.

DULEEK—THE DISTRICT ELECTORAL DIVISIONS OF—
Duleek, Mellifont, St. Mary's.

DUNBOYNE—THE DISTRICT ELECTORAL DIVISIONS OF—
Culmullin, Dunboyne, Gallow, Kilmore, Rodanstown.

DUNSHAUGHLIN—THE DISTRICT ELECTORAL DIVISIONS OF
Donaghmore, Dunshaughlin, Kilbrew, Rathfeigh, Ratoath.

INNFIELD—THE DISTRICT ELECTORAL DIVISIONS OF—
Innfield, Rahinstown, Rathmoylon, Summerhill.

KELLS—THE DISTRICT ELECTORAL DIVISIONS OF—
Boherboy, Kells Rural, Kells Urban.

KILDALKEY—THE DISTRICT ELECTORAL DIVISIONS OF—
Ballyconnell, Cloghbrack, Kildalkey, Killaconnigan.

MOYNALTY—THE DISTRICT ELECTORAL DIVISIONS OF—
Castlekeeran, Loughan, Maperath, Moynalty, Newcastle, Newtown.

NAVAN—THE DISTRICT ELECTORAL DIVISION OF—
Navan Urban.

NOBBER—THE DISTRICT ELECTORAL DIVISIONS OF—
Carrickleck, Cruicetown, Kilmainham, Moybolgue, Nobber, Posseckstown, Trohanny.

OLDCASTLE—THE DISTRICT ELECTORAL DIVISIONS OF—
Killeagh, Moylagh, Oldcastle.

SLANE—The District Electoral Divisions of—
Grangegeeth, Painestown, Slane, Stackallan.

STAMULLEN—The District Electoral Divisions of—
Ardcath, Julianstown, Stamullen.

TARA—The District Electoral Divisions of—
Kentstown, Kilcooly, Killeen, Kilmessan, Skreen, Tara.

TRIM—The District Electoral Divisions of—
'Galtrim, Laracor, Trim Rural, Trim Urban.

Note.—In the above schedule, District Electoral Divisions mean the existing Poor Law Electoral Divisions having the same name.

MONAGHAN.

SCHEDULE A.

Name of Administrative County and Contents.

COUNTY OF MONAGHAN—The existing judicial county of Monaghan.

SCHEDULE B.

County Electoral Divisions and Contents.

AGHABOG—The District Electoral Divisions of—
Aghabog, Caddagh, Lisnaveane.

BALLYBAY—The District Electoral Divisions of—
Ballybay Rural, Ballybay Urban, Tullycorbet.

BELLATRAIN—The District Electoral Divisions of—
Bellatrain, Corracharra, Drumgurra, Raferagh.

BROOMFIELD—The District Electoral Divisions of—
Bocks, Broomfield, Laragh.

CARRICKMACROSS—District Electoral Divisions of—
Carrickmacross Rural, Carrickmacross Urban, Drumcarrow.

CASTLEBLAYNEY—District Electoral Divisions of—
Castleblayney Rural, Castleblayney Urban, Church Hill.

CLONES—The District Electoral Divisions of—
Clones Rural, Clones Urban, St. Tierney.

CLONTIBRET—The District Electoral Divisions of—
Annayalla, Castleshane, Clontibret.

CREEVE—The District Electoral Divisions of—
Carrickatee, Creeve, Greagh.

CREMARTIN—The District Electoral Divisions of—
Carrickaslane, Cremartin, Mullyash.

DRUM—The District Electoral Divisions of—
Anny, Cormeen, Dawsongrove, Drum.

EMYVALE—The District Electoral Divisions of—
Anketell Grove, Derrygorry, Emyvale, Figullar, Shanmullagh.

GLASLOUGH—The District Electoral Divisions of—
Enagh, Glaslough, Rackwallace, Tehallan.

INISHKEEN—The District Electoral Divisions of—
Crossalare, Inishkeen, Kilmurry, Kiltybegs.

KILLEEVAN—The District Electoral Divisions of—
Drumhillagh, Drumsnat, Killeevan, Kilmore.

LOUGH FEA—The District Electoral Divisions of—
Ballymackney, Donaghmoyne, Drumboory, Enagh,
Lough Fea.

MONAGHAN—The District Electoral Divisions of—
Monaghan Rural, Monaghan Urban.

NEWBLISS—The District Electoral Divisions of—
Currin, Drummully, Killynenagh, Newbliss.

SCOTSTOWN—The District Electoral Divisions of—
Clones (Monaghan), Scotstown, Sheskin.

TEDAVNET—The District Electoral Divisions of—
Bellanode, Bragan, Killylough, Tedavnet.

Note.—In the above schedule, District Electoral Divisions mean
the existing Poor Law Electoral Divisions having the same name.

QUEEN'S COUNTY.

SCHEDULE A.

Name of Administrative County and Contents.

QUEEN'S COUNTY—The existing judicial county named
Queen's County (except the portion of the town of
Carlow situated therein).

SCHEDULE B.

County Electoral Divisions and Contents.

ABBEYLEIX—The District Electoral Division of—
Abbeyleix.

ARLESS—THE DISTRICT ELECTORAL DIVISIONS OF—
 Arless, Ballickmoyler, Ballylynan, Barrowhouse, Killabban, Shrule, Tankardstown.

BALLINAKILL—THE DISTRICT ELECTORAL DIVISIONS OF—
 Ballinakill, Blandsfort, Dysartgallen, Timahoe.

BALLYBRITTAS—THE DISTRICT ELECTORAL DIVISIONS OF—
 Ballybrittas, Curraclone, Kilmurry, Moyanna, Sallyford, Vicarstown.

BORRIS-IN-OSSORY—DISTRICT ELECTORAL DIVISIONS OF—
 Ballybrophy, Borris-in-Ossory, Clonmore, Kilcoke, Kyle, Moneenalassa, Moneymore.

CASTLETOWN—THE DISTRICT ELECTORAL DIVISIONS OF—
 Caher, Castletown, Clash, Donore, Raheen.

CLONASLEE—THE DISTRICT ELECTORAL DIVISIONS OF—
 Arderin, Cardtown, Castlecuffe, Clonaslee, Marymount, Nealstown.

COOLRAIN—THE DISTRICT ELECTORAL DIVISIONS OF—
 Ballyfin, Brisha, Capard, Clonin, Coolrain, Lacka.

CULLENAGH—THE DISTRICT ELECTORAL DIVISIONS OF—
 Ballyroan, Clonkeen, Colt, Cullenagh, Kilcolmanbane.

DONAGHMORE—THE DISTRICT ELECTORAL DIVISIONS OF—
 Cuffsborough, Donaghmore, Dunmore, Grantstown, Kildellig, Killermogh.

DURROW—THE DISTRICT ELECTORAL DIVISIONS OF—
 Aughmacart, Cullahill, Durrow, Kilnaseer.

EMO—THE DISTRICT ELECTORAL DIVISIONS OF—
 Dangans, Emo, Mountmelick Rural, Shaen.

LUGGACURREN—THE DISTRICT ELECTORAL DIVISIONS OF—
 Ballylehane, Doonane, Farnans, Fossy, Luggacurren, Rathaspick.

MARYBOROUGH—THE DISTRICT ELECTORAL DIVISION OF—
 Maryborough Urban.

MOUNTMELICK—THE DISTRICT ELECTORAL DIVISION OF—
 Mountmelick Urban.

MOUNTRATH—THE DISTRICT ELECTORAL DIVISIONS OF—
 Mountrath, Trumra.

NEWTOWN—THE DISTRICT ELECTORAL DIVISIONS OF—
 Ardough, Graigue Rural, Newtown, Rossmore, Turra.

O'MORESFOREST—THE DISTRICT ELECTORAL DIVISIONS OF
 Borris, Clondarrig, Maryborough Rural, O'Moresforest.

PORTARLINGTON STH.—DISTRICT ELECTORAL DIVS. OF
 Jamestown, Kilmullen, Portarlington South. .

RATHDOWNEY—The District Electoral Divisions of—
    Errill, Kyle South, Rathdowney, Rathsaran.

STRADBALLY—The District Electoral Divisions of—
    Ballyadams, Ballycarroll, Stradbally, Timogue.

TINNAHINCH—The District Electoral Divisions of—
    Cappalough, Garrymore, Graigue, Meelick, Reary-
    more, Rosenallis, Tinnahinch.

Note.—In the above schedule, District Electoral Divisions mean
the existing Poor Law Electoral Divisions having the same name.

ROSCOMMON.

SCHEDULE A.

Name of Administrative County and Contents.

COUNTY OF ROSCOMMON—The existing judicial county
    of Roscommon (except the portion of the town of
    Ballinasloe and of the town of Athlone situated
    therein):
    So much of the existing judicial county of Galway as
    comprises the district electoral division of Rosmoy-
    lan: and
    So much of the existing judicial county of Mayo as
    comprises the district electoral divisions of Ballagh-
    aderreen and Edmondstown.

SCHEDULE B.

County Electoral Divisions and Contents.

ATHLEAGUE—The District Electoral Divisions of—
    Athleague East, Athleague West, Cams, Cloonygor-
    mican, Dunamon, Fuerty, Rosmoylan.

AUGHRIM—The District Electoral Divisions of—
    Aughrim East, Aughrim West, Cloonteen, Creeve
    (Carrick-on-Shannon), Croghan, Danesfort, Killukin
    (Carrick-on-Shannon), Killummod.

BALLAGHADERREEN—District Electoral Divisions of
    Ballaghaderreen, Edmondstown.

BALLINLOUGH—The District Electoral Divisions of—
    Ballinlough, Kiltullagh.

BALLYFARNAN—The District Electoral Divisions of—
    Aghafin, Altagowlan, Ballyfarnan, Crossna, Keadew,
    Lough Allen.

BELLANAGARE—THE DISTRICT ELECTORAL DIVISIONS OF—
Bellanagare, Buckill, Fairymount.

BOYLE—THE DISTRICT ELECTORAL DIVISIONS OF—
Boyle Rural, Boyle Urban, Rushfield, Tivannagh.

CALTRAGH—THE DISTRICT ELECTORAL DIVISIONS OF—
Caltragh, Carnagh, Kilcar, Lackan, Lecarrow, Lis-
maha, Rock Hill, Scregg, Taghboy, Turrock.

CASTLEPLUNKET—THE DISTRICT ELECTORAL DIVISIONS OF
Carrowduff, Castleplunket, Castleteheen, Cloonfin-
lough, Kilbride North, Kilbride South, Kilgefin,
Killukin (Strokestown), Ogulla.

CASTLEREA—THE DISTRICT ELECTORAL DIVISIONS OF—
Ballintober, Baslick, Castlerea.

CLOONFOWER—THE DISTRICT ELECTORAL DIVISIONS OF—
Artagh South, Cloonfower, Coolougher.

CREAGH—THE DISTRICT ELECTORAL DIVISIONS OF—
Ballydangan, Cloonburren, Cloonown, Crannagh,
Creagh, Culliagh, Drumlosh, Moore.

ELPHIN—THE DISTRICT ELECTORAL DIVISIONS OF—
Annaghmore, Cloonyquin, Cregga, Elphin, Lisgarve,
Rossmore, Tulsk.

FRENCHPARK—THE DISTRICT ELECTORAL DIVISIONS OF—
Breedoge, Estersnow, Frenchpark, Kilcolagh, Kilma-
cumsy, Mantua.

KILGLASS—THE DISTRICT ELECTORAL DIVISIONS OF—
Creeve (Strokestown), Elia, Kilglass North, Kilglass
South, Kilmore, Roosky.

KILTOOM—THE DISTRICT ELECTORAL DIVISIONS OF—
Athlone West Rural, Ballynamona, Carrowreagh,
Castlesampson, Dysart, Kiltoom, Taghmaconnell,
Thomastown.

LOUGHGLINN—THE DISTRICT ELECTORAL DIVISIONS OF—
Artagh North, Loughglinn.

ROCKINGHAM—THE DISTRICT ELECTORAL DIVISIONS OF—
Ballyformoyle, Kilbryan, Oakport, Rockingham,
Tumna North, Tumna South.

ROSCOMMON—THE DISTRICT ELECTORAL DIVISIONS OF—
Cloontuskert, Drumdaff, Kilteevan, Mote, Roscommon
Rural, Roscommon Urban.

STROKESTOWN—THE DISTRICT ELECTORAL DIVISIONS OF—
Ballygarden, Bumlin, Killavackan, Lissonuffy,
Strokestown, Termonbarry.

Note.—In the above schedule, District Electoral Divisions mean
the existing Poor Law Electoral Divisions having the same name.

SLIGO.

SCHEDULE A.

Name of Administrative County and Contents.

COUNTY OF SLIGO—The existing judicial county of Sligo except the district electoral divisions of Ardnaree North, Ardnaree South Rural, and ,Adrnaree South Urban).

SCHEDULE B.

County Electoral Divisions and Contents.

ACLARE—THE DISTRICT ELECTORAL DIVISIONS OF—
Aclare, Breencorragh, Cloonacool, Glendarragh, Kilmacteige.

BALLYMOTE—THE DISTRICT ELECTORAL DIVISIONS OF—
Ballymote, Carrickbanagher, Drumfin.

BALLYSADARE—THE DISTRICT ELECTORAL DIVISIONS OF—
Annagh, Ballysadare East, Ballysadare West, Carrownaskeagh, Coolaney, Dromard East, Dromard West.

BANADA—THE DISTRICT ELECTORAL DIVISIONS OF—
Achonry West, Banada.

CASTLECONNOR—THE DISTRICT ELECTORAL DIVISIONS OF—
Buncrowey, Castleconnor East, Castleconnor West, Kilglass, Mullagheruse.

CLIFFONY—THE DISTRICT ELECTORAL DIVISIONS OF—
Cliffony, North, Cliffony South, Rossinver East, Rossinver West.

COLLOONEY—THE DISTRICT ELECTORAL DIVISIONS OF—
Collooney, Drumcolumb, Lisconny, Riverstown.

COOLAVIN—THE DISTRICT ELECTORAL DIVISIONS OF—
Coolavin, Kilfree, Killaraght.

DROMORE—THE DISTRICT ELECTORAL DIVISIONS OF—
Aughris, Dromore, Skreen, Templeboy North, Templeboy South, Toberpatrick East, Toberpatrick West.

DRUMCLIFF—THE DISTRICT ELECTORAL DIVISIONS OF—
,llintogher East, Calry, Carney, Drumcliff East, Drumcliff West, Glencar.

EASKY—THE DISTRICT ELECTORAL DIVISIONS OF—
Easky, Easky West, Rathmacurkey.

KILMACOWEN—The District Electoral Divisions of—
Ballintogher ; West, Ballynakill, Kilmacowen, Knock-
aree.

KILMACTRANNY—The District Electoral Divisions of
Ballynashee, Killadoon, Kilmactranny, Lakeview,
Shancough.

KILSHALVY—The District Electoral Divisions of—
Cloonoghill, Cuilmore, Kilshalvy, Kilturra.

LISSADILL—The District Electoral Divisions of—
Lissadill East, Lissadill North, Lissadill West.

OWENMORE—The District Electoral Divisions of—
Branchfield, Cartron, Leitrim, Loughil, Owenmore,
Streamstown, Temple.

SLIGO—The District·Electoral Divisions of—
Sligo East, Sligo North, Sligo West.

TEMPLEVANNY—The District Electoral Divisions of—
Aghanagh, Bricklieve, Drumrat, Toomour, Templevanny.

TOBERCURRY—The District Electoral Divisions of—
Achonry East, Tobercurry.

Note.—In·the above schedule, District Electoral Divisions mean
the existing Poor Law Electoral Divisions having the same name.

TIPPERARY (NORTH RIDING).

SCHEDULE A.

Name of Administrative County and Contents.

COUNTY OF TIPPERARY, NORTH RIDING—The
existing judicial county of the North Riding of the
county of Tipperary (except the district electoral divisions of Cappagh, Curraheen, and Glengar).

SCHEDULE B.

County Electoral Divisions and Contents.

ABINGTON—The District Electoral Divisions of—
Abington, Dolla, Foilnaman, Templederry.

ARDCRONY—The District Electoral Divisions of—
Ardcrony, Ballygibbon, Ballylusky, Cloghprior, Knigh,
Monsea.

BALLYNACLOGH—The District Electoral Divisions of
Ballynaclogh, Carrigatogher, Kilmore, Nenagh Rural.

BIRDHILL—The District Electoral Divisions of—
Ballina, Birdhill, Greenhall, Kileomenty.

BORRISOKANE—The District Electoral Divisions of—
Borrisokane, Finnoe, Kilbarron, Terryglass.

BORRISOLEIGH—The District Electoral Divisions of—
Aghnameadle, Borrisnafarney, Borrisnoe, Borrisoleigh,
Glenkeen.

BOURNEY—The District Electoral Divisions of—
Bourney East, Bourney West, Killavinoge, Killea,
Rathnaveoge, Timoney.

CLOGHJORDAN—The District Electoral Divisions of—
Aglishcloghane, Ballingarry, Cloghjordan, Mertonhall,
Uskane.

DERRYCASTLE—The District Electoral Divisions of—
Burgesbeg, Castletown, Derrycastle, Youghalarra.

HOLYCROSS—The District Electoral Divisions of—
Ballycahill, Holycross, Kilrush, Thurles Rural.

LATTERAGH—The District Electoral Divisions of—
Ballymackey, Kilkeary, Kilnaneave, Latteragh.

LITTLETON—The District Electoral Divisions of—
Ballymurreen, Littleton, Longford Pass, Moycarky,
Rahelty, Two-mile-borris.

LORRHA—The District Electoral Divisions of—
Carrig, Clohaskin, Graigue, Lorrha East, Lorrha
West, Rathcabban, Redwood, Riverstown.

MOYALIFF—The District Electoral Divisions of—
Gortkelly, Inch, Moyaliff, Upperchurch.

NENAGH—The District Electoral Divisions of—
Nenagh East Urban, Nenagh West Urban.

NEWPORT—The District Electoral Divisions of—
Killoscully, Kilnarath, Lackagh, Newport.

ROSCREA—The District Electoral Division of—
Roscrea.

TEMPLEMORE—The District Electoral Divisions of—
Drom, Templemore.

TEMPLETOUHY—The District Electoral Divisions of—
Loughmore, Moyne, Templetouhy.

THURLES—The District Electoral Division of—
Thurles Urban.

Note.—In the above schedule, District Electoral Divisions mean
the existing Poor Law Electoral Divisions having the same name.

TIPPERARY (SOUTH RIDING).

SCHEDULE A.

Name of Administrative County and Contents.

COUNTY OF TIPPERARY, SOUTH RIDING—The existing judicial county of the South Riding of the county of Tipperary;

So much of the existing judicial county of the North Riding of the county of Tipperary as comprises the district electoral divisions of Cappagh, Curraheen, and Glengar;

So much of the existing judicial county of Waterford as comprises the portion of the town of Carrick-on-Suir, situated therein; and

So much of the existing judicial county of Waterford as comprises the portion of the borough of Clonmel, situated therein.

SCHEDULE B.

County Electoral Divisions and Contents.

ARDFINNAN—The District Electoral Divisions of— Ardfinnan, Ballybacon, Derrygrath, Newcastle, Tullaghmelan.

ARDMAYLE—The District Electoral Divisions of— Ardmayle, Ballysheehan, Clonoulty East, Gaile, Graystown, Nodstown.

BALLYKISTEEN—The District Electoral Divisions of Ballykisteen, Drumwood, Kilmucklin, Rathlynin, Solloghodbeg.

BALLYPOREEN—The District Electoral Divisions of— Ballyporeen, Burncourt, Coolagarranroe, Kilcoran.

BANSHA—The District Electoral Divisions of— Ballycarron, Bansha, Golden, Kilfeakle, Killadriffe, Thomastown.

CAHER—The District Electoral Divisions of— Caher, Mortlestown.

CAPPAGH—The District Electoral Divisions of— Cappagh, Curraheen, Donohill, Glengar.

CARRICK-ON-SUIR—District Electoral Divisions of— Carrickbeg Urban, Carrick-on-Suir Urban.

CASHEL—The District Electoral Divisions of— Cashel Rural, Cashel Urban.

CLONBEG—The District Electoral Divisions of—
Bruis, Clonbeg, Templeneiry, Tipperary Rural.

CLOGHEEN—The District Electoral Divisions of—
Clogheen, Tubbrid, Tullaghorton.

CLONMEL—The District Electoral Divisions of—
Clonmel East Urban, Clonmel West Urban.

EMLY—The District Electoral Divisions of—
Cullen, Emly, Lattin, Rodus, Shronell.

FENNOR—The District Electoral Divisions of—
Ballyphilip, Buolick, Farranrory, Fennor, Kilcooly, Poyntstown.

FETHARD—The District Electoral Divisions of—
Anner, Cloneen, Fethard, Kilvemnon, Peppardstown.

GARRANGIBBON—The District Electoral Divisions of
Carrick-on-Suir Rural, Garrangibbon, Kilcash, Kilmurry, Newtown.

KILLENAULE—The District Electoral Divisions of—
Ardsallagh, Cooleagh, Killenaule, Magorban, New Birmingham.

KILPATRICK—The District Electoral Divisions of—
Ballygriffin, Clogher, Clonoulty West, Kilpatrick, Oughterleague.

KILSHEELAN—The District Electoral Divisions of—
Clonmel Rural, Colman, Killaloan, Kilsheelan, Kiltinan, Lisronagh.

MULLINAHONE—The District Electoral Divisions of
Ballingarry, Crohane, Drangan, Modeshil, Mullinahone.

TIPPERARY—The District Electoral Divisions of—
Tipperary East Urban, Tipperary West Urban.

TULLAMAIN—The District Electoral Divisions of—
Ballyclerahan, Graigue, Inishlounaght, Killeenasteena, Knockgraffon, Tullamain.

Note.—In the above schedule, District Electoral Divisions mean the existing Poor Law Electoral Divisions having the same name.

TYRONE.

SCHEDULE A.

Name of Administrative County and Contents.

COUNTY OF TYRONE—The existing judicial county of Tyrone.

SCHEDULE B.

County Electoral Divisions and Contents.

AUGHNACLOY—THE DISTRICT ELECTORAL DIVISIONS OF—
Aughnacloy Rural, Aughnacloy 'Urban, Ballymagran, Brantry, Caledon, Clonaneese, Minterburn.

BALLYGAWLEY—THE DISTRICT ELECTORAL DIVISIONS OF—
Ballygawley, Carryglass, Cecil, Draughton, Errigal, Foremass, Killyfaddy, Tattymoyle.

CASTLE CAULFIELD—DISTRICT ELECTORAL DIVISIONS OF
Aghnahoe, Altmore, Athenry, Castle Caulfield, Clonavaddy.

CASTLEDERG—THE DISTRICT ELECTORAL DIVISIONS OF—
Castlederg, Clare, Corgary, Killen, Killeter, Lisnacloon, Magheranageeragh, West Longfield.

CLOGHER—THE DISTRICT ELECTORAL DIVISIONS OF—
Aghintain, Augher, Ballagh, Clogher, Cole, Cullamore, Favor Royal, Fivemiletown, Tullyvar.

COAGH—THE DISTRICT ELECTORAL DIVISIONS OF—
Ballyclog, Coagh, Killycolpy, Munterevlin, Tullyhog.

COOKSTOWN—THE DISTRICT ELECTORAL DIVISIONS OF—
Ballynasollus, Cookstown Rural, Cookstown Urban, Lissan Lower, Oritor.

DRUMQUIN—THE DISTRICT ELECTORAL DIVISIONS OF—
Baron's Court, Bomackatall, Castlebane, Clunahill, Drumquin (Castlederg), Drumquin (Omagh), Lisnacreaght, Listymore, Magheracreggan, Mullagharn.

DUNGANNON—THE DISTRICT ELECTORAL DIVISIONS OF—
Benburb, Bernagh, Derrygortrevy, Dungannon.

DUNNAMANAGH—THE DISTRICT ELECTORAL DIVISIONS OF
Ballymagorry, Ballyneaner, Dunnalong, Dunnamanagh, Glenmornan, Loughash, Mountcastle, Stranagalwilly.

FINTONA—THE DISTRICT ELECTORAL DIVISIONS OF—
Camderry, Clanabogan, Derrybard, Dervaghroy, Fallaghearn, Fintona, Loughmuck, Seskinore.

MOY—THE DISTRICT ELECTORAL DIVISIONS OF—
Drumaspil, Meenagh, Mountjoy, Moy.

NEWTOWNSTEWART—DISTRICT ELECTORAL DIVISIONS OF
Camus, Church Lands, Douglas Burn, Gortin, Lislea, Moyle, Newtownstewart.

z

OMAGH—THE DISTRICT ELECTORAL DIVISIONS OF—
Dunbreen, Gortgranagh, Mountjoy Forest East, Mountjoy Forest West, Omagh Rural, Omagh Urban.

POMEROY—THE DISTRICT ELECTORAL DIVISIONS OF—
Beaghmore, Creggan, Killeenan, Oaklands, Pomeroy, The Rock, The Sandholes.

PLUMB BRIDGE—THE DISTRICT ELECTORAL DIVISIONS OF—
Crockanboy, Fallagh, Glenchiel, Glenlark, Glenroan, Loughmacrory, Mount Hamilton, Plumb Bridge, Trinamadan.

SIX MILE CROSS—THE DISTRICT ELECTORAL DIVISIONS OF—
Beragh, Camowen, Carrickmore, Drumnakilly, Killyclogher, Mountfield, Mullaghslin, Six Mile Cross.

STEWARTSTOWN—THE DISTRICT ELECTORAL DIVISIONS OF
Crossdernot, Donaghmore, Stewartstown, Tullyniskan.

STRABANE—THE DISTRICT ELECTORAL DIVISIONS OF—
Altaclady, East Urney, Strabane.

TRILLICK—THE DISTRICT ELECTORAL DIVISIONS OF—
Dromore, Drumharvey, Greenan, Kilskeery, Moorfield, Trillick, Tullyclunagh.

Note—In the above schedule, District Electoral Divisions mean the existing Poor Law Electoral Divisions having the same name.

WATERFORD.

SCHEDULE A.

Name of Administrative County and Contents.

COUNTY OF WATERFORD—The existing judicial county of Waterford (except the portion of the town of Carrick-on-Suir and of the borough of Clonmel situated therein, and the district electoral division of Kilculliheen).

SCHEDULE B.

County Electoral Divisions and Contents.

ARDMORE—THE DISTRICT ELECTORAL DIVISIONS OF—
Ardmore (Youghal), Ballyheeny, Grallagh, Grange, Kinsalebeg.

BALLYDUFF—THE DISTRICT ELECTORAL DIVISIONS OF—
Ballyduff, Ballyin, Ballysaggartmore, Gortnapeaky,
Mocollop.
BALLYNAKILL—THE DISTRICT ELECTORAL DIVISIONS OF—
Ballynakill, Faithlegg, Woodstown.
CAPPOQUIN—THE DISTRICT ELECTORAL DIVISIONS OF—
Ballyhane, Cappoquin.
CLASHMORE—THE DISTRICT ELECTORAL DIVISIONS OF—
Clashmore, Dromore, Kilcockan, Templemichael.
CLONEA—THE DISTRICT ELECTORAL DIVISIONS OF—
Bohadoon, Clonea, Coumaraglin, Knockaunbrandaun,
Mount Kennedy, Tinnasaggart.
DROMANA—THE DISTRICT ELECTORAL DIVISIONS OF—
Cappagh, Carriglea, Dromana, Keereen, Mountstuart,
Whitechurch.
DUNGARVAN—THE DISTRICT ELECTORAL DIVISIONS OF—
Dungarvan No. 1 Urban, Dungarvan No. 2 Urban.
KILBARRY—THE DISTRICT ELECTORAL DIVISIONS OF—
Drumcannon, Kilbarry, Killea, Killoteran, Kilmac-
league, Rathmoylan, Waterford Rural.
KILMACTHOMAS—THE DISTRICT ELECTORAL DIVISIONS OF
Comeragh, Fews, Fox's Castle, Kilmacthomas, Strad-
bally.
KILMEADAN—THE DISTRICT ELECTORAL DIVISIONS OF—
Kilmeadan (Waterford), Newcastle, Newtown, Pem-
brokestown, Reisk.
KILRONAN—THE DISTRICT ELECTORAL DIVISIONS OF—
Ballymacarbry, Graignagower, Kilmacomma, Kil-
ronan, St. Mary's.
KNOCKMAHON—THE DISTRICT ELECTORAL DIVISIONS OF—
Annestown, Ballylaneen, Carrigcastle, Dunhill, Gar-
denmorris, Georgestown, Kilbarrymeaden, Knock-
mahon.
LISMORE—THE DISTRICT ELECTORAL DIVISIONS OF—
Drumroe, Lismore Rural, Lismore Urban.
MODELLIGO—THE DISTRICT ELECTORAL DIVISIONS OF—
Ballynamult, Colligan, Modelligo (Dungarvan), Model-
ligo (Lismore), Seskinan.
PORTLAW—THE DISTRICT ELECTORAL DIVISIONS OF—
Ballydurn, Clonea, Fenoagh, Kilmeadan (Carrick-on-
Suir), Portlaw.
RATHGORMUCK—THE DISTRICT ELECTORAL DIVISIONS OF
Carrickbeg Rural, Glen, Gurteen Mothel, Rathgor-
muck, Ross.

RINGVILLE—THE DISTRICT ELECTORAL DIVISIONS OF—
    Ardmore (Dungarvan), Ballymacart, Dungarvan
    Rural, Glenwilliam, Ringville.

TALLOW—THE DISTRICT ELECTORAL DIVISIONS OF—
    Castlerichard, Kilwatermoy East, Kilwatermoy West,
    Tallow.

TRAMORE—THE DISTRICT ELECTORAL DIVISIONS OF—
    Islandikane, Tramore.

Note.—In the above schedule, District Electoral Divisions mean
the existing Poor Law Electoral Divisions having the same name.

WESTMEATH.

SCHEDULE A.

Name of Administrative County and Contents.

COUNTY OF WESTMEATH—The existing judicial county
    of Westmeath; and
    So much of the existing judicial county of Roscommon
    as comprises the portion of the town of Athlone
    situated therein.

SCHEDULE B.

County Electoral Divisions and Contents.

ATHLONE—THE DISTRICT ELECTORAL DIVISIONS OF—
    Athlone East Urban, Athlone West Urban.

AUBURN—THE DISTRICT ELECTORAL DIVISIONS OF—
    Auburn, Glassan, Killinure, Muckanagh.

BALLYMORE—THE DISTRICT ELECTORAL DIVISIONS OF—
    Ballymore, Ballymorin, Churchtown, Dysart, Killare.

BELVIDERE—THE DISTRICT ELECTORAL DIVISIONS OF—
    Belvidere, Carrick, Greenpark, Hopestown, Mullingar
    Rural.

CASTLETOWN—THE DISTRICT ELECTORAL DIVISIONS OF—
    Ballynagore, Castletown, Jamestown, Middleton,
    Streamstown.

COOLE—THE DISTRICT ELECTORAL DIVISIONS OF—
    Boherquill, Coole, Coolure, Lackan, Multyfarnham,
    Street.

DELVIN—The District Electoral Divisions of—
Ballinlough, Ballyhealy, Clonarney, Copperalley, Delvin, Killua, Rosmead.

DRUMRANEY—The District Electoral Divisions of—
Ardnagragh, Doonis, Drumraney, Noughaval, Templepatrick, Winetown.

FINNEA—The District Electoral Divisions of—
Finnea, Fore West, Glore, Hilltown, Knockarrow.

KILBEGGAN—The District Electoral Divisions of—
Ardnaglew, Kilbeggan, Lauree, Rahugh.

KILLUCAN—The District Electoral Divisions of—
Cloghan, Derrymore, Heathstown, Huntingdon, Killuean.

KINNEGAD—The District Electoral Divisions of—
Castle, Enniscoffey, Griffinstown, Kinnegad, Russellstown.

KINTURK—The District Electoral Divisions of—
Collinstown, Faughalstown, Fore East, Kilcummy, Kilpatrick, Kinturk.

MILLTOWN—The District Electoral Divisions of—
Ballykilmore, Castlelost, Clonfad, Gaybrook, Milltown, Newtown.

MOATE—The District Electoral Divisions of—
Castledaly, Moate.

MOUNT TEMPLE—The District Electoral Divisions of
Ballybroder, Bellanlack, Kilcumreragh, Mount Temple Umma.

MOYDRUM—The District Electoral Divisions of—
Athlone East Rural, Carn, Moydrum, Tubbrit.

MULLINGAR—The District Electoral Divisions of—
Mullingar North Urban, Mullingar South Urban.

OWEL—The District Electoral Divisions of—
Knockdrin, Owel, Portloman, Stonehall, Tullaghan, Woodland.

RAHARNEY—The District Electoral Divisions of—
Ballynaskeagh, Bracklin, Clonlost, Killulagh, Raharney, Riverdale, Taghmon.

RATHCONRATH—The District Electoral Divisions of—
Emper, Piercetown, Rathconrath, Skeagh, Sonna.

RATHOWEN—The District Electoral Divisions of—
Ballinalack, Glenlough, Kilbixy, Rathowen.

Note.—In the above schedule, District Electoral Divisions mean the existing Poor Law Electoral Divisions having the same name.

WEXFORD.

SCHEDULE A.

Name of Administrative County and Contents.

COUNTY OF WEXFORD—The existing judicial county of Wexford; and
So much of the existing judicial county of Kilkenny as comprises the portion of the town of New Ross situated therein.

SCHEDULE B.

County Electoral Divisions and Contents.

BALLYHUSKARD—THE DISTRICT ELECTORAL DIVISIONS OF Ardcavan, Ardcolm, Ballyhuskard, Castle Ellis, Kilmallock.

BANNOW—THE DISTRICT ELECTORAL DIVISIONS OF—
Ballymitty, Bannow, Clongeen, Duncormick, Harperstown, Harristown, Horetown, Newbawn.

BRIDGETOWN—THE DISTRICT ELECTORAL DIVISIONS OF—
Aughwilliam, Bridgetown, Kilcowan, Killag, Kilmore, Mayglass, Newcastle, Rathaspick.

COOLGREANY—THE DISTRICT ELECTORAL DIVISIONS OF—
Ballylarkin, Ballynestragh, Coolgreany, Gorey Rural, Kilgorman, Kilnahue, Limerick, Monaseed, Wingfield.

ENNISCORTHY—THE DISTRICT ELECTORAL DIVISIONS OF—
Enniscorthy Rural, Enniscorthy Urban.

FERNS—THE DISTRICT ELECTORAL DIVISIONS OF—
Balloughter, Ballycanew, Ballycarney, Ballymore, Ferns, Huntingtown, Kilbora, Kilcomb, Rossminoge, The Harrow, Tinnacross.

FETHARD—THE DISTRICT ELECTORAL DIVISIONS OF—
Ballyhack, Fethard, Kilmokea, Rathroe, Templetown.

GOREY—THE DISTRICT ELECTORAL DIVISIONS OF—
Ardmaine, Ballygarrett, Cahore, Courtown, Gorey Urban, Killenagh.

KILLURIN—THE DISTRICT ELECTORAL DIVISIONS OF—
Artramon, Ballyhoge, Bree, Edermine, Killurin, Kilpatrick, The Leap.

KILTEALY—THE DISTRICT ELECTORAL DIVISIONS OF—
Ballindaggan, Castleborough, Killann, Killoughrum, Kiltealy, Marshalstown, Rossard.

MONAMOLIN—The District Electoral Divisions of—
  Ballyvaldon, Bolaboy, Castle Talbot, Ford, Kilcormick,
  Killincooly, Monamolin, Wells.

NEW ROSS—The District Electoral Divisions of—
  New Ross Rural, New Ross Urban, Rosbercon Urban.

NEWTOWNBARRY—District Electoral Divisions of—
  Ballybeg, Ballyellis, Castledockrell, Kilrush, Moyacomb, Newtownbarry, St. Mary's, Tombrack.

OLD ROSS—The District Electoral Divisions of—
  Ballyanne, Barrack Village, Barronstown, Carrig-
  byrne, Clonleigh, Clonroche, Old Ross, Templeu-
  digan, Whitemoor.

ROSSLARE—The District Electoral Divisions of—
  Drinagh, Killinick, Kilscoran, Lady's *I*sland, Rosslare, St. Helen's Tacumshin, Tomhaggard.

TAGHMON—The District Electoral Divisions of—
  Adamstown, Carrick, Forth, Glynn, Kilbride, Kilgarvan, Taghmon, Wexford Rural, Whitechurch.

TINTERN—The District Electoral Divisions of—
  Carnagh, Dunmain, Inch, Killesk, Oldcourt, Roches-
  town, Tintern, Whitechurch.

WEXFORD—The District Electoral Divisions of—
  Wexford No. 1 Urban, Wexford No. 2 Urban, Wexford No. 3 Urban.

Note.—In the above schedule, District Electoral Divisions mean
the existing Poor Law Electoral Divisions having the same name.

WICKLOW.

SCHEDULE A.

Name of Administrative County and Contents.

COUNTY OF WICKLOW—The existing judicial county of
  Wicklow; and
  So much of the existing judicial county of Dublin as
  comprises the portion of the township of Bray,
  situated therein.

SCHEDULE B.

County Electoral Divisions and Contents.

ARKLOW—The District Electoral Divisions of—
  Arklow No. 1 Urban, Arklow No. 2 Urban.

BALLYARTHUR—The District Electoral Divisions of—
  Arklow Rural, Ballyarthur, Kilbride, (Rathdrum).

BALTINGLASS—The District Electoral Divisions of—
Baltinglass, Hartstown, Stratford, The Grange, Tuckmill.

BLESSINGTON—The District Electoral Divisions of—
Blessington, Kilbride (Naas), Lackan.

BRAY—The District Electoral Divisions of—
Bray No. 1, Bray No. 2, Bray No. 3.

CARNEW—The District Electoral Divisions of—
Ballingate, Carnew, Coolattin, Coolboy, Kilpipe.

DELGANY—The District Electoral Division of—
Delgany.

DUNLAVIN—The District Electoral Divisions of—
Donoughmore, Donard, Dunlavin, Imael North, Imael South, Rathsallagh.

GLENDALOUGH—The District Electoral Divisions of—
Ballycullen, Brockagh, Glendalough, Killiskey, Moneystown, Oldtown.

GLENEALY—The District Electoral Divisions of—
Dunganstown East, Dunganstown South, Dunganstown West, Ennereilly, Glenealy.

HOLLYWOOD—The District Electoral Divisions of—
Burgage, Hollywood, Lugglass, Tober, Togher (Baltinglass).

NEWCASTLE—The District Electoral Divisions of—
Altidore, Kilcoole, Lower Newcastle, Upper Newcastle.

OVOCA—The District Electoral Divisions of—
Aughrim, Ballinacor, Ballinaclash, Kilballyowen, Knockrath, Ovoca.

POWERSCOURT—The District Electoral Divisions of—
Calary, Powerscourt, Togher (Rathdrum).

RATHDANGAN—The District Electoral Divisions of—
Ballinguile, Eadestown, Humewood, Rathdangan, Talbotstown.

RATHDRUM—The District Electoral Divisions of—
Ballinderry, Cronebane, Rathdrum, Trooperstown.

SHILLELAGH—The District Electoral Divisions of—
Aghowle, Cronelea, Killinure, Money, Rath, Shillelagh

TINAHELY—The District Electoral Divisions of—
Ballinglen, Ballybeg, Coolballintaggart, Tinahely.

WICKLOW—The District Electoral Divisions of—
Wicklow Rural, Wicklow Urban.

Note.—In the above schedule, District Electoral Divisions mean the existing Poor Law Electoral Divisions having the same name.

To the Guardians of the Poor of the several Unions named in the Schedule hereinunder annexed; to the Paid Officers of such Unions and of Dispensary Districts therein; and to all others whom it may concern.

WHEREAS, in pursuance of the authorities vested in us by Statute in that behalf, We, the Local Government Board for Ireland, have, from time to time, by General Orders under our Seal regulated the appointment, duties, and tenure of offiee, of the Officers of the several Unions and Dispensary Districts in . Ireland :

AND WHEREAS no paid Officer engaged in the administration of the Poor Relief (Ireland) Acts, 1838 to 1898, is capable of serving as a Poor Law Guardian; and we think fit to make similar provision in regard to eligibility for the Office of County Councillor under the Local Government (Ireland) Act, 1898.

NOW, THEREFORE, in exercise of the powers vested in Us, We, the Local Government Board for Ireland, do hereby order and declare that no such paid Officer as aforesaid shall be eligible to serve as a County Councillor under the Local Government (Ireland) Act, 1898.

> Sealed with our Seal, this Seventeenth day of Jannary in the Year of our Lord One Thousand Eight Hundred and Ninety-nine.

> (Signed),

> H. A. ROBINSON.
> WM. L. MICKS.
> T. J. STAFFORD.
> R. BAGWELL.

CADOGAN.

WE, GEORGE HENRY, EARL CADOGAN, Lord Lieutenant-General and General Governor of Ireland, do hereby approve this Order.

> By Command of His Excellency.

> D. HARREL.

SCHEDULE.

[The Schedule contains the names of all the unions in Ireland].

WHEREAS by Order bearing date the 1st day of November, 1898, We, the Local Government Board for Ireland did provide and declare, in pursuance of the Local Government (Ireland) Act, 1898, that the several divisions in the administrative County of Dublin for the election of county councillors should be the several county electoral divisions defined in Schedule B to that Order.

AND WHEREAS we deem it expedient to vary the said Order in so far as it relates to the county electoral divisions named respectively Coolock and Drumcondra :—

NOW, THEREFORE, We, the Local Government Board for Ireland, do hereby order and declare :

1. That the said county electoral division of Coolock shall consist of the district electoral divisions of Coolock, Drumcondra Rural, and Finglas, in lieu of those mentioned in Schedule B to the said Order of the 1st day of November, 1898; and

2. That the said county electoral division of Drumcondra shall consist of the district electoral divisions of Drumcondra No. 1 Urban, Drumcondra No. 2 Urban, Drumcondra No. 3 Urban, and Glasnevin, in lieu of those mentioned in Schedule B to the said Order of the 1st day of November, 1898.

And we do further declare that this Order shall be in force and take effect at such time as may be necessary for the purposes of the first election of county councillors, and shall be read as one with the said Order of the 1st day of November, 1898.

Given under our Hands and Seal of Office, this Seventeenth day of January, in the Year of our Lord One Thousand Eight Hundred and Ninety-nine.

(Signed),

H. A. ROBINSON.
WM. M. MICKS.
T. J. STAFFORD.
R. BAGWELL.

GENERAL ORDER.

COUNTY AND RURAL DISTRICT COUNCILLORS.

Rules as to Nomination and Election.

To the County Council of every Administrative County in Ireland, and to the Clerk of every such Council.

To the District Council of every Rural District in Ireland and to the Clerk of every such Council, and to all others whom it may concern :—

WHEREAS, by an Order made the Twenty-second day of December, 1898, by the Lord Lieutenant-General and General Governor of Ireland, in pursuance of the Local Government (Ireland) Act, 1898, sec. 104, it is amongst other things ordered that the election of County and Rural District Councils in Ireland shall, subject to the provisions of the Act, be conducted according to rules framed under the said Order by the Local Government Board for Ireland, and that the rules provide for the matters and things in the said Order mentioned.

Now We, the Local Government Board for Ireland, do hereby order that, subject to any directions which may be given by us and until we otherwise order, the following rules shall be observed in connection with the election of County and Rural District Councils in Ireland.

Returning Officer.

1. (1.) The Returning Officer for the election of County Councillors for every County Electoral Division in the County shall be appointed by the County Council.

(2.) The person appointed under Sub-Section (1) shall also be the Returning Officer for the election of Rural District Councillors in every Rural District of the County and in every District Electoral Division of such Rural District.

(3.) If the person so appointed from illness or other cause is unable or unwilling to perform or to complete the performance of the duties specified in Sub-Sections (1) and (2) the Council shall appoint some other person to act as Returning Officer under the said sub-sections, or to perform such of the duties of the Returning Officer as then remain to be performed, as the case may be.

(4.) The Returning Officer shall appoint some place or places within the administrative County as an office or offices for the purpose of the election of County Councillors, and some place or places within each Rural District as an office or offices for the election of Rural District Councillors.

(5.) The Returning Officer may, in writing, appoint a fit person or persons to be his Deputy or Deputies for all or any of the purposes relating to the election of County or Rural District Councillors, provided that, so far as regards the carrying out of Rules 3 to 10 of this Order in respect of the election of Rural District Councillors in Rural Districts, he shall in every case appoint a Deputy, and the Clerk of the Rural District Council shall be the Deputy so appointed.

(6.) If the Clerk of the Rural District Council is, in the opinion of the Local Government Board, unable to perform the duties referred to in Sub-Section (5) of this Rule, or if such Clerk becomes unable to complete the performance of the said duties, or if the ofhee of Clerk is vacant, the Returning Officer shall appoint some other fit person to perform the said duties, or to complete the performance of the said duties, as the case may be.

(7.) A Deputy Returning Officer shall·have all the powers, duties, and liabilities of the Returning Officer in relation to the matters in respect of which he is appointed as Deputy.

Day of Election.

2. The Day of Election of County and Rural District Councillors shall be that fixed for the purpose by the County Council in accordance with the provisions of Section 94 (7) of the Local Government (Ireland) Act, 1898.

Notice of Election.

3. Not later than the day prescribed for that purpose by the First Schedule to this Order, the Returning Officer or his Deputy shall prepare and sign Notices of the Election of County and Rural District Councillors, and shall cause public Notice to be given of the same in accordance with Rule 30 of this Order in each County Electoral Division and in each District Electoral Division respectively. The notice shall be in the Form No. 1 in the Second Schedule to this Order, or in a form to the like effect.

Nomination of Candidates.

4. (1.) Each candidate for election as a County or Rural District Councillor shall be nominated in writing.

(2.) The nomination paper shall state the name of the County Electoral Division or District Electoral Division for which the candidate is nominated, the surname and other name or names in full of the candidate, and his place of abode and description, and if he is qualified as a Local Government Elector for the County, or for the Rural District as the case may be, or in the case of a candidate for the office of Rural District Councillor by having, during the whole of the twelve months preceding the election, resided, and continuing to reside, in the District. It shall be signed in the case of a candidate for the office of County Councillor by two Local Government Electors of the County Electoral Division, and in the case of a candidate for the office of Rural District Councillor, by two Local Government Electors of the District Electoral Division as proposer and seconder, and no more, and shall state their respective places of abode. It should be in the form set out in the notice in Form No. 1 in the Second Schedule to this Order, or in a form to the like effect.

(3.) The name of more than one candidate shall not be inserted in any one nomination paper.

(4.) A Local Government Elector shall not sign more nomination papers than there are County or Rural District Councillors to be elected for the County Electoral Division or District Electoral Division respectively; nor shall he sign a nomination paper for any County Electoral Division or District Electoral Division other than one in respect of which he is registered as a Local Government Elector. Neither shall he sign nomination papers for more than one County Electoral Division or for more than one District Electoral Division.

(5.) If any Local Government Elector shall sign nomination papers for more than one County Electoral Division or District Electoral Division, the nomination paper signed by him relating to the first County Electoral Division or District Electoral Division as the case may be, for which a nomination paper signed by him is received by the Returning Officer shall alone be valid, and of the nomination papers signed by him which relate to that County Electoral Division or District Electoral Division such as are first received by the Returning Officer up to the number of County or Rural District Councillors to be elected for such County Electoral Division or District Electoral Division shall alone be valid. Provided that for the purposes of this paragraph nomination papers not properly filled up and signed shall be excluded.

Nomination Papers to be Provided.

5. The Returning Officer shall provide nomination papers. Any Local Government Elector may obtain nomination papers from either the returning Officer or his Deputy free of charge.

Time for sending in Nomination Papers.

6. Every nomination paper shall be sent to the Returning Officer or his Deputy so that it shall be received at his office within the time prescribed for that purpose by the First Schedule to this Order. A nomination paper received after that time shall not be valid. The Returning Officer shall note on each nomination paper whether it was received before or after that time.

Dealing with Nominations by Returning Officer.

7. (1.) The Returning Officer or his Deputy shall number the nomination papers in the order in which they are received by him ; and the first valid nomination paper received for a candidate shall be deemed to be the nomination of that candidate.

(2.) The Returning Officer or his Deputy shall, as soon as practicable after the receipt of any nomination paper, examine and decide whether it has or has not been properly filled up and signed by two Local Government Electors, and whether it is or is not invalid under Rule 4 (5) or Rule 6. His decision that a nomination paper has been so filled up and signed, and is not invalid as aforesaid, shall be final, and shall not be questioned in any proceeding whatever.

(3.) If the Returning Officer or his Deputy shall decide that a nomination paper is invalid, he shall put a note on it to this effect, stating the grounds of his decision, and he shall sign such note.

(4.) After deciding that the nomination of any candidate is valid, or (except where some other nomination of the candidate has been decided to be valid) that a nomination paper for any candidate is invalid, the Returning Officer or his Deputy shall, not later than the day prescribed for that purpose by the First Schedule to this Order, send, by post or otherwise, notice of his decision to the candidate.

Statement as to Persons Nominated.

8. Not later than the day prescribed for that purpose by the First Schedule to this Order, the Returning Officer shall make out a Statement in the Form No. 2 in the Second Schedule to this Order, or in a form to the like effect, containing the names, places of abode, and descriptions of the persons nominated for election as County Councillors for the several County Electoral Divisions, and his Deputy appointed under 'Rule 1 (5) shall make out a similar statement containing the names, places of abode, and descriptions of the persons nominated for election as Rural District Councillors for the several District Electoral Divisions of the District, or of each of the Districts, in respect

of which he is appointed Deputy. Every such statement, whether it refer to nominations for election to the office of County Councillor, or to that of Rural District Councillor, shall contain a notice of the decision of the Returning Officer or his Deputy, as the case may be, with respect to each candidate as to whether he has been nominated by a valid nomination paper or not. He shall forthwith cause a copy thereof to be suspended in the Court House or Room in which the meetings of the County Council, or the Rural District Council, as the case may be, are held, and in the Board Room of the Guardians of the Union, in which any of the County or District Electoral Divisions affected by the statement are situate, and also a copy to be affixed on the principal external gate or door of the Workhouse of every such Union, and on that of the Court House or other office of the County Council.

Withdrawal of Candidate.

9. Any candidate may withdraw his candidature by delivering, or causing to be delivered, within the time prescribed for that purpose by the First Schedule to this Order, at the office of the Returning Officer or his Deputy at which his nomination was delivered, a notice in writing of such withdrawal, signed by him.

Relation of Nomination to Election.

10. Section 56 of the Municipal Corporations Act, 1882, shall be altered and adapted in its application to the election of County and Rural District Councillors so as to be read as follows :—

(1.) If the number of candidates who receive valid nominations for election to the office of County or Rural District Councillor for any County Electoral Division or District Electoral Division as the case may be, and who do not withdraw their candidature under Rule 9, exceeds the number of County or Rural District Councillors respectively to be elected for the County Electoral Division or District Electoral Division, the County or Rural District Councillor or Councillors, as the case may be, shall be elected from among the persons in each case respectively so nominated.

(2.) If the number of candidates who receive valid nominations is in any case equal to, or is, by the withdrawal of any candidate as provided by Rule 9 or otherwise in any case reduced to a number equal to the number of vacancies, the Returning Officer or his Deputy shall, as early as practicable, give public notice, in accordance with Rule 30 of this Order, that no poll will be taken and that the candidate or candidates so nominated will be declared to be elected.

(3.) If the number of candidates at any election of County or Rural District Councillors for a County Electoral Division or District Electoral Division, respectively, who receive valid nominations is less than, or is, by the withdrawal of any candidate, as provided by Rule 9, or otherwise, reduced to a number less than the number of vacancies, the Returning Officer or his Deputy shall give public notice, in accordance with Rule 30 of this Order, that no poll will be taken, and that the candidate or candidates so nominated will be declared to be elected; and also that such of any retiring County or Rural District Councillors for the County Electoral Division or District Electoral Division, respectively, as were highest on the poll at their election, or if the poll was equal or there was no poll, as shall have been selected by the Returning Officer or his Deputy by lot to make up the required number will be declared to be deemed to be re-elected.

(4.) If after due notice has been given of an ordinary election to fill the office of County or Rural District Councillor for a County Electoral Division or District Electoral Division, respectively, no candidate receives a valid nomination, the Returning Officer or his Deputy shall give public notice in such County or District Electoral Division, in accordance with Rule 30 of this Order, that the retiring County Councillor or Councillors, or the retiring Rural District Councillors as the case may be, will be declared to be deemed to be re-elected.

(5.) The Returning Officer or his Deputy shall forthwith send, by post or otherwise, a copy of any notice under this Rule to each of the persons who will be declared to be elected or to be deemed to be re-elected.

(6.) The notice shall be in the Form No. 3 or the Form No. 4, as the case may be, in the Second Schedule to this Order, or in a form to the like effect.

Day and Hours of Poll.

11. (1.) The poll, if any, shall be held on the day of election as fixed by the County Council in accordance with the provisions of section 94 (7) of the Local Government (Ireland) Act,

1898, and the hours during which the poll shall be open shall be such as shall be fixed by the County Council by any general or special order, or if no such order is in force in the County Electoral Division or District Electoral Division, then such hours as were applicable at the last ordinary election of County or Rural District Councillors in the County Electoral Division or District Electoral Division, respectively, so, however, that the poll shall always be open between the hours of six and eight in the evening.

(2.) Provided that in any Urban District forming a separate County Electoral Division the hours during which the poll shall be taken for the election of County Councillors shall be between 8 a.m. and 8 p.m.

12. Whenever polls have to be taken both for the election of Rural District Councillors, for a District Electoral Division, and for that of a County Councillor for the County Electoral Division in which such District Electoral Division is situated, the polls for these elections shall be taken together.

13. The Returning Officer shall determine the number and situation of the polling places and stations.

Provided as follows —:

(a) No premises licensed for the sale of intoxicating liquor shall be used for a polling station.

(b) The polling stations for the election of County and Rural District Councillors in any District Electoral Division when the polls for the two elections are taken together shall be the same.

Notice of Poll.

14. (1.) If a poll has to be taken, the Returning Officer shall, within the time prescribed for that purpose by the First Schedule to this Order, give public notice thereof in accordance with Rule 30 of this Order. The notice shall specify :—

(a) The day and hours fixed for the poll;

(b) The names, place of abode, and description of each candidate for the County Electoral Division or District Electoral Division whom he has decided to have been nominated by a valid nomination paper, and who has not withdrawn his candidature;

(c) The names of the proposer and seconder who signed the nomination paper of each candidate;

(d) A description of the polling districts; and

(e) The situation and allotment of the polling places and polling stations, and the description of the persons entitled to vote thereat.

2 A

(2.) The notice shall be in the Form No. 5, or in the Form No. 6, as the case requires, in the Second Schedule to this Order, or in a form to the like effect.

Presiding Officers.

15. The Returning Officer, or some person appointed by him for the purpose, shall preside at each polling station. The person presiding at any polling station shall be called the Presiding Officer.

Compartments of Polling Stations—Ballot Papers.

16. The Returning Officer shall furnish every polling station with a sufficient number of compartments in which the voters can mark their votes screened from observation, and shall furnish each Presiding Officer with such number of ballot papers as may be necessary for effectually taking the poll at the election.

Polling Agents.

17. Polling agents, either paid or unpaid, may be appointed for each polling station, subject to the following conditions:

(1.) The number appointed shall in no case exceed four.

(2.) When the number of candidates does not exceed four, each candidate may, in writing, appoint a polling agent.

(3.) When the number of candidates exceeds four, any number of such candidates being not less than one-fourth of the whole number, may jointly appoint in writing a polling agent. Any such appointment shall be delivered at the office of the Returning Officer not less than two clear days before the day of the poll. Except as aforesaid, no polling or personation agent, whether paid or unpaid, shall be appointed for the purposes of the election.

Prohibition of Voting in more than one County or District Electoral Division—Questions to Elector.

18. (1.) A Local Government Elector shall not in the case of an Election of County Councillors vote in more than one County Electoral Division in the County, nor in the case of an Election of Rural District Councillors in more than one District Electoral Division in the Rural District.

(2.) The Presiding Officer may, and if required by any polling agent appointed under Rule 17, shall, put to any elector at the time of his applying for a ballot paper, but not afterwards, the following questions, or one of them, and no other :—

    (*a.*) Are you the person entered in the register for this County [or District] Electoral Division as follows (read the whole entry from the register)?

    (*b.*) Have you already voted at the present election of County [or Rural District] Councillors in this or any other County [or District] Electoral Division of the County?

(3.) A person required to answer either of these questions shall not receive a ballot paper or be permitted to vote until he has answered it, in the manner and to the effect prescribed in Rule 27 of the First Schedule to the Ballot Act, 1872, as adapted and printed in the Third Schedule to this Order, notwithstanding the fact that no person has already voted as therein mentioned.

Forwarding of Ballot Boxes, &c., after the Poll.

19. Immediately on the close of the Poll the Presiding Officer at every Polling Station shall forward with all possible despatch the Ballot Boxes, together with the several other sealed packets referred to in rule 29 of the First Schedule of the Ballot Act, 1872, as adapted in the Third Schedule to this Order as follows, namely, those relating to the election of County Councillors to the County Court House or such other place as the Returning Officer may direct, and those relating to the election of Rural District Councillors to the Offices of the Rural District Council.

Counting the Votes.

20. (1.) If the Returning Officer appoints a person to act as Deputy Returning Officer for the County Electoral Division or District Electoral Division, as the case may be, in respect of the custody and opening of the ballot boxes, the counting and recording of the votes, and the declaration of the number of votes given for each candidate, and of the election of the candidate or candidates to whom the largest number of votes has been given, the person so appointed shall, in addition to his other powers and duties, have all the powers and duties of the Returning Officer in relation to the decision of any question as to any ballot paper and otherwise as to the ballot papers.

(2.) The votes shall be counted as soon as practicable after the close of the poll: those for the Election of County Councillors at the County Court House or some other convenient place appointed by the Returning Officer, and those for the Election of Rural District Councilors at the Offices of the Rural District Council.

Equality of Votes.

21. If an equality of votes is found to exist between any candidates, and the addition of a vote would entitle any of such candidates to be declared elected, the Returning Officer or Deputy Returning Officer, as the case may be, shall determine by lot which of the candidates whose votes are equal shall be elected.

Declaration of Result of Poll.

22. (1.) The declaration of the result of the poll shall be in the Form No. 7 in the Second Schedule to this Order, or in a form to the like effect.

(2.) The Returning Officer or Deputy Returning Officer, as the case may be, making the declaration shall forthwith cause a copy of it to be affixed to the front of the building in which the votes have been counted. If the declaration is made by a Deputy Returning Officer, he shall forthwith send it to the Returning Officer.

Publication of Result of Elections.

23. (1.) The Returning Officer shall prepare and sign notices of the result of the elections in all the County Electoral Divisions in the Administrative County and in all the District Electoral Divisions of the Rural District, and shall by such notices declare to be elected or to be deemed to be re-elected the persons who, under Rule 10, are to be declared to be elected or to be deemed to be re-elected without a poll being taken. The notices shall be in the Form No. 8 in the Second Schedule to this Order, or in a form to the like effect.

(2.) The notice shall be sent by the Returning Officer as early as practicable, in the case of an Election of County Councillors, to the Clerk of the County Council, and in the case of an Election of Rural District Councillors to the Clerk of the Rural District Council, and copies of the notice shall be sent by the Returning Officer to the persons elected or deemed to be re-elected.

Application and Adaptation of Ballot Act, 1872.

24. The provisions of the Ballot Act, 1872, which, with adaptations and alterations, are set out in the Third Schedule to this Order, and only such provisions of that Act shall, subject to such adaptations and alterations, apply to the election of County Councillors.

Provided as follows:—

    (a) For every Rural District Electoral Division for which a poll has to be taken there shall be provided a separate polling station, and the Presiding Officer at such polling station shall be appointed by the Returning Officer.

(b) At every polling station for a Rural District Electoral Division there shall be provided a ballot box for the reception of ballot papers for the election of Rural District Councillors for such District Electoral Division.

(c) Every polling station for a Rural District Electoral Division shall also be a polling station if a poll has to be taken for the election of a County Councillor for the County Electoral Division in which such District Electoral Division is situated, and a separate ballot box shall be provided for the reception of ballot papers for such election of a County Councillor

(d) Where there are polls to be taken both for the election of Rural District Councillors for a District Electoral Division and for the election of a County Councillor for the County Electoral Division in which such District Electoral Division is situated, these polls shall be taken together by means of ballot papers differently coloured, and the ballot boxes mentioned in sub-sections (b) and (c) of this Rule shall be coloured respectively to correspond with the colour of the ballot papers for the reception of which each such ballot box is provided, and the colours shall be fixed by the Returning Officer, and shall be the same for every election throughout the county.

(e) Where polls are taken together in accordance with sub-section (d) of this Rule the same person shall act as Presiding Officer in respect of the polling for both elections.

Adaptation of Municipal Corporations Act, 1882.

25. (1.) The provisions of Sections 74 and 75 of the Municipal Corporations Act, 1882, which with adaptations and alterations are set out in the Fourth Schedule to this Order, shall, subject to such adaptations and alterations, apply to the election of County and Rural District Councillors, and to the persons elected or deemed to be re-elected thereat.

(2.) In the application of Part IV. of the Municipal Corporations Act, 1882 (relating to Corrupt Practices and Election Petitions), as amended by the Municipal Elections (Corrupt and Illegal Practices) Act, 1884, the following adaptations and alterations shall have effect:—

(a) Such application shall be subject to the provisions of this Order.

(*b*) All references to a municipal election or to an election to a corporate office shall be construed as referring to the election of County or Rural District Councillors, and in Section 93 (2) "County," shall be deemed to be substituted for "Borough"; "County Electoral Division or District Electoral Division" shall be deemed to be substituted for "Borough or Ward" or "Borough or Ward of a Borough"; "Poor Rate" shall be deemed to be substituted for "Borough Fund or Borough Rate." The "Returning Officer" shall be substituted for the "Town Clerk," and

(*c*) In all cases "Voter" shall mean a Local Government Elector or a person who votes or claims to vote at an election of County or Rural District Councillors as the case may be.

(*d*) In the application of Sub-section (2) of Section 89 such Sub-section shall be adapted and altered so as to read as follows:—

"(2.) The security shall be to the amount of "Fifty Pounds, unless in any case the High "Court of Justice in Ireland, or a Judge "thereof, on summons, order that the same "shall be to a lesser amount, or to a larger "amount not exceeding Three Hundred "Pounds, and shall be given in the pre- "scribed manner, either by a deposit of "money or by a recognizance entered into "by not more than four sureties, or partly "in one way and partly in the other."

Adaptation of Municipal Elections (Corrupt and Illegal Practices) Act, 1884.

26. In the application of the Municipal Elections (Corrupt and Illegal Practices) Act, 1884, the following adaptations and alterations shall have effect:—

(1.) Such application shall be subject to the provisions of this Order.

(2.) The expressions "County Electoral Division or District Electoral Division," "Returning Officer of County or Rural District Councillors," and "Poor Rate," shall be deemed to be substituted in the Act for "Borough," "Town Clerk," and "Borough Fund or Rate," respectively.

(3.) The expression "Corporate Office" in the Act shall mean the office of County or Rural District Councillor, and a "Municipal Election" shall mean an

Election of one or more County or Rural District Councillors, and the expressions "Municipal Election Court," "Municipal Election List," and "Municipal Election Petition" shall be construed accordingly.

(4.) So much of Section 13 of the Act as permits one polling agent to be employed in each polling station shall not apply except so far as the employment of polling agents is permitted by Rule 17 of this Order.

(5.) An election petition complaining of the Election on the ground of an illegal practice, may be presented at any time within six weeks after the Day of Election.

(6.) In Section 34 of the Act "Burgess Roll' 'shall mean the Register of Local Government Electors.

(7.) Section 37 of the Act shall be read as if a reference to an Election of County or Rural District Councillors was substituted for a reference to any of the Elections mentioned in the First Schedule to the Act.

27. For the purposes of this Order the words "High Court and Judge of the High Court" in the Municipal Corporations Act, 1882, and the Municipal Corporations (Corrupt and Illegal Practices) Act, 1884, shall mean the High Court of Justice in Ireland and a Judge of the said Court respectively, and the words "Director of Public Prosecutions" shall mean the Attorney-General for Ireland.

Non-acceptance of Office.

28. Non-acceptance of office by a person elected or deemed to be re-elected shall in every case create a Casual Vacancy, which shall be filled as directed by Section 94 (4) of the Local Government (Ireland) Act, 1898.

Expenses.

29. Any sum which may be payable to the Returning Officer in respect of his services in taking a poll in the County Electoral Division or District Electoral Division, or in respect of expenses incurred in relation to such poll, and any other sum which may be payable to such Returning Officer in respect of his services in the conduct of the Election, or in respect of expenses incurred in relation to the Election, shall be paid as directed by Section 6 (2) of the Schedule to the Local Government (Application of Enactments) Order, 1898.

Publication of Notices.

30. Any public notice required by this Order shall be given by posting copies of the same at, on, or near the principal entrance of every Church and other House of Worship, and at every Court House, Police Station, Market House, and other usual place for posting public notices within the County Electoral Division or District Electoral Division as the case may require.

Mark instead of Signature.

31. In place of any signature required by this Order it shall be sufficient for the signatory to affix his mark if the same is witnessed by two electors.

Misnomer—Inaccurate Descriptions.

32. No misnomer or inaccurate description of any person or place named in any notice or nomination paper under this Order shall hinder the full operation of such notice or paper with respect to that person or place, provided the description of that person or place is such as to be commonly understood.

Definition of " Ordinary Election."

33. In this Order the expression " Ordinary Election " means the triennial election of County and Rural District Councillors.

34. This Order may be cited as the " COUNTY AND RURAL DISTRICT COUNCILLORS (IRELAND) ELECTION ORDER, 1899."

Sealed with our Seal this Twenty-fifth day of January, in the Year of our Lord One Thousand Eight Hundred and Ninety-nine.

(Signed)   H. A. ROBINSON.
                  WILLIAM L. MICKS.
                  T. J. STAFFORD.
                  R. BAGWELL.

[SCHEDULES

SCHEDULES

TO

COUNTY AND RURAL DISTRICT COUNCILLORS (IRELAND) ELECTION ORDER. 1899.

FIRST SCHEDULE.

TIMES FOR THE PROCEEDINGS AT THE ORDINARY TRIENNIAL ELECTION OF COUNTY AND RURAL DISTRICT COUNTY COUNCILLORS.

Proceeding.	Time.
1. Notice of Election . ` .	Not less than thirty-five clear days before the day of Election.
2. Receipt of Nomination Papers.	Not later than five o'clock p.m. on the seventh day after the Notice of Election was given.
3. Sending notice of decision as to validity of Nomination Papers.	As soon as practicable after receipt, but in any case not later than the third day after the last day for the receipt of Nomination Papers.
4. Making out Statement as to persons nominated.	
5. Withdrawal of Candidates	Not later than five o'clock p.m. on the seventh day after the last day for the receipt of Nomination Papers.
6. Notice of Poll . .	Ten clear days at least, before the day of Election.
7. Day of Election . .	Such day as the County Council may fix in accordance with Section 94 (7) of the Local Government (Ireland) Act, 1898.

SECOND SECHEDULE.

Form No. 1.

Notice of Election.

County of $\left\{ {COUNTY \atop DISTRICT} \right\}$ Electoral Division of

Election of $\left\{ {\text{A } COUNTY COUNCILLOR \text{ [or } COUNCILLORS]} \atop \text{Rural District Councillors.} \right\}$

Notice is hereby given that—

1. The day of election of $\left\{ {\text{a } Councillor \text{ [or } Councillors]} \atop \text{Rural District Councillors}} \right\}$ for

the said $\left\{ {County \atop District} \right\}$ Electoral Division will be

the   day of   18

2. The number of $\left\{ {County \atop \text{Rural District}} \right\}$ Councillors to be elected

for the said $\left\{ {County \atop District} \right\}$ Electoral Division is

3. Each Candidate for Election as a $\left\{ {County \atop \text{Rural District}} \right\}$ Councillor must be nominated in writing, and the nomination
paper must be sent to me, so that it shall be received at
     (which is my office for the purpose of
the election) not later than five o'clock p.m. on   ,
the   day of   , 18 .

4. A Local Government Elector must not sign more than one
nomination paper for the $\left\{ {County \atop District} \right\}$ Electoral Division,
and he must not sign a nomination paper for such
$\left\{ {County \atop District} \right\}$ Electoral Division unless he is registered as a
Local Government Elector in respect of a qualification
therein.

5. Forms of nomination paper may be obtained, free of charge,
from me at the above-named office.

6. The nomination paper must be in the following form or in
a form to the like effect :—

                [Form.

FORM OF NOMINATION PAPER.

COUNTY OF $\left\{\begin{array}{l}COUNTY\\ \text{DISTRICT}\end{array}\right\}$ ELECTORAL DIVISION OF

ELECTION OF $\left\{\begin{array}{l}COUNTY\\ \text{RURAL DISTRICT}\end{array}\right\}$ COUNCILLOR $\left\{\begin{array}{l}County\\ \text{District}\end{array}\right\}$ for the above Electoral

Division in the year 18

. We, the undersigned, being respectively Local Government Electors of the said $\left\{\begin{array}{l}County\\ \text{District}\end{array}\right\}$ Electoral Division, do hereby nominate the undermentioned person as a candidate at the said Election.

Names of Candidate.		Place of Abode.	Description.
Surname.	Other Names in full.		
1.	2.	3.	4.

Signature of PROPOSER,_____

Place of Abode,_____

Signature of SECONDER,_____

Place of Abode,_____

*Instructions for filling up Nomination Papers.**

* These instructions form part of the Nomination Paper.

(1.) The surname of only one candidate for election must be inserted in Column 1.

(2.) The other names of the candidate must be inserted in full in Column 2.

(3.) Insert in Column 3 the place of abode of the candidate.

(4.) In column 4 state the occupation, if any, of the candidate. If the candidate has no occupation, insert some such description as "gentleman," or "married woman," or "spinster," or "widow," as the case may be.

(5.) No person is eligible as a County Councillor for any County Electoral Division unless he is registered as a Local Government Elector in respect of a qualification in the County of which such County Electoral Division forms a part.

(2.) No person is eligible as a Rural District Councillor for any District Electoral Division unless he or she is registered as a Local Government Elector in respect of a qualification in the Rural District of which such District Electoral Division forms a part, and unless he or she has during the whole of the twelve months preceding the Election resided, and continues to reside, in such Rural District.

6. (1.) The paper must be signed by two Local Government Electors of the $\left\{\begin{array}{c}County \\ District\end{array}\right\}$ Electoral Division and no more; by one as Proposer, and by the other as Seconder. The places of abode of the Proposer and Seconder must also be inserted. Instead of signing, the Proposer or Seconder may affix his mark, if it is witnessed by two Local Government Electors.

(2.) A Local Government Elector must not sign more than one nomination paper for the $\left\{\begin{array}{c}County \\ District\end{array}\right\}$ Electoral Division, and he must not sign a nomination paper for such $\left\{\begin{array}{c}County \\ District\end{array}\right\}$ Electoral Division unless he is registered as a Local Government Elector in respect of a qualification therein.

---

7. Not later than   , the   day of   , 18   I shall cause a copy of a statement containing the names, places of abode, and descriptions of the persons nominated for the office of $\left\{\begin{array}{c}County \\ Rural District\end{array}\right\}$ Councillor for the said $\left\{\begin{array}{c}County \\ District\end{array}\right\}$ Electoral Division, and also containing a notice of my decision as regards each candidate as to whether he [or she] has been nominated by a valid nomination paper or not, to be suspended in the Board Room of the County Council, and another to be affixed on the principal external gate or door of the offices of the County Council.

8. Any candidate nominated for election may, not later than five o'clock p.m., on   , the   day of   , 18 withdraw his [or her] candidature by delivering or causing to be delivered at my office for the purposes of the election a notice in writing of such withdrawal signed by him [or her].

9. If more than $\left\{\begin{array}{l}\textit{candidate is}\\\text{candidates are}\end{array}\right\}$ validly nominated for the $\left\{\begin{array}{l}County\\\text{District}\end{array}\right\}$ Electoral Division, and the number is not from any cause reduced to , a poll will be taken on the day of , 18 , of which due notice will be given.

Dated this day of , 18

_____

Returning Officer.
[Deputy Returning Officer.]

_____

Office for purpose of election.

Note.—There shall be added to every notice of election to be published under Rule 3 of this Order the notification following with respect to claims against returning officers; namely:

Take notice, that every person having any claim against a Returning Officer for work, labour, material, services, or expenses in respect of any contract made with him by or on behalf of the Returning Officer, for the purposes of an election shall, within fourteen days after the day on which the return is made of the person or persons elected at the election, transmit to the Returning Officer the detailed particulars of such claim in writing, and the Returning Officer shall not be liable in respect of anything which is not duly stated in such particulars.

FORM No. 2.

Statement as to Persons nominated.

COUNTY OF

$\left.\begin{array}{l}COUNTY\\\text{DISTRICT}\end{array}\right\}$ ELECTORAL DIVISION OF

The following is a statement as to the persons nominated for election as $\left\{\begin{array}{l}County\\\text{Rural District}\end{array}\right\}$ Councillor [or Councillors] for the above-named $\left\{\begin{array}{l}County\\\text{District}\end{array}\right\}$ Electoral Division.

Division.	Persons nominated.			Decision of Returning Officer that Candidate has not been nominated by a valid Nomination Paper.
1.	Names. (Surnames first) 2.	Place of Abode. 3.	Description 4.	5.

The Candidates opposite whose names no entry is made in Column 5 have been validly nominated.

Dated this   day of   , 18

_____
                              Returning Officer.
                     [Deputy Returning Officer.]
_____
Office for purpose of election.

———

FORM No. 3.
Notice that no Poll will be taken.

COUNTY OF $\left\{\begin{matrix}County\\District\end{matrix}\right\}$ ELECTORAL DIVISION OF

WHEREAS the following candidates have been duly nominated for election to the office of $\left\{\begin{matrix}County\\ \text{Rural District}\end{matrix}\right\}$ Councillor for the

$\left\{\begin{matrix}County\\District\end{matrix}\right\}$ Electoral Division [*Insert names, places of abode, and description of candidates.*]

And whereas the said [*insert name or names*] has [*or* have] since withdrawn his [*or her or their*] candidature [*or if some other event has occurred causing a person to cease to be a candidate state what it is*], and $\left\{\begin{matrix}candidate\\candidates\end{matrix}\right\}$ only $\left\{\begin{matrix}remains\\ \text{rer ain}\end{matrix}\right\}$ to be elected to the office of $\left\{\begin{matrix}County\\ \text{Rural District}\end{matrix}\right\}$ Councillor for the said Electoral Division [*or* whereas the following $\left\{\begin{matrix}candidate\\candidates\end{matrix}\right\}$ only $\left\{\begin{matrix}has\\have\end{matrix}\right\}$ been duly nominated for election to the office of $\left\{\begin{matrix}County\\ \text{Rural District}\end{matrix}\right\}$ Councillor for the $\left\{\begin{matrix}County\\District\end{matrix}\right\}$ Electoral Division of   ].

I do hereby give notice that a Poll will not be taken and that the said [*insert names*] will be declared to be elected as $\left\{\begin{matrix}County\\ \text{Rural District}\end{matrix}\right\}$ $\left\{\begin{matrix}Councillor\\Councillors\end{matrix}\right\}$ for the said Division [and that [*insert names*]

* Not appli-
cable at a first
Election; and
at the ordinary
Election only
applicable when
the number of
Candidates
validly nomin-
ated is less than
the number of
vacancies to be
filled.

retiring $\left\{\begin{matrix}County\\ \text{Rural District}\end{matrix}\right\}$ Councillor [or Councillors] will be declared to be deemed to be re-elected].*

Dated this   day of   , 18

_____
                              Returning Officer
                     [Deputy Returning Officer.]

FORM No. 4.

Notice where no Candidates are Nominated.

COUNTY OF   ELECTORAL DIVISION OF

I do hereby give notice that no candidate has been duly nominated for election to the office of $\left\{\begin{array}{l} County \\ \text{Rural District} \end{array}\right\}$ Councillor for the said Division,* and that [*insert names*] the retiring $\left\{\begin{array}{l} County\ Councillor \\ \text{Rural District Councillors} \end{array}\right\}$ for the said Division will be declared to be deemed to be re-elected.

> *If the election is a first election omit from* to the end of the sentence.

Dated this   day of   , 18   .

Returning Officer.
[Deputy Returning Officer.]

FORM No. 5.

Notice of Poll.

(For use when the Poll is to be taken either for the Election of a County Councillor [*or* Councillors] only, or for that of Rural District Councillors only.)

COUNTY OF $\left\{\begin{array}{l} COUNTY \\ \text{DISTRICT} \end{array}\right\}$ ELECTORAL DIVISION OF

ELECTION OF $\left\{\begin{array}{l} A\ COUNTY\ COUNCILLOR \\ \text{RURAL DISTRICT COUNCILLORS} \end{array}\right\}$

for the above $\left\{\begin{array}{l} County \\ \text{District} \end{array}\right\}$ Electoral Division in the year 18 .

NOTICE IS HEREBY GIVEN—

1. That a poll for the election of $\left\{\begin{array}{l} a\ County\ Councillor\ [or \\ \text{Rural District} \end{array}\right.$ $\left.\begin{array}{l} Councillors] \\ \text{Councillors} \end{array}\right\}$ for the above-named $\left\{\begin{array}{l} County \\ \text{District} \end{array}\right\}$ Electoral Division will be held on   the   day of 18 , between the hours of   and   .

2. That the names in alphabetical order, places of abode, and descriptions of the Candidates for election, and the names of their respective Proposers and Seconders are as follows:—

Names of Candidates (Surname first)†	Place of Abode.	Description.	Names of Proposer (Surname first.)	Names of Seconder (Surname first).

> † Insert particulars as to each Candidate for the Electoral Division whose nomination is valid, and who has not withdrawn his candidature.

† If the Electoral Division is not divided into PollingDistricts for the purposes of the election, paragraph 3 should be omitted.

3.† (1). That each elector must vote in the Polling District in which the property in respect of which he votes is situate, and if it is situate in more than one Polling District he may vote in any one (but in one only) of such Polling Districts.

(2). The Polling Districts are as follows :—

‡ If only one Polling Place or Station, adapt form accordingly.

4.‡ The situation and allotment of the Polling Places and Polling Stations and the description of the persons entitled to vote thereat are as follows :—

5. The poll will be taken by ballot, and the colour of the ordinary ballot paper used in the election will be (*insert colour*).

Dated this   day of   , 18

Returning Officer.

Office for purpose of election.

FORM No. 6.

(For use when the poll is to be taken both for the Election of a County Councillor [or Councillors] and for that of Rural District Councillors).

COUNTY OF

COUNTY ELECTORAL DIVISION OF

DISTRICT ELECTORAL DIVISION OF

ELECTION OF A COUNTY COUNCILLOR [or COUNCILLORS] for the above-named COUNTY ELECTORAL DIVISION, and of RURAL DISTRICT COUNCILLORS for the above-named DISTRICT ELECTORAL DIVISION,   in the year 18   .

NOTICE IS HEREBY GIVEN—

1. That polls for the election of a County Councillor [or Councillors] for the above-named County Electoral Division, and for that of Rural District Councillors for the above-named District Electoral Division, will be held on   , the   day of   , 18   , between the hours of and   .

2. That the number of County Councillors to be elected for the County Electoral Division is   .

3. That the number of Rural District Councillors to be elected for the District Electoral Division is   .

4. That the names in alphabetical order, places of abode, and description of the Candidates for election, and the names of their respective Proposers and Seconders, are as follows :—

As County Councillor [or Councillors].

Names of Candidate (Surname first).	Place of Abode.	Description	Names of Proposer (Surname first).	Names of Seconder (Surname first).

As Rural District Councillors.

Names of Candidate (Surname first).	Place of Abode.	Description	Names of Proposer (Surname first).	Names of Seconder (Surname first).

*5. (1). That each Local Government Elector must vote in the Polling District in which the property in respect of which he votes is situate, and if it is situate in more than one Polling District he may vote in any one (but in one only) of such Polling Districts.

(2). The Polling Districts are as follows :—

*If the County or District Electoral Division is not divided into Polling Districts for the purposes of the election, paragraph 5 should be omitted.

†6. The situation and allotment of the Polling Places and Polling Stations and the description of the persons entitled to vote thereat are as follows :—

† If only one Polling place or Station, adapt form accordingly.

7. The poll will be taken by ballot, and the colour of the ordinary ballot paper used in the Election of a County Councillor [or Councillors] will be [insert colour], and that used in the Election of Rural District Councillors will be [insert colour].

Dated this   day of   , 18 .

_____
Returning Officer.
[or Deputy Returning Officer].
for the election of

_____
Office for the purpose of election.

2 B

FORM No. 7.

Declaration of Poll.

COUNTY OF

$\left. {County \atop DISTRICT} \right\}$ELECTORAL DIVISION OF

ELECTION OF$\left\{ {COUNTY\ COUNCILLOR\ [or\ COUNCILLORS] \atop \text{RURAL DISTRICT COUNCILLORS}} \right\}$

for the above-named$\left\{ {County \atop District} \right\}$Electoral Division in the year 18

I, the undersigned, being the Returning Officer [*or* Deputy Returning Officer duly authorised in that behalf] at the poll for the election of$\left\{ {County\ Councillor\ [or\ Councillors] \atop \text{Rural District Councillors}} \right\}$ for the said $\left\{ {County \atop District} \right\}$Electoral Division held on the   day of   , 18 , do hereby give notice that the number of votes recorded for each candidate at the election is as follows :—

Names of Candidates.		Places of Abode.	Number of Votes recorded.
Surnames.	Other Names.		

And I do hereby declare that the said $\left\{ {is \atop are} \right\}$duly elected$\left\{ {County\ Councillor\ [or\ Councillors] \atop \text{Rural District Councillors}} \right\}$ for the said$\left\{ {County \atop District} \right\}$Electoral Division.

Dated this   day of   18

Returning Officer
[*or* Deputy Returning Officer].

FORM No. 8.

Notice of Result of Elections.

{ COUNTY OF }
{ RURAL DISTRICT OF }

ELECTION OF { COUNTY }COUNCILLORS.
{ RURAL DISTRICT }

for the above-named { County }in the year 18 .
{ Rural District }

I, the undersigned, being the Returning Officer at the election of { County Councillors }for the said{ County } do
{ Rural District Councillors } { Rural District }
hereby give notice that the persons whose names are entered in column 6 of the Statement hereunder opposite to the numbers entered in column 5 have been declared duly elected { County Councillors }; and I hereby declare that the persons
{ Rural District Councillors }
whose names are entered in the said column 6 [or in column 7],*   * If the Elec-
and opposite to whose names no numbers are entered in column 5,   tion is a first
where no Polls have been taken, were duly elected [or are to be   Election omit
these words and
deemed to be re-elected]* { County Councillors } for the   column 7.
{ Rural District Councillors }

{ County }Electoral Divisions opposite to the names of which in
{ District }
column 1 the names of such candidates are entered.

{ County } { District } Electoral Division.	Names of Candidates		Places of Abode	Number of Votes recorded	Names of Candidates elected	Names of retiring Councillors deemed to be re-elected
	Surnames	Other Names				
	2	3	4	5	6	

Dated this   day of   , 18

Returning Officer.

THIRD SCHEDULE.

PROVISIONS OF THE BALLOT ACT, 1872, AS ADAPTED AND ALTERED
IN THEIR APPLICATION TO THE ELECTION OF COUNTY AND
RURAL DISTRICT COUNCILLORS.

PROCEDURE AT ELECTIONS OF COUNTY AND RURAL DISTRICT
COUNCILLORS.

Poll at Elections.

2. The ballot of each voter shall consist of a paper (in this Act
called a ballot paper) showing the names and description of the
candidates. Each ballot paper shall have a number printed on the
back, and shall have attached a counterfoil with the same number
printed on the face. At the time of voting, the ballot paper shall
be marked on both sides with an official mark, and delivered to the
voter within the polling station, and the number of such voter on
the register of voters shall be marked on the counterfoil, and the
voter having secretly marked his vote on the paper, and folded it
up so as to conceal his vote, shall place it in a closed box in the
presence of the officer presiding at the polling station (in this
Act called "the presiding officer") after having shown to him the
official mark at the back.

If in the register of electors for a County Electoral Division
the same number is placed opposite to the name of more than
one elector, the Returning Officer shall put a distinguishing
mark on each part of the register which contains numbers used
in other parts of the register, and when the number of any voter
on any part of the register is entered on the counterfoil of a
ballot paper, the mark on that part shall also be entered thereon.

Any ballot paper which has not on its back the official mark,
or on which votes are given to more candidates than the voter is
entitled to vote for, or on which anything, except the said number
on the back, is written or marked by which the voter can be
identified, shall be void and not counted.

After the close of the poll the ballot boxes shall be sealed up,
so as to prevent the introduction of additional ballot papers, and
shall be taken charge of by the Returning Officer, and that officer
shall, in the presence of such agents, if any, of the candidates as
may be in attendance, open the ballot boxes, and ascertain the
result of the poll by counting the votes given to each candidate,
and shall forthwith declare to be elected the candidate to whom
the majority of votes have been given. The decision of the
Returning Officer as to any question arising in respect of any
ballot paper shall be final, subject to reversal on petition questioning the election or return.

OFFENCES.

Offences in respect of Ballot Papers and Ballot Boxes.

3. Every person who—

(1.) Forges and counterfeits or fraudulently defaces or fraudulently destroys any ballot paper, or the official mark on any ballot paper ; or

(2.) Without due authority supplies any ballot paper to any person ; or

(3.) Fraudulently puts into any ballot box any paper other than the ballot paper which he is authorised by law to put in ; or

(4.) Fraudulently takes out of the polling station any ballot paper ; or

(5.) Without due authority destroys, takes, opens, or otherwise interferes with any ballot box or packet of ballot papers then in use for the purposes of the election ;

shall be guilty of a misdemeanor, and be liable, if he is a returning officer, or an officer or clerk in attendance at a polling station, to imprisonment for any term not exceeding two years, with or without hard labour, and if he is any other person to imprisonment for any term not exceeding six months, with or without hard labour.

Any attempt to commit any offence specified in this section shall be punishable in the manner in which the offence itself is punishable.

In any indictment or other prosecution for an offence in relation to the ballot boxes, ballot papers, and marking instruments at an election, the property in such papers, boxes, and instruments may be stated to be in the returning officer at such election, as well as the property in the counterfoils.

Infringement of Secrecy.

4. Every officer, clerk, and agent in attendance at a polling station shall maintain and aid in maintaining the secrecy of the voting in such station, and shall not communicate, except for some purpose authorised by law, before the poll is closed, to any person any information as to the name or number on the register of electors of any elector who has or has not applied for a ballot paper or voted at that station, or as to the official mark, and no such officer, clerk or agent, and no person whosoever, shall interfere with or attempt to interfere with a voter when marking his vote, or otherwise attempt to obtain in the polling station information as to the candidate for whom any voter in such station is about to vote or has voted, or communicate at any time to any person any information obtained in a polling station as to the candidate for whom any voter in such station is about to vote or has voted, or as to the number on the back of the ballot paper given to any voter at such station. Every officer,

clerk, agent, and person in attendance at the counting of the votes shall maintain and aid in maintaining the secrecy of the voting, and shall not attempt to ascertain at such counting the number on the back of any ballot paper, or communicate any information obtained at such counting as to the candidate for whom any vote is given in any particular ballot paper. No person shall directly or indirectly induce any voter to display his ballot paper after he shall have marked the same, so as to make known to any person the name of the candidate for or against whom he has so marked his vote.

Every person who acts in contravention of the provisions of this section shall be liable, on summary conviction before two justices of the peace, to imprisonment for any term not exceeding six months, with or without hard labour.

Use of School and Public Room for Poll.

6. The returning officer at an election of $\left\{ \begin{array}{l} County \\ Rural\ District \end{array} \right\}$ Councillors may use free of charge for the purpose of taking poll, hearing objections to nomination papers, and for counting the votes at such election, any room in a school receiving a grant out of moneys provided by Parliament, and any room the expense of maintaining which is payable out of any local rate, but he shall make good any damage done to such room, and defray any expense incurred by the person or body of persons, corporate or unincorporate, having control over the same on account of its being used for the purpose of taking the poll or for counting the votes as aforesaid. This section shall not apply to any school adjoining or adjacent to any church or other place of worship, nor to a school connected with a convent or other religious establishment.

The use of any room in an unoccupied house for taking the poll shall not render any person liable to be rated or to pay any rate for such house.

Duties of Returning and Election Officers.

General Powers and Duties of Returning Officer.

8. Subject to the provisions of this Act, every returning officer shall provide such nomination papers, polling stations, ballot boxes, ballot papers, stamping instruments, copies of register of electors, and other things, appoint and pay such officers, and do such other acts and things as may be necessary for effectually conducting the election.

Every deputy returning officer shall, in so far as he acts as returning officer, be deemed to be included in the term returning officer.

Keeping of Order in Station.

9. If any person misconducts himself in the polling station, or fails to obey the lawful orders of the presiding officer, he may

immediately, by order of the presiding officer, be removed from the polling station by any constable in or near that station, or any other person authorised in writing by the returning officer to remove him ; and the person so removed shall not, unless with the permission of the presiding officer, again be allowed to enter the polling station during the day.

Any person so removed as aforesaid, if charged with the commission in such station of any offence, may be kept in custody until he can be brought before a justice of the peace.

Provided that the powers conferred by this section shall not be exercised so as to prevent any elector who is otherwise entitled to vote at any polling station from having an opportunity of voting at such station.

Powers of Presiding Officer and Administration of Oaths, &c.

10. For the purpose of the adjournment of the poll, a presiding officer shall have the power by law belonging to a deputy returning officer in a parliamentary election ; and any presiding officer and any clerk appointed by the returning officer to attend at a polling station shall have the power of asking the questions and administering the oath authorised by law to be asked of and administered to voters, and any justice of the peace and any returning officer may take and receive any declaration authorised by this Act to be taken before him.

Liability of Officers for Misconduct.

11. Every returning officer, presiding officer, and clerk who is guilty of any wilful misfeasance or any wilful act or omission in contravention of this Act shall, in addition to any other penalty or liability to which he may be subject, forfeit to any person aggrieved by such misfeasance, act, or omission a penal sum not exceeding one hundred pounds.

No returning officer or officer appointed by him in connection with the election of $\left\{ \begin{array}{c} a \ County \ Councillor \ [or \ Councillors] \\ \text{Rural District Councillors} \end{array} \right\}$

for any $\left\{ \begin{array}{c} County \\ District \end{array} \right\}$ Electoral Division, nor any partner or clerk of any such officer, shall act as agent for any candidate in the management or conduct of his election as $\left\{ \begin{array}{c} County \ Councillor \\ \text{Rural District Councillor} \end{array} \right\}$ If any returning officer or officer appointed by him, or the partner or clerk of any such officer, shall so act he shall be guilty of a misdemeanor.

MISCELLANEOUS.

Prohibition of Disclosure of Vote.

12. No person who has voted at an election shall, in any legal proceeding to question the election or return, be required to state for whom he has voted.

Non-compliance with Rules.

13. No election shall be declared invalid by reason of a defect in the title or appointment of the returning officer or deputy returning officer or of a non-compliance with the rules contained in the First Schedule to this Act or in the County and Rural District Councillors (Ireland) Election Order, 1899, or any mistake in the use of the forms in the Second Schedule to this Act or in the said Order, if it appears to the tribunal having cognizance of the question that the election was conducted in accordance with the principles laid down in the body of this Act and in the Local Goverment (Ireland) Act, 1898, and that such non-compliance or mistake did not affect the result of the election.

PERSONATION.

Definition and Punishment of Personation.

24. The following enactments shall be made with respect to personation at an Election of $\left\{\begin{array}{l}County\ Councillors \\ \text{Rural District Councillors}\end{array}\right\}$:

It shall be the duty of the returning officer to institute a prosecution against any person whom he may believe to have been guilty of personation, or of aiding, abetting, counselling, or procuring the commission of the offence of personation by any person, at the election for which he is returning officer, and the costs and expenses of the prosecutor and the witnesses in such case, together with compensation for their trouble and loss of time, shall be allowed by the court in the same manner in which courts are empowered to allow the same in cases of felony.

Sections 93 to 96, both inclusive, of the Representation of the People (Ireland) Act, 1850, shall apply to personation at an election of $\left\{\begin{array}{l}County\ Councillors \\ \text{Rural District Councillors}\end{array}\right\}$ in the same manner as they apply to a person who knowingly personates and falsely assumes to vote in the name of another person as mentioned in the said Act, but with the substitution of the words "any agent appointed under the County and Rural District Councillors (Ireland) Election Order, 1899," for " any such agent so appointed as aforesaid" or for any reference to any such agent, and of " the presiding officer" for "the returning officer or his respective deputy."

EFFECT OF SCHEDULES.

28. The schedules to this Act, and the notes thereto, and directions therein shall be construed and have effect as part of this Act.

SCHEDULES TO ACT.

FIRST SCHEDULE TO ACT.

RULES FOR ELECTIONS OF COUNTY AND RURAL DISTRICT COUNCILLORS.

The Poll.

15. At every polling place the returning officer shall, subject to the provisions of the County and Rural District Councillors (Ireland) Election Order, 1899, provide a sufficient number of polling stations for the accommodation of the electors entitled to vote at such polling place and shall distribute the polling stations amongst those electors in such manner as he thinks most convenient.

17. A separate room or separate booth may contain a separate polling station, or several polling stations may be constructed in the same room or booth.

18. No person shall be admitted to vote at any polling station except the one allotted to him.

20. The returning officer shall provide each polling station with materials for voters to mark the ballot papers, with instruments for stamping thereon the official mark, and with copies of the register of voters, or such part thereof as contains the names of the voters allotted to vote at such station. He shall keep the official mark secret.

21. The presiding officer appointed to preside at each station shall keep order at his station, shall regulate the number of electors to be admitted at a time, and shall exclude all other persons except the clerks, the agents of the candidates, and the constables on duty.

22. Every ballot paper shall contain a list of the candidates described as in their respective nomination papers, and arranged alphabetically in the order of their surnames, and (if there are two or more candidates with the same surname) of their other names ; it shall be in the form set forth in the Second Schedule to this Act or as near thereto as circumstances admit, and shall be capable of being folded up.

23. Every ballot box shall be so constructed that the ballot papers can be introduced therein, but cannot be withdrawn therefrom, without the box being unlocked. The presiding officer at any polling station, just before the commencement of the poll, shall show the ballot box empty to such persons, if any, as may be present in such station, so that they may see that it is empty, and shall then lock it up, and place his seal upon it in such manner as to prevent its being opened without breaking such seal, and shall place it in his view for the receipt of ballot papers, and keep it so locked and sealed.

24. Immediately before a ballot paper is delivered to an elector, it shall be marked on both sides with the official mark either stamped or perforated, and the number, name, and description of the elector as stated in the copy of the register shall be called out, and the number of such elector, together with the distinguishing mark, if any, of the part of the register in which the number occurs, shall, as required by Section 2 of this Act as adapted, be marked on the counterfoil, and a mark shall be placed in the register against the number of the elector, to denote that he has received a ballot paper, but without showing the particular ballot paper which he has received.

25. The elector, on receiving the ballot paper, shall forthwith proceed into one of the compartments in the polling station, and there mark his paper, and fold it up so as to conceal his vote, and shall then put his ballot paper, so folded up, into the ballot box ; he shall vote without undue delay, and shall quit the polling station as soon as he has put his ballot paper into the ballot box.

26. The presiding officer, on the application of any voter who is incapacitated by blindness or other physical cause from voting in manner prescribed by this Act, or (if the poll be taken on Saturday) of any voter who declares that he is of the Jewish persuasion, and objects on religious grounds to vote in manner prescribed by this Act, or of any voter who makes such a declaration as hereinafter mentioned that he is unable to read, shall, in the presence of the agents of the candidates, cause the vote of such voter to be marked on a ballot paper in manner directed by such voter, and the ballot paper to be placed in the ballot box, and the name and number on the register of voters of every voter whose vote is marked in pursuance of this rule, and the reason why it is so marked shall be entered on a list, in this Act called " the list of votes marked by the presiding officer."

The said declaration, in this Act referred to as " the declaration of inability to read," shall be made by the voter at the time of polling, before the presiding officer, who shall attest it in the form hereinafter mentioned, and no fee, stamp, or other payment shall be charged in respect of such declaration, and the said declaration shall be given to the presiding officer at the time of voting.

27. If a person, representing himself to be a particular elector named on the register, applies for a ballot paper after another person has voted as such elector, the applicant shall, upon duly answering the questions permitted by the County Councillors (Ireland) Election Order, 1899, to be asked of voters at the time of polling, and upon taking an oath in the form hereinafter set out, which the presiding officer shall administer, be entitled to mark a ballot paper in the same manner as any other voter, but the ballot paper (in this Act called a tendered ballot paper) shall be of a colour differing from the other ballot papers, and, instead of being put into the ballot box, shall be given to the presiding officer and endorsed by him with the name of the voter and his number in the register of voters,

and set aside in a separate packet, and shall not be counted by the returning officer. And the name of the voter and his number on the register shall be entered on a list, in this Act called "the tendered votes list."

The oath shall be administered in the following form :—

"You do swear that you are the same person whose name appears "as *A.B.* on the Register of Local Government Electors for "the $\left\{{County \atop District}\right\}$ Electoral Division of   , and "that you have not already voted at the present election " for such$\left\{{County \atop District}\right\}$Electoral Division."

"So Help you God."

Provided that any person entitled to affirm in lieu of taking an oath may affirm in the following form :—

" I, *A.B.*, do solemnly, sincerely, and truly declare and affirm that "I am the same person whose name appears as *A.B.* on the "Register of Local Government Electors for the $\left\{{County \atop District}\right\}$ " Electoral Division of   and that I have not "already voted at the present election for such$\left\{{County \atop District}\right\}$ " Electoral Division."

28. A voter who has inadvertently dealt with his ballot paper in such manner that it cannot be conveniently used as a ballot paper, may, on delivering to the presiding officer the ballot paper so inadvertently dealt with and proving the fact of the inadvertence to the satisfaction of the presiding officer, obtain another ballot paper in the place of the ballot paper so delivered up (in this Act called a spoilt ballot paper) and the spoilt ballot paper shall be immediately cancelled.

29. The presiding officer of each station, as soon as practicable after the close of the poll, shall make up into separate packets sealed with his seal,—

(1.) Each ballot box in use at his station, unopened but with the key attached ; and
(2.) The unused and spoilt ballot papers, placed together ; and
(3.) The tendered ballot papers ; and
(4.) The marked copies of the register of electors, and the counterfoils of the ballot papers ; and
(5.) The tendered votes list, and the list of votes marked by the presiding officer, and a statement of the number of the voters whose votes are so marked by the presiding officer under the heads "physical incapacity," "Jews," and "unable to read," and the declarations of inability to read ;

and shall deliver such packets to the returning officer, or deputy returning officer by whom the votes are to be counted, unless he is himself such officer.

30. The packets shall be accompanied by a statement made by such presiding officer, showing the number of ballot papers entrusted to him

and accounting for them under the heads of ballot papers in the ballot box, unused, spoilt, and tendered ballot papers, which statement is in this Act referred to as the ballot paper account.

Counting Votes.

31. Each candidate may appoint an agent to attend the counting of the votes.

32. The returning officer shall make arrangements for counting the votes in the presence of the agents of the candidates as soon as practicable after the close of the poll, and shall give to the agents of the candidates appointed to attend at the counting of the votes notice in writing of the time and place at which he will begin to count the same.

33. The returning officer, his assistants and clerks, the agents of the candidates, and any person to whom Rule 51 of this Schedule applies, and no other person, except with the sanction of the returning officer, may be present at the counting of the votes.

34. Before the returning officer proceeds to count the votes, he shall, in the presence of the agents of the candidates, open each ballot box, and taking out the papers therein, shall count and record the number thereof, and then mix together the whole of the ballot papers contained in the ballot boxes. He shall then proceed to count the votes.

The returning officer, while counting and recording the number of ballot papers and counting the votes, shall keep the ballot papers with their faces upwards, and take all proper precautions for preventing any person from seeing the numbers printed on the backs of such papers.

35. The returning officer shall, so far as practicable, proceed continuously with counting the votes, allowing only time for refreshment, and excluding, if and so far as he thinks it necessary, the hours between the close of the poll and nine o'clock on the succeeding morning. During the excluded time the returning officer shall place the ballot papers and other documents relating to the election under his own seal and the seals of such of the agents of the candidates as desire to affix their seals, and shall otherwise take proper precautions for the security of such papers and documents.

36. The returning officer shall endorse "rejected" on any ballot paper which he may reject as invalid, and shall add to the endorsement "rejection objected to," if an objection be in fact made by any agent to his decision. The returning officer shall draw up a statement showing the number of ballot papers rejected and not counted by him under the several heads of—

1. Want of official mark ;
2. Voting for more candidates than entitled to ;
3. Writing or mark by which voter could be identified ;
4. Unmarked or void for uncertainty ;

and shall on request allow any agents of the candidates to copy such statement. If the votes are counted by a deputy returning officer he shall, with the declaration of the result of the poll, report to the returning officer the number of ballot papers rejected and not counted by him, under the above heads, and no such statement as aforesaid shall be drawn up by the returning officer. The deputy returning officer shall, on request, allow any agents of the candidates, before such report is sent in, to copy it.

37. Upon the completion of the counting, the returning officer shall seal up in separate packets the counted and rejected ballot papers. He shall not open the sealed packet of tendered ballot papers or marked copy of the register of voters and counterfoils, but shall proceed, in the presence of the agents of the candidates, to verify the ballot paper account given by each presiding officer by comparing it with the number of ballot papers recorded by him as aforesaid, and the unused and spoilt ballot papers in his possession and the tendered votes list, and shall reseal each sealed packet after examination. The returning officer shall draw up a statement as to the result of such verification, and shall, on request, allow any agents of the candidates to copy it.

If the votes are counted by a deputy returning officer, he shall report to the returning officer the result of the verification, and no such statement as aforesaid shall be drawn up by the returning officer. The deputy returning officer shall, on request, allow any agents of the candidates, before such report is sent in, to copy it. He shall with his report send to the returning officer the sealed packets of counted and rejected ballot papers, and the unopened sealed packets which he has received from any presiding officer.

38. Lastly, the returning officer shall carefully preserve for the period hereinafter mentioned all the packets of ballot papers in his possession, together with the said reports, the ballot paper accounts, tendered votes list, list of votes marked by the presiding officer, statements relating thereto, declarations of inability to read, and packets of counterfoils, and marked copies of registers, endorsing on each packet a description of its contents and the date of the election to which they relate, and the name of the district for which such election was held.

39. The returning officer shall retain for six months all documents relating to an election of $\left\{\begin{array}{l} County \\ \text{Rural District} \end{array}\right\}$ Councillors, and then, unless otherwise directed by an order of a court having jurisdiction in the matter, or of any tribunal in which the election is questioned, shall cause them to be destroyed.

40. No person shall be allowed to inspect any rejected ballot papers in the custody of the returning officer, except under the order of the court or tribunal aforesaid, to be granted by such court or tribunal on being satisfied by evidence on oath that the inspection or production of such ballot papers is required for the purpose of instituting or maintaining a prosecution for an offence in relation to ballot papers, or for the purpose of a petition questioning an election or return ; and any such order for the inspection or production of ballot papers may be made subject to such conditions as to persons, time, place, and mode of inspection or production as the court or tribunal making the same may think expedient, and shall be obeyed by the returning officer.

41. No person shall, except by order of a court, or of any tribunal having cognizance of any question relating to the elec-

tion, open the sealed packet of counterfoils after the same has been once sealed up, or be allowed to inspect any counted ballot papers in the custody of the returning officer. Such order may be made subject to such conditions as to persons, time, place, and mode of opening or inspection as the court or tribunal making the order may think expedient : Provided that on making and carrying into effect any such order, care shall be taken that the mode in which any particular elector has voted shall not be discovered until he has been proved to have voted, and his vote has been declared by a competent court to be invalid.

42. All documents in the custody of a returning officer in pursuance of this Act, other than ballot papers and counterfoils, shall be open to public inspection at such time and under such regulations as may have been or may hereafter be prescribed by the Council of the County in which the $\left\{\begin{array}{c} County \\ District \end{array}\right\}$ Electoral Division is situate, and the returning officer shall supply copies of or extracts from the said documents to any person demanding the same, on payment of such fees and subject to such regulations as may have been or may hereafter be prescribed by the County Council.

43· Where an order is made for the production by the returning officer of any document in his possession relating to any specified election of $\left\{\begin{array}{c} County \\ Rural District \end{array}\right\}$ Councillors, the production by such officer or his agent of the document ordered, in such manner as may be directed by such order, or by an order of the court having power to make such first-mentioned order, shall be conclusive evidence that such document relates to the specified election; and any endorsement appearing on any packet of ballot papers produced by such returning officer or his agent shall be evidence of such papers being what they are stated to be by the endorsement. The production from proper custody of a ballot paper purporting to have been used at any election, and of a counterfoil marked with the same printed number and having a number marked thereon in writing, shall be primâ facie evidence that the person who voted by such ballot paper was the person who at the time of such election had affixed to his name in the register of voters at such election the same number as the number written on such counterfoil.

General Provisions.

47. If the returning officer presides at any polling station, the provisions of this Act relating to a presiding officer shall apply to such returning officer, with the necessary modifications as to things to be done by the returning officer to the presiding officer, or the presiding officer to the returning officer.

48. The returning officer may, in addition to any clerks, appoint ompetent persons to assist him in counting the votes.

49. No person shall be appointed by a returning officer for the purposes of an election who has been employed by any other person in or about the election.

50. The presiding officer may do, by the clerks appointed to assist him, any act which he is required or authorised to do by this Act at a polling station, except ordering the arrest, exclusion, or ejection from the polling station of any person.

51. A candidate may himself undertake the duties which any agent of his, if appointed under Rule 31 of this Schedule, might have undertaken, and may, if he does not appoint such an agent, be present at the counting of the votes, or may himself take the place of such agent : Provided that any persons acting under this Rule may, at any time before so acting, make the statutory declaration as to secrecy required by Rule 54 of this Schedule, but he shall not so act until he has made such declaration.

52. The name and address of every agent of a candidate appointed to attend the counting of the votes shall be transmitted to the returning officer one clear day at the least before the opening of the poll ; and the returning officer may refuse to admit to the place where the votes are counted any agent whose name and address has not been so transmitted, notwithstanding that his appointment may be otherwise valid, and any notice required to be given to an agent by the returning officer may be delivered at or sent by post to such address.

53. If any person appointed an agent for the purposes of attending a polling station, or at the counting of the votes, dies, or becomes incapable of acting during the time of the election, another agent may be appointed in his place, and notice shall forthwith be given to the returning officer in writing of the name and address of any agent so appointed.

54. Every returning officer, and every officer, clerk, or agent authorised to attend at a polling station, and also every officer, clerk, or agent authorised to attend at the counting of the votes, shall, before the opening of the poll, make a statutory declaration of secrecy, in the presence, if he is the returning officer, of a justice of the peace, and if he is any other officer or an agent, of a justice of the peace or of the returning officer ; but no such returning officer, clerk, or agent as aforesaid shall, save as aforesaid, be required, as such, to make any declaration or take any oath on the occasion of any election.

55. Where in this Act any expressions are used requiring or authorising or inferring that any act or thing is to be done in the presence of the agents of the candidates, such expressions shall be deemed to refer to the presence of such agents of the candidates as may be authorised to attend, and as have in fact attended, at the time and place where such act or thing is being done, and the non-attendance of any agents or agent at such time and place shall not, if such act or thing be otherwise duly done, in anywise invalidate the act or thing done.

SECOND SCHEDULE TO ACT.

Note.—The forms contained in this schedule, or forms as nearly resembling the same as circumstances will admit shall be used in all cases to which they refer and are applicable, and when so used shall be sufficient in law.

FORM OF BALLOT PAPER.

Form of Front of Ballot Paper.

ELECTION OF { COUNTY COUNCILLORS / RURAL DISTRICT COUNCILLORS. }

Counterfoil No

* Women are not eligible as County Councillors.

NOTE—
The counterfoil is to have a number to correspond with that on the back of the Ballot Paper.

1	DOYLE (James Doyle, of 10 High Street, Oilman.)	
2	LYNCH * (Jane Ellen Lynch, of 12 Main Street, Grocer).	*
3	O'BRIEN (John O'Brien, of 22 Wellclose Place, Accountant).	
4	O'CONOR (Charles O'Conor, of 7 Green Street, Gentleman.)	
5	THOMPSON (William Henry Thompson, of 14 Queen street, Silversmith.)	
6	WILSON (Robert Wilson, of 22 Ranelagh Square, Chemist.)	

Form of Back of Ballot Paper.

No.

Election of a { County / Rural District } Councillor for the

{ County / District } Electoral Division.

, 18

Note.—The number on the ballot paper is to correspond with that on the counterfoil.

Directions as to printing Ballot Paper.

Nothing is to be printed on the ballot paper except in accordance with this schedule.

The surname of each candidate, and if there are two or more candidates of the same surname, also the other names of such candidates, shall be printed in large characters, and the names, places of abode, and descriptions, and the number on the back of the paper, shall be printed in small characters.

Form of Directions for the Guidance of the Voter in voting, which shall be printed in conspicuous Characters, and placarded outside every Polling Station and in every Compartment of every Polling Station.

The voter may vote for $\left\{ \begin{array}{c} candidate \\ candidates \end{array} \right\}$ only as $\left\{ \begin{array}{l} County\ Councillor\ [or\ Councillors] \\ \quad Rural\ District\ Councillors. \end{array} \right\}$

The voter will go into one of the compartments, and, with the pencil provided in the compartment, place a cross on the right-hand side, opposite the name of the candidate for whom he votes, thus **X.**

The voter will then fold up the ballot paper so as to show the official mark on the back; and leaving the compartment will, without showing the front of the paper to any person, show the official mark on the back to the presiding officer, and then in the presence of the presiding officer, put the paper into the ballot box and forthwith quit the polling station.

If the voter inadvertently spoils a ballot paper, he can return it to the officer, who will, if satisfied of such inadvertence, give him another paper.

If the voter votes for more than $\left\{ \begin{array}{l} candidate, \\ candidates, \end{array} \right\}$ or places any mark on the paper by which he may be afterwards identified, his ballot paper will be void, and will not be counted.

If the voter takes a ballot paper out of the polling station, or deposits in the ballot box any other paper than the one given him by the officer, he will be guilty of a misdemeanor and be subject to imprisonment for any term not exceeding six months, with or without hard labour.

Note.—These directions shall be illustrated by examples of the ballot paper.

Form of Statutory Declaration of Secrecy.

I solemnly promise and declare, That I will not at this election of $\left\{ \begin{array}{l} a\ County\ Councillor\ [or\ Councillors] \\ \quad Rural\ District\ Councillors. \end{array} \right\}$ for the $\left\{ \begin{array}{l} County \\ District \end{array} \right\}$ Electoral Division of   of do anything forbidden by section four of The Ballot Act, 1872, which has been read to me.

Note.—The section must be read to the declarant by the person taking the declaration.

2 c

Form of Declaration of inability to read.

I, *A.B.*, of   , being numbered   on
the Register of Local Government Electors for the $\left\{\begin{array}{l}County\\District\end{array}\right\}$
Electoral Division of   , do hereby
declare that I am unable to read.

                                        A.B.,   his mark.
            day of   , 18 .

I, the undersigned, being the presiding officer at the
            polling station for the $\left\{\begin{array}{l}County\\District\end{array}\right\}$ Electoral
Division of   do hereby certify that
the above declaration, having been first read to the above-named
A.B., was signed by him in my presence with his mark.

                        Signed, *C.D.*,
            Presiding Officer at   polling
station for the $\left\{\begin{array}{l}County\\District\end{array}\right\}$ Electoral Division of
                        day of   , 18

FOURTH SCHEDULE.

SECTIONS 74 AND 75 OF THE MUNICIPAL CORPORATIONS ACTS,
1882, AS ADAPTED AND ALTERED IN THEIR APPLICATION TO
THE ELECTION OF A COUNTY COUNCILLOR IN A DISTRICT
OTHER THAN A BOROUGH.

Offences in relation to Nomination Papers.

74.—(1.) If any person forges or fraudulently defaces or
fraudulently destroys any nomination paper or delivers to the
Returning Officer any forged nomination paper, knowing it to be
forged, he shall be guilty of a misdemeanor, and shall be liable to
imprisonment for any term not exceeding six months, with or
without hard labour.

(2.) An attempt to commit any such offence shall be punishable as the offence is punishable.

*Neglect of Duty by Returning Officer or Deputy Returning
Officer.*

75.—(1.) If a person who has undertaken to act as
returning officer or deputy returning officer, at an election of
$\left\{\begin{array}{l}County\\Rural District\end{array}\right\}$ Councillors neglects or refuses to conduct or
declare the election in manner provided by the Local Government
(Ireland) Act, 1898, and the County and Rural District Councillors (Ireland) Election Order, 1899, he shall for every such offence
be liable to a fine not exceeding one hundred pounds, recoverable
by action.

(2.) An action under this section shall not lie after three
months from the neglect or refusal.

GENERAL ORDER.

TRANSITORY PROVISIONS for FIRST ELECTIONS under the Local
Government (Ireland) Act, 1898,

OF

COUNTY AND RURAL DISTRICT COUNCILLORS.

WHEREAS by Section 111, sub-section (1) of the Local
Government (Ireland) Act, 1898, it is enacted that the First
Elections under the said Act of County and Rural District
Councillors, shall be held on the twenty-fifth day of March next
after the passing of the said Act, or on such day within fourteen
days before or after that day as the Local Government Board
for Ireland may appoint:

AND WHEREAS by Section 5 of the Schedule to an Order
made the twenty-second day of December, 1898, by His Excellency the Lord Lieutenant in Council, under Section 104 of the
said Local Government (Ireland) Act, it is ordered that the
Election of County and Rural District Councillors shall be conducted in accordance with Rules framed under the said Order
by the Local Government Board for Ireland:

AND WHEREAS, We, the Local Government Board for
Ireland, acting in pursuance of the powers given us by the said
Order in Council have made and issued a General Order for the
regulation of the Ordinary Elections of such County and Rural
District Councillors:

NOW, THEREFORE, We do further order and direct with
respect to the First Elections of such County and Rural District
Councillors as is hereinafter set forth:—

1. The First Elections of County Councillors for every County
Electoral Division, and the First Elections of Rural District
Councillors for every District Electoral Division in Ireland shall
take place on the sixth day of April in the year One Thousand
Eight Hundred and Ninety-nine, and all proceedings relating
to such First Elections shall be taken at or within the times
prescribed in the Table contained in the Schedule to this Order.

2. (1.) The Under-Sheriff of each County provided he signify
to the Local Government Board within Seven days
of the date of this Order that he is willing so to act,
shall be the Returning Officer for the First Election
of County Councillors under the Local Government
(Ireland) Act, 1898, for such County and for every
County Electoral Division of such County.

(2.) Such Under-Sheriff of each County shall also be the Returning Officer for the First Election of Rural District Councillors under the said Act for each Rural District of the County and for each District Electoral Division of every such Rural District.

(3.) Provided that no such Under-Sheriff or other person appointed under any provisions of this Order shall act under Sub-Section (1) of the present Rule who does not also act under Sub-Section (2) of the said Rule, nor shall any Under-Sheriff or other person appointed as aforesaid act under Sub-Section (2) who does not also act under Sub-Section (1).

3. In the case of any County the Under-Sheriff of which has not signified within the time prescribed that he is willing to act as Returning Officer under the foregoing Rule, the Returning Officer shall be a person appointed by the Local Government Board.

4. (1.) In every County Electoral Division comprised by or containing an Urban District, the Returning Officer shall appoint as his Deputy for all purposes relating to the Election of a County Councillor or Councillors for such County Electoral Division if such Urban District is a Borough, the Town Clerk, and if such Urban District is not a Borough the Clerk of the Urban District Council.

(2.) If the office of Town Clerk or Clerk of the Urban District Council is vacant, or if the Town Clerk or Clerk of the Urban District Council is in the opinion of the Local Government Board for Ireland unable to perform the duties of Deputy Returning Officer for all the purposes referred to in Sub-Section (1) of this Rule, or if such Town Clerk or Clerk becomes unable to complete the performance of such duties the Returning Officer shall appoint some other fit and competent person to perform the said duties, or to complete the performance of the said duties, as the case may be.

5. (1.) In every Rural District the Returning Officer shall appoint the Clerk of the Union in which such District is comprised or situated to be his Deputy for the carrying out of Rules 3-10 of the County and Rural District Councillors (Ireland) Election Order, 1899, with respect to the Rural District and every District Electoral Division of such District.

(2.) If the Clerk of the Union is in the opinion of the Local Government Board unable to perform the duties referred to in Sub-Section (1) of this Rule, or if such

Clerk becomes unable to complete the performance of the said duties, or if the office of Clerk is vacant, the Returning Officer shall appoint some other fit person to perform the said duties, or to complete the performance of the said duties, as the case may be.

6. Every Deputy Returning Officer appointed for a County Electoral Division shall be also Deputy Returning Officer in respect of giving notice of arranging for, and declaring the result of the poll or polls, for the Election of Rural District Councillors in every Rural District Electoral Division contained in the said County Electoral Division, in which the Clerk of Union or other person acting as the Deputy of the Returning Officer under Rule 5 of this Order has certified that a poll must be taken in accordance with the provisions of Rule 10, subsection (1) of the above-mentioned County and Rural District Councillors (Ireland) Election Order, 1899.

7. At every first Election of County and Rural District Councillors under the provisions of the Local Government (Ireland) Act, 1898, the poll, if any, shall be open between the hours of 10 a.m. and 8 p.m., provided that in any Urban District forming a separate County Electoral Division the hours during which the poll shall be open shall be from 8 a.m. to 8 p.m.

8. In the case of the First Election of Rural District Councillors for a Rural District the ballot boxes, together with the several other sealed packets referred to in Rule 29 of the First Schedule to the Ballot Act, 1872, as adapted in the Third Schedule to the County and Rural Districts (Ireland) Election Order, 1899, shall be forwarded to the Workhouse of the Union in which the Rural District to which they relate is comprised or situated, or to such other convenient place as the Returning Officer may direct, and the Votes shall be counted at the said Workhouse or at the said other place, as the case may be.

9. Subject, as aforesaid, the County and Rural District Councillors (Ireland) Election Order, 1899, shall apply as if the First Elections were the ordinary Elections therein referred to.

10. This Order may be cited as the " County and Rural District Councillors (Ireland) First Elections Order, 1899."

Sealed with our Seal this Twenty-fifth day of January, in the Year of our Lord One Thousand Eight Hundred and Ninety-nine.

(Signed)   H. A. ROBINSON.
WM. L. MICKS.
T. J. STAFFORD.
R. BAGWELL.

[SCHEDULE.

SCHEDULE.

TIMES FOR THE PROCEEDINGS AT THE FIRST ELECTIONS OF COUNTY AND RURAL DISTRICT COUNCILLORS UNDER THE LOCAL GOVERNMENT (IRELAND) ACT, 1898.

Proceeding.	Time.
1. Notice of Election . .	Not later than February 25.
2. Receipt of Nomination Papers.	Not later than 5 o'clock p.m. on March 6.
3. Sending notice of decision as to validity of Nomination Papers.	As soon as practicable after receipt, but in any case not later than March 8.
4. Making out Statement as to persons nominated.	Not later than March 9.
5. Withdrawal of Candidates	Not later than 5 o'clock p.m. on March 13.
6. Notice of Poll . .	Not later than March 27.
7. Day of Election . .	April 6.

COUNTY OF ROSCOMMON.

COUNTY ELECTORAL DIVISIONS AMENDING ORDER

WHEREAS by Order bearing date the 1st day of November, 1898, We, the Local Government Board for Ireland, did provide and declare, in pursuance of the Local Government (Ireland) Act, 1898, that the several divisions in the administrative County of Roscommon for the election of county Councillors should be the several county electoral divisions defined in Schedule B to that Order:

AND WHEREAS We deem it expedient to vary the said Order in so far as it relates to the number of county electoral divisions of the said administrative county, and to the county electoral divisions named respectively Castleplunket, Elphin, and Roscommon:—

NOW, THEREFORE, We, the Local Government Board for Ireland, do hereby order and declare:

1. That the number of the county electoral divisions of the administrative county of Roscommon shall be increased from twenty to twenty-one:

2. That the said county electoral division of Castleplunket shall consist of the district electoral divisions of Carrow-duff, Castleplunket, Castleteheen, Cloonfinlough, Kil-bride North, Killukin (Strokestown), Ogulla, and Tulsk, in lieu of those mentioned in Schedule B to the said Order of the 1st day of November, 1898:

3. That the said county electoral division of Elphin shall consist of the district electoral divisions of Annaghmore, Cloonyquin, Cregga, Elphin, Lisgarve, and Rossmore, in lieu of those mentioned in Schedule B to the said Order of the 1st day of November, 1898:

4. That the said county electoral division of Roscommon shall consist of the district electoral divisions of Kil-bride South, Mote, Roscommon Rural, and Roscommon Urban, in lieu of those mentioned in Schedule B to the said Order of the 1st day of November, 1898: and

5. That an additional county electoral division to be named the Drumdaff county electoral division shall be constituted, and shall consist of the district electoral divisions of Cloontuskert, Drumdaff, Kilgefin and Kilteevan.

And We do further declare that this Order shall be in force and take effect at such time as may be necessary for the purposes of the first election of county councillors, and shall be read as one with the said Order of the 1st day of November, 1898.

Given under our Hands and Seal of Office, this Thirty-first day of January, in the Year of our Lord One Thousand Eight Hundred and Ninety-nine.

(Signed)   H. A. ROBINSON.
              WILLIAM L. MICKS.
              T. J. STAFFORD.

FIRST ELECTIONS.

ADDITIONAL RURAL DISTRICT COUNCILLORS.

WHEREAS by section 111 (3) (b) of the Local Government (Ireland) Act, 1898, it is provided that the Local Government Board for Ireland, if in the case of the first election they are of opinion that any district electoral division ought to be divided, may allow more than two rural district councillors to be elected for that division:

NOW, THEREFORE, We, the Local Government Board for Ireland, do hereby order that the number of rural district councillors specified in column 4 of the schedule hereunto annexed may at the first election under the aforesaid Act be elected for the district electoral division set out on the same line in column 3 of the said schedule and situated respectively in the relative administrative county and rural district mentioned in columns 1 and 2 of such schedule.

AND We do further declare that this Order shall be in force and take effect at such time as may be necessary for the purposes of the first election of rural district councillors.

SCHEDULE.

Administrative County.	Rural District.	District Electoral Division.	No. of Rural District Councillors to be elected.
1	2	3	4
Cavan ...	Bailieborough ...	Bailieborough ...	3
	Oldcastle No. 2 ...	Virginia ...	3
Cork ...	Clonakilty ...	Rosscarbery ...	3
Donegal ...	Dunfanaghy ...	Crossroads ...	3
	,, ...	Dunfanaghy ...	3
	Glenties ...	Killybegs ...	3
	Milford ...	Rathmelton ...	3
	Stranorlar ...	Convoy ...	3
	,, ...	Stranorlar ...	4
Down ...	Downpatrick ...	Ballynahinch ...	3
	,, ...	Castlewellan ...	3
	,, ...	Killyleagh ...	3
	,, ...	Portaferry ...	3
	Kilkeel ...	Kilkeel ...	3
	Lurgan No. 2 ...	Moira ...	3

Administrative County.	Rural District.	District Electoral Division.	No. of Rural District Councillors to be elected.
1	2	3	4
Dublin ...	Balrothery ...	Garristown ...	3
	,, ...	Lusk ...	3
	,, ...	Swords ...	3
	Dublin South ...	Tallaght ...	3
Galway ...	Galway ...	Inishmore ...	3
Kerry ...	Dingle ...	Dingle ...	3
Kilkenny ...	Castlecomer ...	Castlecomer ...	5
King's ...	Edenderry No. 1 ...	Edenderry ...	3
Longford ...	Ballymahon No. 1 ...	Ballymahon ...	3
	,, ...	Kilglass ...	3
Louth ...	Dundalk ...	Carlingford ...	3
Meath ...	Dunshaughlin ...	Dunboyne ...	3
	Navan ...	Ardbraccan ...	3
Queen's ...	Abbeyleix ...	Abbeyleix ...	3
	Roscrea No. 3 ...	Borris-in-Ossory	3
Tipperary N.R. ...	Nenagh ...	Newport ...	3
	Roscrea No. 1 ...	Roscrea ...	4
Tipperary S.R. ...	Clogheen ...	Caher ...	4
	,, ...	Clogheen ...	3
Tyrone ...	Clogher ...	Augher ...	3
	,, ...	Ballygawley ...	3
	,, ...	Cecil ...	3
	,, ...	Clogher ...	3
	,, ...	Favour Royal ...	3
	,, ...	Fivemiletown ...	3
Wicklow ...	Rathdown No. 2 ...	Delgany ...	4
	,, ...	Powerscourt ...	4

Given under our Hands and Seal of Office this Fourth day of February, in the Year of Our Lord One Thousand Eight Hundred and Ninety-nine.

(Signed),

G. W. BALFOUR.
H. A. ROBINSON.
WM. L. MICKS.
T. J. STAFFORD.
R. BAGWELL.

RURAL DISTRICT COUNCILLORS FOR TOWNS.

WHEREAS by section 23 (3) of the Local Government (Ireland) Act, 1898, it is provided that two councillors shall be elected for each district electoral division in a rural district except where the Local Government Board for Ireland assign more than two councillors to a town or part of a town forming one district electoral division :

NOW, THEREFORE, We, the Local Government Board for Ireland, do hereby order and declare that the number of rural district councillors specified in column 4 of the schedule hereunto annexed shall be assigned to the town, or part of a town, as the case may be, forming the district electoral division set out on the same line in column 3 of the said schedule and situated respectively in the relative administrative county and rural district mentioned in columns 1 and 2 of such schedule.

AND We do further declare that this Order shall be in force and take effect at such time as may be necessary for the purposes of the first election of rural district councillors.

SCHEDULE.

Administrative County.	Rural District.	District Electoral Division.	No. of Rural District Councillors to be elected.
1	2	3	4
Antrim ...	Antrim ...	Antrim Urban ...	4
Cork ...	Macroom ...	Macroom ...	4
	Mallow ...	Mallow N'th Urb	3
	,, ...	Mallow S'th Urb	3
	Midleton ...	Midleton Urban	5
	Skibbereen ...	Skibbereen Urb	4
Down ...	Downpatrick ...	Downpatrick Urb	4
Dublin ...	Balrothery ...	Balbriggan Urb	4
Kildare ...	Athy No. 1 ...	Athy East Urb	2
	,, ...	Athy West Urb	2
	Naas No. 1 ...	Naas Urban ...	4
		Newbridge Urban	3
Kilkenny ...	Callan No. 1 ...	Callan Urban .	5
King's ...	Tullamore No. 1 ...	Tullamore Urban	4

Administrative County.	Rural District.	District Electoral Division.	No. of Rural District Councillors to be elected.
1	2	3	4
Longford ...	Longford ...	Longford No. 1 Urban ...	3
	,, ...	Longford No. 2 Urban	2
Louth ...	Ardee No. 1 ...	Ardee Urban ...	5
Monaghan ...	Carrickmacross ...	Carrickmacross Urban ...	4
Tipperary N.R. ...	Nenagh ...	Nenagh East. Urb	3
	,, ...	Nenagh West Urb	3
Tipperary S.R. ...	Tipperary No. 1 ...	Tipperary East Urban ...	3
	...	Tipperary West Urban ...	3
Tyrone ...	Dungannon ...	Dungannon ...	3
	Omagh ...	Omagh Urban ...	3
	Strabane No. 1 ...	Strabane ...	4
Waterford ...	Lismore ...	Lismore Urban ...	4
Westmeath ...	Mullingar ...	Mullingar North Urban ...	2
	. ...	Mullingar South Urban ...	2
Wexford ...	Gorey ...	Gorey Urban ...	4
Wicklow ...	Rathdrum ...	Arklow No. 1 Urban ...	4
	...	Arklow No. 2 Urban ...	2

Given under our Hands and Seal of Office this Fourth day of February, in the Year of Our Lord One Thousand Eight Hundred and Ninety-nine.

(Signed),

G. W. BALFOUR.
H. A. ROBINSON.
WM. L. MICKS.
T. J. STAFFORD.
R. BAGWELL.

LOCAL GOVERNMENT IN IRELAND.

GUARDIANS FOR COUNTY BOROUGHS AND URBAN COUNTY DISTRICTS.

WHEREAS by section 24 of the Local Government (Ireland) Act, 1898, it is provided that guardians of a poor law union shall be elected for any district electoral division in an urban district, and that where the Local Government Board for Ireland constitute any urban county district, or part thereof, or part of a county borough, a district electoral division, they may assign to that division two or more guardians:

NOW, THEREFORE, We, the Local Government Board for Ireland, do hereby order and declare that the number of poor law guardians specified in column 4 of the schedule hereunto annexed shall be assigned to the district electoral division set out on the same line in column 3 of the said schedule and situated respectively in the relative poor law union and urban county district or county borough mentioned in columns 1 and 2 of such schedule.

AND We do further declare that this Order shall be in force and take effect at such time as may be necessary for the purposes of the first election of poor law guardians.

SCHEDULE.

Name of Union.	Name of Urban County District, or County Borough.	Name of District Electoral Division comprised in Urban County District or County Borough.	No. of Guardians to be elected.
1	2	3	4
Armagh	Armagh	Armagh N'th Urb	2
	,,	,, East Urb	2
	,,	,, S'th Urb	2
Athlone	Athlone	Athlone East Urb	3
	,,	,, West Urb	3
Ballinasloe	Ballinasloe	Ballinasloe Urban	4
Ballymena	Ballymena	Ballymena	4
Ballymoney	Ballymoney	Ballymoney	4
	Portrush	Portrush Urban	3
Banbridge	Banbridge	Banbridge E. Urb	2
	,,	,, W. Urb	3
	Dromore	Dromore Urban	3
	Tanderagee	Tanderagee Urb	2

Name of Union.	Name of Urban County District, or County Borough.	Name of District Electoral Division comprised in Urban County District or County Borough.	No. of Guardians to be elected.
1	2	3	4
Belfast ...	Belfast ...	Clifton ...	2
	,, ...	Court ...	2
	,, ...	Dock ...	2
		... Duncairn	2
		... Falls ...	2
		... Pottinger ...	2
		... Shankill ...	2
		... Smithfield ...	2
		... St. George's ...	2
		... Victoria ...	2
		... Woodvale ...	2
		... Cromac ...	2
		... Ormeau ...	2
	,, ...	Windsor ...	2
	,, ...	St. Anne's ...	2
	Holywood ...	Holywood Urban	2
Carlow ...	Carlow ...	Carlow Urban ...	3
	,, ...	Graigue Urban...	2
Carrick-on-Suir ...	Carrick-on-Suir ...	Carrick-on-Suir Urban ...	4
	,, ...	Carrickbeg Urb	2
Cashel ...	Cashel ...	Cashel Urban	4
Cavan ...	Belturbet ...	Belturbet ...	2
Clonakilty ...	Clonakilty ...	Clonakilty Urban	3
Clones ...	Clones ...	Clones Urban ...	4
Clonmel ..	Clonmel ...	Clonmel E. Urban	6
	,, ...	,, W. ,,	6
Coleraine ...	Coleraine ...	Coleraine ...	8
Cootehill ...	Cootehill ...	Cootehill Urban	2
Cork ...	Cork ..	Cork No. 1 Urb	4
	,, ...	,, 2 Urb	4
	...	,, 3 Urb	4
	...	,, 4 Urb	6
	...	,, 5 Urb	6
	,, ...	,, 6 Urb	4
	,, ...	,, 7 Urb	4
	Queenstown ...	Queenstown Urb	4
Drogheda ...	Drogheda ...	Fair Gate ...	4
	,, ...	St. Lawrence Gate ...	6
	,, ...	West Gate ...	4

Name of Union.	Name of Urban County District, or County Borough.	Name of District Electoral Division comprised in Urban County District or County Borough.	No. of Guardians to be elected.
1	2	3	4
Dublin North ...	Dublin ...	Arran-quay ...	5
	,, ...	Inns-quay ...	5
	...	Mountjoy ...	5
	...	North City ...	5
	,, ...	North Dock ...	5
	,, ...	Rotunda ...	5
	Clontarf ...	Clontarf ...	4
	Drumcondra, Clonliffe, and Glasnevin ...	Drumcondra No. 1 Urban ...	4
	,,	Drumcondra No. 2 Urban ...	2
		Drumcondra No. 3 Urban ...	2
Dublin South ...	Dublin ...	Fitzwilliam ...	4
	,, ...	Mansion House...	4
	...	Merchant's-quay ...	4
	...	Royal Exchange ...	4
	...	South City ...	4
	...	South Dock ...	4
	...	Trinity ...	4
	,, ...	Usher's-quay ...	4
	,, ...	Wood-quay ...	4
	Pembroke ...	Pembroke East ...	5
	,, ...	Pembroke West ...	5
	Rathmines and Rathgar	Rathmines and Rathgar East	5
		Rathmines and Rathgar West	5
	New Kilmainham ...	New Kilmainham	3
Dundalk ...	Dundalk ...	Dundalk No. 1 Urban ...	3
	...	Dundalk No. 2 Urban ...	3
	...	Dundalk No. 3 Urban ...	3
	...	Dundalk No. 4 Urban ...	3
Dungarvan ...	Dungarvan ...	Dungarvan No. 1 Urban ...	5
	...	Dungarvan No. 2 Urban ...	2

Name of Union.	Name of Urban County District, or County Borough.	Name of District Electoral Division comprised in Urban County District or County Borough.	No. of Guardians to be elected.
1	2	3	4
Ennis	... Ennis	... Ennis No. 1 Urb	2
	,,	... ,, 2 Urb	2
	,,	... ,, 3 Urb	2
	,,	... ,, 4 Urb	2
Enniscorthy	... Enniscorthy	... Enniscorthy Urb	4
Enniskillen	... Enniskillen	... Enniskillen Urb	6
Fermoy	... Fermoy	... Fermoy Urban	4
Galway	... Galway	... Galway N. Urb	4
	,,	... ,, E. Urb	4
	,,	... ,, S. Urb	4
	,,	... ,, W. Urb	4
Granard	... Granard	... Granard Urban	2
Kells	... Kells	... Kells Urban ...	4
Kilkenny	... Kilkenny	... Kilkenny No. 1 Urban ...	8
		... Kilkenny No 2 Urban ...	6
Killarney	... Killarney	... Killarney Urban	5
Kilrush	... Kilrush	... Kilrush Urban ...	3
Kinsale	... Kinsale	... Kinsale Urban ...	6
Larne	... Larne	... Larne ...	6
	Carrickfergus	... Carrickfergus Urb	5
Letterkenny	... Letterkenny	... Letterkenny Urb	4
Limavady	... Limavady	... Limavady ...	2
Limerick	... Limerick	... Limerick No. 1 Urban ...	2
		... Limerick No. 2 Urban ...	2
		... Limerick No. 3 Urban ...	2
		... Limerick No. 4 Urban ...	2
		... Limerick No. 5 Urban ...	2
		... Limerick No. 6 Urban ...	2
		... Limerick No. 7 Urban ...	2
		... Limerick No. 8 Urban ...	2

Name of Union.	Name of Urban County District, or County Borough.	Name of District Electoral Division comprised in Urban County District or County Borough.	No. of Guardians to be elected.
1	2	3	4
Lisburn	Lisburn ...	Lisburn ...	8
Listowel	Listowel ...	Listowel Urban	3
Londonderry	Londonderry ...	Londonderry No. 1 Urban ...	3
		... Londonderry No. 2 Urban ...	3
		... Londonderry No. 3 Urban ...	3
		... Londonderry No. 4 Urban ...	3
		... Londonderry No. 5 Urban ...	3
.Lurgan	Lurgan ...	Lurgan Urban ...	6
	Portadown	Portadown Urb	4
Monaghan	Monaghan ...	Monaghan Urb	4
Navan	Navan ...	Navan Urban ...	6
New Ross	New Ross ...	New Ross Urb	6
	,,	Rosbercon Urb	2
Newry	Newry ...	Newry N. Urb	3
	,,	,, S. Urb	3
	,,	,, W. Urb	3
	Warrenpoint	Warrenpoint Urb	2
Newtownards	Newtownards ..	N'wtownards Urb	5
	Bangor	Bangor Urban ...	6
Parsonstown	Parsonstown ...	Parsonstown Urb	4
Rathdown	Blackrock ...	Blackrock No. 1	2
	,,	,, 2	4
	,,	,, 3	2
	Bray	Bray No. 1 ...	2
	,,	,, 2 ...	2
	,,	,, 3 ...	3
	Dalkey	Dalkey ...	2
	Killiney and Ballybrack	Killiney ...	2
	Kingstown	Kingstown No. 1	2
	,,	,, 2	4
	,,	,, 3	6
	,,	,, 4	4
Rathdrum	Wicklow ...	Wicklow Urban	3
Sligo	Sligo ...	Sligo North ...	4
	,,	,, East ...	4
	,,	,, West ...	4

Name of Union.	Name of Urban County District, or County Borough.	Name of District Electoral Division comprised in Urban County District or County Borough.	No. of Guard-ians to be elected.
1	2	3	4
Thurles ...	Thurles	... Thurles Urban	6
	Templemore	... Templemore ...	3
Tralee ...	Tralee	... Tralee Urban ...	6
Trim ...	Trim	... Trim Urban ...	3
Waterford ...	Waterford	... Waterford No. 1 Urban ...	3
		... Waterford No. 2 Urban ...	3
		... Waterford No. 3 Urban ...	3
		... Waterford No. 4 Urban ...	3
	,,	... Waterford No. 5 Urban ...	3
Wexford ...	Wexford	... Wexford No. 1 Urban ...	3
		... Wexford No. 2 Urban ...	3
		... Wexford No. 3 Urban ...	3
Youghal ...	Youghal	... Youghal Urban	8

Given under our Hands and Seal of Office this Fourth day of February, in the Year of Our Lord One Thousand Eight Hundred and Ninety-nine.

(Signed),

G. W. BALFOUR.
H. A. ROBINSON.
WM. L. MICKS.
T. J. STAFFORD.
R. BAGWELL.

GENERAL ORDER.

GUARDIANS IN URBAN DISTRICTS.
Rules as to Nomination and Election.

WHEREAS by an Order made the twenty-second day of December, 1898, by the Lord Lieutenant-General and General Governor of Ireland, by and with the advice and consent of Her Majesty's Privy Council in Ireland, in pursuance of the Local Government (Ireland) Act, 1898, Section 104, it is ordered that the election of Guardians in Urban Districts shall, subject to the provisions of the said Act be conducted according to Rules framed under the said Order by the Local Government Board for Ireland, and that the Rules so framed should notwithstanding any other Act, provide for the matters mentioned in the said Order.

Now, We, the Local Government Board for Ireland, do hereby order that, subject to any directions which may be given by us and until we otherwise order, the following Rules shall be observed in connection with the election of Guardians in Urban Districts in Ireland as hereinafter set forth, that is to say—

(a) The ordinary election to fill ordinary vacancies.

(b) The first election of Guardians for any Urban District which may hereafter be constituted.

Returning Officer.

1. (1.) The Town Clerk of the Borough, or in Urban Districts which are not Boroughs, the Clerk to the Urban District Council shall be the Returning Officer.

(2.) If the office of Town Clerk or Clerk is vacant at the time when any duty relative to the Election has to be performed by the Returning Officer, or if the Town Clerk or Clerk from illness or other sufficient cause is unable to perform such duty, or fails to do so, the Council of the Borough or other Urban District shall appoint some other person to act as Returning Officer, or to perform such of the duties of the Returning Officer as then remain to be performed, as the case may be.

(3.) The Returning Officer shall appoint some place within the Borough or other Urban District as an Ofhee for the purpose of the Election.

(4.) The Returning Officer may, in writing, appoint a fit person to be his deputy for all or any of the purposes relating to the Election of any Guardian or Guardians for a District Electoral Division. A Deputy Returning Officer shall have all the powers, duties, and liabilities of the Returning Officer in relation to the matters in respect of which he is appointed as deputy.

Day of Election.

2. The day of election of Guardians in any Urban District shall be that prescribed by Section 24 (b) of the Local Government (Ireland) Act, 1898, and fixed by the County Council in accordance with Section 94 (7) of the said Act, 1898.

Notice of Election.

3. (The same as Rule 3 of the Order regulating the election of County and District Councillors, except that mention of County and District Councillors and divisions is omitted).

Nomination of Candidates.

4. (1.) Each candidate for election as Guardian in an Urban District shall be nominated in writing.

(2.) The nomination paper shall state the name of the District Electoral Division for which the candidate is nominated, the surname and other name or names in full, the place of abode, and description of the candidate, who must be qualified as a Local Government elector for the Urban District, or by having during the whole of the twelve months preceding the election resided and continuing to reside in such Urban District. It shall be signed by two Local Government electors of the District Electoral Division as proposer and seconder, and no more, and shall state their respective places of abode. It shall be in the form set out in the Notice in the Form No. 1 in the Second Schedule to this Order, or in a form to the like effect.

(3.) The name of more than one candidate shall not be inserted in any one nomination paper.

(4.) A Local Government elector shall not sign more nomination papers than there are Guardians to be elected for the District Electoral Division for which the election is to be held, nor shall he sign a nomination paper for the District Electoral Division unless he is registered as a Local Government elector in respect of a qualification therein. Neither shall he sign nomination papers for more than one District Electoral Division in the same Union, nor shall he sign any nomination paper at an Election of Guardians if he has already signed one or more at an Election of Rural District Councillors for any District Electoral Division in the same Union.

(5.) If any Local Government elector shall sign nomination papers for more than one District Electoral Division in the Urban District, or shall sign a number of nomination papers larger than the number of Guardians to be elected for the District Electoral Division, such of the nomination papers signed by him as relate to the first District Electoral Division for which a nomination paper signed by him is received by the Returning Officer shall alone be valid, and of the nomination papers signed by him which relate to such District Electoral Division such as are first received by the Returning Officer up to the number of Guardians to be elected, shall alone be valid. Provided that for the purposes of this paragraph nomination papers not properly filled up and signed shall be excluded.

Nomination Papers to be provided.

5. The Returning Officer shall provide nomination papers. Any Local Government Elector may obtain nomination papers from the Returning Officer free of charge.

Time for sending in Nomination Papers.

6. Every nomination paper shall be sent to the Returning Officer so that it shall be received at his Office within the time prescribed for that purpose by the First Schedule to this Order. A nomination paper received after that time shall not be valid. The Returning Officer shall note on each nomination paper whether it was received before or after that time.

Dealing with Nominations by Returning Officer.

7. (The same as Rule 7 of County and Rural District Council Elections, except that there is no mention made of the Deputy of the Returning Officer).

Statement as to Persons nominated.

8. Not later than the day prescribed for that purpose by the First Schedule to this Order, the Returning Officer shall make out a statement in the Form No. 2 in the Second Schedule to this Order, or in a form to the like effect, containing the names, places of abode, and descriptions of the persons nominated for election to the office of Guardian for the several District Electoral Divisions of the Urban District for which the election is to be held, and also containing a notice of his decision as regards each candidate as to whether he has been nominated

by a valid nomination paper or not. He shall forthwith cause copies thereof to be suspended in the Town Hall or Room in which the meetings of the Council are held, and in the Board Room of the Guardians of the Union, and another to be affixed on the principal external gate or door of the Town Hall or other offices of the Council of the Borough or District, and on that of the Workhouse of the Union.

Withdrawal of Candidate.

9. Any candidate may withdraw his candidature by delivering or causing to be delivered at the office of the Returning Officer within the time prescribed for that purpose by the First Schedule to this Order, a notice in writing of such withdrawal, signed by him.

Relation of Nomination to Election.

10. (The same as Rule 10 of County and Rural District Council Election Rules, *mutatis mutandis*).

Day and Hours of Poll.

11. The poll, if any, shall be held on the day of election as prescribed by Section 24 (*b*) of the Local Government (Ireland) Act, 1898, and fixed by the County Council in accordance with Section 94 (7) of the said Act, and the hours during which the poll shall be open shall be such as shall be fixed by the County Council by any general or special order, or if no such order is in force in the District then such hours as were applicable at the last ordinary election of Guardians so, however, that the poll shall always be open between the hours of six and eight in the evening.

12. If a poll is to be taken for the election of a County Councillor or Councillors for the County Electoral Division in which any District Electoral Division is situated, and also for the election of a Guardian or Guardians for such District Electoral Division the polls for both elections shall be taken together, unless this is impracticable.

13. The Returning Officer shall determine the number and situation of the polling places and stations.
Provided as follows:—

(*a*) No premises licensed for the sale of intoxicating liquor shall be used for a polling station.

(*b*) The polling stations for the election of Guardians and County Councillors in any District Electoral Division when the polls for the two elections are taken together shall be the same.

(c) Where the number of Local Government Electors in a District Electoral Division is not more than five hundred, only one polling station shall, unless the Council otherwise direct, be provided for such District Electoral Division; and so on for each additional five hundred Local Government Electors, or for any number of Local Government Electors over and above the last five hundred.

(d) The foregoing provision shall not be deemed to make it obligatory on the Returning Officer to provide a separate polling station for each five hundred Local Government Electors in the District Electoral Division.

Notice of Poll.

14. (The same as Rule 14 of County and Rural District Election Rules, *mutatis mutandis*, and with the addition of "the number of Guardians to be elected," to the particulars to be given in the notice of the poll).

Presiding Officers.

15. The Returning Officer, or some person appointed by him for the purpose, shall preside at each polling station. The person presiding at any polling station shall be called the Presiding Officer. Provided that at any polling station the same person shall act as Presiding Officer for the Election of a County Councillor or Councillors and for that of Guardians when the polls for the two elections are taken together.

Compartments of Polling Stations—Ballot Papers.

16. (Same as Rule 16 of County and Rural District Election Rules).

Polling Agents.

17. (The same as Rule 17 of County and Rural District Election Rules).

Prohibition against Voting in more than one District Electoral Division—Questions to Elector

18. (1.) A Local Government Elector shall not be permitted to vote in more than one District Electoral Division of a Union for the members, whether Rural District Councillors or Guardians, of the Board of Guardians of that Union.

(2.) The Presiding Officer may, and if required by any polling agent appointed under Rule 17, shall, put to any elector at the time of his applying for a ballot paper, but not after-wards, the following questions, or one of them, and no other :—

    (*a*) Are you the person entered in the Local Government Register for this District Electoral Division as follows (read the whole entry from the Register)?

    (*b*) Have you already voted at the present election of Guardians in this Urban District of
or at the Election of Rural District Councillors or Guardians in any other District Electoral Division of the   Union?

(3.) The same as Rule 18 (3) of County and Rural District Election Rules).

Counting the Votes.

19. (1.) If the Returning Officer appoints a person to act as Deputy Returning Officer for the District Electoral Division as regards the custody and opening of the ballot boxes, the counting and recording of the votes, and the declaration of the number of votes given for each candidate, and of the election of the candidate or candidates to whom the largest number of votes has been given, the person so appointed shall, in addition to his other powers and duties, have all the powers and duties of the Returning Officer in relation to the matters aforesaid, and to the decision of any questions as to any ballot paper and otherwise as to the ballot papers. Provided that, in the case of a Borough or other Urban District comprising more than one District Electoral Division, the Returning Officer shall in every District Electoral Division in which he does not himself preside at a polling station appoint some one of the Presiding Officers to act as Deputy Returning Officer for such District Electoral Division.

(2.) The votes shall be counted in the District Electoral Division for which the election is held, or in some place near thereto as soon as practicable after the close of the poll.

Equality of Votes.

20. (Same as Rule 21 of County and Rural District Election Rules).

Declaration of Result of Poll.

21. (Same as Rule 22 of County and Rural District Council Elections).

Publication of Result of Elections.

22. (1.) The Returning Officer shall prepare and sign a notice of the result of the election in all the District Electoral Divisions for which he acts as Returning Officer, and shall by such notice declare to be elected or to be deemed to be re-elected the persons who, under Rule 10, are to be declared to be elected or to be deemed to be re-elected without a poll being taken. The Notice shall be in the Form No. 8 in the Second Schedule to this Order, or in a form to the like effect.

(2.) The Returning Officer shall cause copies of the notice to be suspended in the Town Hall or room in which the meetings of the Council are held, and in the Board Room of the Guardians of the Union, and another copy to be affixed to the principal external gate or door of the Town Hall or other offices of the Council, and another to the principal external gate or door of the Workhouse of the Union, and he shall also cause public notice thereof to be given in accordance with Rule 30 of this Order. The Returning Officer shall also send copies to the persons elected or deemed to be re-elected.

Application and Adaptation of Ballot Act, 1872.

23. The provisions of the Ballot Act, 1872, which, with adaptations and alterations, are set out in the Third Schedule to this Order, and only such provisions of that Act shall, subject to such adaptations and alterations, apply to the election of all Guardians in Urban Districts.

Provided as follows:—

(a) Such application shall be subject to the provisions of this Order.

(b) The ballot papers used at the election of a County Councillor or Councillors shall be of a different colour from that of any ballot papers used in the election of any Guardians for the District Electoral Division when the polls for both elections are taken together.

(c) Whether the polls for both elections are taken together or not, the ballot papers for the election of a County Councillor or Councillors shall be of the colour fixed by the Returning Officer for the Election of County Councillors, under Rule 24 (d) of the County Rural District Councillors (Ireland) Election Order, 1899; and the ballot boxes shall be painted to correspond with the colour of the ballot papers for the reception of which each ballot box is provided.

Adaptation of Municipal Corporations Act, 1882.

24. (The same, *mutatis mutandis,* as Rule 25 of County and Rural District Election Rules).

Adaptation of Municipal Elections (Corrupt and Illegal Practices) Act, 1884.

25. (The same, *mutatis mutandis,* as Rule 26 of County and Rural District Election Rules).

26. (The same as Rule 27 of County and Rural District Election Rules).

Casual Vacancies.

27. Casual vacancies in the office of Guardian for an Urban District shall be filled by the Board in accordance with Section 94 (5) of the Local Government (Ireland) Act, 1898, and every person so chosen to fill a casual vacancy shall hold office until the time when the person in whose place he has been chosen would regularly have gone out of office.

Non-acceptance of Office.

28. Non-acceptance of office by a person elected or deemed to be re-elected, shall in every case create a casual vacancy.

Expenses.

29. (1.) Any sum which may be payable to the Returning Officer in respect of his services in taking a poll in the District Electoral Division, or in respect of expenses incurred in relation to such poll, shall be defrayed by the Council of the Borough or other Urban District out of the Borough or District Fund.

(2.) Any other sum which may be payable to the Returning Officer in respect of his services in the conduct of the election shall, in like manner, be defrayed by the Council of the Borough or other Urban District.

Publication of Notices.

30. (Same as Rule 30 of County and Rural District Election Rules).

Mark instead of Signature.

31. (Same as Rule 31 of County and Rural District Election Rules).

Misnomer.—Inaccurate Descriptions.

32. (Same as Rule 32 of County and Rural District Election Rules).

Definition of " Ordinary Election."

33. The expression " ordinary election " means the triennial election of Guardians in Urban Districts, and includes any first election of Guardians for any Urban District which may hereafter be constituted.

This Order may be cited as the " Guardians (Ireland) Election Order, 1899."

> Sealed with our Seal this Seventh day of February, in the Year of our Lord One Thousand Eight Hundred and Ninety-nine.
>
> (Signed),
>
> H. A. ROBINSON.
> WM. L. MICKS.
> T. J. STAFFORD.
> R. BAGWELL.

[The Schedules are the same, *mutatis mutandis*, as those attached to the County and Rural District Election Rules.

The Oath to be tendered, when required, to voters in the polling booths is to be administered in the following form:—

> " You do swear that you are the same person whose name
> " appears as *A.B.* on the Register of   ,
> " and that you have not already voted at the present
> " Election of Guardians or at the Election of Rural Dis-
> " trict Councillors or Guardians in this or any other Dis-
> " trict Electoral Division in the   Union.
>
> " SO HELP YOU GOD."

Provided that any person entitled to affirm in lieu of taking an oath may affirm in the following form:—

> " I, *A.B.*, do solemnly, sincerely, and truly declare and affirm
> " that I am the same person whose name appears as *A.B.*
> " on the Register of Electors for the District Electoral
> " Division of   , and that I have not
> " already voted at the present Election of Guardians, or
> " at the Election of Rural District Councillors or Guar-
> " dians, in this or any other Electoral Division in the
> "   Union."

The declaration of secrecy to be made by the Returning Officer may be made at one and the same time, in respect of all the District Electoral Divisions, for which he is Returning Officer.]

GENERAL ORDER.

TRANSITORY PROVISIONS FOR FIRST ELECTIONS UNDER THE LOCAL GOVERNMENT (IRELAND) ACT, 1898,

OF

GUARDIANS IN URBAN DISTRICTS.

WHEREAS by Section 24, Sub-Section (*b*) of the Local Government (Ireland) Act, 1898, it is enacted that in an Urban District the Guardians for any District Electoral Division therein shall be elected by the Local Government Electors for that Division, subject to the like provisions in the like manner and at the like time as District Councillors for a Rural District :

AND WHEREAS by Section 5 of the Schedule to an Order, made the twenty-second day of December, 1898, by His Excellency the Lord Lieutenant in Council, under Section 104 of the said Local Government (Ireland) Act, it is ordered that the Election of Guardians in Boroughs and Urban County Districts shall, subject to the provisions of the Act, be conducted according to rules framed under the above-cited Order by the Local Government Board for Ireland :

AND WHEREAS We, the said Local Government Board for Ireland, acting in pursuance of the powers given us by the said Order, have made and issued General Orders regulating the procedure to be followed at the First Election of Rural District Councillors under the said Local Government (Ireland) Act, 1898, and also a General Order regulating in like manner the procedure to be followed at the ordinary Election of Guardians in Urban Districts :

AND WHEREAS We, the said Local Government Board for Ireland, acting in pursuance of powers given to us by Section 111, Sub-Section (1) of the said Local Government (Ireland) Act, 1898, did, by Section 1 of the County and Rural District Councillors (Ireland) First Elections Order, 1899, being one of the General Orders above mentioned, direct that the First Election of Rural District Councillors in every County of Ireland should take place on the sixth day of April, in the year One Thousand Eight Hundred and Ninety-nine, and by the same Order did also fix certain dates for the various proceedings required by said General Orders to be taken :

NOW, THEREFORE, We do further order and direct with respect to the First Election of Guardians in Urban Districts as is hereinafter set forth—

1. The First Election of Guardians in Boroughs and other Urban Districts for every District Electoral Division contained in or comprised by any such Borough or other Urban District shall take place on the sixth day of April, in the year One Thousand Eight Hundred and Ninety-nine, and all proceedings relating to such First Election shall be taken at or within the times prescribed in the Table contained in the Schedule to this Order.

2. (1.) If the Town Clerk of any Borough or the Clerk to the Council of any Urban District other than a Borough is either unwilling, or, in the opinion of the Local Government Board, unable to perform the duties of Returning Officer under Rule 1 of the Guardians (Ireland) Election Order, 1899, or if the office of Town Clerk or Clerk to the Urban District Council is vacant, the Returning Officer shall be a person appointed by the Local Government Board.

(2.) If the Town Clerk, Clerk, or other person appointed under Sub-Section (1) of this Rule becomes for any reason unable to perform or complete the performance of any of the said duties, the Local Government Board shall appoint some other person to perform or complete the performance of the said duties as the case may require.

3. At every First Election of Guardians in Boroughs and other Urban Districts under the provisions of the Local Government (Ireland) Act, 1898, the Poll, if any, shall be open between the hours of 8 a.m. and 8 p.m.

4. Subject as aforesaid, the Guardians (Ireland) Election Order, 1899, shall apply as if the First Elections were the ordinary Elections therein referred to.

5. This Order may be cited as the GUARDIANS (IRELAND) FIRST ELECTIONS ORDER, 1899.

[SCHEDULE

SCHEDULE.

TIMES FOR THE PROCEEDINGS AT THE FIRST ELECTIONS OF
GUARDIANS IN URBAN DISTRICTS UNDER THE LOCAL
GOVERNMENT (IRELAND) ACT, 1898.

Proceeding.	Time.
1. Notice of Election, ...	Not later than February 25. ... ...
2. Receipt of Nomination Papers, ...	Not later than 5 o'clock p.m. on March 6.
3. Sending notice of decision as to validity of Nomination Papers.	As soon as practicable after receipt, but in any case not later than March 8.
4. Making out Statement as to persons nominated	Not later than March 9.
5. Withdrawal of Candidates, ...	Not later than 5 o'clock p.m. on March 13.
6. Notice of Poll, ...	Not later than March 27.
7. Day of Election, ...	April 6.

Sealed with our Seal this Seventh day of February, in the
Year of our Lord One Thousand Eight Hundred and
Ninety-nine.

(Signed),

H. A. ROBINSON.
WM. L. MICKS.
T. J. STAFFORD.
R. BAGWELL.

PAWNBROKERS' LICENCE DUTY.

In exercise of the power given to Us by the Local Government (Ireland) Act, 1898, section 124, We, the Local Government Board for Ireland, hereby order and appoint that the provisions of section 67 of the said Act shall come into operation on the 1st March, 1899.

Given under our Hands and Seal of Office, this Twenty-third day of January, in the Year of Our Lord One Thousand Eight Hundred and Ninety-nine.

(Signed),

H. A. ROBINSON.
WM. L. MICKS.
T. J. STAFFORD.

GENERAL ORDER, No. 2.

COUNTY AND RURAL DISTRICT COUNCILLORS.
Rules as to Nomination and Election.

To the County Council of every Administrative County in Ireland, and to the Clerk of every such Council.

To the District Council of every Rural District in Ireland and to the Clerk of every such Council, and to all others whom it may concern.

WHEREAS, by an Order made the Twenty-second day of December, 1898, by the Lord Lieutenant-General and General Governor of Ireland, in pursuance of the Local Government (Ireland) Act, 1898, sec. 104, it is amongst other things ordered that the election of County and Rural District Councils in Ireland shall, subject to the provisions of the Act, be conducted according to rules framed under the said Order by the Local Government Board for Ireland, and that the rules provide for the matters and things in the said Order mentioned:

AND WHEREAS We, the said Local Government Board for Ireland, did, on the Twenty-fifth day of January, 1899, make and issue a General Order entitled "The County and

Rural District Councillors (Ireland) Election Order, 1899,"
regulating the procédure to be followed with respect to the
nomination and election of County and Rural District Councillors in Ireland:

AND WHEREAS We did, by the above-mentioned General
Order, direct that the same should remain in force until we
should otherwise order:

AND WHEREAS We do now deem it expedient that the
said General Order should be modified in certain particulars:.

NOW, THEREFORE, We, acting in further pursuance of
the above-cited Order in Council, do hereby order and direct
that, notwithstanding anything to the .contrary in the said
General Order contained, subject to any directions that may be
given by Us, and until We otherwise order, the following rules
shall be observed in connection with the election of County and
Rural District Councillors in Ireland:—

Returning Officer.

1. (1.) (Same as corresponding Rule in original Order).
(2.) (Same as corresponding Rule in original Order).
(3.) (Same as corresponding Rule in original Order).
(4.) Same as corresponding Rule in original Order, with the
following addition:—"Provided that where the Workhouse
of the Union in which such Rural District is situated is within
an Urban District in the same county, such Workhouse may
be used as an office for the election of Rural District Councillors
for the Rural District."
(5.) (Same as corresponding Rule in original Order).
(6.) (Same as corresponding Rule in original Order).
(7.) Where a Union extends into two or more counties, the
Returning Officer in any such county other than that in which
the Workhouse of the said Union is situated may, if he thinks
fit, appoint some person to act as Assistant Deputy to the Clerk
of the Council of the Rural District formed by the part of the
Union situate within the said County, for the purpose of carrying out any or all of the duties referred to in Sub-section (5)
of this Rule in respect of the said Rural District.
(8.) (Same as corresponding Rule in original Order).

Day of Election.

2. The day of Election of County and Rural District Councillors shall be that fixed for the purpose by the County Council
in accordance with the provisions of Section 94 (7) of the Local
Government (Ireland) Act, 1898.

Notice of Election.

3. (Same as corresponding Rule in original Order).

Nomination of Candidates.

4. (1.) (Same as corresponding Rule in original Order).

(2.) The nomination paper shall state the name of the County Electoral Division or District Electoral Division for which the candidate is nominated, the surname and other name or names in full, the place of abode, and description of the candidate, who must be qualified as a Local Government Elector for the County or for the Rural District, as the case may be, or, in the case of a candidate for the office of Rural District Councillor, by having, during the whole of the twelve months preceding the Election, resided, and continuing to reside in the Rural District. It shall be signed in the case of a candidate for the offiee of County Councillor by two Local Government Electors of the County Electoral Division, and in the case of a candidate for the ofhee of Rural District Councillor by two Local Government Electors of the District Electoral Division, as proposer and seconder, and no more, and shall state their respective places of abode. It should be in the form set out in the notice in Form No. 1 in the Second Schedule to this Order, or in a form to the like effect.

(3.) (Same as corresponding Rule in original Order).

(4.) Same as corresponding Rule in original Order, with the following addition:—"Neither shall he sign nomination papers for more than one County Electoral Division in the same County, or for more than one District Electoral Division in the same Union, whether the Election for such District Electoral Division be of Guardians or of Rural District Councillors."

(5.) (Same as corresponding Rule in original Order).

Nomination Papers to be provided.

5. (Same as corresponding Rule in original Order).

Time for sending in Nomination Papers.

6. (Same as corresponding Rule in original Order).

Dealing with Nominations by Returning Officer.

7. (Same as corresponding Rule in original Order).

Statement as to Persons nominated.

8. (Same as corresponding Rule in original Order).

Withdrawal of Candidate.

9. (Same as corresponding Rule in original Order).

2 E

Relation of Nomination to Election.

10. (Same as corresponding Rule in original Order).

Day and Hours of Poll.

11. (Same as corresponding Rule in original Order).

12. Whenever polls have to be taken both for the election of Rural District Councillors, or in an Urban District of Guardians, for a District Electoral Division, and for that of a County Councillor or Councillors, for the County Electoral Division in which such District Electoral Division is situated, these polls for these elections shall be taken together.

13. Same as corresponding Rule in original Order, except as follows :—

> "(*b*) The polling stations for the election of County and Rural District Councillors or, in an Urban District for the election of County Councillors and Guardians in any District Electoral Division when the polls for the two elections are taken together, shall be the same."

Notice of Poll.

14. (Same as corresponding Rule in original Order).

Presiding Officers.

15. (1.) The Returning Officer, or some person appointed by him for the purpose, shall preside at each polling station, save only that at any polling station in an Urban District at which polls are taken together for the election of a County Councillor or Councillors and for that of Guardians a person appointed by the Returning Officer or Guardians shall preside at both Elections. The person presiding at any polling station shall be called the Presiding Officer.

(2.) At a polling station in a Rural District the same person shall act as Presiding Officer for the Election of a County Councillor or Councillors and for that of Rural District Councillors when the polls for the two Elections are taken together.

Compartments of Polling Stations—Ballot Papers.

16. (Same as corresponding Rule in original Order).

Polling Agents.

17. Polling Agents, either paid or unpaid, may be appointed subject to the following conditions :—

> (1.) Where there is only one polling station in the same room or booth, each candidate may appoint one polling agent and no more for such polling station.

(2.) Where more than one polling station is constructed in the same room or booth each candidate may appoint one polling agent and no more for such room or booth.

Except as aforesaid no polling or personation agent, whether paid or unpaid, shall be appointed for the purposes of the election.

Prohibition of Voting in more than one County or District Electoral Division—Questions to Elector.

18. (1.) A Local Government Elector shall not in the case of an Election of County Councillors vote in more than one County Electoral Division in the County, nor in the case of an Election of Rural District Councillors in more than one District Electoral Division in the Rural District; and he shall not vote at any Election of Rural District Councillors for a Rural District if he has already voted at an Election of Guardians in any District Electoral Division in the same Union.

(2.) The Presiding Officer may, and if required by any polling agent appointed under Rule 17, shall, put to any Elector at the time of his applying for a ballot paper, but not afterwards one or more of the following questions, and no other:—

(*a*) Are you the person entered in the register for this County [or District] Electoral Division as follows (read the whole entry from the register)?

(*b*) Have you already voted at the present election of County Councillors in this or any other County Electoral Division of the County?

(*c*) Have you already voted at the present Election of Rural District Councillors in this or any other District Electoral Division of the Rural District or at any Election of Guardians or Rural District Councillors in any District Electoral Division in the Union of

(3.) A person required to answer any one or more of these questions shall not receive a ballot paper or be permitted to vote until he has answered it, in the manner and to the effect prescribed in Rule 27 of the First Schedule to the Ballot Act, 1872, as adapted and printed in the Third Schedule to this Order, notwithstanding the fact that no person has already voted as therein mentioned.

Forwarding of Ballot Boxes, &c., after the Poll.

19. (Same as corresponding Rule in original Order).

Counting the Votes.

20. (Same as corresponding Rule in original Order).

Equality of Votes.

21. (Same as corresponding Rule in original Order).

Declaration of Result of Poll.

22. (Same as corresponding Rule in original Order).

Publication of Result of Elections

23. Same as corresponding Rule in original Order, with the following addition to sub-rule (2): " The Returning Officer shall also cause copies of each Notice to be suspended in the Room in which the meetings of the County Council, or Rural District Council, as the case may be, are respectively held, and shall cause public notice to be given thereof in accordance with Rule 30 of this Order. He shall also send copies of the Notice to the persons elected or deemed to be re-elected."

Application and Adaptation of Ballot Act, 1872.

24. Same as corresponding Rule in original Order, with the following addition to sub-rule (a): " Where more than one polling station is constructed in the same room or booth the same person may act as Presiding Officer, for all or any number of such polling stations."

Adaptation of Municipal Corporations Act, 1882.

25. Same as corresponding Rule in original Order, with the following alteration, sub-rule (1) (b): " County or District Fund " shall be deemed to be substituted for " Borough Fund or Borough Rate."

Adaptation of Municipal Elections (Corrupt and Illegal Practices) Act, 1884.

26. Same as corresponding Rule in original Order, with the following:

"(2.) The expressions " County Electoral Division or District Electoral Division," and " County or District Fund," shall be deemed to be substituted in the Act for " Borough," or " Municipal Borough," " Borough or Ward," or " Borough or Ward of a Borough," and " Borough Fund or Rate," respectively."

"(3.) And " Burgess List " shall mean a list of Local Government Electors."

"(5.) The duties imposed upon the Town Clerk by section 24 of the Act shall be performed by some person appointed for that purpose by the County Council."

27. (Same as corresponding Rule in original Order).

Non-acceptance of Office.

28. (Same as corresponding Rule in original Order).

Expenses.

29. (Same as corresponding Rule in original Order).

Publication of Notices.

30. (Same as corresponding Rule in original Order).

Mark instead of Signature.

31. In place of any signature required by this Order it shall be sufficient for the signatory to affix his mark if the same is witnessed by two Local Government Electors.

Misnomer—Inaccurate Descriptions.

32. (Same as corresponding Rule in original Order).

Definition of "Election."

33. In this Order the expression "Election" means the triennial election of County and Rural District Councillors.

34. This Order may be cited as the "COUNTY AND RURAL DISTRICT COUNCILLORS (IRELAND) No. 2. ELECTION ORDER, 1899."

Sealed with our Seal this Sixteenth day of February, in the Year of Our Lord, One Thousand Eight Hundred and Ninety-nine.

(Signed),

G. W. BALFOUR.
H. A. ROBINSON.
WM. L. MICKS.
T. J. STAFFORD.

SCHEDULES

TO

COUNTY AND RURAL DISTRICT COUNCILLORS (IRELAND) ELECTION ORDER, 1899.

(The same as in original Order with the following alterations). See pages 353 to 378.

In Rule 27 of Rules for taking the poll :—

The oath shall be administered in the following form :—

> "You do swear that you are the same person whose name
> "appears as *A.B.* on the Register of Local Government
> "Electors for the $\left\{\begin{array}{l} County \\ District \end{array}\right\}$ Electoral Division of
> "   , and that you have not already voted at the
> "present election of $\left\{\begin{array}{l} County \\ Rural\ District \end{array}\right\}$ Councillors for the
> "$\left\{\begin{array}{l} County \\ Rural\ District \end{array}\right\}$ of   , in this or any other
> "$\left\{\begin{array}{l} County \\ District \end{array}\right\}$ Electoral Division of the said $\left\{\begin{array}{l} County \\ Rural\ District \end{array}\right\}$
> "of   , and that you have not already voted at
> "an Election either of Rural District Councillors or Guard-
> "ians in any other District Electoral Division of the Union
> "of   .
>
> "SO HELP YOU GOD."

Provided that any person entitled to affirm in lieu of taking an oath may affirm in the following form :—

> "I, *A.B.*, do solemnly, sincerely, and truly declare and affirm
> "that I am the same person whose name appears as *A.B.*,
> "on the Register of Local Government Electors for the
> "$\left\{\begin{array}{l} County \\ District \end{array}\right\}$ Electoral Division of   , and
> "that I have not already voted at the present election of
> "$\left\{\begin{array}{l} County \\ Rural\ District \end{array}\right\}$ Councillors for the $\left\{\begin{array}{l} County \\ Rural\ District \end{array}\right\}$ of
> "   , in this or any other $\left\{\begin{array}{l} County \\ District \end{array}\right\}$ Electoral
> "Division of the said $\left\{\begin{array}{l} County \\ Rural\ District \end{array}\right\}$ of   ,
> "and that I have not already voted at an Election either of
> "Rural District Councillors or Guardians in any other
> "District Electoral Division of the Union of   ."

FOURTH SCHEDULE.

Corresponding heading in original Order, altered as follows :

"SECTIONS 74 AND 75 OF THE MUNICIPAL CORPORATIONS
ACT, 1882, AS ADAPTED AND ALTERED IN THEIR APPLICA-
TION TO THE ELECTION OF COUNTY AND RURAL DISTRICT
COUNCILLORS IN IRELAND."

EXISTING OFFICERS, URBAN DISTRICT COUNCILS, AND TOWN COMMISSIONERS.

In exercise of the power given to Us by the Local Government (Ireland) Act, 1898, section 124, We, the Local Government Board for Ireland, hereby order and appoint that the provisions of sections 115 to 119, inclusive, of the said Act so far as they relate to all existing Officers of Municipal Corporations, Urban District Councils and Town Commissioners shall come into operation on this date.

Given under our Hands and Seal of Office, this Twenty-first day of February, in the Year of Our Lord· One Thousand Eight Hundred and Ninety-nine.

(Signed),

G. W. BALFOUR.
H. A. ROBINSON.
T. J. STAFFORD.
R. BAGWELL.

GUARDIANS FOR COUNTY BOROUGHS AND URBAN COUNTY DISTRICTS.

AMENDING ORDER—URBAN DISTRICT OF BRAY.

WHEREAS by section 24 of the Local Government (Ireland) Act, 1898, it is provided that guardians of a poor law union shall be elected for any district electoral division in an urban district, and that where the Local Government Board for Ireland constitute any urban county district, or part thereof, or part of a county borough, a district electoral division, they may assign to that division two or more guardians:

AND WHEREAS We, the Local Government Board for Ireland, did by Order dated the 4th day of February, 1899, assign a certain number of guardians to each district electoral division comprised in an urban district:

AND WHEREAS We deem it expedient to vary the said Order in so far as it relates to the district electoral divisions named respectively Bray No. 2 and Bray No· 3 situated in the urban district of Bray, and poor law union of Rathdown:

NOW, THEREFORE, We, the Local Government Board
for Ireland, do hereby order and declare:—

    1. That the number of poor law guardians assigned to the
district electoral division of Bray No. 2 shall be three,
in lieu of the number mentioned in the schedule to
the said Order of the 4th day of February, 1899: and

    2. That the number of poor law guardians assigned to the
district electoral division of Bray No. 3 shall be two,
in lieu of the number mentioned in the schedule to
the said Order of the 4th day of February, 1899,

And we do further declare that this Order shall be in force
and take effect at such time as may be necessary for the purposes of the first election of poor law guardians, and shall be
read as one with the said Order of the 4th day of February,
1899.

    Given under our Hands and Seal of Office this Twenty-
second day of February, in the year of Our Lord One
Thousand Eight Hundred and Ninety-nine.

    (Signed),

                H. A. ROBINSON.
                T. J. STAFFORD.

GENERAL ORDER.

Transitory Provisions (No. 2) for First Elections under the
Local Government (Ireland) Act, 1898, of County and
Rural District Councillors.

    WHEREAS We, the Local Government Board for Ireland,
did, on the twenty-fifth day of January, 1899, in virtue of
powers given to Us by Section 111, Sub-section (1), of the
Local Government (Ireland) Act, 1898, and by Section 5 of
the Schedule to an Order in Council made the twenty-second
day of December, 1898, by His Excellency the Lord Lieutenant
in Council, make and issue a General Order entitled the County
and Rural District Councillors (Ireland) First Elections Order,
1899:

    AND WHEREAS We do now deem it expedient to supple-
ment the said General Order in some particulars:

NOW, THEREFORE, We, in further pursuance of the powers given to Us by the said Act and Order in Council, do hereby order and direct with respect to the First Elections of County and Rural District Councillors in Ireland as is hereinafter set forth :—

1. If any doubt arises as to the person entitled as Under-Sheriff to act as Returning Officer, the Returning Officer shall be a person appointed by the Local Government Board.

2. In any County Electoral Division containing, but not co-extensive with, an Urban District or Districts, the Returning Officer may, if in his judgment such a course is necessary for the proper conduct of the Election of County and Rural District Councillors within such County Electoral Division, appoint a person in addition to any Town Clerk or Clerk of an Urban District Council to be his Deputy therein, and he shall apportion between any such Town Clerk or Clerk and the person so appointed the various duties imposed by any Order of the Local Government Board upon a Deputy Returning Officer for a County Electoral Division.

3. Where a Union extends into two or more Counties the Returning Officer in any such County other than that in which the Workhouse of the said Union is situated may, if he thinks fit, appoint some person to act as Assistant Deputy to the Clerk of Union in the Rural District formed by the part of the Union within the said County for the purpose of carrying out Rules 3—10 of the County and Rural District Councillors (Ireland), (No. 2) Election Order, 1899.

4. Where a County Electoral Division does not contain, or is not comprised by an Urban District, but includes ten or more than ten District Electoral Divisions, the Returning Officer may, if in his judgment such a course is necessary for the proper conduct of the election of County and Rural District Councillors within such County Electoral Division, appoint two persons as his Deputies therein, and may apportion between them the various duties connected with the Elections in respect of which they are appointed as Deputies.

5. Where the County Court House or Sheriff's Office of any administrative County is situated within a County Borough, such Court House or Office shall be deemed for the purposes of these rules to be within such administrative County.

6. The Notices of the result of the Elections referred to in Rule 23 of the County and Rural District Councillors (Ireland), (No. 2) Election Order, 1899, shall be sent, in the case of an Election of County Councillors to the Local Government Board, and in the case of an Election of Rural District Councillors to the Clerk of the Union in which the Rural District for which the Election has been held is situated.

7. References contained in the County and Rural District Councillors (Ireland) First Elections Order, 1899, to the County and Rural District Councillors (Ireland) Election Order, 1899, shall be construed as referring to the County and Rural District Councillors (Ireland), (No. 2) Election Order, 1899.

8. Subject as aforesaid, the County and Rural District Councillors (Ireland) First Elections Order, 1899, shall apply to all such First Elections, and the County and Rural District Councillors (Ireland), (No. 2) Election Order, 1899, shall apply as if the First Elections were the Elections therein referred to.

9. This Order may be cited as the "County and Rural District Councillors (Ireland) (No. 2) First Elections Order, 1899."

Sealed with our Seal this Twenty-second day of February, in the Year of Our Lord One Thousand Eight Hundred and Ninety-nine.

(Signed),

H. A. ROBINSON.
T. J. STAFFORD.
R. BAGWELL.

RURAL DISTRICT COUNCILLORS FOR TOWNS.

TOWN OF BANDON.

WHEREAS by section 23 (3) of the Local Government (Ireland) Act, 1898, it is provided that two councillors shall be elected for each district electoral division in a rural district except where the Local Government Board for Ireland assign more than two councillors to a town or part of a town forming one district electoral division:

NOW, THEREFORE, We, the Local Government Board for Ireland, do hereby order and declare that the number of rural district councillors specified in column 4 of the schedule hereunto annexed shall be assigned to the town forming the district electoral division set out in column 3 of the said schedule and situated respectively in the administrative county and rural district mentioned in columns 1 and 2 of such schedule.

AND We do further declare that this Order shall be in force and take effect at such time as may be necessary for the purposes of the first election of rural district councillors.

SCHEDULE.

Administrative County. 1	Rural District. 2	District Electoral Division. 3	Number of Rural District Councillors to be elected. 4
Cork ...	Bandon ...	Bandon ...	3

Given under our Hands and Seal of Office this Twenty-third day of February, in the Year of Our Lord One Thousand Eight Hundred and Ninety-nine.

(Signed),

H. A. ROBINSON.

T. J. STAFFORD.

R. BAGWELL.

APPENDIX IV.

ALTERATIONS OF BOUNDARIES SÚMMARISED.

THE FOLLOWING STATEMENT SHOWS:—

  I.—Alterations in County Boundaries.

  II.—Alterations in Union Boundaries.

  III.—Adjustment of Urban Districts previously situated in two Counties.

  IV.—Alterations in each County altered with List of County Districts in such County.

  V.—Alterations in Electoral Divisions.

I.—ALTERATIONS IN COUNTIES.

PROVINCE OF CONNAUGHT:—

Electoral Divisions of Owenbrin and Ballinchalla in Ballinrobe Union and County Galway transferred to County Mayo.

Electoral Division of Rosmoylan in Roscommon Union and County Galway transferred to County Roscommon.

Electoral Divisions of Drummaan, Inishcaltra North and Mountshannon in Scariff Union and County Galway transferred to County Clare.

Electoral Divisions of Ballaghaderreen and Edmondstown in Castlerea Union and County Mayo transferred to County Roscommon.

Electoral Divisions of Ardnaree North, Ardnaree South Rural, and Ardnaree South Urban in Ballina Union and County Sligo transferred to County Mayo.

PROVINCE OF LEINSTER:—

Electoral Division of Kilculliheen in Waterford Union and County Waterford transferred to County Kilkenny.

PROVINCE OF MUNSTER:—

Electoral Divisions of Drumaan, Inishcaltra North and Mountshannon transferred to County Clare. (*See* under Province of Connaught.)

Electoral Division of Kilculliheen transferred from County Waterford. (*See* under Province of Leinster.)

II.—ALTERATIONS IN UNION BOUNDARIES.

ARMAGH UNION—
Electoral Division of Caledon in County Tyrone transferred to Dungannon Union.

BAILIEBOROUGH UNION—
(*See* under Kells Union.)

BALLYMONEY UNION—
Electoral Divisions of Hervey Hill, Kilrea, Tamlaght, and The Grove in County Londonderry transferred to Coleraine Union. (*See* also under Coleraine Union.)

BALROTHERY UNION—
(*See* under Dunshaughlin Union.)

BALTINGLASS UNION—
(*See* under Shillelagh Union.)

BELFAST UNION—
(*See* under Lisburn Union.)

CARLOW UNION—
(*See* under Baltinglass Union and Enniscorthy Union.)

CARRICKMACROSS UNION—
(*See* under Dundalk Union.)

CASTLEBLAYNEY UNION—
(*See* under Dundalk Union.)

CELBRIDGE UNION—
Electoral Division of Rodanstown in County Meath transferred to Dunshaughlin Union.

CLOGHER UNION—·
Electoral Divisions of Bragan, Derrygorry, and Shanmullagh in County Monaghan transferred to Monaghan Union.

COLRAINE UNION—
Electoral Divisions of Beardiville, Bushmills, and Portrush in County Antrim transferred to Ballymoney Union. (*See* also under Ballymoney Union.)

DUNDALK UNION—·
Electoral Division of Lower Creggan in County Armagh transferred to Castleblaney Union.
Electoral Division of Inishkeen in County Monaghan transferred to Carrickmacross Union.

DUNGANNON UNION—
(*See* under Armagh Union.)

DUNSHAUGHLIN UNION—
Electoral Division of Garristown in County Dublin transferred to Balrothery Union.
(*See* also under Celbridge Union.)

ENNISCORTHY UNION—
Electoral Division of Cranemore in County Carlow transferred to Carlow Union.
(*See* also under Shillelagh Union.)

ENNISKILLEN UNION—
Electoral Division of Kilskerry in County Tyrone transferred to Irvinestown Union.

IRVINESTOWN UNION—
(*See* under Enniskillen Union.)

KELLS UNION—
Electoral Division of Mullagh in County Cavan transferred to Bailieborough Union.

LISBURN UNION—
Electoral Divisions of Malone East Urban and Malone West Urban (County Antrim), and Breda Urban (County Down) in the Lisburn Union transferred to Belfast Union.

MONAGHAN UNION—
(*See* under Clogher Union.)

ROSCREA UNION—
(*See* under Urlingford Union.)

SHILLELAGH UNION—
town in County Carlow transferred to Baltinglass
Union.
Electoral Division of Clonegall in County Carlow transferred
to Carlow Union.
Electoral Division of Moyacomb in County Wexford trans-
ferred to Enniscorthy Union.
Electoral Divisions of Clonmore, Hacketstown and Harolds-

URLINGFORD UNION—
Electoral Division of Kyle South in Queen's County transferred to Roscrea Union.

III.—ADJUSTMENT OF URBAN DISTRICTS.

TOWNS.

Portion of Athlone in Co. Roscommon added to Co. Westmeath.
    ,,   Ballinasloe in Co. Roscommon   ,,   Co. Galway.
    ,,   Bray in Co. Dublin   ,,   Co. Wicklow.
    ,,   Carlow in Queen's Co.   ,,   Co. Carlow.
    ,,   Carrick-on-Suir in Co. Waterford,,   Co. Tipperary
    ,,   Clonmel in Co. Waterford   ,,   Co. Tipperary.
    ,,   Drogheda in Co. Meath   ,,   Co. Louth.
    ,,   Lisburn in Co. Down   ,,   Co. Antrim.
    ,,   New Ross in Co. Kilkenny   ,,   Co. Wexford.
    ,,   Newry in Co. Armagh   ,,   Co. Down.

IV.—ALTERATIONS IN EACH COUNTY ALTERED WITH LIST OF COUNTY DISTRICTS IN SUCH COUNTY.

PROVINCE OF CONNAUGHT.

GALWAY COUNTY—
Electoral Divisions of Owenbrin and Ballinchalla trans-
ferred to County Mayo.
Electoral Division of Rosmoylan transferred to County
Roscommon.
Electoral Divisions of Drummaan, Inishcaltra North and
Mountshannon transferred to County Clare.
Portion of Urban Sanitary District of Ballinasloe in the
County Roscommon added to County Galway.

Unions—unchanged.

The Rural Districts are:—

Ballinasloe No 1 (being that portion of Ballinasloe Union situated in County Galway less Urban Sanitary District of Ballinasloe).

Clifden (Union).

Galway (being Galway Union less Urban Sanitary District of Galway).

Glennamaddy (Union).

Gort (Union).

Loughrea (Union).

Mount Bellew (Union).

Oughterard (Union).

Portumna (Union).

Tuam (Union).

Urban Districts are:—

Ballinasloe (in Union of Ballinasloe).

Galway (in Union of Galway).

LEITRIM COUNTY—

County—unchanged.

Unions—unchanged.

Rural Districts are:—

Ballyshannon No. 3 (being that portion of Balyshannon Union in County Leitrim).

Bawnboy No. 2 (being that portion of Bawnboy Union in County Leitrim).

Carrick-on-Shannon No 1 (being that portion of Carrick-on-Shannon Union in County Leitrim).

Manorhamilton (Union).

Mohill (Union).

Urban Districts.—None.

MAYO COUNTY—

Electoral Divisions of Owenbrin and Ballinchalla transferred to County Mayo from County Galway.

Electoral Divisions of Ardnaree North, Ardnaree South Rural, and Ardnaree South Urban transferred to County Mayo from County Sligo.

Electoral Divisions of Ballaghaderreen and Edmondstown transferred from County Mayo to County Roscommon.

Unions—unchanged

Rural Districts are :—

Ballina (Union).
Ballinrobe (Union).
Belmullet (Union).
Castlebar (Union).
Claremorris (Union).
Killala (Union).
Swineford (Union).
Westport (Union).

Urban Districts.—None.

ROSCOMMON COUNTY—

Electoral Divisions of Ballaghaderreen and Edmondstown transferred to County Roscommon from County Mayo.

Electoral Division of Rosmoylan transferred to County Roscommon from County Galway.

That portion of Urban Sanitary District of Ballinasloe in County Roscommon transferred from County Roscommon to County Galway.

That portion of Urban Sanitary District of Athlone in County Roscommon transferred from County Roscommon to County Westmeath.

Unions—unchanged.

Rural Districts are :—

Athlone No. 2 (being that portion of Athlone Union in County Roscommon).

Ballinasloe No. 2 (being that portion of Ballinasloe Union in County Roscommon).

Boyle No 1 (being that portion of Boyle Union in County Roscommon).

Carrick-on-Shannon No. 2 (being that portion of Carrick-on-Shannon Union in County Roscommon).

Castlerea (Union).
Roscommon (Union).
Strokestown (Union).

Urban Districts.—None.

SLIGO COUNTY—

Electoral Divisions of Ardnaree North, Ardnaree South Rural, and Ardnaree South Urban transferred from County Sligo to County Mayo.

Unions—unchanged.

2 F

Rural Districts are:—

Boyle No. 2 (being that portion of Boyle Union in County
Sligo).
Dromore West (Union).
Sligo (being Sligo Union less Urban Sanitary District of
Sligo).
Tobercurry (Union).

Urban District:—
Sligo (in Union of Sligo).

PROVINCE OF LEINSTER.

CARLOW COUNTY—

Portion of Urban Sanitary District of Carlow in Queen's
County added to County Carlow.

Unions altered:—

Electoral Divisions of Clonmore, Hacketstown, and Haroldstown, in County Carlow, transferred to Baltinglass Union from Union of Shillelagh.
Electoral Division of Clonegall in County Carlow transferred to Carlow Union from Shillelagh Union.
Electoral Division of Cranemore in County Carlow transferred to Carlow Union from Enniscorthy Union.

Rural Districts are:—

Baltinglass No. 2 (being that portion of Baltinglass Union
in County Carlow).
Carlow No. 1 (being that portion of Carlow Union in
County Carlow less Urban Sanitary District of
Carlow).
New Ross No 3 (being that portion of New Ross Union in
County Carlow).

Urban District:—
Carlow (in Union of Carlow).

DUBLIN COUNTY—

Portion of the Urban Sanitary District of Bray in County
Dublin added to County Wicklow.
City of Dublin, a County Borough.

Union altered:—

Electoral Division of Garristown in County Dublin transferred to Balrothery Union from Union of Dunshaughlin.

Rural Districts are:—

Balrothery (Union).
Celbridge No. 2 (being that portion of Celbridge Union in County Dublin).
Dublin North (being the Union of Dublin North less the portion of the County Borough of Dublin situated therein and the Urban Sanitary Districts of Clontarf and Drumcondra).
Dublin South (being the Union of Dublin South less the portion of the County Borough of Dublin situated therein and the Urban Sanitary Districts of New Kilmainham, Pembroke, and Rathmines and Rathgar).
Rathdown No. 1 (being that portion of the Union of Rathdown less the Urban Sanitary Districts of Blackrock, Dalkey, Killiney and Ballybrack, and Kingstown, in County Dublin).

Urban Districts are:—

Blackrock (in Union of Rathdown).
Clontarf (in Union of North Dublin).
Dalkey (in Union of Rathdown).
Drumcondra, Clonliffe, and Glasnevin (in Union of North Dublin).
Killiney and Ballybrack (in Union of Rathdown).
Kingstown (in Union of Rathdown).
New Kilmainham (in Union of South Dublin).
Pembroke (in Union of South Dublin).
Rathmines and Rathgar (in Union of South Dublin).

KILDARE COUNTY—

County—unchanged.

Union altered:—

Electoral Division of Rodanstown in County Meath transferred from Celbridge Union to Union of Dunshaughlin.

Rural Districts are: —

Athy No 1 (being that portion of Athy Union in County Kildare).
Baltinglass No. 3 (being that portion of Baltinglass Union in County Kildare).
Celbridge No. 1 (being that portion of Celbridge Union in County Kildare).
Edenderry No. 2 (being that portion of Edenderry Union in County Kildare).
Naas No. 1 (being that portion of Naas Union in County Kildare).

Urban Districts.—None.

KILKENNY COUNTY— ،

Portion of Urban Sanitary District of New Ross in County Kilkenny added to County Wexford.
Electoral Division of Kilculliheen in County Waterford added to County Kilkenny.

Union altered: - -

Electoral Division of Kyle South in Queen's County transferred from Urlingford Union to Union of Roscrea.

Rural Districts are: —

Callan No. 1 (being that portion of Callan Union in County Kilkenny).
Carrick-on-Suir No. 3 (being that portion of Carrick-on-Suir Union in County Kilkenny).
Castlecomer (Union).
Kilkenny (being Kilkenny Union less Urban Sanitary District of Kilkenny).
New Ross No 2 (being that portion of New Ross Union in County Kilkenny).
Thomastown (Union).
Urlingford No. 1 (being that portion of Urlingford Union in County Kilkenny).
Waterford No. 2 (being that portion of Waterford Union in County Kilkenny).

Urban District: —

Kilkenny (in Union of Kilkenny).

KING'S COUNTY—

County—unchanged.

Unions—unchanged. (*See* County Kilkenny and Queen's County as to change in Roscrea Union.)

Rural Districts are:—
Edenderry No 1 (being that portion of Edenderry Union in King's County).
Mountmelick No. 2 (being that portion of Mountmelick Union in King's County).
Parsonstown No. 1 (being that portion of Parsonstown Union in King's County, less Urban Sanitary District of Parsonstown).
Roscrea No. 2 (being that portion of Roscrea Union in King's County).
Tullamore No. 1 (being that portion of Tullamore Union in King's County).

Urban District:—
Parsonstown (in Union of Parsonstown).

LONGFORD COUNTY—

County—unchanged.

Unions—unchanged.

Rural Districts are:—
Ballymahon No. 1 (being that portion of Ballymahon Union in County Longford).
Granard No. 1 (being that portion of Granard Union in County Longford less Urban Sanitary District of Granard).
Longford (Union).

Urban District:—
Granard (in Union of Granard).

LOUTH COUNTY—

Portion of the Urban Sanitary District of Drogheda in County Meath added to County Louth.

Unions altered : —

Electoral Division of Lower Creggan in County Armagh transferred from Dundalk Union to Union of Castleblayney.

Electoral Division of Inishkeen in County Monaghan transferred from Dundalk Union to Union of Carrickmacross.

Rural Districts are : —

Ardee No. 1 (being that portion of Ardee Union in County Louth).

Drogheda No. 1 (being that portion of Drogheda Union less Urban Sanitary District of Drogheda in County Louth).

Dundalk (being Dundalk Union less Urban Sanitary District of Dundalk).

Urban Districts are : —

Drogheda (in Drogheda Union).
Dundalk (in Dundalk Union).

MEATH COUNTY—

Portion of Urban Sanitary District of Drogheda in County Meath added to County Louth.

Unions altered —:

Electoral Division of Garristown in County Dublin transferred from Dunshaughlin Union to Union of Balrothery.

Electoral Division of Rodanstown in County Meath transferred to Dunshaughlin Union from Union of Celbridge.

Electoral Division of Mullagh in County Cavan transferred to Bailieborough Union from Union of Kells.

Rural Districts are : —

Ardee No. 2 (being that portion of Ardee Union in County Meath).

Drogheda No. 2 (being that portion of Drogheda Union in County Meath).

Dunshaughlin (Union).

Edenderry No. 3 (being that portion of Edenderry Union in County Meath).

Kells (being Kells Union less Urban Sanitary District of Kells).

Navan (being Navan Union less Urban Sanitary District of Navan).

Oldcastle No. 1 (being that portion of Oldcastle Union in County Meath).

Trim (being Trim Union less Urban Sanitary District of Trim).

Urban Districts are:—

Kells (in Union of Kells).

Navan (in Union of Navan).

Trim (in Union of Trim).

QUEEN'S COUNTY—

Portion of Urban Sanitary District of Carlow in Queen's County added to County Carlow.

Union altered: —

Electoral Division of Kyle South in Queen's County transferred to Roscrea Union from Union of Urlingford.

Rural Districts are:—

Abbeyleix (Union).

Athy No. 2 (being that portion of Athy Union in Queen's County).

Carlow No. 2 (being that portion of Carlow Union in Union in Queen's County).

Mountmelick No. 1 (being that portion of Mountmelick Union in Queen's County).

Roscrea No. 3 (being that portion of Roscrea Union in Queen's County).

Urban Districts.—None.

WESTMEATH COUNTY—

Portion of Urban Sanitary District of Athlone in County Roscommon added to County Westmeath.

Unions—unchanged.

Rural Districts are:—

Athlone No. 1 (being that portion of Athlone Union less Urban Sanitary District of Athlone in County Westmeath).

Ballymahon No. 2 (being that portion of Ballymahon
    Union in County Westmeath).
Delvin (Union).
Granard No. 3 (being that portion of Granard Union in
    County Westmeath).
Mullingar (Union).
Tullamore No. 2 (being that portion of Tullamore Union
    in County Westmeath).

Urban District: —

Athlone (in Union of Athlone).

WEXFORD COUNTY—

Portion of Urban Sanitary District of New Ross in County
    Kilkenny added to County Wexford.

Unions altered: —

Electoral Division of Moyacomb in County Wexford trans-
    ferred to Enniscorthy Union from Union of Shil-
    lelagh.
Electoral Division of Cranemore in County Carlow trans-
    ferred from Enniscorthy Union to Union of Carlow.

Rural Districts are: —

Enniscorthy (being Enniscorthy Union less Urban Sani-
    tary District of Enniscorthy).
Gorey (Union).
New Ross No. 1 (being that portion of New Ross Union
    in County Wexford less Urban Sanitary District
    of New Ross).
Wexford (being Wexford Union less Urban Sanitary Dis-
    trict of Wexford).

Urban Districts are: —

Enniscorthy (in Union of Enniscorthy).
New Ross (in Union of New Ross).
Wexford (in Union of Wexford).

WICKLOW COUNTY—

Portion of Urban Sanitary District of Bray in County
    Dublin added to County Wicklow.

Unions altered:—

Electoral Divisions of Clonmore, Hacketstown, and Haroldstown in County Carlow transferred to Baltinglass Union from Shillelagh Union.

Electoral Division of Clonegall in County Carlow transferred from Shillelagh Union to Union of Carlow.

Electoral Division of Moyacomb in County Wexford transferred from Shillelagh Union to Union of Enniscorthy.

Rural Districts are:—

Baltinglass No. 1 (being that portion of Baltinglass Union in County Wicklow).

Naas No. 2 (being that portion of Naas Union in County Wicklow).

Rathdown No. 2 (being that portion of Rathdown Union in County Wicklow less Urban Sanitary District of Bray).

Rathdrum (being Rathdrum Union less Urban Sanitary District of Wicklow).

Shillelagh (Union).

Urban Districts are:—
Bray (in Union of Rathdown).
Wicklow (in Union of Rathdrum).

PROVINCE OF MUNSTER.

CLARE COUNTY—

Electoral Divisions of Drummaan, Inishcaltra North and Mountshannon in County Galway added to County Clare.

Unions—unchanged.

Rural Districts are:—
Ballyvaghan (Union).
Corrofin (Union).
Ennis (being Ennis Union less Urban Sanitary District of Ennis).
Ennistymon (Union).
Killadysert (Union).

Kilrush (being Kilrush Union less Urban Sanitary District of Kilrush).

Limerick No. 2 (being that portion of Limerick Union in County Clare).

Scariff (Union).

Tulla (Union).

Urban Districts are:—

Ennis (in Union of Ennis).

Kilrush (in Union of Kilrush).

CORK COUNTY—

County—unchanged.

City of Cork a County Borough.

Unions—unchanged.

Rural Districts are:—

Bandon (Union).

Bantry (Union).

Castletown (Union).

Clonakilty (being Clonakilty Union less Urban Sanitary District of Clonakilty).

Cork (being Cork Union less County Borough of Cork and Urban Sanitary District of Queenstown).

Dunmanway (Union).

Fermoy (being Fermoy Union less Urban Sanitary District of Fermoy).

Kanturk (Union).

Kilmallock No. 2 (being that portion of Kilmallock Union in County Cork).

Kinsale (being Kinsale Union less Urban Sanitary District of Kinsale).

Macroom (Union).

Mallow (Union).

Midleton (Union).

Millstreet (Union).

Mitchelstown No. 1 (being that portion of Mitchelstown Union in County Cork).

Skibbereen (Union).

Skull (Union).

Youghal No. 1 (being that portion of Youghal Union in County Cork less Urban Sanitary District of Youghal).

Urban Districts are:—

Clonakilty (in Union of Clonakilty).
Fermoy (in Union of Fermoy).
Kinsale (in Union of Kinsale).
Queenstown (in Union of Cork).
Youghal (in Union of Youghal).

KERRY COUNTY—

County—unchanged.

Unions—unchanged.

Rural Districts are:—
Caherciveen (Union).
Dingle (Union).
Kenmare (Union).
Killarney (being Killarney Union less Urban Sanitary
District of Killarney).
Listowel No. 1 (being that portion of Listowel Union in
County Kerry less Urban Sanitary District of Lis-
towel).
Tralee (being Tralee Union less Urban Sanitary District
of Tralee).

Urban Districts are:—

Killarney (in Union of Killarney).
Listowel (in Union of Listowel).
Tralee (in Union of Tralee).

LIMERICK COUNTY—

County—unchanged.

City of Limerick a County Borough.

Unions—unchanged.

Rural Districts are:—
Croom (Union).
Kilmallock No. 1 (being that portion of Kilmallock Union
in County Limerick).
Limerick No. 1 (being that portion of Limerick Union in
County Limerick less County Borough of Lim-
erick).
Listowel No. 2 (being that portion of Listowel Union in
County Limerick).

Mitchelstown No. 2 (being that portion of Mitchelstown
Union in County Limerick).
Newcastle (Union).
Rathkeale (Union).
Tipperary No. 2 (being that portion of Tipperary Union
in County Limerick).

Urban Districts.—None.

TIPPERARY COUNTY (North Riding)—

The boundaries of the North and South Ridings of Tipperary for Assize purposes are not exactly followed
in the division for administrative purposes. The
Electoral Divisions of Cappagh, Curraheen, and
Glengar in Union of Tipperary are transferred to
the administrative County of the South Riding.

Unions—unchanged.

Rural Districts are :—
Borrisokane (Union).
Nenagh (Union).
Parsonstown No. 2 (being that portion of Parsonstown
Union in County Tipperary).
Roscrea No. 1 (being that portion of Roscrea Union in
County Tipperary).
Thurles (being Thurles Union less the Urban Sanitary
Districts of Templemore and Thurles).

Urban Districts are :—
Templemore (in Union of Thurles).
Thurles (in Union of Thurles).

TIPPERARY COUNTY (South Riding)—

Portion of Urban Sanitary District of Clonmel in County
Waterford added to County Tipperary, South
Riding).
Portion of Urban Sanitary District of Carrick-on-Suir in
County Waterford added to County Tipperary,
South Riding.
Electoral Divisions of Cappagh, Curraheen. and Glengar in
Tipperary Union transferred to the South Riding.

Unions—unchanged.

Rural Districts are :—
Callan No. 2 (being that portion of Callan Union in
County Tipperary, South Riding).

Carrick-on-Suir No. 1 (being that portion of Carrick-on-Suir Union less Urban Sanitary District of Carrick-on-Suir in County Tipperary, South Riding).

Cashel (being Cashel Union less Urban Sanitary District of Cashel).

Clogheen (Union).

Clonmel No. 1 (being that portion of Clonmel Union less Urban Sanitary District of Clonmel in County Tipperary, South Riding).

Tipperary No. 1 (being that portion of Tipperary Union in County Tipperary, South Riding).

Urlingford No. 2 (being that portion of Urlingford Union in County Tipperary, South Riding).

Urban Districts are :—

Carrick-on-Suir (in Union of Carrick-on-Suir).

Cashel (in Union of Cashel).

Clonmel (in Union of Clonmel).

WATERFORD COUNTY—

City of Waterford a County Borough.

Electoral Division of Kilculliheen in County Waterford added to County Kilkenny.

Portion of Urban Sanitary District of Clonmel in County Waterford added to Co. Tipperary, South Riding.

Portion of Urban Sanitary District of Carrick-on-Suir in County Waterford added to Co. Tipperary, South Riding.

Unions—unchanged.

Rural Districts are :—

Carrick-on-Suir No. 2 (being that portion of Carrick-on-Suir Union in County Waterford).

Clonmel No. 2 (being that portion of Clonmel Union in County Waterford).

Dungarvan (being Dungarvan Union less Urban Sanitary District of Dungarvan).

Kilmacthomas (Union).

Lismore (Union).

Waterford No. 1 (being that portion of Waterford Union in Co. Waterford less County Borough of Waterford).

Youghal No. 2 (being that portion of Youghal Union in County Waterford).

Urban District :—

Dungarvan (in Union of Dungarvan).

PROVINCE OF ULSTER.

ANTRIM COUNTY—

City of Belfast a County Borough.

Portion of Urban Sanitary District of Lisburn in County Down transferred to County Antrim.

Unions altered:—

The Electoral Divisions of Beardiville, Bushmills and Portrush transferred to Ballymoney Union from Coleraine Union.

The Electoral Divisions of Hervey Hill, Kilrea, Tamlaght and The Grove transferred from Ballymoney Union to Coleraine Union.

The portion of Malone Electoral Division in the City of Belfast transferred from Lisburn Union to Belfast Union.

Rural Districts are:—

Antrim (Union).

Ballycastle (Union).

Ballymena (being Union of Ballymena, less Urban Sanitary District of Ballymena).

Ballymoney (being Union of Ballymoney less Urban Sanitary Districts of Ballymoney and Portrush).

Belfast No. 1 (being that portion of Belfast Union in County Antrim, less portion of County Borough of Belfast situated therein).

Larne (being Union of Larne less Urban Sanitary District of Larne and Urban portion of present Urban Sanitary District of Carrickfergus).

Lisburn No. 1 (being that portion of Union of Lisburn less Urban Sanitary District of Lisburn in County Antrim).

Lurgan No. 3 (being that portion of Lurgan Union in the County Antrim).

Urban Districts are:—

Ballymena (in Ballymena Union).

Ballymoney (in Ballymoney Union).

Carrickfergus (in Larne Union).

Larne (in Larne Union).

Lisburn (in Lisburn Union).

Portrush (in Ballymoney Union).

ARMAGH COUNTY—

Portion of Urban Sanitary District of Newry in County Armagh transferred from County Armagh to County Down.

Unions altered:—

Electoral Division of Lower Creggan in County Armagh transferred to Castleblaney Union from Union of Dundalk.

Electoral Division of Caledon in County Tyrone transferred from Armagh Union to Dungannon Union.

Rural Districts are:—

Armagh (being Union of Armagh less Urban Sanitary District of Armagh).

Banbridge No. 2 (being that portion of Banbridge Union in County Armagh less Urban Sanitary District of Tanderagee).

Castleblayney No. 2 (being that portion of Castleblayney Union in County Armagh).

Lurgan No. 1 (being that portion of Lurgan Union in County Armagh less Urban Sanitary Districts of Lurgan and Portadown).

Newry No. 2 (being that portion of Newry Union in County Armagh).

Urban Districts are:—

Armagh (in Union of Armagh).
Lurgan (in Union of Lurgan).
Portadown (in Union of Lurgan).
Tanderagee (in Union of Banbridge).

CAVAN COUNTY—

County—unchanged.

Union altered:—

The Electoral Division of Mullagh in County Cavan transferred from Kells Union to Bailieborough Union.

Rural Districts are:—

Bailieborough (Union).

Bawnboy No. 1 (being that portion of Bawnboy Union in County Cavan).

Cavan (being Cavan Union less Urban Sanitary District of Belturbet).

Cootehill No. 1 (being that portion of Cootehill Union in County Cavan less Urban Sanitary District of Cootehill).

Enniskillen No. 2 (being that portion of Enniskillen Union in County Cavan).

Granard No. 2 (being that portion of Granard Union in County Cavan).

Oldcastle No. 2 (being that portion of Oldcastle Union in County Cavan).

Urban Districts are: —

Belturbet (in Union of Cavan).
Cootehill (in Union of Cootehill).

DONEGAL COUNTY—

County—unchanged.

Unions—unchanged.

Rural Districts are: —

Ballyshannon No. 1 (being that portion of Ballyshannon Union in County Donegal).

Donegal (Union).
Dunfanaghy (Union).
Glenties (Union).
Inishowen (Union).
Letterkenny (being Letterkenny Union less Urban Sanitary District of Letterkenny).

Londonderry No. 2 (being that portion of Londonderry Union in County Donegal).

Milford (Union).
Strabane No. 2 (being that portion of Strabane Union in County Donegal).

Stranorlar (Union).

Urban District: —

Letterkenny (in Union of Letterkenny).

DOWN COUNTY—

City of Belfast a County Borough.

Portion of Urban Sanitary District of Lisburn in County Down transferred from County Down to County Antrim.

Portion of Urban Sanitary District of Newry in County Armagh transferred to County Down from County Armagh.

Union altered: —

Portion of Electoral Division of Breda in Lisburn Union and comprised in County Borough of Belfast transferred to Belfast Union.

Rural Districts are: —

Banbridge No. 1 (being that portion of Banbridge Union in County Down less Urban Sanitary Districts of Banbridge and Dromore).

Belfast No. 2 (being that portion of Belfast Union in County Down less County Down portion of County Borough of Belfast and the Urban Sanitary District of Holywood).

Downpatrick (Union).

Kilkeel (Union).

Lisburn No. 2 (being that portion of Lisburn Union in County Down).

Lurgan No. 2 (being that portion of Lurgan Union in County Down).

Newry No. 1 (being that portion of Newry Union in County Down less Urban Sanitary Districts of Newry and Warrenpoint).

Newtownards (being Newtownards Union less Urban Sanitary Districts of Bangor and Newtownards).

Urban Districts are: —

Banbridge (in Union of Banbridge).
Bangor (in Union of Newtownards).
Dromore (in Union of Banbridge).
Holywood (in Union of Belfast).
Newry (in Union of Newry).
Newtownards (in Union of Newtownards).
Warrenpoint (in Union of Newry).

FERMANAGH COUNTY—

County—unchanged.

Union altered: —

Electoral Division of Kilskerry in County Tyrone transferred from Enniskillen Union to Irvinestown Union.

Rural Districts are: —

Ballyshannon No. 2 (being that portion of Balyshannon Union in County Fermanagh).

Clones No. 2 (being that portion of Clones Union in County Fermanagh).

Enniskillen No. 1 (being that portion of Union of Enniskillen in County Fermanagh less Urban Sanitary
District of Enniskillen).

Irvinestown No. 1 (being that portion of Irvinestown
Union in County Fermanagh).

Lisnaskea (Union).

Urban District: —

Enniskillen (in the Union of Enniskillen).

LONDONDERRY COUNTY—

County—unchanged.

City of Londonderry a County Borough.

Unions altered : —

Electoral Divisions of Beardiville, Bushmills, and Portrush
in County Antrim transferred from Coleraine Union
to Ballymoney Union.

Electoral Divisions of Hervey Hill, Kilrea, Tamlaght,
and The Grove in County Londonderry transferred
to Coleraine Union from Ballymoney Union.

Rural Districts are : —

Coleraine (being Union of Coleraine less Urban Sanitary
District of Coleraine).

Limavady (being Union of Limavady less Urban Sanitary
District of Limavady).

Londonderry No. 1 (being that portion of Union of Londonderry in County Londonderry less County
Borough of Londonderry).

Magherafelt (Union).

Urban Districts are : —

Coleraine (in Union of Coleraine).

Limavady (in Union of Limavady).

MONAGHAN COUNTY—

County—unchanged.

Unions altered :—

Electoral Divisions of Bragan, Derrygorry, and Shanmullagh in County Monaghan transferred to Monaghan Union from Union of Clogher.

Electoral Division of Inishkeen in County Monaghan
transferred from Dundalk Union to Union of Carrickmacross.

Rural Districts are :—-

Carrickmacross (Union).

Castleblayney No. 1 (being that portion of Castleblayney Union in County Monaghan).

Clones No. 1 (being that portion of Clones Union in County Monaghan less Urban Sanitary District of Clones).

Cootehill No. 2 (being that portion of Cootehill Union in County Monaghan).

Monaghan (being Union of Monaghan less Urban Sanitary District of Monaghan).

Urban Districts are :—

Clones (in Union of Clones).

Monaghan (in Union of Monaghan).

TYRONE COUNTY—

County—unchanged.

Unions altered :—

Electoral Division of Caledon in County Tyrone transferred to Dungannon Union from Union of Armagh.

Electoral Division of Kilskerry in County Tyrone transferred to Irvinestown Union from Enniskillen Union.

Electoral Divisions of Bragan, Derrygorry, and Shanmullagh in County Monaghan transferred from Clogher Union to Union of Monaghan.

Rural Districts are :—-

Castlederg (Union).

Clogher (Union).

Cookstown (Union).

Dungannon (Union).

Irvinestown No. 2 (being that portion of Irvinestown Union in County Tyrone).

Omagh (Union).

Strabane No. 1 (being that portion of Strabane Union in County Tyrone).

Urban Districts.—None.

V.—ALTERATIONS IN ELECTORAL DIVISIONS.

Unions	Electoral Divisions Altered	Electoral Divisions Constituted
Antrim	Antrim	Antrim Urban. ,, Rural
Ardee	Ardee	Ardee Urban. ,, Rural

Armagh	Armagh	Armagh N'th Urban.
		    ,, East Urban.
		    ,, S'th Urban.
		    ,, Rural.

Armagh	Keady Crossmore	Keady Urban. ,, Rural. Crossmore.
Athlone	Athlone East	Athlone East Urban. ,, Rural.
Athlone	Athlone West	Athlone West Urban ,, Rural.

Athy	Athy	Athy West Urban.
		    ,, East Urban.
		    ,, Rural.

Ballina	Ballina	Ballina Urban. ,, Rural.
Ballina	Ardnaree South	Ardnaree S'th Urban ,, Rural.
Ballinasloe	Ballinasloe Creagh	Ballinasloe Urban. ,, Rural. Creagh.
Ballymena	Ballymena Ballyclug	Ballymena. Ballyclug.
Ballymoney	Ballymoney Enagh	Ballymoney. Enagh.
Ballyshannon	Ballyshannon Bundoran Carrickboy	Ballyshannon Urban ,, Rural. Bundoran. Carrickboy.
Balrothery	Balbriggan	Balbriggan Urban. ,, Rural.

Banbridge	Banbridge	Banbridge East Urb.
		    ,, W'st Urb.
		    ,, Rural.

UNIONS	Electoral Divisions Altered	Electoral Divisions Constituted
Banbridge ...	Dromore ... Quilly ...	Dromore Urban. ,, Rural. Quilly.
Banbridge ...	Tullylish ...	Gilford. Tullylish.
Banbridge ...	Tanderagee ... Mullahead ...	Tanderagee Urban. ,, Rural. Mullahead.
Bandon ...	Ballymodan ... Kilbrogan ...	Bandon. Ballymodan. Kilbrogan.
Bantry ...	Bantry ...	Bantry Urban. ,, Rural.
Belfast ...	Holywood ...	Holywood Urban. ,, Rural.
Belfast and Lisburn ...	Belfast Ballygomartin Ballyhackamore Ballymacarrett Ballymurphy Ballysillan Castlereagh Greencastle Breda Malone	Clifton. Court. Dock. Duncairn. Falls. Pottinger. Shankill. Smithfield. St. George's. Victoria. Woodvale. Cromac. Ormeau. Windsor. St. Anne's. Ballyhackamore. Castlereagh. Ballygomartin. Ballysillan. Breda. Malone.
Boyle ...	Boyle ...	Boyle Urban. ,, Rural.
Callan ..	Callan ...	Callan Urban. ,, Rural.
Carlow ...	Bagenalstown ...	Bagenalstown Urban ,, Rural.

UNIONS	Electoral Divisions Altered	Electoral Divisions Constituted
Carlow ...	Carlow ...	Carlow Urban. „ Rural.
Carlow ...	Graigue	Graigue Urban. „ Rural.
Carrickmacross ...	Carrickmacross ...	Carrickmacross Urb. „ Rural
Carrick-on-Suir ...	Carrick-on-Suir ...	Carrick-on-Suir Urb. „ Rural
Carrick-on-Suir ...	Carrickbeg Fenoagh ...	Carrickbeg Urban. „ Rural. Fenoagh.
Cashel ...	Cashel	Cashel Urban. „ Rural.
Cashel ...	Fethard ... Peppardstown ...	Fethard. Peppardstown.
Castlebar ...	Castlebar ...	Castlebar Urban. „ Rural.
Castleblayney ...	Castleblayney ...	Castleblayney Urban „ Rural.
Castleblayney ...	Ballybay ...	Ballybay Urban. „ Rural.
Cavan ...	Cavan ...	Cavan Urban. „ Rural.
Cavan • ...	Belturbet ... Kilconny ... Grilly ...	Belturbet. Kilconny. Grilly.
Clogher ...	Aughnacloy ...	Aughnacloy Urban. „ Rural.
Clonakilty ...	Clonakilty ...	Clonakilty Urban. „ Rural.
Clones ...	Clones ...	Clones Urban. „ Rural.
Clonmel ...	Clonmel ... Inishlounaght ... Kilmacomma ... St. Mary's ... Kilmanahan ...	Clonmel East Urban. „ West Urban „ Rural. Inishlounaght. St. Mary's. Kilmacomma.
Coleraine ...	Coleraine ... Bannbrook ... Knockantern ...	Coleraine Bannbrook. Knockantern.
Coleraine ...	Portrush ...	Portrush Urban. „ Rural.

UNIONS	Electoral Divisions Altered	Electoral Divisions Constituted
Cookstown ...	Cookstown ...	Cookstown Urban.
		„ Rural.
Cootehill ...	Cootehill ...	Cootehill Urban.
		„ Rural.
Cork ...	Cork ...	Cork No. 1 Urban.
		„ 2 Urban.
		„ 3 Urban.
		„ 4 Urban.
		„ 5 Urban.
		„ 6 Urban.
		„ 7 Urban.
		Bishopstown.
		Blackrock.
		St. Mary's.
Cork ...	Queenstown ...	Queenstown Urban.
		„ Rural.
Downpatrick ...	Downpatrick ...	Downpatrick Urban.
		„. Rural.
Drogheda ...	St. Peters' ...	Fair Gate.
	St. Mary's ...	St. Lawrence Gate.
		West Gate.
		St. Peter's.
		St. Mary's.
Dublin North ...	Clontarf ...	Clontarf ...
	Drumcondra ...	Drumcondra No. 1 Urban.
	Finglas ...	Drumcondra No. 2 Urban.
	Glasnevin ...	Drumcondra No. 3 Urban.
	North City ...	Drumcondra Rural.
		Finglas.
		Glasnevin.
		⎧ Arran Quay.
		⎪ Inn's Quay.
		⎨ Mountjoy.
		⎪ North City.
		⎪ North Dock
		⎩ Rotunda.
Dublin South ...	Clondalkin ...	New Kilmainham.
	Palmerstown ...	Clondalkin.
	Rathfarnham ...	Palmerstown.

Unions	Electoral Divisions Altered	Electoral Divisions Constituted
Dublin South—*con.*	Rathmines ...	Rathfarnham.
	Donnybrook ...	Pembroke East.
	South City ...	,, West.
		Rathmines and Rathgar West
		Rathmines and Rathgar East.
		Donnybrook
		Fitzwilliam.
		Mansion House.
		Merchant's Quay.
		Royal Exchange.
		South City.
		South Dock.
		Trinity.
		Usher's Quay.
		Wood Quay.
Dundalk ...	Dundalk ...	Dundalk No. 1 Urb.
		,, 2 Urb.
		,, 3 Urb.
		,, 4 Urb.
		,, Rural.
Dungannon ...	Dungannon ...	Dungannon
	Derrygortrevy ...	Derrygortrevy.
Dungarvan ...	Dungarvan ...	Dungarvan No.1 Urb
		,, 2 Urb
		,, Rural.
Ennis ...	Ennis ...	Ennis No. 1 Urban.
		,, 2 Urban.
		,, 3 Urban.
		,, 4 Urban.
		,, Rural.
Enniscorthy ...	Enniscorthy ...	Enniscorthy Urban.
		,, Rural.
Enniskillen ...	Enniskillen ...	Enniskillen Urban.
		,, Rural.
Fermoy ...	Fermoy ...	Fermoy Urban.
		,, Rural.
Galway ...	Galway ...	Galway North Urb.

Unions	Electoral Divisions Altered	Electoral Divisions Constituted
Galway—*con.*	Barna ...	Galway East Urb.
		„ South Urb.
		„ West Urb.
		„ Rural.
		Barna.
Gorey ...	Gorey ...	Gorey Urban.
	Courtown ...	„ Rural.
		Courtown.
Granard ...	Granard ...	Granard Urban.
		„ Rural.
Kells ...	Kells ...	Kells Urban.
		.. Rural
Kilkenny ...	Kilkenny ...	Kilkenny No 1 Urb.
		„ 2 Urb.
		„ Rural.
Killarney ...	Killarney ...	Killarney Urban.
		„ Rural.
Kilrush ...	Kilrush ...	Kilrush Urban.
		„ Rural.
Kinsale ...	Kinsale ..	Kinsale Urban.
		„ Rural.
Larne ...	Carrickfergus ...	Carrickfergus Urb.
		„ Rural.
Larne ...	Larne ...	Larne
	Kilwaughter ...	Kilwaughter.
Letterkenny ...	Letterkenny ...	Letterkenny Urban.
		„ Rural.
Limavady ...	Limavady ...	Limavady.
	Fruithill ...	Fruithill.
Limerick ...	Limerick ...	Limerick No 1 Urb.
		„ 2 Urb.
		„ 3 Urb.
		„ 4 Urb.
		„ 5 Urb.
		„ 6 Urb.
		„ 7 Urb.
		„ 8 Urb.
		„ North Rural
		„ South Rural
Lisburn ...	Lisburn ...	Lisburn.
	Blaris ...	Blaris.

Unions	Electoral Divisions Altered	Electoral Divisions Constituted
Lisburn—*con.*	Derryaghy ... Lissue ... Lambeg ... [*see* also under Belfast]	Derryaghy. Lissue.
Lismore ...	Lismore ...	Lismore Urban. ,, Rural.
Listowel ...	Listowel ...	Listowel Urban. ,, Rural.
Londonderry ...	City and Suburbs ... Lower Liberties ... Upper Liberties ... Waterside ...	Londonderry No. 1 Urban. Londonderry No. 2 Urban. Londonderry No. 3 Urban. Londonderry No. 4 Urban. Londonderry No. 5 Urban. Lower Liberties. Upper Liberties. Waterside.
Longford ...	Longford ...	Longford No. 1 Urb. ,, 2 Urb. ,, Rural.
Loughrea ...	Loughrea ...	Loughrea Urban. ,, Rural.
Lurgan ...	Lurgan ...	Lurgan Urban. ,, Rural.
Lurgan ...	Portadown ... Carrowbrack ...	Portadown Urban. ,, Rural. Carrowbrack.
Macroom ...	Macroom ... Macloneigh ...	Macroom. Macloneigh.
Mallow ...	Mallow ...	Mallow North Urb. ,, South Urb. ,, Rural.
Midleton ...	Midleton ...	Midleton Urban. ,, Rural.
Monaghan ...	Monaghan ...	Monaghan Urban. ,, Rural.
Mountmelick ...	Maryborough ...	Maryborough Urban ,, Rural.

Unions	Electoral Divisions Altered	Electoral Divisions Constituted
Mountmelick ...	Mountmelick ... Dangans ...	Mountmelick Urban ,, Rural. Dangans.

Mullingar ...	Mullingar ...	Mullingar N'th Urb.
		    ,, S'th Urb.
		    ,, Rural.

Naas ...	Newbridge ... Morristownbiller ... Oldconnell ...	Newbridge Urban. ,, Rural. Morristownbiller. Oldconnell.
Naas ...	Naas ...	Naas Urban. ,, Rural.
Navan ...	Navan ...	Navan Urban ,, Rural.

Nenagh ...	Nenagh ...	Nenagh East Urban
		    ,, West Urban
		    ,, Rural.

New Ross ...	New Ross ...	New Ross Urban. ,, Rural.
New Ross ...	Rosbercon ...	Rosbercon Urban. ,, Rural.
Newry ...	Ballybot ...	Newry West Urban. Ballybot.

Newry ...	Newry ...	Newry North Urban
		    ,, South Urban
		    ,, Rural.

Newry ...	Warrenpoint ...	Warrenpoint Urban. ,, Rural.

Newtownards.	Newtownards.
	Newtownards South
		Newtownards Urban.
		    ,, North.
		    ,, South.

Newtownards.	Bangor ...	Bangor Urban. ,, Rural.
Omagh ...	Omagh ...	Omagh Urban. ,, Rural.
Parsonstown ...	Parsonstown ... Eglish ...	Parsonstown Urban. ,, Rural. Eglish.

UNIONS	Electoral Divisions Altered	Electoral Divisions Constituted
Rathdown ...	Blackrock ...	Blackrock No. 1.
	Dundrum ...	,, 2.
	Kingstown ...	,, 3.
	Stillorgan ...	Kingstown No. 1.
	Killiney ...	,, 2.
	Rathmichael ...	,, 3.
	Bray ...	,, 4.
	Delgany ...	Dalkey.
		Killiney.
		Bray No. 1.
		,, 2.
		,, 3.
		Dundrum.
		Stillorgan.
		Ballybrack.
		Rathmichael.
		Delgany.
Rathdrum ...	Arklow ...	Arklow No. 1 Urban
		,, Rural.
Rathdrum ...	Kilbride ...	Arklow No. 2 Urban
		Kilbride.
Rathdrum ...	Wicklow ...	Wicklow Urban.
		,, Rural.
Rathkeale ...	Rathkeale ...	Rathkeale Urban.
	Ballyallinan ...	,, Rural.
		Ballyallinan.
Roscommon ...	Roscommon ...	Roscommon Urban.
		,, Rural.
Roscrea ...	Kyle ... (Transferred from Urlingford.)	Kyle South.
Skibbereen ...	Skibbereen ...	Skibbereen Urban.
		,, Rural.
Sligo ...	Sligo ...	Sligo North.
		,, East.
		,, West.
Strabane ...	Strabane ...	Strabane.
	Camus ...	Camus.
Thurles ...	Templemore ...	Templemore.
	Drom ...	Drom.
Thurles ...	Thurles ...	Thurles Urban.
		,, Rural.

UNIONS	Electoral Divisions Altered	Electoral Divisions Constituted
Tipperary ...	Tipperary ...	Tipperary East Urb. „ West Urb. „ Rural.
Tralee ...	Tralee ... Blennerville ...	Tralee Urban. „ Rural. Blennerville.
Trim ...	Trim ...	Trim Urban. „ Rural.
Tuam ...	Tuam ...	Tuam Urban. „ Rural.
Tullamore ...	Tullamore ...	Tullamore Urban. „ Rural.
Urlingford ...	[see under Roscrea.]	
Waterford ...	Waterford ...	Waterford No. 1 Urb „ 2 Urb „ 3 Urb „ 4 Urb „ 5 Urb Kilculliheen. Waterford Rural.
Westport ...	Westport ... Kilmeena ...	Westport Urban. „ Rural. Kilmeena.
Wexford ...	Wexford ...	Wexford No. 1 Urb. „ 2 Urb. „ 3 Urb. „ Rural.
Youghal ...	Youghal ...	Youghal Urban. „ Rural.

APPENDIX V.

URBAN SANITARY DISTRICTS.

TABLE showing the towns in Ireland which are Urban Sanitary Districts, and the Acts under which those towns are constituted.

Total number of Urban Sanitary Districts   74

URBAN SANITARY DISTRICTS AND ACTS UNDER WHICH CONSTITUTED.

ARMAGH—17 and 18 Vic., cap. 103, and 59 and 60 Vic., cap. ccxxxv.

ATHLONE—17 and 18 Vic., cap. 103.

*BALLINASLOE— Do.,   and 43 and 44 Vic., cap. xxxviii.

BALLYMENA—17 and 18 Vic., cap. 103.

*BALLYMONEY—   Do.,   and 51 and 52 Vic., cap. cxxiv.

*BANBRIDGE—   Do.,   and 43 and 44 Vic., cap. xl.

*BANGOR—   Do., .   and 42 and 43 Vic., cap. lx., and 51 and 52 Vic., cap. xxxiii.

BELFAST—3 and 4 Vic., cap 108, and special Acts.

*BELTURBET—17 and 18 Vic., cap. 103, and 57 Vic., cap. ii.

BLACKROCK—26 and 27 Vic., cap. cxxi.

BRAY—29 and 30 Vic., cap. cclxi.

CARLOW—17 and 18 Vic., cap. 103.

CARRICKFERGUS—3 and 4 Vic., cap. 108, sec. 16, 6 and 7 Vic., cap. 93, sec. 26, and 58 and 59 Vic., cap. lxxi.

CARRICK-ON-SUIR—17 and 18 Vic., cap. 103.

*CASHEL—   Do.,   and 42 and 43 Vic., cap. lvii.

*CLONAKILTY—   Do.,   and 44 Vic., cap. iii.

*CLONES—   Do.,   and 51 and 52 Vic., cap. cxxiv.

CLONMEL—3 and 4 Vic., cap. 108, and 58 and 59 Vic., cap. cxxxi.

CLONTARF—32 and 33 Vic., cap. lxxxv.

COLERAINE—17 and 18 Vic., cap. 103.

*COOTEHILL—   Do.,   and 48 and 49 Vic., cap. xcviii.

CORK—3 and 4 Vic., cap. 108, and special Acts.

DALKEY—30 and 31 Vic., cap. cxxxiv.

DROGHEDA—3 and 4 Vic., cap. 108.

*DROMORE—17 and 18 Vic., cap. 103, and 44 Vic., cap. iii.

DRUMCONDRA, CLONLIFFE, AND GLASNEVIN—41 and 42 Vic., cap. clvii.

DUBLIN—3 and 4 Vic., cap. 108, and special Acts.

DUNDALK—17 and 18 Vic., cap. 103.

DUNGARVAN—17 and 18 Vic., cap. 103, and 26 Vic., cap. xlv.

ENNIS—17 and 18 Vic., cap. 103.

*ENNISCORTHY—Do., and 42 and 43 Vic., cap. lvii.

ENNISKILLEN—33 and 34 Vic., cap. cxliii.

FERMOY—17 and 18 Vic., cap. 103.

GALWAY—16 and 17 Vic., cap. cc.

*GRANARD—17 and 18 Vic., cap. 103, and 56 and 57 Vic., cap. cxxi.

*HOLYWOOD—17 and 18 Vic., cap. 103, and 42 and 43 Vic., cap. lvii.

*KELLS— Do., do.

KILKENNY—3 and 4 Vic., cap. 108.

*KILLARNEY—17 and 18 Vic., cap. 103, and 42 and 43 Vic., cap. lxxxvii.

*KILLINEY AND BALLYBRACK—17 and 18 Vic., cap. 103, and 50 and 51 Vic., cap. cxiii.

KILMAINHAM (NEW)—31 and 32 Vic., cap. cx.

*KILRUSH—17 and 18 Vic., cap. 103, and 49 and 50 Vic., cap. liv.

KINGSTOWN—32 and 33 Vic., cap. cxxxiii., and 37 and 38 Vic., cap. clxvii.

KINSALE—17 and 18 Vic., cap. 103.

*LARNE— Do., and 55 Vic., cap. xxxii.

*LETTERKENNY— Do., and 45 Vic., cap. xxxii.

*LIMAVADY— Do., and 60 and 61 Vic., cap. lxxxi.

LIMERICK—3 and 4 Vic., cap. 108, and special Acts.

LISBURN—17 and 18 Vic., cap. 103.

*LISTOWEL— Do., and 46 and 47 Vic., cap. lxxxiii.

LONDONDERRY—3 and 4 Vic., cap. 108, and special Acts.

LURGAN—17 and 18 Vic., cap. 103.

*MONAGHAN—9 Geo. IV., cap. 82, and 43 and 44 Vic., cap. xl.

*NAVAN—17 and 18 Vic., cap. 103, and 44 Vic., cap. iii.

NEW ROSS—17 and 18 Vic., cap. 103.

NEWRY—34 and 35 Vic., cap. cxcviii.

NEWTOWNARDS—17 and 18 Vic., cap. 103.

*PARSONSTOWN— Do., and 42 and 43 Vic., cap. lxxxvii

PEMBROKE—26 and 27 Vic., cap. lxxii.

PORTADOWN—17 and 18 Vic., cap. 103.

*PORTRUSH—   Do.,   and 59 and 60 Vic., cap. lxxxvii.

QUEENSTOWN—17 and 18 Vic., cap. 103.

RATHMINES AND RATHGAR—10 and 11 Vic., cap. ccliii., and other Acts.

SLIGO—3 and 4 Vic., cap. 108, and special Act.

*TANDERAGEE—17 and 18 Vic., cap. 103, and 51 and 52 Vic., cap. lxxxix.

*TEMPLEMORE—   Do.,   and 42 and 43 Vic., cap. lvii.

*THURLES—   Do.,   and 43 and 44 Vic., cap. xl.

TRALEE—17 and 18 Vic., cap. 103.

*TRIM—   Do.,   and 43 and 44 Vic., cap. xl.

*WARRENPOINT—Do.,   and 46 Vic., cap. xl.

WATERFORD—3 and 4 Vic., cap. 108.

WEXFORD—   Do.

*WICKLOW—9 Geo. IV., cap. 82, and 42 and 43 Vic., cap. lvii.

*YOUGHAL—17 and 18 Vic., cap. 103, and 42 and 43 Vic., cap. lvii.

Note.—Forty-two of the towns in the above table were constituted urban sanitary districts by section 4 of the Public Health (Ireland) Act, 1878, but each of those marked with an asterisk has been so constituted by provisional order under section 7. The confirming Act in each such case is given in the above table.

INDEX.

2 H

INDEX. 459

CRIMINAL INJURIES :
List of Acts Relating to, 185
Provisions Relating to, 45-7, 110, 111, 122, 173, 185

CURRENT RATES :
Saving of Remedies for Collection of, 244

DESTRUCTIVE INSECTS ACT :
Provision as to Administration of, 15, 111

DIFFICULTIES :
Removal of, as to first elections, Councils, etc., 9, 22, 220

DISEASES OF ANIMALS ACTS :
Officers under, 82-3, 163

DISPENSARY COMMITTEES IN RURAL DISTRICTS :
Provisions as to, 40, 129

DISPENSARY HOUSES :
Provisions as to, 44, 101, 162, 276

DISPENSARY MEDICAL OFFICERS :
Salaries of, as Medical Officers of Health, by whom to be paid, 82, 161

DISTRICT CHARGES :
What are, 54, 132

DISTRICT ELECTORAL DIVISIONS :
Identical with Poor Law Electoral Divisions, 33, 123
May be grouped for First Elections, 86, 176
May be divided, 123
Number of Rural District Councillors for, 33, 123
Number of Rural District Councillors in certain towns, 33, 123, 387

DISTRICT FUND :
Establishment of, 133

DISURBANISING :
Provisions as to, 32, 131

DROGHEDA :
Special Provisions as to, 51, 152, 153

DUBLIN COLLECTOR-GENERAL AND STAFF :
Provisions as to, 96

DUBLIN RATES :
Changes Regarding, 29, 76-8, 147-50
List of Acts Relating to, 186

DUNGANNON :
Provisions Relating to, 43, 389

ECCLESIASTICAL DIGNITARIES :
Relation of, to County Infirmaries, 100

ELECTION EXPENSES :
Candidates, 7, 8, 217
Official, By whom paid, 218
,, Returning Officer's Account of, 7, 218-9
Scale of, Official, at Elections, 6, 218
Taxation of, Official, 7, 219
,, Candidates', 7, 219

ENGLISH AND SCOTCH ACTS APPLIED :
List of, 188

EPIDEMIC AND INFECTIOUS DISEASES :
Provision as to, 37, 127

EXCEPTIONAL DISTRESS :
Provisions as to Relief of, 19, 117

EXCLUDED CHARGES :
Area of Levy of, 65, 142-3
What are, 65, 141-3

EXISTING JUDICIAL COUNTIES :
Definition of, 1, 150
First Councils to be elected for, 1, 150
,, ,, with certain exceptions, 1, 151
First Councils subject to alteration of boundaries, 1, 151
List of alterations in, 420, et seq.

EXISTING OFFICERS :
Provisions as to, 89-96

EXISTING SECURITIES :
Saving for, 245

EXPENSES :
Local Officers', 258
Raising of, in Rural Districts, 55, 137
,, ,, ,, Urban ,, 56, 132, 137
,, ,, ,, County Boroughs, 56, 133
To be paid within half-year, 137
What, paid by Poor-rate, 55, 56, 132, 136, 137

EXPLOSIVES ACT :
Provisions as to Administration of, 15, 111

FERTILIZING AND FEEDING STUFFS ACT :
Provision as to administration of, 14

FINANCIAL RELATIONS :
Adjustment of, Amongst new areas, 258-9

FIRST COUNCILLORS AND COMMISSIONERS :
Retirement of, 87, 88, 256, 257

FIRST COUNCILS :
Special Provisions as to, 87, 251, 253

Printed by SEALY, BRYERS & WALKER, Abbey Street, Dublin.

Lightning Source UK Ltd.
Milton Keynes UK
UKHW02f0743160818
327336UK00010B/625/P